Promises to Keep

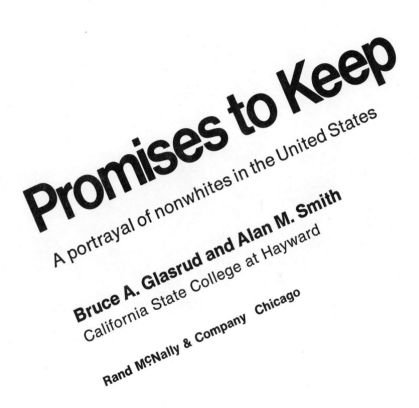

Promises to Keep

A portrayal of nonwhites in the United States

Bruce A. Glasrud and Alan M. Smith
California State College at Hayward

Rand McNally & Company   Chicago

Preface

This book is designed to provide a series of collateral readings on the history of nonwhite Americans for students of United States history. Although many standard American history textbooks have recently been revised to correct their almost total neglect of these minorities, the result in most cases is a token appearance of dark-skinned characters in what is essentially a white man's story. The obvious need for materials treating nonwhites in American history courses has been met by a number of readers on specific minority groups. This book presents readings dealing with the history of all the major nonwhite groups that have played a part in the development of America.

The term "nonwhite" is difficult to define. In this work, we have included articles about Americans who have viewed themselves, or who have been viewed by the white majority, as distinct and different because of their skin color. The groups included—the Indians, blacks, Mexican-Americans, Chinese-Americans, Japanese-Americans, Filipino-Americans, and Puerto Ricans—differ greatly in their roles and experiences in American history, but all have encountered prejudice and difficulties on account of their skin color.

The articles which compose this volume are arranged under six chronological headings covering American history from the founding of Jamestown to the present. In each historical period there is an article concerning the nonwhite groups in American society at that particular time; there are also several articles which cover the relationships among nonwhite groups. The articles are the work of scholarly students of America, most of them historians, writing during the past thirty years. The authors vary in their focuses and points of view, but all are concerned with the interaction between the non-white minorities and the white majority in the United States. In most cases, the articles have been edited for the sake of brevity, but citations of sources have been retained and introductory material has been supplied to place the essays in a larger context.

We hope that these readings will aid students of American history in discovering the richness and diversity of the peoples of the United States and in understanding the origins of the racial problems which still plague the nation.

We wish to thank three people for their help in developing this volume: Richard J. Orsi for his suggestion of potential selections, Ann S. Jablin, our editor at Rand McNally, for her careful reading of the manuscript, and Pearlene V. Glasrud for her incisive and instructive comments as the work progressed.

Bruce A. Glasrud

Hayward, California   Alan M. Smith

Table of Contents

Part I
Introduction

Introduction

Nonwhites in the United States comprise a substantial minority whose experience and life style differ significantly from that of the white majority. White Americans developed a social system in which race, color, and culture were important distinguishing criteria. With these factors as broad indicators of status in society, red, yellow, brown, or black skin marked a man as inferior in the eyes of the white majority and set limits on the extent to which he could share in the benefits of an expanding and upwardly mobile society.

As did the various white ethnic groups, nonwhites arrived in substantial blocs at specific junctures in the national development. There has been an increase in the population of nonwhites, although until recently Native Americans, called Indians because of a well-known mistake, were an exception. The population of Native Americans had declined as a result of incessant warfare, and in the process they lost much of their land, heritage, and livelihood. The first nonwhites to immigrate to North America were blacks from Africa who began to populate the continent at the same time as the Europeans since they were imported as slaves for profit-seeking whites. Even after the abolition of slavery, blacks faced a harsh caste system which severely regulated their lives.

The incorporation of other nonwhite groups awaited the mid-nineteenth century when the United States waged war against Mexico, conquered vast stretches of territory, and added to its population former citizens of her southern neighbor. Other Mexicans entered the United States as impoverished agricultural and industrial workers in the twentieth century, and, because of barriers created by language, culture, religion, and alien status, they were easily exploited.

Beginning in 1848, Chinese also entered the United States. They sought gold to take back to China; but racial and cultural differences again precluded equitable treatment, and they became poorly paid laborers. When some were able to achieve success despite the obstacles, alarmed whites brought about the enactment of the Chinese Exclusion Act. Other Orientals, Japanese, Filipinos, and Koreans, trailed the Chinese to the United States. Recently, additional minorities including Hawaiians, Eskimos, Puerto Ricans, and lesser numbers from Southeast Asia, India, and the Middle East have migrated to the United States.

Relations among the nonwhites varied with the predicament of each group. Often they competed with one another for the few menial positions or favors offered to minorities. At other times they joined forces against the white majority in a bid for privileges that were denied them. Some nonwhites strove for acceptance by the majority, which meant adopting white values, but usually they were restricted to separate and unequal areas where they developed their own cultures and societies apart from those of the whites.

Three themes stand out in the history of nonwhites in the United States. First, nonwhites confronted total domination by the white majority. Their subjugation took the forms of slavery, war, annihilation, physical torture, cultural deprivation, economic restriction, political exclusion, geographical removal, and social ostracism. Second, segregation became a way of life as the paramount white society forced physical separation upon them. Whenever the nonwhites sought apartheid, the whites, fearful of collective action directed against them, took reluctant steps to modify legal segregation. But there have been few meaningful steps toward integration, and the result remains in the confinement of blacks in ghettos, Chinese in Chinatowns, Chicanos in barrios, and Indians on reservations. Third, nonwhites resisted white encroachments. Their defiance assumed overt and covert forms, often at the same time. Overt resistance included riots, revolts, warfare, and murder; covert resistance often hid behind smiles, good behavior, and the signing of treaties. But dislike of whites and the white dominated society was obvious, even to those whites who insisted that nonwhites were happy with their second-class status.

The United States, a nation which has prided itself on its equalitarian nature, is, in actuality, a heterogeneous society that exhibits major schisms between the groups which comprise it. The tensions of American society are particularly apparent between the dominant white majority and the various nonwhite minorities. The nonwhites, subjugated, segregated, and defiant, remain a challenge to the nation's capacities for providing the promise of equality to all its citizens.

Accounts of the manner in which immigrants or minority groups
become, or fail to become, "Americanized" too often portray
the myths, rather than the realities, of that process. Milton M.
Gordon, in "Assimilation in America," asserts that Americans have
used three concepts to explain both what has happened and
what should happen to immigrants and the manner in which
newcomers have interacted with the dominant society: (1) Anglo-
conformity, (2) the melting pot, and (3) cultural pluralism.
Although cultural pluralism is the most accurate of the three, none
are apt descriptions of assimilation; rather, Gordon concludes,
the phrase "structural pluralism" better interprets the American
experience. In the United States acculturation which stresses
secondary and impersonal relationships takes place, but structural
assimilation which emphasizes primary and personal relationships is
often lacking. For racial minorities, however, even acculturation
has been limited. Instead, nonwhites have established separate
communities within the prevailing white society.

Assimilation in America:
Theory and Reality

Milton M. Gordon

Three ideologies or conceptual models have competed for attention on the American scene as explanations of the way in which a nation, in the beginning largely white, Anglo-Saxon, and Protestant, has absorbed over 41 million immigrants and their descendants from variegated sources and welded them into the contemporary American people. These ideologies are Anglo-conformity, the melting pot, and cultural pluralism. They have served at various times, and often simultaneously, as explanations of what has happened—descriptive models—and of what should happen—goal models. Not infrequently they have been used in such a fashion that it is difficult to tell which of these two usages the writer has had in mind. In fact, one of the more remarkable omissions in the history of American intellectual thought is the relative lack of close analytical attention given to the theory of immigrant adjustment in the United States by its social scientists.

The result has been that this field of discussion—an overridingly

Abridged from Milton M. Gordon, "Assimilation in America: Theory and Reality," Daedalus, XC (1961), pp. 163–185. Reprinted by permission of Daedalus, Journal of the American Academy of Arts and Sciences, Boston, Mass., Spring 1961, Ethnic Groups in American Life. Some footnotes have been re-numbered.

important one since it has significant implications for the more familiar problems of prejudice, discrimination, and majority-minority group relations generally—has been largely preempted by laymen, representatives of belles lettres, philosophers, and apologists of various persuasions. Even from these sources the amount of attention devoted to ideologies of assimilation is hardly extensive. Consequently, the work of improving intergroup relations in America is carried out by dedicated professional agencies and individuals who deal as best they can with day-to-day problems of discriminatory behavior, but who for the most part are unable to relate their efforts to an adequate conceptual apparatus. Such an apparatus would, at one and the same time, accurately describe the present structure of American society with respect to its ethnic groups (I shall use the term "ethnic group" to refer to any racial, religious, or national origins collectively), and allow for a considered formulation of its assimilation or integration goals for the foreseeable future. One is reminded of Alice's distraught question in her travels in Wonderland: "Would you tell me, please, which way I ought to go from here?" "That depends a good deal," replied the Cat with irrefutable logic, "on where you want to get to."

The story of America's immigration can be quickly told for our present purposes. The white American population at the time of the Revolution was largely English and Protestant in origin, but had already absorbed substantial groups of Germans and Scotch-Irish and smaller contingents of Frenchmen, Dutchmen, Swedes, Swiss, South Irish, Poles, and a handful of migrants from other European nations. Catholics were represented in modest numbers, particularly in the middle colonies, and a small number of Jews were residents of the incipient nation. With the exception of the Quakers and a few missionaries, the colonists had generally treated the Indians and their cultures with contempt and hostility, driving them from the coastal plains and making the western frontier a bloody battleground where eternal vigilance was the price of survival.

Although the Negro at that time made up nearly one-fifth of the total population, his predominantly slave status, together with racial and cultural prejudice, barred him from serious consideration as an assimilable element of the society. And while many groups of European origin started out as determined ethnic enclaves, eventually, most historians believe, considerable ethnic intermixture within the white population took place. "People of different blood" [sic]—write two American historians about the colonial period, "English, Irish, German, Huguenot, Dutch, Swedish—mingled and intermarried with little thought of any difference."[1] In such a society, its people predominantly English, its white immigrants of other ethnic origins either English-speaking or derived largely from countries of northern and western Europe whose cultural divergences from the English were not great, and its dominant white population excluding by fiat the claims and considerations of welfare of the non-Caucasian minorities, the problem of assimilation understandably did not loom unduly large or complex.

The unfolding events of the next century and a half with increasing momentum dispelled the complacency which rested upon the relative simplicity of colonial and immediate post-Revolutionary conditions. The large-scale immigration to America of the famine-fleeing Irish, the Germans, and later the Scandinavians (along with additional Englishmen and other peoples of northern and western Europe) in the middle of the nineteenth century (the so-called "old immigration"), the emancipation of the Negro slaves and the problems created by post-Civil War reconstruction, the placing of the conquered Indian with his broken culture on government reservations, the arrival of the Oriental, first attracted by the discovery of gold and other opportunities in the West, and finally, beginning in the last quarter of the nineteenth century and continuing to the early 1920's, the swelling to proportions hitherto unimagined of the tide of immigration from the peasantries and "pales" of southern and eastern Europe—the Italians, Jews, and Slavs of the so-called "new immigration," fleeing the persecutions and industrial dislocations of the day—all these events constitute the background against which we may consider the rise of the theories of assimilation mentioned above. After a necessarily foreshortened description of each of these theories and their historical emergence, we shall suggest analytical distinctions designed to aid in clarifying the nature of the assimilation process, and then conclude by focusing on the American scene.

1. Allan Nevins and Henry Steele Commager, America: The Story of a Free People (Boston, Little, Brown, 1942), p. 58.

Anglo-Conformity

"Anglo-conformity"[2] is a broad term used to cover a variety of viewpoints about assimilation and immigration; they all assume the desirability of maintaining English institutions (as modified by the American Revolution), the English language, and English-oriented cultural patterns as dominant and standard in American life. However, bound up with this assumption are related attitudes. These may range from discredited notions about race and "Nordic" and "Aryan" racial superiority, together with the nativist political programs and exclusionist immigration policies which such notions entail, through an intermediate position of favoring immigration from northern and western Europe on amorphous, unreflective grounds ("They are more like us"), to a lack of opposition to any source of immigration, as long as these immigrants and their descendants duly adopt the standard Anglo-Saxon cultural patterns. There is by no means any necessary equation between Anglo-conformity and racist attitudes.

It is quite likely that "Anglo-conformity" in its more moderate aspects, however explicit its formulation, has been the most prevalent ideology of assimilation goals in America throughout the nation's history. . . .

Anglo-conformity received its fullest expression in the so-called Americanization movement which gripped the nation during World War I. While "Americanization" in its various stages had more than one emphasis, it was essentially a consciously articulated movement to strip the immigrant of his native culture and attachments and make him over into an American along Anglo-Saxon lines—all this to be accomplished with great rapidity. To use an image of a later day, it was an attempt at "pressure-cooking assimilation." It had prewar antecedents, but it was during the height of the world conflict that federal agencies, state governments, municipalities, and a host of private organizations joined in the effort to persuade the immigrant to learn English, take out naturalization papers, buy war bonds, forget his former origins and culture, and give himself over to patriotic hysteria.

2. The phrase is the Coles's. See Stewart G. Cole and Mildred Wiese Cole, *Minorities and the American Promise* (New York, Harper & Brothers, 1954), ch. 6.

After the war and the "Red scare" which followed, the excesses of the Americanization movement subsided. In its place, however, came the restriction of immigration through federal law. Foiled at first by presidential vetoes, and later by the failure of the 1917 literacy test to halt the immigrant tide, the proponents of restriction finally put through in the early 1920's a series of acts culminating in the well-known national-origins formula for immigrant quotas which went into effect in 1929. Whatever the merits of a quantitative limit on the number of immigrants to be admitted to the United States, the provisions of the formula, which discriminated sharply against the countries of southern and eastern Europe, in effect institutionalized the assumptions of the rightful dominance of Anglo-Saxon patterns in the land. Reaffirmed with only slight modifications in the Mc-Carran-Walter Act of 1952, these laws, then, stand as a legal monument to the creed of Anglo-conformity and a telling reminder that this ideological system still has numerous and powerful adherents on the American scene.

The Melting Pot

While Anglo-conformity in various guises has probably been the most prevalent ideology of assimilation in the American historical experience, a competing viewpoint with more generous and idealistic overtones has had its adherents and exponents from the eighteenth century onward. Conditions in the virgin continent, it was clear, were modifying the institutions which the English colonists brought with them from the mother country. Arrivals from non-English homelands such as Germany, Sweden, and France were similarly exposed to this fresh environment. Was it not possible, then, to think of the evolving American society not as a slightly modified England but rather as a totally new blend, culturally and biologically, in which the stocks and folkways of Europe, figuratively speaking, were indiscriminately mixed in the political pot of the emerging nation and fused by the fires of American influence and interaction into a distinctly new type?

Such, at any rate, was the conception of the new society which motivated that eighteenth-century French-born writer and agriculturalist, J. Hector St. John Crèvecoeur, who, after many years of

American residence, published his reflections and observations in *Letters from an American Farmer.*[3] Who, he asks, is the American?

> He is either an European, or the descendant of an European, hence that strange mixture of blood, which you find in no other country. I could point out to you a family whose grandfather was an Englishman, whose wife was Dutch, whose son married a French woman, and whose present four sons have now four wives of different nations. *He* is an American, who leaving behind him all his ancient prejudices and manners, receives new ones from the new mode of life he has embraced, the new government he obeys, and the new rank he holds. He becomes an American by being received in the broad lap of our great *Alma Mater.* Here individuals of all nations are melted into a new race of men, whose labours and posterity will one day cause great changes in the world.

Some observers have interpreted the open-door policy on immigration of the first three-quarters of the nineteenth century as reflecting an underlying faith in the effectiveness of the American melting pot, in the belief "that all could be absorbed and that all could contribute to an emerging national character."[4] ...

... Around the turn of the [twentieth] century the melting-pot idea became embedded in the ideals of the age as one response to the immigrant receiving experience of the nation. Soon to be challenged by a new philosophy of group adjustment ... and always competing with the more pervasive adherence to Anglo-conformity, the melting-pot image, however, continued to draw a portion of the attention consciously directed toward this aspect of the American scene in the first half of the twentieth century. In the mid-1940's a sociologist who had carried out an investigation of intermarriage trends in New Haven, Connecticut, described a revised conception of the melting process in that city and suggested a basic modification of the theory

3. J. Hector St. John Crèvecoeur, *Letters from an American Farmer* (New York, Albert and Charles Boni, 1925; reprinted from the 1st edn., London, 1782), pp. 54–55.

4. Oscar Handlin, ed., *Immigration as a Factor in American History* (Englewood, Prentice-Hall, 1959), p. 146.

of that process. In New Haven, Ruby Jo Reeves Kennedy[5] reported from a study of intermarriages from 1870 to 1940 that there was a distinct tendency for the British-Americans, Germans, and Scandinavians to marry among themselves—that is, within a Protestant "pool"; for the Irish, Italians, and Poles to marry among themselves—a Catholic "pool"; and for the Jews to marry other Jews. In other words, intermarriage was taking place across lines of nationality background, but there was a strong tendency for it to stay confined within one or the other of the three major religious groups, Protestants, Catholics, and Jews. Thus, declared Mrs. Kennedy, the picture in New Haven resembled a "triple melting pot" based on religious divisions, rather than a "single melting pot." Her study indicated, she stated, that "while strict endogamy is loosening, religious endogamy is persisting and the future cleavages will be along religious lines rather than along nationality lines as in the past. If this is the case, then the traditional 'single-melting-pot' idea must be abandoned, and a new conception, which we term the 'triple-melting-pot' theory of American assimilation, will take its place as the true expression of what is happening to the various nationality groups in the United States."[6] The triple-melting-pot thesis was later taken up by the theologian Will Herberg and formed an important sociological frame of reference for his analysis of religious trends in American society, *Protestant-Catholic-Jew.*[7] But the triple-melting-pot hypothesis patently takes us into the realm of a society pluralistically conceived. We turn now to the rise of an ideology which attempts to justify such a conception.

Cultural Pluralism

Probably all the non-English immigrants who came to American shores in any significant numbers from colonial times onward—settling either in the forbidding wilderness, the lonely prairie, or in

5. Ruby J. Reeves Kennedy, "Single or Triple Melting-Pot? Intermarriage Trends in New Haven, 1870–1940," *American Journal of Sociology,* 1944, 49:331–339. See also her "Single or Triple Melting-Pot? Intermarriage in New Haven, 1870–1950," *ibid.,* 1952, 58:56–59.

6. *Ibid.,* "Single or Triple Melting-Pot? . . . 1870–1940," p. 332 (author's italics omitted).

7. Will Herberg, *Protestant-Catholic-Jew* (Garden City, Doubleday, 1955).

some accessible urban slum—created ethnic enclaves and looked forward to the preservation of at least some of their native cultural patterns. Such a development, natural as breathing, was supported by the later accretion of friends, relatives, and countrymen seeking out oases of familiarity in a strange land, by the desire of the settlers to rebuild (necessarily in miniature) a society in which they could communicate in the familiar tongue and maintain familiar institutions, and, finally, by the necessity to band together for mutual aid and mutual protection against the uncertainties of a strange and frequently hostile environment. This was as true of the "old" immigrants as of the "new." In fact, some of the liberal intellectuals who fled to America from an inhospitable political climate in Germany in the 1830's, 1840's, and 1850's looked forward to the creation of an all-German state within the union, or, even more hopefully, to the eventual formation of a separate German nation, as soon as the expected dissolution of the union under the impact of the slavery controversy should have taken place.[8] Oscar Handlin, writing of the sons of Erin in mid-nineteenth-century Boston, recent refugees from famine and economic degradation in their homeland, points out: "Unable to participate in the normal associational affairs of the community, the Irish felt obliged to erect a society within a society, to act together in their own way. In every contact therefore the group, acting apart from other sections of the community, became intensely aware of its peculiar and exclusive identity."[9] Thus cultural pluralism was a fact in American society before it became a theory—a theory with explicit relevance for the nation as a whole, and articulated and discussed in the English-speaking circles of American intellectual life. . . .

The classic statement of the cultural pluralist position [appeared early in 1915 in two articles entitled] "Democracy versus the Melting-Pot." Their author was Horace Kallen, a Harvard-educated philos-

8. Nathan Glazer, "Ethnic Groups in America: From National Culture to Ideology," in Morroe Berger, Theodore Abel, and Charles H. Page, eds., *Freedom and Control in Modern Society* (New York, D. Van Nostrand, 1954), p. 161; Marcus Lee Hansen, *The Immigrant in American History* (Cambridge, Harvard University Press, 1940), pp. 129–140; John A. Hawgood, *The Tragedy of German-America* (New York, Putnam's, 1940), *passim*.

9. Oscar Handlin, *Boston's Immigrants* (Cambridge, Harvard University Press, 1959, rev. edn.), p. 176.

opher with a concern for the application of philosophy to societal affairs, and, as an American Jew, himself derivative of an ethnic background which was subject to the contemporary pressures for dissolution implicit in the "Americanization," or Anglo-conformity, and the melting-pot theories. In these articles Kallen vigorously rejected the usefulness of these theories as models of what was actually transpiring in American life or as ideals for the future. Rather he was impressed by the way in which the various ethnic groups in America were coincident with particular areas and regions, and with the tendency for each group to preserve its own language, religion, communal institutions, and ancestral culture. All the while, he pointed out, the immigrant has been learning to speak English as the language of general communication, and has participated in the over-all economic and political life of the nation. These developments in which "the United States are in the process of becoming a federal state not merely as a union of geographical and administrative unities, but also as a cooperation of cultural diversities, as a federation or commonwealth of national cultures,"[10] the author argued, far from constituting a violation of historic American political principles, as the "Americanizers" claimed, actually represented the inevitable consequences of democratic ideals, since individuals are implicated in groups, and since democracy for the individual must by extension also mean democracy for his group.

The processes just described, however, as Kallen develops his argument, are far from having been thoroughly realized. They are menaced by "Americanization" programs, assumptions of Anglo-Saxon superiority, and misguided attempts to promote "racial" amalgamation. Thus America stands at a kind of cultural crossroads. It can attempt to impose by force an artificial, Anglo-Saxon oriented uniformity on its peoples, or it can consciously allow and encourage its ethnic groups to develop democratically, each emphasizing its particular cultural heritage. If the latter course is followed, as Kallen puts it at the close of his essay, then,[11]

---

10. Horace M. Kallen, "Democracy versus the Melting-Pot," *The Nation*, 18 and 25 February 1915; reprinted in his *Culture and Democracy in the United States*, Boni and Liveright, 1924; the quotation is on p. 116.
11. Kallen, *Culture and Democracy . . .*, p. 124.

The outlines of a possible great and truly democratic common-wealth become discernible. Its form would be that of the federal republic; its substance a democracy of nationalities, cooperating voluntarily and autonomously through common institutions in the enterprise of self-realization through the perfection of men according to their kind. The common language of the commonwealth, the language of its great tradition, would be English, but each nationality would have for its emotional and involuntary life its own peculiar dialect or speech, its own individual and inevitable esthetic and intellectual forms. The political and economic life of the commonwealth is a single unit and serves as the foundation and background for the realization of the distinctive individuality of each *nation* that composes it and of the pooling of these in a harmony above them all. Thus "American civilization" may come to mean the perfection of the cooperative harmonies of "European civilization"—the waste, the squalor and the distress of Europe being eliminated—a multiplicity in a unity, an orchestration of mankind.

...In the twentieth century, particularly since World War II, "cultural pluralism" has become a concept which has worked its way into the vocabulary and imagery of specialists in intergroup relations and leaders of ethnic communal groups. In view of this new pluralistic emphasis, some writers now prefer to speak of the "integration" of immigrants rather than of their "assimilation."[12] However, with a few exceptions,[13] no close analytical attention has been given either by social scientists or practitioners of intergroup relations to the meaning of cultural pluralism, its nature and relevance for a modern industrialized society, and its implications for problems of prejudice

12. See W. D. Borrie *et al.*, *The Cultural Integration of Immigrants* (a survey based on the papers and proceedings of the UNESCO Conference in Havana, April 1956), Paris, UNESCO, 1959; and William S. Bernard. "The Integration of Immigrants in the United States" (mimeographed), one of the papers for this conference.

13. See particularly Milton M. Gordon, "Social Structure and Goals in Group Relations"; and Nathan Glazer, "Ethnic Groups in America; From National Culture to Ideology," both articles in Berger, Abel, and Page, *op. cit.*; S. N. Eisenstadt, *The Absorption of Immigrants* (London, Routledge and Kegan Paul, 1954); and W. D. Borrie *et al.*, *ibid.*

and discrimination—a point to which we referred at the outset of this discussion.

Conclusions

In the remaining pages I can make only a few analytical comments which I shall apply in context to the American scene, historical and current. My view of the American situation will not be documented here, but may be considered as a series of hypotheses in which I shall attempt to outline the American assimilation process.

First of all, it must be realized that "assimilation" is a blanket term which in reality covers a multitude of subprocesses. The most crucial distinction is one often ignored—the distinction between what I have elsewhere called "behavioral assimilation" and "structural assimilation."[14] The first refers to the absorption of the cultural behavior patterns of the "host" society. (At the same time, there is frequently some modification of the cultural patterns of the immigrant-receiving country, as well.) There is a special term for this process of cultural modification or "behavioral assimilation"—namely, "acculturation." "Structural assimilation," on the other hand, refers to the entrance of the immigrants and their descendants into the social cliques, organizations, institutional activities, and general civic life of the receiving society. If this process takes place on a large enough scale, then a high frequency of intermarriage must result. A further distinction must be made between, on the one hand, those activities of the general civic life which involve earning a living, carrying out political responsibilities, and engaging in the instrumental affairs of the larger community, and, on the other hand, activities which create personal friendship patterns, frequent home intervisiting, communal worship, and communal recreation. The first type usually develops so-called "secondary relationships," which tend to be relatively impersonal and segmental; the latter type leads to "primary relationships," which are warm, intimate, and personal.

With these various distinctions in mind, we may then proceed.

Built on the base of the original immigrant "colony" but frequently extending into the life of successive generations, the characteristic ethnic group experience is this: within the ethnic group there devel-

14. Milton M. Gordon, "Social Structure and Goals in Group Relations," p. 151.

ops a network of organizations and informal social relationships which permits and encourages the members of the ethnic group to remain within the confines of the group for all of their primary relationships and some of their secondary relationships throughout all the stages of the life cycle. From the cradle in the sectarian hospital to the child's play group, the social clique in high school, the fraternity and religious center in college, the dating group within which he searches for a spouse, the marriage partner, the neighborhood of his residence, the church affiliation and the church clubs, the men's and the women's social and service organizations, the adult clique of "marrieds," the vacation resort, and then, as the age cycle nears completion, the rest home for the elderly and, finally, the sectarian cemetery—in all these activities and relationships which are close to the core of personality and selfhood—the member of the ethnic group may if he wishes follow a path which never takes him across the boundaries of his ethnic structural network.

The picture is made more complex by the existence of social class divisions which cut across ethnic group lines just as they do those of the white Protestant population in America. As each ethnic group which has been here for the requisite time has developed second, third, or in some cases, succeeding generations, it has produced a college-educated group which composes an upper middle class (and sometimes upper class, as well) segment of the larger groups. Such class divisions tend to restrict primary group relations even further, for although the ethnic-group member feels a general sense of identification with all the bearers of his ethnic heritage, he feels comfortable in intimate social relations only with those who also share his own class background or attainment.

In short, my point is that, while *behavioral assimilation* or acculturation has taken place in America to a considerable degree, *structural assimilation*, with some important exceptions, has not been extensive.[15] The exceptions are of two types. The first brings us back to the "triple-melting-pot" thesis of Ruby Jo Reeves Kennedy and Will Herberg. The "nationality" ethnic groups have tended to merge within each of the three major religious groups. This has been particularly true of the Protestant and Jewish communities. Those

15. See Erich Rosenthal, "Acculturation without Assimilation?" *American Journal of Sociology*, 1960, 66:275–288.

descendants of the "old" immigration of the nineteenth century, who were Protestant (many of the Germans and all the Scandinavians), have in considerable part gradually merged into the white Protestant "subsociety." Jews of Sephardic, German, and Eastern-European origins have similarly tended to come together in their communal life. The process of absorbing the various Catholic nationalities, such as the Italians, Poles, and French Canadians, into an American Catholic community hitherto dominated by the Irish has begun, although I do not believe that it is by any means close to completion. Racial and quasi-racial groups such as the Negroes, Indians, Mexican-Americans, and Puerto Ricans still retain their separate sociological structures. The outcome of all this in contemporary American life is thus pluralism—but it is more than "triple" and it is more accurately described as *structural pluralism* than as cultural pluralism, although some of the latter also remains.

My second exception refers to the social structures which implicate intellectuals. There is no space to develop the issue here, but I would argue that there is a social world or subsociety of the intellectuals in America in which true structural intermixture among persons of various ethnic backgrounds, including the religious, has markedly taken place.

My final point deals with the reasons for these developments. If structural assimilation has been retarded in America by religious and racial lines, we must ask why. The answer lies in the attitudes of both the majority and the minority groups and in the way these attitudes have interacted. A saying of the current day is, "It takes two to tango." To apply the analogy, there is no good reason to believe that white Protestant America has ever extended a firm and cordial invitation to its minorities to dance. Furthermore, the attitudes of the minority-group members themselves on the matter have been divided and ambiguous. Particularly for the minority religious groups, there is a certain logic in ethnic communality, since there is a commitment to the perpetuation of the religious ideology and since structural intermixture leads to intermarriage and the possible loss to the group of the intermarried family. Let us, then, examine the situation serially for various types of minorities.

With regard to the immigrant, in his characteristic numbers and socioeconomic background, structural assimilation was out of the question. He did not want it, and he had a positive need for the comfort of his own communal institutions. The native American, moreover, whatever the implications of his public pronouncements, had no intention of opening up his primary group life to entrance by these hordes of alien newcomers. The situation was a functionally complementary standoff.

The second generation found a much more complex situation. Many believed they heard the siren call of welcome to the social cliques, clubs, and institutions of white Protestant America. After all, it was simply a matter of learning American ways, was it not? Had they not grown up as Americans, and were they not culturally different from their parents, the "greenhorns"? Or perhaps an especially eager one reasoned (like the Jewish protagonist of Myron Kaufmann's novel, *Remember Me To God*, aspiring to membership in the prestigious club system of Harvard undergraduate social life) "If only I can go the last few steps in Ivy League manners and behavior, they will surely recognize that I am one of them and take me in." But, alas, Brooks Brothers suit notwithstanding, the doors of the fraternity house, the city men's club, and the country club were slammed in the face of the immigrant's offspring. That invitation was not really there in the first place; or, to the extent it was, in Joshua Fishman's phrase, it was a " 'look me over but don't touch me' invitation to the American minority group child."[16] And so the rebuffed one returned to the homelier but dependable comfort of the communal institutions of his ancestral group. There he found his fellows of the same generation who had never stirred from the home fires. Some of these had been too timid to stray; others were ethnic ideologists committed to the group's survival; still others had never really believed in the authenticity of the siren call or were simply too passive to do more than go along the familiar way. All could now join in the task that was well within the realm of the sociologically possible—the build-up of social institutions and organizations within the ethnic enclave, manned increasingly by members of the second generation and suitably separated by social class.

Those who had for a time ventured out gingerly or confidently, as the case might be, had been lured by the vision of an "American"

16. Joshua A. Fishman, "Childhood Indoctrination for Minority-Group Membership and the Quest for Minority-Group Biculturism in America," in Oscar Handlin, ed., *Group Life in America* (Cambridge, Harvard University Press, forthcoming).

social structure that was somehow larger than all subgroups and was ethnically neutral. Were they, too, not Americans? But they found to their dismay that at the primary group level a neutral American social structure was a mirage. What at a distance seemed to be a quasi-public edifice flying only the all-inclusive flag of American nationality turned out on closer inspection to be the clubhouse of a particular ethnic group—the white Anglo-Saxon Protestants, its operation shot through with the premises and expectations of its parental ethnicity. In these terms, the desirability of whatever invitation was grudgingly extended to those of other ethnic backgrounds could only become a considerably attenuated one.

With the racial minorities, there was not even the pretense of an invitation. Negroes, to take the most salient example, have for the most part been determinedly barred from the cliques, social clubs, and churches of white America. Consequently, with due allowance for internal class differences, they have constructed their own network of organizations and institutions, their own "social world." There are now many vested interests served by the preservation of this separate communal life, and doubtless many Negroes are psychologically comfortable in it, even though at the same time they keenly desire that discrimination in such areas as employment, education, housing, and public accommodations be eliminated. However, the ideological attachment of Negroes to their communal separation is not conspicuous. Their sense of identification with ancestral African national cultures is virtually nonexistent, although Pan-Africanism engages the interest of some intellectuals and although "black nationalist" and "black racist" fringe groups have recently made an appearance at the other end of the communal spectrum. As for their religion, they are either Protestant or Catholic (overwhelmingly the former). Thus, there are no "logical" ideological reasons for their separate communality; dual social structures are created solely by the dynamics of prejudice and discrimination, rather than being reinforced by the ideological commitments of the minority itself.

Structural assimilation, then, has turned out to be the rock on which the ships of Anglo-conformity and the melting pot have foundered. To understand that behavioral assimilation (or acculturation) without massive structural intermingling in primary relationships has been the dominant motif in the American experience of creating and developing a nation out of diverse peoples is to comprehend the most essential sociological fact of that experience. It is against the background of "structural pluralism" that strategies of strengthening intergroup harmony, reducing ethnic discrimination and prejudice, and maintaining the rights of both those who stay within and those who venture beyond their ethnic boundaries must be thoughtfully devised.

Part II
Clash of Cultures, 1607-1763

Clash of Cultures, 1607–1763

On the eve of the American Revolution the thirteen British North American colonies contained approximately two-and-a-half-million people, the majority of whom were whites of European origin. Over 60 percent of the white inhabitants were of English stock, and English institutions and culture dominated the society of the colonies. There were also two sizeable nonwhite minorities, red and black, which lived within the colonies but outside the framework of the dominant European culture.

Indians were a majority when the English first established permanent North American settlements. In the early seventeenth century nearly one million Indians inhabited the area which became the United States. The English, deriving their first ideas about American colonization from reports of the Spanish experience, expected to encounter tractable Indians who could easily be subdued and relegated to the status of servants and slaves. Initial contacts with Indians quickly dashed such expectations. The Indians tolerated the white intruders as a harmless and unimpressive minority. Later they resisted the increasing number of Europeans as a threat to Indian land and culture. The English, on the other hand, refused to acknowledge Indian culture and engaged in weak and sporadic efforts to incorporate the red men into their civilization, mainly through religious proselytization. The Indians generally spurned such advances.

The steady growth of English population and a pattern of settlement which relied heavily on agriculture to provide an economic raison d'être for the colonies created continual clashes between whites and Indians over the use and possession of land. On some occasions the whites secured land by sale and treaty. When Indians were unwilling to relinquish the land, warfare often followed. The results of persistent white aggression were disasterous for the Indians. Some nations were driven west beyond the frontier of white settlement, often into the territory of hostile Indian rivals. Other tribes, such as the Pequots of Connecticut, were annihilated by the whites. Still others made their peace with the whites; they were frequently absorbed by the English society in a subservient and segregated position. This latter result led to the rapid modification of Indian culture. Despite some concerted efforts to retake the land, such as King Philip's War in Massachusetts (1675–76), the Indians were unable to stem the white tide. Technological superiority, increasing numbers, and a more acquisitive attitude toward land insured white domination.

The other nonwhite minority in British North America, the blacks, began to arrive a decade after the founding of Virginia when twenty Africans were brought to Jamestown in 1619 by a Dutch slave trader and sold to white settlers as bound servants. The forced immigration of Africans to the colonies continued on a very limited scale throughout the seventeenth century, but accelerated with the development of commercial agriculture in the southern colonies as white planters sought new sources of labor. White indentured servants proved to be an expensive, unruly, and often inefficient labor force, and the relationship which developed between the English and the Indians prevented, in most cases, the development of red slavery. By the mid-seventeenth century white masters in Virginia and Maryland began to experiment with black labor, and the laws of these colonies reflected the concurrent development of a slave system. Toward the end of the century the expansion of the African slave trade, the rapid growth of American plantation agriculture, and the decline of competing slave markets in the West Indies combined to assure the large scale importation and enslavement of Africans in the southern colonies. Blacks constituted a large portion of the population in every colony from Maryland south by mid-eighteenth century, and almost all were enslaved by a system of perpetual servitude which gave masters virtually unlimited authority over their lives and labor.

While both minorities, red and black, lived within the American colonies, they were not in any real sense a part of the white culture or society. Socially, legally, and physically, they existed apart from and subservient to the white majority.

Nancy Oestreich Lurie,
*"Indian Cultural Adjustment
to European Civilization"*

Conflict between Indians and whites has been a persistent theme in American history. Although this racial antagonism is often presented as a simple economic struggle over occupation of the land, Nancy Lurie, in "Indian Cultural Adjustment to European Civilization," demonstrates that much more was involved. The sections of Professor Lurie's article, which appear here, cover the early years of Indian-white relationships in the first permanent English colony in North America and reveal a clash of cultures which led to the supremacy of one at the expense of the other. Particularly significant is the author's observation that upon initial contact the two cultures were different but not unequal. Yet, initiating a pattern which would appear many times in American history, white Virginians succeeded in destroying the Powhatan Confederacy in less than four decades.

Indian Cultural Adjustment to European Civilization

Nancy Oestreich Lurie

... During much of the sixteenth century Europeans were active in regions immediately adjacent to Virginia and possibly in Virginia itself. Their activity was often associated with violence, and there was sufficient time for rumors concerning them to have reached the Virginia natives before any direct contacts were made. By the time the English attempted to found colonies on the east coast toward the close of the sixteenth century, they encountered difficulties which may have been more than the simple result of European inexperience in developing techniques for survival in the New World. Raleigh's enterprise, for example, may have been singulary ill-timed. A general unrest in Indian-white relationships marked the period from 1577 to 1597 in the Carolina region where Raleigh's followers chose to remain. Pemisipan, a Secotan chief who attempted to organize opposition to the British in 1585, could hardly have been blamed if he saw a curious similarity to accounts he may have heard concerning the Spanish when, for the trifling matter of the theft

Abridged from Nancy Oestreich Lurie, "Indian Cultural Adjustment to European Civilization," *Seventeenth-Century America: Essays in Colonial History*, edited by James Morton Smith (Chapel Hill: University of North Carolina Press, 1959), pp. 33–60. Reprinted by permission of the publisher and the Institute of Early American History and Culture. Footnotes have been renumbered.

of a silver cup, the English burned the corn and destroyed the buildings at his village of Aquascogoc.[1] The later events at Cape Henry, the first landfall of the Jamestown colonists, suggest that the immediate hostility expressed by the Indians was inspired by fear of reprisals for the fate of Raleigh's colony. The Indians who attacked the English belonged to the Chesapeake tribe, immediately adjacent to the tribes with whom Pemisipan conspired.[2] It is also possible, as James Mooney implies, that by 1607 the Virginia Indians evaluated any sudden appearance of Europeans as evil and took immediate measures to repel them. However, this view oversimplifies several important factors. Long before any Europeans arrived at Jamestown, the Indians had been fighting over matters of principle important to them, such as possession of land and tribal leadership. If they were aware of the fate of other Indians at the hands of Europeans, there was no reason for them to assume that their fate would be similar; they were not necessarily allied with the beleaguered tribes, nor did they share a sense of racial kinship. Sharp cultural differences and even sharper linguistic differences separated the various Indian societies. While there was reason to fear and hate the Europeans as invaders who made indiscriminate war on all Indians, the fear was only that of being taken unawares and the hate could be modified if the tribes which had fallen victim thus far were strangers or even enemies. If the Indians of Virginia had any knowledge of Europeans, they must have been aware that the white men were fundamentally outnumbered, frequently unable to support themselves in an environment which the Indians found eminently satisfactory, and that European settlements were usually short lived. The appearance of the English was probably far less alarming than 350 years of hindsight indicate ought to have been the case.

This is demonstrated by the fact that the Virginia Indians under

1. Maurice A. Mook, "Algonkian Ethnohistory of the Carolina Sound," *Jour. of The Washington Academy of Sciences*, 34 (1944), 185–86, quotes and discusses the journal of 1585, usually attributed to Sir Richard Grenville, regarding this incident and also establishes the location of Aquascogoc in North Carolina.

2. [George Percy], "Observations gathered out of *A Discourse of the Plantation of the Southerne Colonie in Virginia by the English, 1606*; written by that Honorable Gentleman, Master George Percy," in Edward Arber, ed., *Captain John Smith ... Works, 1608–1631* (Birmingham, Eng., 1884), xl–li.

the leadership of Powhatan seem to have made their first adjustments to Europeans in terms of existing native conditions.[3] Primary among these conditions were Powhatan's efforts to gain firmer control over his subject tribes and to fight tribes traditionally at enmity with his followers. It was expedient to help the settlers stay alive, for they could be useful allies in his established plans; but at the same time he could not allow them to gain ascendancy. The situation was complicated by factionalism in Powhatan's ranks and lack of accord among the settlers. However, recognition of the fundamental aboriginal situation makes the early events at Jamestown understandable on a rational basis. It offers a logical foundation for subsequent developments in Indian-white relationships and Indian adjustments to European civilization as the result of something more than barbaric cupidity and a thirst for the white man's blood.

Certainly a wary sensitivity to any sign of hostility or treachery characterized the behavior of both whites and Indians at the outset of settlement at Jamestown. The Europeans were still seriously concerned about the probable fate of Raleigh's colony and they had already been attacked by the Indians at Cape Henry. The Indians, in turn, may well have possessed information concerning the alarmingly retributive temperament of Europeans, at least in terms of the incident at nearby Aquascogoc, if not through generalized opinions derived from the long history of intermittent European contact along the east coast.

Nevertheless, the party of Europeans that set out on exploration of the country about Jamestown encountered a welcome at the various Indian villages different from the greetings offered at Cape Henry. Except for one cold but not overtly hostile reception in the Weanoc country, the white men were feted, fed, and flattered. At the same time a suggestion of the uncertainty of the next years occurred before the exploring party had even returned to their head-

---

3. There are many data to indicate that in culture contact situations, generally regular processes of cultural acceptance and rejection can be traced to the formulation of analogies between innovations and existing phenomena on the part of the recipient culture. See Melville J. Herskovits, *Man and His Works* (New York, 1950), 553–58, for a discussion of the processes of reinterpretation and syncretism; Ralph Linton, *The Study of Man* (New York, 1936), 317–18, and Homer G. Barnett, "Cultural Processes," *Amer. Anthropologist*, 42 (1940), 21–48, give similar but independent analyses of analogy formulation on the basis of form, function, meaning, and use or principle of given traits.

quarters—at Jamestown the remaining colonists were attacked by a party of local Indians.[4] Events of this nature as well as the general observations recorded during the first two years at Jamestown are particularly instructive in any attempt to understand Indian motivations and policy regarding the British.

The narratives are difficult to follow because of the variety of orthographies employed for Indian words. Certain features remain speculative because initial communication between whites and Indians was limited to the use of signs and the few native words that could be learned readily.[5] However, it is possible to see native culture in terms of regularities and consistencies which were not obvious to the colonists. Likewise, the apparent inconsistencies on the part of the natives, recounted by the settlers as innate savage treachery, indicate that the aboriginal culture was in a process of growth, elaboration, and internal change. These phases of culture, which included both extensive tendencies of intertribal confederation and divisive reactions expressed by individual tribes, were interrupted and redirected but not initiated by the arrival of Europeans in 1607.

From the viewpoint of the twentieth century, it is difficult to realize that the material differences between the Indians and the European colonists, who lived before the full development of the industrial revolution, were equalled if not outweighed by the similarities of culture. This was especially true in Virginia, where a local florescence of culture and a demonstrated ability to prevail over other tribes gave the Indians a sense of strength which blinded them to the enormity of the threat posed by the presence of Europeans. There was actually little in the Europeans' imported bag of tricks which the Indians could not syncretize with their own experience. Metal was not unknown to them: they used native copper, brought in from the West, for decorative purposes. Metal weapons and domestic utensils were simply new and effective forms of familiar objects to accomplish familiar tasks. Even guns were readily mas-

4. [Captain Gabriel Archer], "A Relayton of the Discovery &c. 21 May–22 June, 1607," in Arber, ed., *Works of John Smith*, li–lii. It is worth noting that news of the attack was apparently communicated to the Indians who were entertaining the exploring party, but that Powhatan had either been unable to prevent the attack or had not known of the plan until it was accomplished.
5. Throughout the present study, spelling of Indian words, apart from direct quotations, has been regularized according to the pattern of Mook's publications.

tered after the noise, which evoked astonishment at first, was understood as necessary to their operation. Likewise, fabrics and articles of personal adornment were part of Indian technology. Many utilitarian objects such as nets, weirs, and gardening implements were very similar in both Indian and European culture. European ships were simply larger and different, as was fitting for a people interested in traveling greater distances by open water than the Indians had ever cared to do.

Expansive accounts of the size and permanence of the great European cities could easily have been likened by the natives to the impressive aboriginal developments in the lower Mississippi Valley; archeological evidence suggests that knowledge of this cultural complex was widespread.[6] Even if these Indian models of nascent urbanization are discounted, the statements made by Europeans about their country and king may well have sounded like the exaggerations of outnumbered strangers endeavoring to buttress their weaknesses with talk of powerful but distant brothers. This explanation is admittedly conjectural, although we find ample documentation of the Indians' disinclination to admit any significant superiority in white culture at a somewhat later period. During the early nineteenth century, when the industrial revolution was underway and the eastern United States was heavily populated by whites, Indian visitors were brought from the West in the hope that they would be cowed by the white man's power and cease resistance to the forces of civilization. The Indians remained singularly unimpressed.[7] Furthermore, at the time Jamestown was founded in the seventeenth century, the only knowledge Indians possessed concerning Europeans indicated that Indians were well able to oppose white settlement. Raleigh's ill-fated colony was a clear reminder of the European's mortality.

6. Paul Martin, George Quimby, and Donald Collier, *Indians Before Columbus* (Chicago, 1947), offer useful illustrations of the far-flung continental diffusion of cultural traits in prehistoric times, although dates assigned have been reassessed during the last ten years.

7. See Katherine C. Turner, *Red Men Calling on the Great White Father* (Norman, Okla., 1951), which presents a series of essays on such visits. Although the Indians considered their trips as entertaining educational experiences, their quoted remarks in the main reveal opinions that the white man had an unnecessarily complex and burdensome way of life at the expense of the finer one enjoyed by the Indians.

Although the early accounts tend to take a patronizing view of the Indians, the points on which the Europeans felt superior had little meaning for the aborigines: literacy, different sexual mores, ideas of modesty, good taste in dress and personal adornment, and Christian religious beliefs. The argument of technological superiority at that time was a weak one; despite guns and large ships the Europeans could not wrest a living from a terrain which, by Indian standards, supported an exceptionally large population. Scientific knowledge of generally predictable group reactions thus suggests that the degree of ethnocentrism was probably equal on both sides of the contact between Indians and Europeans in Virginia. Recognition of the Indians' self-appraisal is necessary for a clear understanding of their basis of motivation and consequent behavior in relation to Europeans.

Moreover, it was evident to the colonists that they were dealing with a fairly complex society, exhibiting many characteristics of leadership, social classes, occupational specialization, social control, and economic concepts that were eminently comprehensible in European terms. If the exploring parties overstated the case when they translated *weroance* as "king" and likened tribal territories to European kingdoms, they at least had a truer understanding of the nature of things than did the democratic Jefferson, who first designated the Virginia tribes as the "Powhatan Confederacy."[8] Since the term "Confederacy" is so firmly entrenched in the literature, it will be retained here as a matter of convenience; but, in reality, Powhatan was in the process of building something that approximated an empire. By 1607 it was not an accomplished fact, but the outlines were apparent. . . .

. . . The Chesapeake Indians are included in the Confederacy, but this southernmost group was not fully under Powhatan's control at the time the settlers arrived. Their attack on the colonists at Cape Henry gave Powhatan the opportunity to gain favor with the English by swiftly avenging the hostile action. Although some historians have implied that Powhatan destroyed the entire tribe, it is far more

8. John Smith observed that "one as Emperour ruleth over many kings or governours." *A Map of Virginia with a Description of the Countrey* . . . and *The General Historie of Virginia* . . ., in Arber, ed., *Works of John Smith*, 79, 375. Mook, "Aboriginal Population of Tidewater Virginia," *Amer. Anthropologist*, 44 (1944), 197, attributes the first use of the term "Powhatan Confederacy" to Jefferson.

likely that he simply killed the leaders and placed trusted kinsmen in these positions.[9]

Powhatan's method of fighting and his policy of expanding political control combined a reasoned plan of action with quick ferocity and a minimum of bloodshed. Indian warfare was generally limited to surprise attacks and sniping from cover. Constant replacements of fighting men kept the enemy occupied and wore down their resistance, while actual casualties were relatively limited in number. Accounts of Powhatan's conquests and the occurrences observed after 1607 point to a carefully devised method of establishing his control over a wide territory. Entire communities might be killed if they proved exceptionally obstinate in rendering homage and paying tribute, but in most cases Powhatan simply defeated groups of questionable loyalty and upon their surrender moved them to areas where he could keep better watch over them. Trusted members of the Confederacy were then sent to occupy the vacated regions, while Powhatan's relatives were distributed throughout the tribes in positions of leadership.[10] Mook's studies indicate that the degree of Powhatan's leadership decreased in almost direct proportion to the increase in geographical distance between the Pamunkey and the location of a given tribe.[11] Throughout the entire region, however, the combination of ample sustenance, effective techniques of production, provident habits of food storage, and distribution of supplies through exchange offset shortcomings in the political framework connecting the tribes and helped to cement social ties and produce a commonality of culture....

...At the outset of colonization in 1607 Powhatan's policies can best be understood in relation to circumstances antedating the arrival of the Jamestown settlers. Powhatan saw the whites in his territory as potential allies and as a source of new and deadly weapons to be used in furthering his own plans for maintaining control over his Confederacy and protecting the Confederacy as a whole against the

9. [Archer], "Relayton," Arber, ed., Works of John Smith, xliv; William Strachey, The Historie of Travaile into Virginia Britannia, Hakluyt Society edn. (London, 1849), 101, 105; James Mooney, "Powhatan Confederacy," Amer. Anthropologist, 9 (1907), 130.

10. Mooney, "Powhatan Confederacy," Amer. Anthropologist, 9 (1907), 136.

11. Mook, "Virginia Ethnology from an Early Relation," Wm. and Mary College Qtly., 2nd ser., 23 (1943), 115.

threat posed by the alien tribes of the piedmont region. Likewise, existing concepts of intertribal trade in foodstuffs and other commodities were extended to include trade with the newly arrived whites. It is worth noting that European novelties, apart from weapons, were of far less interest to Powhatan than the fact that the British possessed copper, an object vested with traditional native values and heretofore obtained with great difficulty.[12]

In the initial stages of contact between the Indians and the whites, therefore, it is hardly surprising that Powhatan and his people felt at least equal to the English. The chieftain could appreciate the foreigners as allies in the familiar business of warfare and trade, but in general there seemed little to emulate in European culture and much to dislike about the white men. However, even in the most difficult phases of their early relationship, Powhatan did not indulge in a full-scale attack against the settlers. At that time he was still engaged in strengthening his Confederacy and perhaps he could not risk extensive Indian defection to the side of the whites. But there is an equal likelihood that Powhatan's primary motivation was the desire to control and use the whites for his own purposes rather than to annihilate them.

At the time Jamestown was founded, native civilization was enjoying a period of expansion, and Powhatan had ample reason for sometimes considering the English as more an annoyance than a serious danger. The unusually rich natural environment and the security offered by the Confederacy stimulated the growth of social institutions and cultural refinements. In addition, the Virginia Indians were exceptionally powerful and, by aboriginal standards, their population was large: the entire Confederacy numbered some 8,500 to 9,000 people, or a density of approximately one person to every square mile.[13] The Indians lived according to a well-ordered and impressively complex system of government. They dwelled in secure

12. "Their manner of trading is for copper, beads, and such like; for which they giue such commodities as they haue, as skins, fowle, fish, flesh, and their country corne." Arber, ed., Works of John Smith. Ibid., 74, 369. Smith reported that Powhatan requested him to abandon the settlement among the Paspehegh and move to his own country: "Hee promised to giue me Corne, Venison, or what I wanted to feede vs: Hatchets and Copper wee should make him, and none should disturb vs." Ibid., 20.

13. Mook, "Aboriginal Population," Amer. Anthropologist, 44 (1944), 201, 208.

villages, had substantial houses and extensive gardens, and had a notable assemblage of artifacts for utilitarian, religious, and decorative purposes.

The Indians won the grudging respect of the colonists for their advanced technology, but the Europeans were contemptuous of their seemingly hopeless commitment to superstition, while their ceremonialism appeared to the whites a ridiculous presumption of dignity.[14] A typical bias of communication between Europeans and Indians is seen in Smith's account of the Quiyoughcohannock chief who begged the settlers to pray to the Christian God for rain because their own deities had not fulfilled the Indians' requests. Smith asserted that the Indians appealed to the whites because they believed the Europeans' God superior to their own, just as the Europeans' guns were superior to bows and arrows. Yet Smith notes with some wonder that the Quiyoughcohannock chief, despite his cordiality and interest in the Christian deity, could not be prevailed upon to "forsake his false Gods."[15] Actually this chief of one of the lesser tribes of the Confederacy illustrated the common logic of polytheistic people who often have no objection to adding foreign deities to their pantheon if it seems to assure more efficient control of the natural universe. The chief was not interested in changing his religious customs in emulation of the Europeans; he merely wished to improve his own culture by judicious borrowing—a gun at one time, a supernatural being at another.

Nor would the chief have dared respond to a new religion in its entirety, even if such an unlikely idea had occurred to him. The whole structure of tribal life relied upon controlling the mysterious aspects of the world by a traditional body of beliefs which required the use of religious functionaries, temples, idols, and rituals. These were awesome arrangements and not to be treated lightly, although improvement by minor innovations might be permitted.[16]

14. [Archer], "Relayton," Arber, ed., *Works of John Smith*, 1, provides a characteristic response of the colonists in his description of Opechancanough, who "so set his Countenance stryving to be stately, as to our seeming he became a fool."

15. Arber, ed., *Works of John Smith*, 79, 374.

16. For a general account of religion derived from the basic sources, see Charles C. Willoughby, "The Virginia Indians of the Seventeenth Century," *Amer. Anthropologist*, 9 (1907), 61–63. The most complete single account in the early narratives based on firsthand observation is included in Henry Spelman, "Relation of Virginea," 1613, in Arber, ed., *Works of John Smith*, cv–cvi.

The geopolitical sophistication of the Virginia tribes is reflected in the secular hierarchy of leadership which extended in orderly and expanding fashion from the villages, through the separate tribes, up to Powhatan as head of the entire Confederacy. A gauge of the complexity of government is the fact that the Confederacy shared with the Europeans such niceties of civilization as capital punishment.[17] In small societies having a precarious economy, indemnities in goods or services are usually preferred to taking the life of a culprit even in crimes as serious as murder. However, where the life of the offender or one of his kinsmen is exacted for the life of the victim, punishment is the concern of the particular families involved; the rest of the group merely signifies approval of the process as a means of restoring social equilibrium after an offense is committed. Powhatan's government, however, was much closer to that of the English than it was to many of the tribes of North America. Punishment was meted out by a designated executioner for an offense against the society as the society was symbolized in the person of the leader.

Nevertheless, despite its elaborate civil structure, the Confederacy exhibited a universal rule of any society: a complex theory of government does not necessarily assure complete success in application. Powhatan not only had unruly subjects to deal with, but entire tribes in his domain could not be trusted. Relations between whites and Indians therefore were always uncertain, largely because of political developments within the Confederacy. When the colonists were supported by Powhatan, they were in mortal danger from those dissatisfied tribes of the Confederacy which had the foresight to realize that the English might one day assist Powhatan to enforce his authority. When Powhatan and his closest associates turned upon the settlers, the less dependable tribes became friendly to the whites.

In view of this morass of political allegiances, it is little wonder that early accounts of the settlers are replete with material which seems to prove the innate treachery of the Indians. Yet the militant phases of Indian activity, as illustrated by the initial attack on Jamestown and Powhatan's vengeance on the offending Chesapeake tribe, must be seen as part of a larger policy involving alternative methods of settling inter-group differences. Although the settlers knew that

17. Arber, ed., *Works of John Smith*, 81–82, 377–78; Spelman, "Relation," *ibid.*, cxi.

dissatisfaction among Powhatan's followers offered a means of preventing a coordinated Indian attack, they also discovered that established mechanisms of diplomacy existed among the Indians that could be employed for their benefit. For example, the Jamestown settlement was located in the territory of the Paspahegh tribe, and relations with this tribe frequently became strained. The Powhatan forces represented by the leaders of the Pamunkey, Arrohattoc, Youghtanund, and Mattaponi offered to act as intermediaries in negotiating peace with the Paspehegh and other hostile tribes or, if necessary, to join forces with the settlers in an armed assault on mutual enemies.[18]

If the Europeans found it difficult to live among the Indians, the Europeans seemed equally unpredictable to the Indians. Early in his relationship with the English, Powhatan was promised five hundred men and supplies for a march on the Monacan and Manahoac; but instead of finding wholehearted support among his allies for this campaign, Powhatan discovered that the whites were helpless to support themselves in the New World. As time wore on and they became increasingly desperate for food, the Europeans were less careful in the difficult business of trying to distinguish friends from enemies. They extorted supplies promiscuously, driving hard bargains by the expedient of burning villages and canoes.[19]

It is problematical whether, as Smith implies, Powhatan was actually unable to destroy the handful of English because he could not organize his tribes for a full-scale offensive or whether he was biding his time in the hope of eventually establishing a clear-cut power structure in which the colonists would be allowed to survive but remain subservient to his designs in native warfare. At any rate, after two years of English occupation at Jamestown, Powhatan moved from his traditional home on the Pamunkey River some fifteen miles from the Europeans and settled in a more remote village upstream on the Chickahominy River. Violence flared periodically during

18. [Archer], "Relayton," *ibid.*, lv.

19. See Mooney, "Powhatan Confederacy," *Amer. Anthropologist*, 9 (1907), 136–39, for an exhaustive review of instances illustrating the ever harsher measures taken by the colonists in coercing the Indians. In his indignation, Mooney scarcely notes that the Indians took measures of revenge by killing whites so that the process of hostilities increased over a period of time, with each side intent on settling some score with the other side.

these early years: colonists were frequently killed and often captured. Sometimes, being far from united in their allegiance, they fled to the Indian villages, where they were usually well treated. Captives and runaways were exchanged as hostages when one side or the other found it convenient. However, if Powhatan was willing to take advantage of dissident feeling among the whites, he was no fool and he finally put to death two colonists who seemed to be traitors to both sides at the same time. The execution was much to Smith's satisfaction, for it saved him from performing the task and assured a far more brutal punishment than he would have been able to inflict upon the renegades.[20]

Throughout the period from 1607 to 1609, the chronicles include a complexity of half-told tales involving alliances and enmities and mutual suspicions, of Indians living among settlers and settlers living among Indians. Although this interaction was of an individual nature, the two groups learned something of each other; yet each side maintained its own values and traditions as a social entity. The Indians were primarily concerned with obtaining new material goods. By theft, trade, and the occupation of European artisans in their villages, they increased their supply of armaments and metal work. With the use of Indian guides and informants, the settlers became familiar with the geography of the region, and they also learned the secrets of exploiting their new environment through techniques of native gardening. For the most part, however, conscious efforts to bridge the cultural gap were unavailing. There was one amusing attempt to syncretize concepts of Indian and European monarchy and thereby bring about closer communication, when Powhatan was treated to an elaborate "coronation." The chief weroance was only made more vain by the ceremonies; he was by no means transformed into a loyal subject of the English sovereign, as the white settlers had intended.[21]

An increasing number of settlers arrived in Virginia and, with the

20. Smith admitted that Powhatan's move to the village of Orapaks was simply to get away from the settlers. Arber, ed., Works of John Smith, 20, 70–71, 366–67; for the execution, see ibid., 487.

21. Ibid., 124–25, 434–35. Smith's disgust was aroused by the coronation because it not only made Powhatan conceited, but it threatened to disrupt the trade in copper. Powhatan had been willing to exchange huge amounts of corn for a pittance, and Smith feared he would be spoiled by the rich coronation gifts.

help of Indians who by this time had ample reason to let the whites perish, managed to weather the hazards of the "starving time." As the whites became more firmly established, competition between Europeans and Indians took on the familiar form of a struggle for land. Armed clashes occurred frequently, but there were no organized hostilities, and the Indians continued to trade with the English. A peace which was formally established in 1614 and lasted until 1622 is often attributed to a refinement of Powhatan's sensibilities because of the marriage of Pocahontas and John Rolfe. Although Pocahontas was indeed the favorite child of Powhatan, it is likely that the chieftain's interest in her marriage was not entirely paternal. This strengthening of the social bond between Indians and Europeans helped solidify Powhatan's power and prestige among the confederated tribes, as he was thus enduringly allied with the whites.

Continuation of harmony between Indians and whites for a period of eight years was doubtless rendered possible because enough land still remained in Virginia for both settlers and Indians to live according to their accustomed habits. The seriousness of the loss of Indian land along the James River was lessened by the existence of a strip of virtually unoccupied territory just east of the fall line which ran the length of the Confederacy's holdings. If properly armed and not disturbed by internal dissensions and skirmishes with the English, the Powhatan tribes could afford to settle at the doorstep of their piedmont neighbors and even hope to expand into enemy territory. Hostilities require weapons, and peaceful trade with the English meant easier access to arms which the Confederacy could turn against the Monacan and Manahoac. It is also possible that by this time Powhatan realized the vast strength of the English across the sea and was persuaded to keep the settlers as friends. Knowledge of Europe would have been available to the chieftain through such Indians as Machumps, described by William Strachey as having spent "somtym in England" as well as moving "to and fro amongst us as he dares and as Powhatan gives him leave."[22]

Whatever were Powhatan's reasons for accepting the peace, it appears that he utilized the lull in hostilities to unify the Confederacy and deal with his traditional enemies. We have no direct evidence of activities against the piedmont tribes, for there is little

22. Strachey, *Historie of Travaile into Virginia*, 54.

historical data regarding the western area at this time. However, by the time the fur trade became important in the West the Monacan and Manahoac had lost the power which had once inspired fear among the tribes of the Confederacy. In view of Powhatan's years of scheming and the probable closer proximity of the Confederacy to the piedmont region after 1614, it may be conjectured that the Virginia chieftain and his people took some part in the downfall of the Monacan and Manahoac.[23]

When Powhatan died in 1618, his brother Opechancanough succeeded him as leader of the Confederacy.[24] Opechancanough continued to observe Powhatan's policy of peace for four years, although relations between Indians and Europeans were again degenerating. The Indians' natural resources were threatened as the increasing tobacco crops encroached on land where berries had grown in abundance and game had once been hunted. In the face of European advance, the Indians became restive and complained of the settlers' activities; but these signs went unnoticed by the colonists.[25] Opechancanough was aware that the real danger to the Confederacy arose from neither internal dissensions nor traditional Indian enemies but from the inexorable growth of European society in Virginia. He was apparently able to convince all the member tribes of this fact, if they had not already drawn their own conclusions. The subsequent uprising of 1622 was a well-planned shock to the English; it was

23. Throughout the accounts of 1607–8 there are references to aiding Powhatan in dealing with the piedmont Siouans and Powhatan's satisfaction in the promises. Arber, ed., *Works of John Smith*, 20, 70–71, 366–67; [Archer], "Relayton," *ibid.*, xlvii. As relations between Powhatan and the settlers became strained, Powhatan discouraged the settlers from going to the Monacan, fearing that the whites might ally themselves with his enemies. Smith quotes Powhatan: "As for the Monacans, I can revenge my own iniuries." *Ibid.*, 124, and see 482–83. For the subsequent decline of the Monacan, see the journal of Batt's expedition reprinted from the British Museum manuscript in Bushnell, "Discoveries Beyond the Appalachian Mountains in September, 1671," *Amer. Anthropologist*, 9 (1907), 46–53.

24. Arber, ed., *Works of John Smith*, 451; Robert Beverley, *The History and Present State of Virginia*, ed. by Louis B. Wright (Chapel Hill, 1947), 61.

25. Edward D. Neill, *History of the Virginia Company of London* (Albany, N. Y., 1869), 317–19, cites references which suggest that the Indians expressed excessive protestations of kindness and friendship in order to lull the settlers' suspicions in 1622. Shortly after Powhatan's death, however, fear of the Indians was so intense that Captain Spelman was harshly dealt with on the belief that he was engaged in inciting the Indians to hostile acts.

alarming not so much for the destruction wrought, since by that time the Europeans could sustain the loss of several hundred people, but for the fact that the Confederacy could now operate as a unified fighting organization. This was a solidarity which Powhatan either had been unable or was disinclined to achieve.

Doubtless Opechancanough expected reprisals, but he was totally unprepared for the unprecedented and utter devastation of his lands and the wholesale slaughter of his people. The tribes were scattered, some far beyond the traditional boundaries of their lands, and several of the smaller groups simply ceased to exist as definable entities. Gradually as the fury of revenge died down, the remnants of the Confederacy regrouped and began to return to their homelands. However, the settlers were no longer complacent about their Indian neighbors. In addition to campaigning against the natives, they erected a string of fortifications between Chesiac and Jamestown, and they tended to settle Virginia in the south rather than toward the north and west.[26] In effect, therefore, Opechancanough accomplished a limited objective; a line was established between Indians and Europeans, but the line was only temporary and the Indians paid a terrible price.

Moreover, the cultural gap widened during the ensuing years. Following the period of reprisals the Indians were left to make a living and manage their affairs as best they could. Many old grievances seemed to be forgotten, and the natives gave the appearance of accepting their defeat for all time. Opechancanough, who had eluded capture immediately after the attack of 1622, remained at large, but the Europeans attempted to win tribes away from his influence rather than hunt him down at the risk of inflaming his followers. Finally, white settlement once more began to spread beyond the safety of concentrated colonial population. Tensions were re-created on the frontier, and there were minor skirmishes; the Indians complained to the English, but they also continued their trading activities. Thus matters continued for more than twenty years until large-scale hostilities again broke out.[27]

The uprising of 1644 was surprisingly effective. It is generally

26. Mook, "Aboriginal Population," *Amer. Anthropologist*, 44 (1944), 204–5, discusses shifts in Indian tribal populations as a response to European movements after 1622.

27. Edward D. Neill, *Virginia Calororum: The Colony under the Rule of Charles the First and Second, A.D. 1625–A.D. 1685* (Albany, N. Y., 1886), 60–61.

known that in both the 1622 and the 1644 uprisings the percentage of Indians killed in relation to the total Indian population was far greater than the percentage of settlers killed in relation to the total white population. Yet with far fewer Indians to do the fighting, Opechancanough managed to kill at least as many Europeans in the second attack as he had in the first.[28] The uprising is another proof that the Indians' method of adjusting to changes wrought by the Europeans continued to be an attempt to prevail over or remove the source of anxiety—the settlers—rather than to adapt themselves to the foreign culture. Certainly the Indians never felt that their difficulties would be resolved by assimilation among the whites, a solution which the colonists at times hoped to effect through the adoption of Indian children, intermarriage, and Indian servitude.[29]

Hopeless though the uprising appears in retrospect, it was entirely logical within Opechancanough's own cultural frame of reasoning. It is impossible to determine whether the Indians were aware of the futility of their action, nor do we know enough about the psychology of these people to ascribe to them such a grim fatalism that they would prefer a quick and honorable death to the indignities of living in subjection to the whites. But there is something impressive about Opechancanough, an old and enfeebled man, being carried on a litter to the scene of battle. Whatever the outcome his days were numbered. His young warriors, however, knew of the horrible reprisals of 1622 and they understood the cost of being defeated by the white man. Yet they too were willing to risk an all-out attack.

There is little doubt that Opechancanough realized the danger inherent in rebellion. He was a shrewd strategist and a respected leader. It is entirely possible that he hoped for assistance from forces outside the Confederacy. Tension had existed between the whites of Virginia and Maryland for a number of years, and in one instance the Virginians had hoped to incite the Confederacy against their neighbors. Maryland had been settled only ten years before the second uprising, and although hostile incidents between whites and Indians had occurred, her Indian policy had been more just and humane than Virginia's. If Opechancanough did expect military

28. Mooney, "Powhatan Confederacy," *Amer. Anthropologist*, 9 (1907), 138–39, discusses reductions in Indian population. Opechancanough's secrecy inspires wonder, but the success of the attack is indicative of the degree of separation that marked the lives of the colonists and the Indians by 1644.

29. Neill, *Virginia Calororum*, 74.

assistance from whites for his uprising against whites, he had historical precedent to inspire him. Powhatan had exploited factionalism among the Jamestown settlers, and it may be that the tension between Virginia and Maryland suggested an extension of his policy to Opechancanough. Whatever the motivations behind Opechancanough's design for rebellion, the second uprising attested to the strength of the old Confederacy and indicated clearly the stubborn resistance of the Indians to cultural annihilation.

Although the usual revenge followed the attack of 1644, Virginia's Indian policy was beginning to change. The Powhatan tribes were too seriously reduced in numbers to benefit greatly by the progress, but their treatment at the hands of the colonists following the uprising marked a new development in Indian-white relations, one which eventually culminated in the modern reservation system. In 1646 a formal treaty was signed with the Powhatan Confederacy establishing a line between Indian and white lands and promising the Indians certain rights and protection in their holdings. While their movements were to be strictly regulated, the natives were guaranteed recognition for redress of wrongs before the law. There were two particularly important features of the treaty. First, the Indians were to act as scouts and allies against the possibility of outside tribes' invading the colony; this policy was in contrast to the earlier device of attempting to win the friendship of peripheral tribes to enforce order among the local Indians.[30] Second, and consistent with the growing importance of the fur trade in colonial economics, the Indians were to pay a tribute each year in beaver skins. During the following years various legislative acts were adopted to protect the Indians in their rights and establish mutual responsibilities with the tribes.[31]

---

30. As early as 1609, the instructions given Thomas Gates as acting governor of the colony indicate the initial policy decided upon: "If you make friendship with any of thiese nations as you must doe, choose to do it with those that are farthest from you & enemies unto those amongst whom you dwell for you shall have least occasion to have differences with them, and by that means a surer league of amity." The entire text of Gates's instructions as they related to the Indians is quoted in Bushnell, "Virginia From Early Records," *Amer. Anthropologist*, 9 (1907), 35.

31. See Wesley Frank Craven, *The Southern Colonies in the Seventeenth Century, 1607–1689* (Baton Rouge, La., 1949), 361–66, for a discussion of changes in Virginia's Indian policy.

Winthrop D. Jordan,
"Modern Tensions
and the Origins of American Slavery"

The conflict between blacks and whites in the United States has caused many scholars to search American history for the origins of racial prejudice. In "Modern Tensions and the Origins of American Slavery," Winthrop Jordan reports on the arguments of earlier historians. Most scholars had followed one of two theses: that slavery was responsible for the growth of prejudice, or that prejudice led to the institution of slavery. Jordan emphasized that the history of white racism in America is inextricably bound to the development of slavery, but the causal relationship is less certain. He concludes that the institution of slavery and white prejudice toward blacks developed gradually and simultaneously, each factor reinforcing the other. In a subsequent work, White Over Black, Jordan found conclusive evidence to indicate a jaundiced English view of black Africans even before contact between them was established. The resulting entrenchment of both slavery and racism by the eighteenth century fixed the pattern of black subjugation which has been an enduring theme of American history.

Modern Tensions
and the Origins of American Slavery
Winthrop D. Jordan

Thanks to John Smith we know that Negroes first came to the British continental colonies in 1619.[1] What we do not know is exactly when Negroes were first enslaved there. This question has been debated by historians for the past seventy years, the critical point being whether Negroes were enslaved almost from their first importation or whether they were at first simply servants and only later reduced to the status of slaves. The long duration and vigor of the controversy suggest that more than a simple question of dating has been involved. In fact certain current tensions in American society have complicated the historical problem and greatly heightened its significance. Dating the origins of slavery has taken on a striking modern relevance.

Winthrop D. Jordan, "Modern Tensions and the Origins of American Slavery," *Journal of Southern History*, XXVIII (February, 1962), pp. 18–30. Copyright © 1962 by the Southern Historical Association. Reprinted by permission of the Managing Editor. A modified and much more complete description of the origin of American slavery is in Winthrop D. Jordan, *White Over Black: American Attitudes Toward the Negro, 1550–1812* (Chapel Hill, 1968).

1. "About the last of August came in a dutch man of warre that sold us twenty Negars." Smith was quoting John Rolfe's account. Edward Arber and A. G. Bradley (eds.), *Travels and Works of Captain John Smith* ... (2 vols., Edinburgh, 1910), II, 541.

During the nineteenth century historians assumed almost universally that the first Negroes came to Virginia as slaves. So close was their acquaintance with the problem of racial slavery that it did not occur to them that Negroes could ever have been anything but slaves. Philip A. Bruce, the first man to probe with some thoroughness into the early years of American slavery, adopted this view in 1896, although he emphasized that the original difference in treatment between white servants and Negroes was merely that Negroes served for life. Just six years later, however, came a challenge from a younger, professionally trained historian, James C. Ballagh. His *A History of Slavery in Virginia* appeared in the *Johns Hopkins University Studies in Historical and Political Science*, an aptly named series which was to usher in the new era of scholarly detachment in the writing of institutional history. Ballagh offered a new and different interpretation; he took the position that the first Negroes served merely as servants and that enslavement did not begin until around 1660, when statutes bearing on slavery were passed for the first time.[2]

There has since been agreement on dating the statutory establishment of slavery, and differences of opinion have centered on when enslavement began in actual practice. Fortunately there has also been general agreement on slavery's distinguishing characteristics: service for life and inheritance of like obligation by any offspring. Writing on the free Negro in Virginia for the Johns Hopkins series, John H. Russell in 1913 tackled the central question and showed that some Negroes were indeed servants but concluded that "between 1640 and 1660 slavery was fast becoming an established fact. In this twenty years the colored population was divided, part being servants and part being slaves, and some who were servants defended themselves with increasing difficulty from the encroachments of slavery."[3] Ulrich B. Phillips, though little interested in the matter, in 1918 accepted Russell's conclusion of early servitude and transition toward slavery after 1640. Helen T. Catterall took much the same position in 1926.

2. Philip A. Bruce, *Economic History of Virginia in the Seventeenth Century* (2 vols., New York, 1896), II, 57–130; James C. Ballagh, *A History of Slavery in Virginia* (Baltimore, 1902), 28–35.

3. John H. Russell, *The Free Negro in Virginia, 1619–1865* (Baltimore, 1913), 29.

On the other hand, in 1921 James M. Wright, discussing the free Negro in Maryland, implied that Negroes were slaves almost from the beginning, and in 1940 Susie M. Ames reviewed several cases in Virginia which seemed to indicate that genuine slavery had existed well before Ballagh's date of 1660.[4]

All this was a very small academic gale, well insulated from the outside world. Yet despite disagreement on dating enslavement, the earlier writers—Bruce, Ballagh, and Russell—shared a common assumption which, though at the time seemingly irrelevant to the main question, has since proved of considerable importance. They assumed that prejudice against the Negro was natural and almost innate in the white man. It would be surprising if they had felt otherwise in this period of segregation statutes, overseas imperialism, immigration restriction, and full-throated Anglo-Saxonism. By the 1920's, however, with the easing of these tensions, the assumption of natural prejudice was dropped unnoticed. Yet only one historian explicitly contradicted that assumption: Ulrich Phillips of Georgia, impressed with the geniality of both slavery and twentieth-century race relations, found no natural prejudice in the white man and expressed his "conviction that Southern racial asperities are mainly superficial, and that the two great elements are fundamentally in accord."[5]

Only when tensions over race relations intensified once more did the older assumption of natural prejudice crop up again. After World War II American Negroes found themselves beneficiaries of New Deal politics and reforms, wartime need for manpower, worldwide repulsion at racist excesses in Nazi Germany, and growingly successful colored anticolonialism. With new militancy Negroes

4. *Ibid.*, 23–39; Ulrich B. Phillips, *American Negro Slavery* (New York, 1918), 75–77, and *Life and Labor in the Old South* (Boston, 1929), 170; Helen T. Catterall (ed.), *Judicial Cases Concerning American Slavery and the Negro* (5 vols., Washington, 1926–1937), I, 54–55, 57–63; James M. Wright, *The Free Negro in Maryland, 1634–1860* (New York, 1921), 21–23; Susie M. Ames, *Studies of the Virginia Eastern Shore in the Seventeenth Century* (Richmond, 1940), 100–106. See also T. R. Davis, "Negro Servitude in the United States," *Journal of Negro History*, VIII (July 1923), 247–83, and Edgar T. Thompson, "The Natural History of Agricultural Labor in the South" in David K. Jackson (ed.), *American Studies in Honor of William Kenneth Boyd* (Durham, N. C., 1940), 127–46.

5. Phillips, *American Negro Slavery*, viii.

mounted an attack on the citadel of separate but equal, and soon it became clear that America was in for a period of self-conscious reappraisal of its racial arrangements. Writing in this period of heightened tension (1949) a practiced and careful scholar, Wesley F. Craven, raised the old question of the Negro's original status, suggesting that Negroes had been enslaved at an early date. Craven also cautiously resuscitated the idea that white men may have had natural distaste for the Negro, an idea which fitted neatly with the suggestion of early enslavement. Original antipathy would mean rapid debasement.[6]

In the next year (1950) came a sophisticated counterstatement, which contradicted both Craven's dating and implicitly any suggestion of early prejudice. Oscar and Mary F. Handlin in "Origins of the Southern Labor System" offered a case for late enslavement, with servitude as the status of Negroes before about 1660. Originally the status of both Negroes and white servants was far short of freedom, the Handlins maintained, but Negroes failed to benefit from increased freedom for servants in mid-century and became less free rather than more.[7] Embedded in this description of diverging status were broader implications: Late and gradual enslavement undercut the possibility of natural, deep-seated antipathy toward Negroes. On the contrary, if whites and Negroes could share the same status of half freedom for forty years in the seventeenth century, why could they not share full freedom in the twentieth?

The same implications were rendered more explicit by Kenneth M. Stampp in a major reassessment of Southern slavery published two years after the Supreme Court's 1954 school decision. Reading physiology with the eye of faith, Stampp frankly stated his assumption "that innately Negroes are, after all, only white men with black skins, nothing more, nothing less."[8] Closely following the Handlins' article on the origins of slavery itself, he almost directly denied any pattern of early and inherent racial antipathy: "... Negro and white

6. Wesley F. Craven, *The Southern Colonies in the Seventeenth Century, 1607–1689* (Baton Rouge, 1949), 217–19, 402–403.

7. *William and Mary Quarterly*, s. 3, VII (April 1950), 199–222.

8. Kenneth M. Stampp, *The Peculiar Institution: Slavery in the Ante-Bellum South* (New York, 1956), vii–viii, 3–33.

servants of the seventeenth century seemed to be remarkably uncon-
cerned about their visible physical differences." As for "the trend toward special treatment" of the Negro, "physical and cultural differences provided handy excuses to justify it."[9] Distaste for the Negro,
then, was in the beginning scarcely more than an appurtenance of
slavery.

These views squared nicely with the hopes of those even more
directly concerned with the problem of contemporary race relations,
sociologists and social psychologists. Liberal on the race question almost to a man, they tended to see slavery as the initial cause of the
Negro's current degradation. The modern Negro was the unhappy
victim of long association with base status. Sociologists, though unin-
terested in tired questions of historical evidence, could not easily
assume a natural prejudice in the white man as the cause of slavery.
Natural or innate prejudice would not only violate their basic assumptions concerning the dominance of culture but would under-
mine the power of their new Baconian science. For if prejudice was
natural there would be little one could do to wipe it out. Prejudice
must have followed enslavement, not vice versa, else any liberal program of action would be badly compromised. One prominent social
scientist suggested in a UNESCO pamphlet that racial prejudice in
the United States commenced with the cotton gin![10]

Just how closely the question of dating had become tied to the
practical matter of action against racial prejudice was made apparent
by the suggestions of still another historian. Carl N. Degler grappled
with the dating problem in an article frankly entitled "Slavery and
the Genesis of American Race Prejudice."[11] The article appeared in

---

9. *Ibid.*, 21–22.

10. Arnold Rose, "The Roots of Prejudice" in UNESCO, *The Race Question
in Modern Science* (New York, 1956), 224. For examples of the more general
view see Frederick G. Detweiler, "The Rise of Modern Race Antagonisms,"
American Journal of Sociology, XXXVII (March 1932), 743; M. F. Ashley
Montagu, *Man's Most Dangerous Myth: The Fallacy of Race* (New York, 1945),
10–11, 19–20; Gunnar Myrdal, *An American Dilemma: The Negro Problem and
Modern Democracy* (New York, 1944), 83–89, 97; Paul Kecskemeti, "The Psychological Theory of Prejudice: Does it Underrate the Role of Social History?"
Commentary, XVIII (October 1954), 364–66.

11. *Comparative Studies in Society and History*, II (October 1959), 49–68. See
also Degler, *Out of Our Past: The Forces that Shaped Modern America* (New
York, 1959), 26–39.

1959, a time when Southern resistance to school desegregation seemed more adamant than ever and the North's hands none too clean, a period of discouragement for those hoping to end racial discrimination. Prejudice against the Negro now appeared firm and deep-seated, less easily eradicated than had been supposed in, say, 1954. It was Degler's view that enslavement began early, as a result of white settlers' prejudice or antipathy toward the first Negroes. Thus not only were the sociologists contradicted but the dating problem was now overtly and consciously tied to the broader question of whether slavery caused prejudice or prejudice caused slavery. A new self-consciousness over the American racial dilemma had snatched an arid historical controversy from the hands of an unsuspecting earlier generation and had tossed it into the arena of current debate.

Ironically there might have been no historical controversy at all if every historian dealing with the subject had exercised greater care with facts and greater restraint in interpretation. Too often the debate entered the realm of inference and assumption. For the crucial early years after 1619 there is simply not enough evidence to indicate with any certainty whether Negroes were treated like white servants or not. No historian has found anything resembling proof one way or the other. The first Negroes were sold to the English settlers, yet so were other Englishmen. It can be said, however, that Negroes were set apart from white men by the word *Negroes*, and a distinct name is not attached to a group unless it is seen as different. The earliest Virginia census reports plainly distinguished Negroes from white men, sometimes giving Negroes no personal name; and in 1629 every commander of the several plantations was ordered to "take a generall muster of all the inhabitants men woemen and Children as well *Englishe* as Negroes."[12] Difference, however, might or might not involve inferiority.

The first evidence as to the actual status of Negroes does not appear until about 1640. Then it becomes clear that *some* Negroes were serving for life and some children inheriting the same obligation. Here it is necessary to suggest with some candor that the Handlins'

12. H. R. McIlwaine (ed.), *Minutes of the Council and General Court of Colonial Virginia, 1622–1632, 1670–1676* (Richmond, 1924), 196. See the lists and musters of 1624 and 1625 in John C. Hotten (ed.), *The Original Lists of Persons of Quality* ... (New York, 1880), 169–265.

statement to the contrary rests on unsatisfactory documentation.[13] That some Negroes were held as slaves after about 1640 is no indication, however, that American slavery popped into the world fully developed at that time. Many historians, most cogently the Handlins, have shown slavery to have been a gradual development, a process not completed until the eighteenth century. The complete deprivation of civil and personal rights, the legal conversion of the Negro into a chattel, in short slavery as Americans came to know it, was not accomplished overnight. Yet these developments practically and logically depended on the practice of hereditary lifetime service, and it is certainly possible to find in the 1640's and 1650's traces of slavery's most essential feature.[14]

The first definite trace appears in 1640 when the Virginia General Court pronounced sentence on three servants who had been retaken after running away to Maryland. Two of them, a Dutchman and a Scot, were ordered to serve their masters for one additional year and then the colony for three more, but "the third being a negro named John Punch shall serve his said master or his assigns for the time of his natural life here or else where." No white servant in America, so

13. "The status of Negroes was that of servants; and so they were identified and treated down to the 1660's." ("Origins," 203.) The footnote to this statement reads, "For disciplinary and revenue laws in Virginia that did not discriminate Negroes from other servants, see Hening, *Statutes*, I, 174, 198, 200, 243, 306 (1631–1645)." But pp. 200 and 243 of William Waller Hening (ed.), *The Statutes at Large; Being a Collection of All the Laws of Virginia* . . . (2nd ed. of vols. 1–4, New York, 1823), I, in fact contain nothing about either servants or Negroes, while a tax provision on p. 242 specifically discriminates against Negro women. The revenue act on p. 306 lists the number of pounds of tobacco levied on land, cattle, sheep, horses, etc., and on tithable persons, and provides for collection of lists of the above so that the colony can compute its tax program; nothing else is said of servants and tithables. To say, as the Handlins did in the same note, that Negroes, English servants, and horses, etc., were listed all together in some early Virginia wills, with the implication that Negroes and English servants were regarded as alike in status, is hardly correct unless one is to assume that the horses were sharing this status as well. (For complete bibliographical information on Hening [ed.], *Statutes*, see E. G. Swem, *Virginia Historical Index* [2 vols., Roanoke, Va., 1934–1936], I, xv–xvi.)
14. Latin-American Negroes did not lose all civil and personal rights, did not become mere chattels, yet we speak of "slavery" in Latin America without hesitation. See Frank Tannenbaum, *Slave and Citizen: The Negro in the Americas* (New York, 1947), and Gilberto Freyre, *The Masters and the Slaves: A Study in the Development of Brazilian Civilization* (New York, 1946).

far as is known, ever received a like sentence.[15] Later the same month a Negro was again singled out from a group of recaptured runaways; six of the seven were assigned additional time while the Negro was given none, presumably because he was already serving for life.[16] After 1640, too, county court records began to mention Negroes, in part because there were more of them than previously—about two per cent of the Virginia population in 1649.[17] Sales for life, often including any future progeny, were recorded in unmistakable language. In 1646 Francis Pott sold a Negro woman and boy to Stephen Charlton "to the use of him ... forever." Similarly, six years later William Whittington sold to John Pott "one Negro girle named Jowan; aged about Ten yeares and with her Issue and produce duringe her (or either of them) for their Life tyme. And their Successors forever"; and a Maryland man in 1649 deeded two Negro men and a woman "and all their issue both male and Female." The executors of a York County estate in 1647 disposed of eight Negroes— four men, two women, and two children—to Captain John Chisman "to have hold occupy posesse and inioy and every one of the afforementioned Negroes forever[.]"[18] The will of Rowland Burnham of "Rapahanocke," made in 1657, dispensed his considerable number of Negroes and white servants in language which clearly differentiated between the two by specifying that the whites were to serve for their "full terme of tyme" and the Negroes "for ever."[19] Nor did anything

15. "Decisions of the General Court," Virginia Magazine of History and Biography, V (January 1898), 236. Abbot Emerson Smith in the standard work on servitude in America, Colonists in Bondage: White Servitude and Convict Labor in America, 1607–1776 (Chapel Hill, 1947), 171, says that "there was never any such thing as perpetual slavery for any white man in any English colony." There were instances in the seventeenth century of white men sold into "slavery," but this was when the meaning of the term was still indefinite and often equated with servitude.

16. "Decisions of the General Court," 236–37.

17. A Perfect Description of Virginia ... (London, 1649), reprinted in Peter Force (ed.), Tracts ... (4 vols., Washington, 1836–1846), II.

18. These four cases may be found in Northampton County Deeds, Wills &c. (Virginia State Library, Richmond), No. 4 (1651–1654), 28 (misnumbered 29), 124; Archives of Maryland (69 vols., Baltimore, 1883–1961), XLI, 261–62; York County Records (Virginia State Library), No. 2 (transcribed Wills & Deeds, 1645–1649), 256–57.

19. Lancaster County Loose Papers (Virginia State Library), Box of Wills, 1650–1719, Folder 1656–1659.

in the will indicate that this distinction was exceptional or novel. In addition to these clear indications that some Negroes were owned for life, there were cases of Negroes held for terms far longer than the normal five or seven years.[20] On the other hand, some Negroes served only the term usual for white servants, and others were completely free.[21] One Negro freeman, Anthony Johnson, himself owned a Negro.[22] Obviously the enslavement of some Negroes did not mean the immediate enslavement of all.

Further evidence of Negroes serving for life lies in the prices paid for them. In many instances the valuations placed on Negroes (in estate inventories and bills of sale) were far higher than for white servants, even those servants with full terms yet to serve. Since there was ordinarily no preference for Negroes as such, higher prices must have meant that Negroes were more highly valued because of their greater length of service. Negro women may have been especially prized, moreover, because their progeny could also be held perpetually. In 1645, for example, two Negro women and a boy were sold for 5,500 pounds of tobacco. Two years earlier William Burdett's inventory listed eight servants (with the time each had still to serve) at valuations ranging from 400 to 1,100 pounds, while a "very antient" Negro was valued at 3,000 and an eight-year-old Negro girl at 2,000 pounds, with no time-remaining indicated for either. In the late 1650's an inventory of Thomas Ludlow's large estate evaluated a white servant with six years to serve at less than an elderly Negro man and only one half of a Negro woman.[23] The labor owned by James Stone in 1648 was evaluated as follows:

20. For examples running for as long as thirty-five years, see William and Mary Quarterly, s. 1, XX (October 1911), 148; Russell, Free Negro in Virginia, 26–27; Ames, Eastern Shore, 105. Compare the cases of a Negro and an Irish servant in Calendar of Virginia State Papers ... (11 vols., Richmond, 1875–1892), I, 9–10, and Maryland Archives, XLI, 476–78; XLIX, 123–24.

21. Russell, Free Negro in Virginia, 24–41. See especially the cases in Virginia Magazine of History and Biography, V (July 1897), 40; York County Deeds, Wills, Orders, etc. (Virginia State Library), No. 1 (1633–1657, 1691–1694), 338–39.

22. John H. Russell, "Colored Freemen As Slave Owners in Virginia," Journal of Negro History, I (July 1916), 234–37.

23. York County Records, No. 2, 63; Northampton County Orders, Deeds, Wills, &c., No. 2 (1640–1645), 224; York County Deeds, Orders, Wills, &c. (1657–1662), 108–109.

	lb tobo
Thomas Groves, 4 yeares to serve	1300
Francis Bomley for 6 yeares	1500
John Thackstone for 3 yeares	1300
Susan Davis for 3 yeares	1000
Emaniell a Negro man	2000
Roger Stone 3 yeares	1300
Mingo a Negro man	2000[24]

Besides setting a higher value on the two Negroes, Stone's inventory, like Burdett's, failed to indicate the number of years they had still to serve. It would seem safe to assume that the time remaining was omitted in this and similar documents simply because the Negroes were regarded as serving for an unlimited time.

The situation in Maryland was apparently the same. In 1643 Governor Leonard Calvert agreed with John Skinner, "mariner," to exchange certain estates for seventeen sound Negro "slaves," fourteen men and three women between sixteen and twenty-six years old. The total value of these was placed at 24,000 pounds of tobacco, which would work out to 1,000 pounds for the women and 1,500 for the men, prices considerably higher than those paid for white servants at the time.[25]

Wherever Negro women were involved, however, higher valuations may have reflected the fact that they could be used for field work while white women generally were not. This discrimination between Negro and white women, of course, fell short of actual enslavement. It meant merely that Negroes were set apart in a way clearly not to their advantage. Yet this is not the only evidence that Negroes were subjected to degrading distinctions not directly related to slavery. In several ways Negroes were singled out for special treatment which suggested a generalized debasing of Negroes as a group. Significantly, the first indications of debasement appeared at about the same time as the first indications of actual enslavement.

The distinction concerning field work is a case in point. It first

24. York County Records, No. 2, 390.
25. Apparently Calvert's deal with Skinner was never consummated. *Maryland Archives*, IV, vii, 189, 320–21. For prices of white servants see *ibid.*, IV, 31, 47–48, 74, 78–79, 81, 83, 92, 98, 108–109, 184, 200, 319.

appeared on the written record in 1643, when Virginia pointedly recognized it in her taxation policy. Previously tithable persons had been defined (1629) as "all those that worke in the ground of what qualitie or condition soever." Now the law stated that all adult men and Negro women were to be tithable, and this distinction was made twice again before 1660. Maryland followed a similar course, beginning in 1654.[26] John Hammond, in a 1656 tract defending the tobacco colonies, wrote that servant women were not put to work in the fields but in domestic employments, "yet som wenches that are nasty, and beastly and not fit to be so imployed are put into the ground."[27] Since all Negro women were taxed as working in the fields, it would seem logical to conclude that Virginians found them "nasty" and "beastly." The essentially racial nature of this discrimination was bared by a 1668 law at the time slavery was crystallizing on the statute books:

> Whereas some doubts have arisen whether negro women set free were still to be accompted tithable according to a former act, *It is declared by this grand assembly* that negro women, though permitted to enjoy their ffreedome yet ought not in all respects to be admitted to a full fruition of the exemptions and impunities of the English, and are still lyable to payment of taxes.[28]

Virginia law set Negroes apart in a second way by denying them the important right and obligation to bear arms. Few restraints could indicate more clearly the denial to Negroes of membership in the white community. This action, in a sense the first foreshadowing of the slave codes, came in 1640, at just the time when other indications first appear that Negroes were subject to special treatment.[29]

26. Hening (ed.), *Statutes*, I, 144, 242, 292, 454. The Handlins erroneously placed the "first sign of discrimination" in this matter at 1668 ("Origins," 217n). For Maryland, see *Maryland Archives*, I, 342; II, 136, 399, 538–39; XIII, 538–39.

27. John Hammond, *Leah and Rachel, or, the Two Fruitful Sisters Virginia, and Mary-land: Their Present Condition, Impartially Stated and Related* . . . (London, 1656), reprinted in Force (ed.), *Tracts*, II.

28. Hening (ed.), *Statutes*, II, 267. The distinction between white and colored women was neatly described at the turn of the century by Robert Beverley, *The History and Present State of Virginia*, Louis B. Wright, ed. (Chapel Hill, 1947), 271–72.

29. Hening (ed.), *Statutes*, I, 226, and for the same act in more detail see *William and Mary Quarterly*, s. 2, IV (July 1924), 147. The Handlins dis-

Finally, an even more compelling sense of the separateness of Negroes was revealed in early distress concerning sexual union between the races. In 1630 a Virginia court pronounced a now famous sentence: "Hugh Davis to be soundly whipped, before an assembly of Negroes and others for abusing himself to the dishonor of God and shame of Christians, by defiling his body in lying with a negro."[30] While there were other instances of punishment for interracial union in the ensuing years, fornication rather than miscegenation may well have been the primary offense, though in 1651 a Maryland man sued someone who he claimed had said "that he had a black bastard in Virginia."[31] There may have been nothing racial about the 1640 case by which Robert Sweet was compelled "to do penance in church according to laws of England, for getting a negroe woman with child and the woman whipt."[32] About 1650 a white man and a Negro woman were required to stand clad in white sheets before a congregation in Lower Norfolk County for having had relations, but this punishment was sometimes used in ordinary cases of fornication between two whites.[33]

---

counted this law: "Until the 1660's the statutes on the Negroes were not at all unique. Nor did they add up to a decided trend." ("Origins," 209.) The note added to this statement reads, "That there was no trend is evident from the fluctuations in naming Negroes slaves or servants and in their right to bear arms. See Hening, Statutes, I, 236, 258, 292, 540; Bruce, Institutional History, II, 5 ff., 190 ff. For similar fluctuations with regard to Indians, see Hening, Statutes, I, 391, 518." But since the terms "servants" and "slaves" did not have precise meaning, as the Handlins themselves asserted, fluctuations in naming Negroes one or the other can not be taken to mean that their status itself was fluctuating. Of the pages cited in Hening, p. 258 is an act encouraging Dutch traders and contains nothing about Negroes, servants, slaves, or arms. Page 292 is an act providing that fifteen tithable persons should support one soldier; Negroes were among those tithable, but nothing was said of allowing them to arm. Page 540 refers to "any negro slaves" and "said negro," but mentions nothing about servants or arms. In the pages dealing with Indians, p. 391 provides that no one is to employ Indian servants with guns, and p. 518 that Indians (not "Indian servants") are to be allowed to use their own guns; the two provisions are not contradictory. Philip A. Bruce, Institutional History of Virginia in the Seventeenth Century (2 vols., New York, 1910), II, 5 ff., indicates that Negroes were barred from arming in 1639 and offers no suggestion that there was any later fluctuation in this practice.

30. Hening (ed.), Statutes, I, 146. "Christianity" appears instead of "Christians" in McIlwaine (ed.), Minutes of the Council, 479.

31. Maryland Archives, X, 114–15.

32. Hening (ed.), Statutes, I, 552; McIlwaine, Minutes of the Council, 477.

33. Bruce, Economic History of Virginia, II, 110.

It is certain, however, that in the early 1660's when slavery was gaining statutory recognition, the colonial assemblies legislated with feeling against miscegenation. Nor was this merely a matter of avoiding confusion of status, as was suggested by the Handlins. In 1662 Virginia declared that "if any christian shall committ ffornication with a negro man or woman, hee or shee soe offending" should pay double the usual fine. Two years later Maryland prohibited interracial marriages:

> forasmuch as divers freeborne English women forgettfull of their free Condicōn and to the disgrace of our Nation doe intermarry with Negro Slaves by which alsoe divers suites may arise touching the Issue of such woemen and a great damage doth befall the Masters of such Negros for prevention whereof for deterring such freeborne women from such shamefull Matches . . . ,

strong language indeed if the problem had only been confusion of status. A Maryland act of 1681 described marriages of white women with Negroes as, among other things, "always to the Satisfaccōn of theire Lascivious & Lustfull desires, & to the disgrace not only of the English butt allso of many other Christian Nations." When Virginia finally prohibited all interracial liaisons in 1691, the assembly vigorously denounced miscegenation and its fruits as "that abominable mixture and spurious issue."[34]

34. Hening (ed.), Statutes, II, 170; III, 86–87; Maryland Archives, I, 533–34; VII, 204. Opinion on this matter apparently was not unanimous, for a petition of several citizens to the Council in 1699 asked repeal of the intermarriage prohibition. H. R. McIlwaine (ed.), Legislative Journals of the Council of Colonial Virginia (3 vols., Richmond, 1918–1919), I, 262. The Handlins wrote ("Origins," 215), "Mixed marriages of free men and servants were particularly frowned upon as complicating status and therefore limited by law." Their citation for this, Hening (ed.), Statutes, II, 114 (1661/62), and Marcus W. Jernegan, Laboring and Dependent Classes in Colonial America, 1607–1783 (Chicago, 1931), 55, 180, gives little backing to the statement. In Virginia secret marriage or bastardy between whites of different status got the same punishment as such between whites of the same status. A white servant might marry any white if his master consented. See Hening (ed.), Statutes, I, 252–53, 438–39; II, 114–15; 167; III, 71–75, 137–40. See also James C. Ballagh, White Servitude in the Colony of Virginia (Baltimore, 1895), 50. For Maryland, see Maryland Archives, I, 73, 373–74, 441–42; II, 396-97; XIII, 501–502. The Handlins also suggested that in the 1691 Virginia law, "spurious" meant simply "illegitimate," and they cited Arthur W. Calhoun, A Social History of the American Family from

One is confronted, then, with the fact that the first evidences of enslavement and of other forms of debasement appeared at about the same time. Such coincidence comports poorly with both views on the causation of prejudice and slavery. If slavery caused prejudice, then invidious distinctions concerning working in the fields, bearing arms, and sexual union should have appeared only after slavery's firm establishment. If prejudice caused slavery, then one would expect to find such lesser discriminations preceding the greater discrimination of outright enslavement.

Perhaps a third explanation of the relationship between slavery and prejudice may be offered, one that might fit the pattern of events as revealed by existing evidence. Both current views share a common starting point: They predicate two factors, prejudice and slavery, and demand a distinct order of causality. No matter how qualified by recognition that the effect may in turn react upon the cause, each approach inevitably tends to deny the validity of its opposite. But what if one were to regard both slavery and prejudice as species of a general debasement of the Negro? Both may have been equally cause and effect, constantly reacting upon each other, dynamically joining hands to hustle the Negro down the road to complete degradation. Mutual causation is, of course, a highly useful concept for describing social situations in the modern world.[35] Indeed it has been widely applied in only slightly altered fashion to the current racial situation: Racial prejudice and the Negro's lowly position are widely accepted as constantly reinforcing each other.

This way of looking at the facts might well fit better with what we know of slavery itself. Slavery was an organized pattern of human relationships. No matter what the law might say, it was of different character than cattle ownership. No matter how degrading, slavery involved human beings. No one seriously pretended otherwise. Slavery was not an isolated economic or institutional phenomenon; it was the practical facet of a general debasement without which slavery could have no rationality. (Prejudice, too, was a form of debasement,

---

Colonial Times to the Present (3 vols., Cleveland, O., 1917–1919), I, 42, which turns out to be one quotation from John Milton. However, "spurious" was used in colonial laws with reference only to unions between white and black, and never in bastardy laws involving whites only. Mulattoes were often labeled "spurious" offspring.

35. For example, George C. Homans, The Human Group (New York, 1950).

a kind of slavery in the mind.) Certainly the urgent need for labor in a virgin country guided the direction which debasement took, molded it, in fact, into an institutional framework. That economic practicalities shaped the external form of debasement should not tempt one to forget, however, that slavery was at bottom a social arrangement, a way of society's ordering its members in its own mind.

William S. Willis,
"Divide and Rule:
Red, White, and Black in the Southeast"

Three races, red, black, and white, resided in the British North
American colonies. In "Divide and Rule," William Willis examines
the relationships among the races in eighteenth-century
South Carolina where a white minority lived among larger black
and red populations. The whites feared both nonwhite majorities
as a threat to their security, and particularly, dreaded a black and red
alliance against their domination. Willis details the means by
which whites attempted to separate and alienate the two
majorities from each other. By making each an accomplice in
the struggle to subjugate the other and by creating hostility
between them, South Carolina whites were able to divide and rule.

Divide and Rule:
Red, White, and Black
in the Southeast

William S. Willis

North of Mexico, the Colonial Southeast was the only place where Indians, Whites, and Negroes met in large numbers.[1] Little of the fascinating story of this contact has been told and some crucial parts may be beyond recall for lack of documents. The early attitude of Indians toward Negroes is obviously of great importance. To some extent, it has been dealt with, but conclusions have differed. Laurence Foster and James Johnston are certain that the early feeling of Indians was one of friendliness.[2] On the other hand, some students, mainly Southern historians, stress hostility.[3] As a matter of fact, a

Abridged from William S. Willis, "Divide and Rule: Red, White, and Black in the Southeast," pp. 157–176. Copyright © by The Association for the Study of Negro Life and History, Inc. Published in *The Journal of Negro History*, XLVIII (July 1963). Some footnotes have been renumbered.

1. Gratitude is extended to Margaret Furcron, Brooklyn College, to Elliott P. Skinner, New York University, and especially to Morton H. Fried, Columbia University, for valuable suggestions, but any infelicities of style or errors of fact are the author's.

2. Laurence Foster, *Negro-Indian Relationships in the Southeast* (Philadelphia, 1935), p. 74; James H. Johnston, "Documentary Evidence of the Relations of Negroes and Indians," *Journal of Negro History*, XIV (January, 1929), pp. 21–23.

3. W. J. Rivers, *A Sketch of the History of South Carolina* (Charleston, 1856), p. 48; W. C. Macleod, *The American Indian Frontier* (New York, 1928), p. 306; Chapman J. Milling, *Red Carolinians* (Chapel Hill, 1940), p. 63.

great deal of hostility seems to have existed in the eighteenth century. In 1752, the Catawba Indians showed great anger and bitter resentment when a Negro came among them as a trader.[4] Perhaps the Cherokee had the strongest color prejudice of all Indians. Even the Spaniards were not "White" enough for them. In 1793, Little Turkey, a prominent chief, declared that Spaniards were not "real white people, and what few I have seen of them looked like mulattoes, and I would never have anything to say to them."[5] According to John Brickell, an early eighteenth century reporter, Indians had a "natural aversion to the Blacks."[6] In 1763, George Milligen Johnston, a South Carolina physician, opined that this hostility was mutual and spoke of the "natural Dislike and Antipathy, that subsists between them [Negroes] and our Indian Neighbors."[7] But the Southern historians have not explained why Indians disliked Negroes. This paper examines this hostility, and that of Negroes to Indians. The story is the familiar one of divide and rule. Specifically, it will be shown that Whites willfully helped create the antagonism between Indians and Negroes in order to preserve themselves and their privileges.

In the Colonial Southeast, Negro slavery and trade with Indians were more prominent in South Carolina than anywhere else. The province sanctioned slavery from its beginnings in 1670, but South Carolinians brought in few Negroes until the late 1690's. From that time, the steady increase in the number of Negro slaves correlates with the steadily increasing demand for labor. First, there was the expansion of rice production on slave-operated plantations. This occurred at about the same time, near the turn of the eighteenth century, that the general supply of slaves in the New World swelled. In the 1720's, the manufacture of pitch and tar, and in the 1740's the growth of indigo production added to the demand for slave labor. Meanwhile other events conspired to curtail other supplies of labor. Indian slavery dwindled and virtually disappeared after the Yamassee War of 1715–1717. This rebellion of tribes trading with the province produced a widespread notion that South Carolina was a dangerous

4. W. L. McDowell (ed.), *Documents relating to Indian Affairs, May 21, 1750–August 7, 1754* (Columbia, 1959), p. 201.
5. *American State Papers, Indian Affairs*, I, 461.
6. John Brickell, *The Natural History of North Carolina* (Dublin, 1737), p. 263.
7. Milling (ed.), *Colonial South Carolina: Two Contemporary Descriptions* (Columbia, 1951), p. 136.

place and few Whites entered for two decades after the fighting. The demand for Negroes grew in tandem with the mounting political power of the planters and the government was increasingly responsive to the latter's demands. By the beginning of the eighteenth century, Negroes outnumbered Whites and they increased their proportion of the population later in the century when various estimates put the ratio at two or three to one and even higher.[8]

Despite allegations about the submissiveness of Negroes and their acquiescence to slavery, eighteenth century Whites were afraid of their slaves. This fear grew as Negroes became more numerous. Whites especially dreaded slave insurrections; to South Carolinians, Negro rebels were an "intestine Enemy the most dreadful of Enemies."[9] The eighteenth century was punctuated by a steady succession of insurrectionary plots and actual insurrections. Indeed, the Charles Town government at times kept half of its soldiers in the capital. Negroes also struck back at their masters in other ways. They poisoned them, they set fires, and they committed suicide. They also employed subtle everyday resistances, such as, malingering and feigned stupidity. They also ran away. Some went for only short periods to nearby places; others went permanently to distant hiding places, to the mountains and swamps, to the Indian country, and to the Spanish in Florida. Running south to Florida became especially common after the Yamassee War when Spain encouraged more Negroes to come and offered them freedom. By the late 1720's, Negro subversion had become the main defense problem of South Carolina.[10]

Indians were also a big problem, and they were feared. The Colonial Southeast was an arena of an unremitting struggle for empire among Whites: English, French, Spanish, and later Americans. Indian tribes were caught in the middle of this struggle; and Whites competed for their allegiance, for their trade and their warriors. Suc-

8. David D. Wallace, *South Carolina: A Short History, 1520–1948* (Chapel Hill, 1951), *passim*; Verner W. Crane, *The Southern Frontier, 1670–1732* (Durham, 1928), *passim*.

9. J. H. Easterby (ed.), *Journals of the Commons House of Assembly, September 12, 1739–March 26, 1741* (Columbia, 1952), p. 97.

10. Herbert Aptheker, *American Negro Slave Revolts* (New York, 1943), *passim*; Alexander Garden to Secretary, October 31, 1759, Society for the Propagation of the Gospel in Foreign Parts MSS (later cited as SPG MSS), Series B, II, Pt. 1, 962 Library of Congress; Robert L. Meriwether, *The Expansion of South Carolina, 1729–1765* (Kingsport, 1940), p. 6.

cess in the empire struggle depended upon success in the Indian country. For a decade at least, the mere survival of South Carolina remained uncertain and the position of the province among Indians was precarious. But even before the eighteenth century, South Carolina had become much more secure and had constructed a remarkable system of Indian alliances. These alliances gave South Carolina sway over the majority of Indians in the South and forced the Spanish and French to keep retreating. Through its successes, South Carolina became confident, perhaps overconfident, of controlling Indians. Then came the Yamassee War. For a time South Carolinians were on the verge of being driven into the sea; however, in the end they had their victory. But with all the devastation, their province emerged from the war weakened and insecure, with Spain and France stronger than ever. The old confidence of managing Indians was gone, and gone for good. They now believed more than ever that Indians could never be really trusted. From now on, they and all Whites lived in dread of the next Indian uprising—an uprising that would be supported by enemy Whites.[11]

The picture in the Colonial Southeast was this: a frightened and dominant White minority faced two exploited colored majorities.[12] To meet the Negro danger, South Carolina devised a harsh slave code; the police control of slaves was comprehensive, specific, and brutal. To meet the Indian danger, the province had a system of trade regulation that was less brutal than the slave code but of approximately equal thoroughness. That Indian tribes were still independent and had some freedom of choice necessitated their being dealt with somewhat like equals. After the Yamassee War, the province played tribe off against tribe; indeed, village against village.[13] They also watched the munitions trade to prevent any stockpiling of arms.[14] In meeting each danger, South Carolinians were plagued by

11. Crane, passim.

12. Around 1750, Whites were estimated at 30–40,000; Indians, 60,000; Negroes, 70–90,000. Kenneth W. Porter, "Negroes on the Southern Frontier," Journal of Negro History, XXXIII (January, 1948), 53–54.

13. Commons House of Assembly to Francis Nicholson, February 3, 1721, Great Britain Public Record Office, Colonial Office (later cited as CO), 5/426, pp. 20–21, Library of Congress.

14. McDowell (ed.), Journals of the Commissioners of the Indian Trade, September 20, 1710–August 29, 1718 (Columbia, 1955), p. 137.

the discrepancy between what they willed and what they could actually do. This discrepancy became greater with time. It did not take much imagination on the part of Whites to put the two dangers, Indians and Negro slaves, together. As early as 1712, Governor Alexander Spotswood, of Virginia, juxtaposed them.[15] In 1729, the French delayed sending an expedition against the Natchez Indians who had slaughtered French citizens because they feared that New Orleans without troops would be attacked by the Choctaw Indians, and Negroes in order to "free themselves from slavery, might join them."[16] This was the biggest fear of all. In 1775, John Stuart, British Superintendent of Southern Indian Affairs, explained that "nothing can be more alarming to Carolinians than the idea of an attack from Indians and Negroes."[17]

What did South Carolinians do about this nightmare? One answer was, keep Indians and Negroes apart—do not let them mix. In 1757, Captain Daniel Pepper, agent to the Creek Indians, stated that "intimacy" between Indians and Negroes should be avoided.[18] In 1767, Stuart expressed this idea again, perhaps even more strongly: "any Intercourse between Indians and Negroes in my opinion ought to be prevented as much as possible."[19] If this were done, Negroes could not establish personal relations with Indians and learn their languages. This would eliminate the dreaded coordinated blow by Indians and Negroes. But Whites also had other goals in mind. Whites believed that whenever Negro and Indian talked in private the talk was against them. The government believed that Negroes could spread discontent among the tribes and foil its schemes in the Indian country. In 1779, the British Indian Service stated that "Negroes infused many very bad notions into their [Indians] minds."[20] To do this, Negroes need not always lie; as servants, they were some-

15. *Colonial Records of North Carolina*, I, 886.

16. Reuben G. Thwaites (ed.), *Jesuit Relations* (Cleveland, 1900), LIX, 189.

17. *Colonial Records of North Carolina*, X, 118.

18. Pepper to Lyttelton, March 30, 1757, South Carolina Indian Book, February 21, 1757–March 6, 1760, p. 19, Library of Congress.

19. Stuart to Gage, November 27, 1767, Thomas Gage Papers, William L. Clements Library, Ann Arbor.

20. Report of Board of Commissioners, August 16, 1779, CO, 5/81, p. 451.

times privy to important secrets. Moreover, the government was double-dealing with its Indian allies; for instance, stirring up trouble between Creeks and Cherokee. On the other hand, Indians could offer freedom to Negroes and tell them how to get to their villages.

To this end of keeping these colored peoples apart, South Carolinians tried to prevent Indians from coming into the province unless they were on official business. In 1742, a Committee on Indian Affairs warned against frequent visiting by Indians because of the hazard of their associating with slaves, "particularly in regard to their talking, and having too great Intercourse with our Slaves, at the outplantations, where they camp."[21] Even when on official missions to Charles Town, chiefs were discouraged from bringing too many aides-de-camp and were hurried away as quickly as possible.[22] The Settlement Indians, those partially detribalized natives living within the province, presented a special problem. Here again the government opposed contact with Negroes; trading and intermarriage were frowned upon.[23] This determination to prevent Indian-Negro contacts within the White settlements was a main cause for curtailing the enslavement of Indians. Indian slaves got to know Negroes and, since they escaped easily into the hinterland, they might carry Negroes along with them. In 1729, Governor Etienne Perier, of Louisiana, explained that "Indian slaves being mixed with our negroes may induce them to desert."[24]

Keeping Negroes and Indians apart had another aim: keep Negroes out of the Indian country. Eighteenth century legislation consistently prohibited any Negro, slave or free, from going to any Indian tribe either as a trader in his own right or as a White trader's helper.[25] Violations of this prohibition almost always led to hasty action to

---

21. Report of Committee on Indian Affairs, May 27, 1742, CO, 5/443, p. 31.
22. McDowell, *Documents*, p. 109.
23. Report of Committee on Indian Affairs, February 29, 1727, CO, 5/430, p. 37.
24. Dunbar Rowland and A. G. Sanders (eds.), *Mississippi Provincial Archives, French Dominion, 1701–1729* (Jackson, 1929), I, 573. Later cited as *MPAFD*.
25. Crane, p. 203; John R. Alden, *John Stuart and the Southern Colonial Frontier, 1754–1775* (Ann Arbor, 1944), pp. 19, 342.

remove these Negroes. Later in the eighteenth century when the westward movement was getting into high gear, opposition to Whites taking their slaves into Indian country became an important obstruction to White settlement of the interior.[26]

Fugitive Negroes among the Indians were the biggest headache. In 1767, Stuart declared that "to prevent the Indian Country [from] becoming an Asylum for Negroes is a Matter of the Utmost consequence to the prosperity of the provinces."[27] To keep slaves from escaping, South Carolina assigned patrols to watch the roads and countryside; to keep Indian raiding parties out of the province, the government built forts at key approaches and sent rangers out to ride along the frontiers. But Indians were excellent slave catchers. The Settlement Indians in particular were regularly employed to track down fugitive slaves; indeed, slave catching was so profitable to them that they readily agreed in 1727 to move their villages so that they could do a better job.[28] . . .

Keeping Negroes and Indians apart had still another aim: keep Negroes out of the swamps and the mountains. Negroes frequently escaped to these out of the way places. These fugitives, called Maroons, preferred the swamps, especially those in the direction of St. Augustine. . . .

Maroons were the most resourceful of all fugitives. They aimed at nothing less than setting up small self-sufficient societies in the most inhospitable places. They had to plan ahead, carefully and secretly. They knew a hard life of hard work and hard fighting awaited them. [For example], fifteen Virginia Maroons carried guns, ammunition, clothing, furniture, and implements into the mountains; before they were captured, they had started clearing land in order to farm. Once established in their fastnesses, Maroons then lived as banditti; they plundered White settlements, killing masters and rescuing slaves. In 1717, a band under the leadership of one Sebastian terrorized the southern parishes of South Carolina.[29] In the early 1770's, a frightened William Bartram, the noted naturalist, encountered a band of

26. Stuart to Gage, March 19, 1765 and December 27, 1767, Gage Papers.
27. Stuart to Gage, September 26, 1767, op. cit.
28. Report of Committee on Indian Affairs, February 29, 1727, CO, 5/430, p. 37.
29. Wallace, The History of South Carolina (New York, 1934), I, 372.

marauders north of Charles Town and later explained that "people were . . . frequently attacked, robbed, and sometimes murdered" by Negro bands in this region.[30] These Maroons were dangerous men and women, and they struck out against slavery. No threat, however, was greater than the possibility of their cooperating with hostile Indians and coordinating their attacks against White settlements. Top priority was given by Whites to the immediate destruction of the Maroons. This job was too important to be handled by a local community. Instead the government sent soldiers into the wilderness to eliminate them.[31] Indians were also called upon to help, and they were especially good at ferreting out Maroons from their lurking places.[32]

In addition to keeping Indians and Negroes apart, Whites pitted the colored groups against each other. In 1725, Richard Ludlam, a South Carolina minister, confessed that "we make use of a Wile for our prest. Security to make Indians & Negro's a checque upon each other least by their Vastly Superior Numbers we should be crushed by one or the other."[33] How did Whites go about this? The essential thing was to make bad blood between them: create suspicion, fear, and hatred. In 1758, James Glen, long governor of South Carolina, explained to William Lyttelton, his inexperienced successor, that "it has been allways the policy of this govert to creat an aversion in them [Indians] to Negroes."[34] . . .

Whites sought to convince Indians that Negroes worked against their best interests. In October, 1715, the Cherokee were on the verge of deserting their Indian confederates in the Yamassee War and joining South Carolina in an attack upon the Creeks. They hoped for a better trade with Charles Town and more security in the South. However, two runaway Negroes from South Carolina came to the Cherokee villages and, according to the South Carolinians, told these Indians a "parcell of lies" which dissuaded the Cherokee from joining

---

30. Mark Van Doren (ed.), *The Travels of William Bartram* (New York, 1940), p. 371.

31. Peter Timothy to Lyttelton, November 13, 1759, Lyttelton Papers.

32. E. Merton Coulter (ed.), *The Journal of William Stephens, 1743–1745* (Athens, 1959), II, 245.

33. Ludlam to Secretary, March, 1725, SPG MSS, A, 19, p. 85.

34. Glen to Lyttelton, January 23, 1758, Lyttelton Papers.

the South Carolinians.[35] Later in January, 1716, the Cherokee finally went over to the province; on their part, the South Carolinians agreed to specific commitments for a larger trade at cheap prices and for military support against all enemies of the Cherokee. For a while, it seemed that the province really intended to live up to these commitments and the Cherokee were happy with their new friends in Charles Town.[36] During this time, Whites lost no chance of reminding the Indians that Negroes had almost prevented this boon from coming their way. . . .

Whites also contributed to this aversion by using Negro slaves as soldiers against Indians. These slaves were rewarded with goods and sometimes with their freedom. Negroes made good soldiers against other Negroes in rebellion; if they did this against their own people, they certainly had no compunction about fighting Indians.[37] In the Yamassee War, trusted Negroes were drafted and armed and then sent against enemy Indians in the province. Later they were also used against enemy Indians in the interior. . . .

Employing Indians as slave catchers encouraged anti-Negro sentiment among the Indians themselves. Whites paid Indians well for returning fugitive slaves; for instance, at the great Augusta Conference in 1763, the price was set at one musket and three blankets for each slave brought in. The Indian trade was largely based on deerskins, and these skins were sold cheaply to the traders; in order to buy a musket and three blankets, an Indian had to pay about thirty-five skins. This required several months of hunting.[38] Moreover, the hunting grounds were dangerous places; enemies were always lurking about. Hence, an Indian often lost time fighting, if he were lucky enough not to lose his life. In a word, Indians were usually short of goods and in debt. The reward for fugitive slaves was, therefore, something they could rarely afford to turn down. Moreover, the avariciousness of Indians was proverbial in the South.[39]

35. Langdon Cheves (ed.), "Journal of the March of the Carolinians into the Cherokee Mountains, 1715–1716," *Year Book of the City of Charleston for 1894*, p. 344.

36. Crane, pp. 180–184, 193–194.

37. Easterby, p. 64.

38. Stuart to Gage, August 31, 1771, Gage Papers.

39. McDowell, *Documents, passim*.

But Indians knew what slavery was like among Whites. They saw its cruelty and brutality whenever they visited the White settlements. They also remembered that Whites had once enslaved Indians in large numbers and occasionally still did so. Indeed, the great fear of Indians was that Whites, and especially South Carolinians, would at some time make slaves of all Indians in the South. This fear was in the background of all their dealings with Whites.[40] All of this worked in two contradictory ways on Indians. Self-interest made the Indian act as an enemy of Negro freedom; but human feelings made him guilty. Like other men in this ambivalence, he suppressed his guilt with a convenient hostility.

Since it was important that Negroes should fear and hate Indians, it is likely that Whites told their slaves many horror stories about Indians, especially those depicting the terrible things that Indians did to Negroes. Actually it was not difficult to portray Indians in a bad light. Indians did kill and they were cruel. Sometimes their raiding parties striking swiftly and with surprise killed Negroes alongside their White masters.[41] Indians also scalped and otherwise mutilated their victims regardless of race.[42] Besides, Indians were known in the early days to subject their male captives to prolonged and deadly tortures; now and then they did this even in the eighteenth century. . . . But atrocities were not the main thing. The main thing was that Indians often behaved as real enemies of Negro freedom. To a large extent, Whites encouraged Indians to act this way. As we shall see, this was partly done to make Negroes fear and hate Indians. Given this aim, we assume that Whites publicized these unfriendly acts of Indians among their slaves—and conveniently overlooked their own responsibility . We will now give attention to some situations in which Indians behaved as enemies of Negro freedom.

As we know, Whites employed Indians as slave catchers, and Indians were eager for these jobs. Moreover, Negroes knew that Indians, being expert woodsmen, were better slave catchers than White soldiers and patrols.[43] Negroes also realized that death sometimes

40. Edmund Atkin to Lyttelton, November 3, 1759, Lyttelton Papers.
41. George Gilmer, *Sketches of Some of the First Settlers of Upper Georgia* (Americus, 1926), p. 251.
42. *American State Papers, Indian Affairs*, I, 452.
43. Glen to Newcastle, April 14, 1748, CO, 5/389, p. 58.

awaited the unsuccessful runaway instead of a return to slavery. The Charles Town government executed leaders of fugitive slave parties and those slaves who ran away repeatedly. This government also instructed slave catchers to kill fugitive Negroes when they could not capture them; therefore, dead fugitives were paid for as well as live ones.[44] This encouraged Indians to be more bloodthirsty than White slave catchers: the labor of these fugitives was not going to benefit them. Besides, scalping was more profitable to them than to Whites: Indians could make one scalp look like two or more scalps. To prevent this cheating, the Charles Town government tried to buy only scalps with two ears.[45] . . .

Indians were *bona fide* slave traders. They stole Negroes from White slaveholders in order to sell them to other White slaveholders. Indians had been prepared for this Negro trade by the earlier trade in Indian slaves; for instance, they had learned that male captives were often too valuable to be done away with. Except for raids by Spanish Indians against South Carolina, Indians did not steal too many Negroes in the first half of the eighteenth century. About the only other Indians that regularly raided for Negro slaves were the Chickasaw and other allied tribes of South Carolina living near the Mississippi River. These tribes raided French settlements in Louisiana and French convoys on the Great River. Negroes captured in these raids were sold to Charles Town traders who carried them to South Carolina.[46] This trade did not bring many slaves into the province; the French were always so short of Negroes. For the Negroes, this trade was a calamity. Their capture meant the substitution of one enslavement by a more severe one. Therefore, these Negroes must have been bitter anti-Indian propagandists among the slaves of South Carolina. . . .

Finally, Whites employed Indians to help crush slave insurrections. In the Stono Rebellion of 1739, the most serious insurrection in South Carolina during the eighteenth century, about eighty Negro slaves killed more than thirty Whites. At the outset, the Charles Town government called upon Settlement Indians for help. These

44. Aptheker, "Maroons within the Present Limits of the United States," *Journal of Negro History*, XXIV (April, 1939), 169.

45. Samuel Hazard (ed.), *Pennsylvania Archives, 1756–1760* (Philadelphia, 1853), III, 200; Easterby, p. 681.

46. *MPAFD*, III, 635.

Indians pursued those slaves who eluded the militia at Stono; in a few weeks, they managed to capture some of these slaves and to kill a few others.[47] Indians also aided the province in suppressing slave insurrections in 1744 and 1765.[48] Slave insurrections in the eighteenth century were small-scale affairs; South Carolinians did not need many Indians to help them restore order in any particular one. What mattered most was speed in putting them down; otherwise, more timid Negroes might respond to the call of liberty and join the rebel slaves. Therefore, for this job, the Charles Town government turned to Settlement Indians and Eastern Siouans. Although few in numbers, these Indians lived closer to White settlements and could be quickly mustered whenever needed.

The Charles Town government paid Indians high wages for helping suppress slave insurrections. In the Stono Rebellion, each Indian was given a coat, a flap, a pair of stockings, a hat, a gun, two pounds of powder, and eight pounds of bullets. The legislature, dominated by large slaveholders whose eyes were on the future, wanted to increase this payment. It declared that "Indians should be encouraged in such manner as to induce them always to offer their Service whenever this Government may have Occasion for them."[49] In 1744, the Natchez, now living as scattered Settlement Indians in South Carolina after their defeat by the French in 1729, informed Governor Glen that they wanted to be "together to be ready to assist the Government in case of any Insurrection, or Rebellion of the Negroes."[50] We can be certain that Negroes knew how eager Indians were to help keep them in slavery.

The Charles Town government did not wait for an uprising before calling on Indians. This government tried to anticipate trouble and then prevent it by using Indians to intimidate Negroes. On November 10, 1739, less than two months after Stono, the legislature ordered its Committee on Indian Affairs to cooperate with its special committee investigating this insurrection in "finding the most effectual

47. Easterby, passim.
48. Milling, Red Carolinians, p. 229; Wallace, South Carolina: Short History, p. 185.
49. Easterby, pp. 65, 76–77.
50. South Carolina Council Journal, December 11, 1743–December 8, 1744, CO, 5/448, pp. 187–188.

means for preventing of such Dangers throughout the province." South Carolinians feared insurrections especially at Christmas, Negroes having so much more free time during these holidays.[51] During the Christmas of 1716, the Charles Town government ordered Settlement Indians to move nearer White settlements to terrorize the slaves. Moreover, the government made a practice of locating Settlement Indians near places at which slaves might become troublesome. In the summer of 1716, it maintained the Wineau Indians around the Santee settlements "for keeping ye Negroes in awe."[52] But South Carolinians did not rely only on Settlement Indians to prevent insurrections. These tribes and even the Catawba were not large enough to intimidate all Negroes in the province; there were not enough Settlement Indians to station at every danger point. As we know, South Carolinians saw the danger of a big insurrection in every little one. For intimidating all slaves, South Carolina needed at least one big inland tribe. Therefore, the government turned to its most trusted ally and probably the tribe most hostile to Negroes: the Cherokee. In 1737, Lieutenant-Governor Thomas Broughton reported that he was sending for Cherokee warriors "to come down to the settlements to be an awe to the negroes."[53] Thus, a special effort was made after the Yamassee War to keep Negroes isolated from the Cherokee. In 1741, the legislature requested that Broughton purchase two Negro slaves owned by a Cherokee chief so that they could be shipped to the "West Indies or Northern Colonies to prevent any Detriment that they might do this Province by getting acquainted with the Cherokees."[54] It is clear that this intimidation by Indians helped prevent slave insurrections.

Conclusion

Hostility between Indians and Negroes in the Colonial Southeast was more pronounced than friendliness. Southern Whites were afraid of these two colored races, each of which outnumbered them. Whites

51. Easterby, pp. 24, 69.
52. Wallace, *History of South Carolina*, I, 185; McDowell, *Journals*, p. 80.
53. Quoted in Wallace, *History of South Carolina*, I, 368.
54. Easterby (ed.), *Journals of the Commons House of Assembly, May 18, 1741–July 10, 1742* (Columbia, 1953), p. 45.

were especially afraid that these two exploited races would combine against them. To prevent this combination, Whites deliberately maintained social distance between Indians and Negroes and created antagonism between them. To maintain this social distance, Whites segregated Indians and Negroes from each other. They did this by keeping Indians out of White settlements as much as possible and by trying to keep Negroes out of the Indian country and other out of the way places where these colored races might meet. To create antagonism, Whites deliberately played Indians and Negroes against each other. They pointed out to these races that each was the enemy of the other. To this end of mutual hostility, Whites also used Negroes as soldiers against Indians; on the other hand, they used Indians to catch runaway slaves and to suppress slave insurrections. In the eyes of Negroes, Indians were enemies of Negro freedom. At times, Whites encouraged Indians and Negroes to murder each other. In these ways, Whites created much of the hostility between Indians and Negroes in the eighteenth century.

Part III
Revolutionary Ideals and Minority Realities, 1763-1842

Revolutionary Ideals and Minority Realities, 1763–1842

In the eight decades between 1763 and 1842, the United States fought a successful war for independence and established a republican government based on the idealistic rhetoric of the American Revolution. American revolutionary ideals, articulated by Thomas Jefferson in the Declaration of Independence, indicated a commitment to the concept "that all men are created equal, that they are endowed by their Creator with certain unalienable Rights, that among these are Life, liberty and the pursuit of Happiness." The history of the nation in the decades following 1776 reveals a steady growth of democracy as a national ideal and reality. The reality, however, was limited to whites because neither blacks nor Indians shared in the "blessings of liberty" secured by the American Revolution.

Most of the Indians in British North America at the beginning of the revolution lived west of the Allegheny Mountains, where the British government attempted to protect them from further incursions by white settlers. The policy of deterring white expansion beyond the Alleghenies irritated many colonists, and some land-hungry whites viewed the break with England as a means of securing new properties. As a result most Indians were hostile to the American cause, and many, like those who fought under the Mohawk warrior, Joseph Brant, actively supported the British. The victory of the colonials opened the West to white settlement. Some Indian lands between the Alleghenies and the Mississippi River were taken by conquest and some by purchase, but the American government never deviated from its policy of populating the new territory with white farmers.

The United States government pursued the different and often conflicting approaches of "civilization" and removal in its dealings with the Indians. "Civilization" involved persuading the Indians to abandon hunting for agriculture and to forsake communal ownership of property. Its proponents reasoned that independent Indian farmers would require less land and be more pliable than roving bands of hunters. Removal was a scheme to dispossess the eastern tribes and resettle them west of the Mississippi. Even those nations which adopted "civilization" were not exempt from removal, and by 1850 approximately one hundred thousand Indians had been relocated. The process, accomplished by a combination of force, threats, tricks, and bribes, took a heavy toll in Indian lives and culture.

As did the Indians, many blacks found themselves participants in, but not beneficiaries of, the American Revolution. Both the British and colonial armies used black troops during the revolution, and in some cases slaves were rewarded with freedom for their service. However, revolutionary rhetoric about freedom had little impact on the institution of slavery. The obvious disparity between revolutionary ideals and the reality of slavery caused many whites, including slaveholders, to question the morality of black bondage. The states north of Maryland abolished slavery in the years following the revolution, but in the South discussion of the economic and moral evils of slavery led only to occasional voluntary manumission.

The debates over slavery during the revolutionary period reveal clearly the manner in which slavery and racism were linked in the minds of white Americans. Many whites argued that, although slavery was evil, abolition would be socially disastrous. A society composed of blacks and whites on an equal footing was unthinkable because of the inferiority of blacks. Such notions led to the popularity of colonization schemes with the goal of freeing blacks and relocating them in Africa or elsewhere beyond the borders of the country. Unrealistic as a means of ending slavery, the chimera of colonization beckoned those who wanted to make the United States a white man's nation.

Abolitionists, beginning in the 1830s, directly attacked the institution of slavery by demanding immediate and unequivocal emancipation. The resistance of the slaves themselves, most dramatically in the form of open revolts, constituted a further challenge to the "peculiar institution." Events such as the slave uprising under Gabriel Prosser near Richmond, Virginia (1800), the conspiracy of Denmark Vesey in Charleston, South Carolina (1822), and Nat Turner's rebellion in Southampton County, Virginia (1831) frightened white southerners. Ironically, the attacks of the abolitionists and the slave revolts stiffened the resolve of southern slaveholders to defend and protect slavery, a process which resulted in an even more repressive institution.

White Americans made significant strides toward the democratic government and equalitarian society seemingly promised by the American Revolution. Yet, the growth and prosperity of the nation was accomplished at the expense of the lives and liberties of the two nonwhite minorities which lived within its borders. Blacks and Indians remained the exploited subjects of a nation which believed in democracy for whites only.

Benjamin Quarles,
"Lord Dunmore As Liberator"

Personal liberty as an avowed aim of the American Revolution stood in direct conflict with the possession of slaves. The obvious disparity between principle and practice led many white American revolutionaries to question the practice of slavery. The war itself also had an unsettling effect on slavery as both sides attempted to recruit black soldiers with promises of freedom. In "Lord Dunmore As Liberator," Benjamin Quarles recounts the efforts of the last royal governor of Virginia to raise a black army by urging slaves of revolutionaries to desert their masters. Virginia slaves welcomed Dunmore's offer of freedom, and almost eight hundred joined him despite considerable obstacles. Yet, like so many proposals which promised an end to slavery during this period, Dunmore's scheme ended in disaster. The American Revolution failed to accord its benefits to the enslaved Americans.

Lord Dunmore As Liberator

Benjamin Quarles

In American patriotic tradition the first full-fledged villain to step from the wings as the Revolutionary War unfolded was John Murray, Earl of Dunmore. Like other royal governors in office as the crisis reached its pitch, the Crown's representative in Virginia would have been a marked man no matter how circumspect his behavior. Dunmore, lacking in diplomatic skills, was destined to furnish the colonists with a convenient hate-symbol. The one act that most thoroughly defamed his name was a deed which in Negro circles cast its author in the role of liberator. This was Dunmore's proclamation inviting slaves to leave their masters and join the royal forces.

Issued as of November 7, 1775, on board the *William* in the harbor at Norfolk, the proclamation announced that in order to defeat "treasonable purposes" the governor was establishing martial law. Colonists who refused "to resort to his Majesty's standard" were to be adjudged traitors. Then came the words which were destined to be quoted far and wide: "and I do hereby further declare all indented servants, Negroes, or others, (appertaining to Rebels,) free, that are able and willing to bear arms, they joining His Majesty's Troops, as

Abridged from Benjamin Quarles, "Lord Dunmore As Liberator," *William and Mary Quarterly*, XV (1958), pp. 494–507. Reprinted by permission. Footnotes have been renumbered.

soon as may be, for the more speedily reducing the Colony to a proper sense of their duty, to His Majesty's crown and dignity."[1] Dunmore's proclamation had its expected effect. "The colonists," wrote a contemporary, "were struck with horror";[2] the "Poet of the American Revolution" implored the heavens to deliver the colonies from the "valiant" Dunmore and "his crew of banditti" ("who plunder Virginians at Williamsburg city").[3] Taking alarm, the Continental Congress lost no time in bestirring itself. On December 2, 1775, the delegates instructed the "Committee for fitting our armed vessels" to engage ships of war for the taking or destroying of the governor's fleet,[4] and the presiding officer urged the commander in chief of the Continental Army to take such measures against his lordship as would "effectually Repel his violences and secure the peace and safety of that Colony."[5] Two days later the Congress recom-

1. Original broadside, 11 by 17 inches, in University of Virginia library. For a facsimile which Patrick Henry circulated, and which differs a little in punctuation from the original, see Francis L. Berkeley, Jr., *Dunmore's Proclamation of Emancipation* (Charlottesville, 1941), frontispiece. See also *American Archives*, comp. Peter Force, 4th Ser. (Washington, 1837–46), III, 1385.

2. David Ramsay, *History of the American Revolution* (Philadelphia, 1789), I, 234.

3. *The Poems of Philip Freneau*, ed. Fred Lewis Pattee (Princeton, 1902–07), I, 140. "Hell itself could not have vomitted anything more black than his design of emancipating our slaves," wrote a Philadelphia correspondent to a friend abroad. *Morning Chronicle and London Advertiser*, Jan. 20, 1776, quoted in *Letters on the American Revolution, 1774–1776*, ed. Margaret W. Willard (Boston, 1925), p. 233. It was the judgment of Edward Rutledge that the proclamation tended "more effectually to work an eternal separation between Great Britain and the Colonies,—than any other expedient, which could possibly have been thought of." Rutledge to Ralph Izard, Dec. 8, 1775, in *Correspondence of Mr. Ralph Izard* (New York, 1844), I, 165.

4. *Journal of the Continental Congress, 1774–1789*, ed. Worthington C. Ford and others (Washington, 1904–37), III, 395.

5. John Hancock to George Washington, Dec. 2, 1775, in *Letters of Members of the Continental Congress*, ed. Edmund C. Burnett (Washington, 1921–36), I, 267. The army commander shared the apprehension of Congress. "If," he wrote to a Virginia delegate, "that man is not crushed before spring, he will become the most formidable enemy America has; his strength will increase as a snow ball by rolling; and faster, if some expedient cannot be hit upon, to convince the slaves and servants of the impotency of his designs." George Washington to Richard Henry Lee, Dec. 26, 1775, in R. H. Lee, *Memoir of the Life of Richard Henry Lee* (Philadelphia, 1825), II, 9. Compare Washington to Joseph Reed, Dec. 15, 1775, in *The Writings of George Washington from the Original Manuscript Sources, 1745–1799*, ed. John C. Fitzpatrick (Washington, 1931–44), IV, 167.

mended to Virginia that she resist Dunmore "to the utmost. . . ."[6]

The apprehension over Dunmore's proclamation was grounded primarily in the fear of its unsettling effect on the slaves, if not in the fear of a servile insurrection—that nightmarish dread in communities where the whites were outnumbered. A policy that would strike off their shackles would obviously have a marked appeal to the inhabitants of slave row. Moreover, there had been recent evidence that the Virginia bondmen were responsive to the offer of freedom.

Dunmore himself had furnished such evidence. For at least eight months prior to the formal proclamation, the governor had seriously considered the idea of enlisting the slaves. His reasons were plain. Rebellious planters who contemplated a resort to arms would be deprived of their workers and would be compelled to return to their homes to protect their families and their property. Moreover, the slaves would help fill the ranks of military laborers for His Majesty's forces, and such human *potentiel de guerre* was badly needed. And Dunmore could expect little help from British headquarters in Boston.[7] Obviously, too, the Crown supporters and their sympathizers counted on the disaffection of the Negroes in the South.[8]

Needing supporters to hold the rebellion-bent Virginians in check, Dunmore let it be known late in April 1775 that he might be driven to set up the royal standard, adding that if he did he believed that

6. *Journals of the Continental Congress*, III, 403.
7. General Thomas Gage wrote to Dunmore on Sept. 10, 1775: "I can neither assist you with Men, arms or ammunition, for I have them not to spare; should you draw upon me I have not the Cash to pay your Bills." Clinton Papers, William L. Clements Library, University of Michigan. For England's continuing great difficulty in getting man power see Edward E. Curtis, *The Organization of the British Army in the American Revolution* (New Haven, 1926), pp. 51–80.
8. "Although Virginia and Maryland are both very populous," wrote Governor Josiah Martin of North Carolina to Dartmouth on June 30, 1775, "the Whites are greatly outnumbered by the Negroes, at least in the former; a circumstance that would facilitate exceedingly the Reduction of those Colonies who are very sensible of their Weakness arising from it." Clinton Papers. This idea of Negro support was a persistent one: "The Negroes may be all deemed so many Intestine Enemies, being all slaves and desirous of Freedom." Joseph Galloway to Dartmouth, Jan. 23, 1778, *Facsimiles of Manuscripts in European Archives Relating to America, 1773–1783*, ed. Benjamin F. Stevens (London, 1889–98), XXIV, no. 2079. For a similar expression from another loyalist, see "Moses Kirkland to His Majesty's Commissioners, Oct. 21, 1778," Clinton Papers.

he could count on "all the Slaves on the side of Government."[9] On May 1 the governor wrote to the Earl of Dartmouth expressing confidence that, once supplied with arms and ammunition, he would be able "to collect from among the Indians,[10] negroes and other persons" a force sufficient to hold his own.[11] Two weeks later, Gage in a letter to Dartmouth touched on Dunmore's proposal: "We hear," wrote the British commander, "that a Declaration his Lordship has made, of proclaiming all the Negroes free, who should join him, has Startled the Insurgents."[12]

In late April a group of slaves, scenting freedom in the air, went to the governor's house and volunteered their services, but Dunmore had them dismissed.[13] He was then not quite ready for the open break, but it would not be long delayed. On June 8, 1775, the governor took the decisive step of quitting Williamsburg and taking asylum aboard the man-of-war *Fowey* at Yorktown, a move he had been turning over in his mind since May 15.[14] "I have thought it best for his Majesty's service," he wrote, "to retire from amidst such hostile appearances around me."[15] The House of Burgesses, taking note of the governor's flight, assured him that his personal safety was in no danger, but pointedly noted its displeasure that "a Scheme, the most diabolical, had been mediated, and generally recommended,

9. "Deposition of Dr. William Pasteur. In Regard to the Removal of Powder from the Williamsburg Magazine," in "Virginia Legislative Papers (from Originals in Virginia State Archives)," *Virginia Magazine of History and Biography*, XIII (July 1905), p. 49.

10. Later that year Dunmore concocted a plan to raise the tribes, as Gage phrased it, "on the back Parts of the Province of Virginia, to be Joined by such Inhabitants and Indians as may be at, and about Detroit." Gage to Guy Carleton, Sept. 11, 1775, Gage MSS. (American Series), Clements Library. This so-called "Connolly Plot" is briefly described in Isaac S. Harrell, *Loyalism in Virginia* (Philadelphia, 1926), pp. 35–37.

11. Dartmouth to Dunmore, Aug. 2, 1775, *Amer. Arch.*, 4th Serv., III, 6. In this passage Dartmouth reports the contents of a letter from Dunmore dated May 1.

12. Gage to Dartmouth, May 15, 1775, Gage MSS. (English Series), Clements Library.

13. "Deposition of John Randolph in Regard to the Removal of the Powder," in "Virginia Legislative Papers," *Va. Mag. of His. and Biog.*, XV (Oct. 1907), 150.

14. Dunmore to Gage, May 15, 1775, Gage MSS. (American Series).

15. *Ibid.*, June 17, 1775.

by a Person of great Influence, to offer Freedom to our Slaves, and turn them against their Masters."[16]

Realizing that there was no turning back, Dunmore initiated a policy of unofficial slave solicitation to augment his tiny force of three hundred white soldiers, seamen, and loyalist recruits. In early August the "Officers of the Volunteer Companies" in Williamsburg informed the Convention that the "Governour's Cutter had carried off a number of Slaves belonging to private gentlemen. . . ."[17] Small sloops, which were employed primarily to intercept intracolonial shipments of powder, invited slaves aboard. "Lord Dunmore sails up and down the river," wrote a Norfolk correspondent on October 28, 1775, to a friend in England, "and where he finds a defenceless place, he lands, plunders the plantation and carries off the negroes."[18]

Now ready to come out into the open, Dunmore was concerned only with his timing. An apparently auspicious moment came in mid-November 1775 when a skirmish took place at Kemp's Landing on the Elizabeth River. In this action the colonial militia was routed and its two commanding colonels were captured. Entering the village in triumph, Dunmore, on November 14, ordered the publication of the proclamation he had drafted a week earlier on board the *William*. The final break had come—the governor had set up his standard and had officially called upon the slaves to join him.

Tidewater Virginia took alarm as rumors spread that the slaves were stampeding to the British.[19] But there were strong deterring factors. Foremost among these was the military alertness of the Virginians themselves. Before any substantial slave migration to Dunmore could get under way the governor suffered a decisive defeat at arms. . . .

16. *Journals of the House of Burgesses of Virginia, 1773–1776*, ed. John Pendleton Kennedy (Richmond, 1905), p. 256.

17. "Proceedings of the Virginia Convention, August 3, 1775," *Amer. Arch.*, 4th Ser., III, 373.

18. *Morning Chronicle and London Advertiser*, Dec. 22, 1775, in Willard, *Letters in the American Revolution*, pp. 271–272. The number of slaves reaching Dunmore during the preproclamation stage is indeterminate; "some accounts make them about 100; others less." Edmund Pendleton and others to Virginia Delegates in Congress, Nov. 11, 1775, Lee Family MSS., U. Va. library.

19. "Letters mention that slaves flock to him in abundance, but I hope it is magnified." Edmund Pendleton to Richard Henry Lee, Nov. 27, 1775, *Amer. Arch.*, 4th Ser., IV, 202.

The military preparation of the colonists was matched by their promptness in adopting "home front" measures to prevent slaves from joining the governor. Newspapers lost no time in publishing the proclamation in full, as information and as a warning. To deter runaways local patrol groups were doubled, highways were carefully watched, and owners of small craft were required to exercise vigilance. Since Dunmore's action had come as no surprise, the Virginians had had time to put the colony in a "tolerable state of defense."[20] Adjacent Maryland, through its Council of Safety, ordered the military to station itself in St. Mary's County "and guard the shores from thence to the river Powtowmack, to prevent any servants, negroes, or others from going on board the Fowey ship of war."[21]

To vigilance the colonists added psychological warfare. In Alexander Purdie's Virginia Gazette was published a letter from a subscriber urging that Negroes be cautioned against joining Dunmore. Slaves should be told that the English ministry, in refusing to stop the slave trade, had proved a far greater enemy to Negroes than their American masters, and that if the colonists were defeated, their slaves would be sold to the West Indies. They should be told, too, continued Mr. Purdie's correspondent, that Dunmore was cruel to his own black servitors. And, finally, they should be urged to place their expectation on "a better condition in the next world." If this information had been spread widely, "not one slave would have joined our enemies."[22] ...

Official action was not long in coming. The Virginia Convention on December 8 appointed a committee to prepare an answer to Dunmore's proclamation. Five days later, when the committee made its report, it was directed to draw up a declaration stating that runaways to the British would be pardoned if they returned in ten days; otherwise they would "be liable to such punishment as shall be directed by the Convention." The following day, with the committee's report at hand, the delegates issued a declaration of policy. Beginning with a reminder that the time-honored penalty for a slave insurrection was

20. Ramsay, American Revolution, I, 234.
21. Journal and Correspondence of the Maryland Council of Safety, Aug. 29, 1775–July 6, 1776, ed. William H. Browne and others, Archives of Maryland (Baltimore, 1883—in progress), XI, 511–512.
22. Purdie's Virginia Gazette, Williamsburg, Nov. 17, 1775. Hereafter cited as Va. Gaz.

death without benefit of clergy, the document stated that Negroes who had been "seduced" to take up arms were liable to punishment. But in order that they might return in safety to their duties, they would be pardoned if they laid down their arms forthwith. The proclamation concluded with a request to "all humane and benevolent persons in the colony" to convey to the slaves this "offer of mercy."[23] To insure a wide circulation, the proclamation was published as a broadside.[24]

The Virginians supplemented techniques of persuasion and sweet reasonableness with alternatives more forthright and punitive. In early December the Convention decreed that slaves taken in arms were to be sold to the foreign West Indies, with the sale money, minus expenses, to go to their masters.[25] Somewhat less severe was the fate of captured runaways who had failed in their attempts to reach the King's forces. Such slaves, if their masters were patriots, were returned to their home plantations, often after first serving a term of imprisonment. An owner of a captured runaway might be ordered to "convey him to some interior part of the Country as soon as may be...."[26] Slaves of British sympathizers were put to work in the lead mines,[27] a practice which became customary in Virginia for the duration of the war. Distrusting all Negroes who had joined the governor, the Convention recommended that military officers "seize and secure" even those who came bearing flags of truce.[28]

The death penalty was used sparingly. In Northampton County the court passed such a sentence on a group of thirteen slaves who

23. *Proceedings of the Convention of the Delegates in the Colony of Virginia* (Richmond, 1816), p. 62.

24. Virginia Broadsides (V. 54), U. Va. library.

25. William Waller Hening, *The Statutes at Large; Being a Collection of All the Laws of Virginia* . . . (Richmond, 1809–23), IX, 106.

26. Such was the language used by the Virginia Council to William Kirby (July 12, 1776) concerning his slave Frank. *Journals of the Council of State of Virginia*, ed. H. R. McIlwaine and Wilmer L. Hall (Richmond, 1931–32, 1952), I, 67.

27. On Dec. 14, 1775, the Convention ordered the Committee of Safety to employ captive slaves "in working the Lead Mine in the County of Fincastle, for the use of this Colony." *Amer. Arch.*, 4th Ser., IV, 85. Shortly afterward four would-be followers of Dunmore who were captured at Accomac were ordered "sent up the country and employed in some publick works." *Ibid.*, VI, 1553.

28. *Ibid.*, VI, 1524.

had seized a schooner at Hungers Creek and sailed into the bay, their destination the James. Overtaken by a whale boat,[29] their execution was set for April 2, 1776. But the Northampton Committee of Safety sent word to Williamsburg inquiring whether the punishment should not be mitigated since the seizing of the boat was more "intended to effect an escape to Dunmore than any other Design of committing a felony."[30] Whenever the death sentence was passed, as in the case of two runaways who mistook an armed vessel of the Virginia navy for a British man-of-war, it was used mainly "as an example to others."[31]

Despite preventive efforts, whether an appeal to common sense or a resort to legal reprisals, many slaves made their way to the British, spurred in part by loyalist propaganda of the governor's good treatment.[32] Some two hundred "immediately joined him,"[33] and within a week after the proclamation the number had reached three hundred.[34] "Numbers of Negros and Cowardly Scoundrels flock to his Standard," wrote a member of the provincial Committee of Safety.[35] ...

The Negroes who reached the British were generally able-bodied men who could be put to many uses.[36] It was as soldiers, however,

29. James Kent and William Henry to Maryland Council of Safety, Feb. 28, 1776, Arch. of Md., XI, 191.

30. Northampton Committee of Safety to General Committee of Safety, Apr. 23, 1776, "Va. Leg. Papers," Va. Mag. of Hist. and Biog., XV (Apr. 1908), 407.

31. Va. Gaz., Apr. 13, 1776.

32. Northampton Committee of Safety to General Committee of Safety, Apr. 23, 1776, "Va. Leg. Papers," Va. Mag. of Hist. and Biog., XV, 407. Dunmore would have every reason to welcome runaways, but perhaps his reception of them fell short of the report, circulated in the Virginia Gazette, that on the evening the governor's forces landed on Gwynn's Island, they amused themselves "with a promiscuous ball, which was opened, we hear, by a certain spruce little gentleman, with one of the black ladies." Va. Gaz., May 31, 1776.

33. Northampton Committee of Safety to Continental Congress, Nov. 25, 1775, "Va. Leg. Papers," Va. Mag. of Hist. and Biog., XIV (Jan. 1907), 251.

34. Andrew Sprowel to Peter Paterson, Nov. 19, 1775, ibid., XIV (Apr. 1907), 387.

35. John Page to Thomas Jefferson, Nov. 24, 1775, The Papers of Thomas Jefferson, ed. Julian P. Boyd (Princeton, 1950—in progress), I, 265.

36. Two women, however, were among a party of nine slaves who were seized in mid-December after putting out to sea in an open boat in an attempt to reach Norfolk. Pennsylvania Gazette, Philadelphia, Dec. 20, 1775.

that Dunmore envisoned them, and he enlisted them from the beginning. By early December he was arming them "as fast as they came in."[37] He made use of Negro privates at the rout of the colonials at Kemp's Landing; indeed, slaves had captured one of the two commanding colonels.[38] In the skirmishes preceding the action at Great Bridge, two runaways who were taken prisoner testified that the garrison was manned by thirty whites and ninety Negroes, and that "all the blacks who are sent to the fort at the great Bridge, are supplied with muskets, Cartridges &c strictly ordered to use them defensively & offensively."[39] By the first of December the British had nearly three hundred slaves outfitted in military garb, with the inscription, "Liberty to Slaves," emblazoned across the breast of each.[40] The governor officially designated them "Lord Dunmore's Ethiopian Regiment."[41]

The first and only major military action in which Dunmore's forces were engaged was the battle of Great Bridge.[42] Of the governor's

37. Dunmore to Sec. of State for the Colonies, Dec. 6, 1775, Peter Force-George Bancroft Transcripts, "Virginia: Official Correspondence," Library of Congress.
38. Edmund Pendleton to R. H. Lee, Nov. 27, 1775, Amer. Arch., 4th Ser., IV, 202.
39. William Woodford to Edmund Pendleton, Dec. 5, 1775, "The Woodford, Howe, and Lee Letters," Richmond College Historical Papers, I (June 1915), 113. Added Woodford, "The bearer brings you one of the Balls taken out of the cartirages found upon the negro Prisoners, as they were extremely well made." Ibid., p. 112.
40. Maryland Gazette, Annapolis, Dec. 14, 1775.
41. Dunmore to Sec. of State for Colonies, Dec. 6, 1775, Force-Bancroft Transcripts.
42. Eyewitness accounts of the action at Great Bridge include: "...a Midshipman on board his Majesty's ship Otter, commanded by Captain Squires, Dec. 9," in Willard, Letters on the American Revolution, pp. 234–235; "Thomas McKnight to Rev. Dr. McKnight, on board the King's Fisher, Dec. 26, 1775," Miscellaneous Collection, Clements Library; "Contemporary English Accounts of the Destruction of Norfolk in 1776," comp. H. S. Parsons, Wm. & Mary Quart., 2d Ser., XIII (Oct. 1933), 219–224; Richard Kidder Meade to Theodorick Bland, Jr., Norfolk Town Camp, Dec. 18, 1775, in The Bland Papers, ed. Charles Campbell (Petersburg, 1840–43), I, 38; "The Woodford, Howe, and Lee Letters," Richmond College Hist. Papers, I, 96–163, passim; William Woodford to Edmund Pendleton, Dec. 10, 1775, in Md. Gaz., Dec. 21, 1775, and Jan. 4, 1776. For Dunmore's account see Dunmore to Secretary of State for the Colonies, Dec. 13, 1775, Force-Bancroft Transcripts. For the story, relished by Virginians, that a well-coached slave had been sent into Dunmore's lines with instructions to misrepresent the strength of the colonial militia, see John Burk, The History of Virginia (Petersburg, 1805–16), IV, 85.

troops of some six hundred men, nearly half were Negroes. Of the eighteen wounded prisoners taken by the Virginians in this rout, two were former slaves. James Anderson was wounded "in the Forearm— Bones shattered and flesh much torn," and Caesar was hit "in the Thigh, by a Ball, and 5 shot—one lodged."[43] After the fiasco at Great Bridge, the governor was forced to operate from his ships. Taking aboard the hardiest of his Negro followers and placing them under officers who exercised them at small arms, he sanguinely awaited recruits.

Dunmore's use of Negroes also embraced sailoring services. On the six tenders sent by the governor to cannonade Hampton in late October 1775, there were colored crewmen. Two of them were captured when the Virginians seized the pilot boat Hawk Tender.[44] To man the small craft that scurried in and out of the river settlements, harassing the plantations, the British depended largely on ex-slaves. Particularly were they needed as pilots. Joseph Harris, a runaway, served as pilot of the Otter, having come to Captain Matthew Squire with the highest recommendation from a fellow naval officer. "I think him too useful to His Majesty's service to take away," wrote the latter, because of "his being well acquainted with many creeks in the Eastern Shore, at York, James River, and Nansemond, and many others, . . ." and "accustomed to pilot. . . ."[45] Two citizens on the Isle of Wight advised the chairman of the Virginia Committee of Safety to go slow on discharging "a Negro fello, named Caesar," who was not only "a very great Scoundrel" but was also "a fello' they can't do well without being an Excellent pilot."[46]

Another service performed by Dunmore's black followers was foraging. The governor's supply of provisions, particularly fresh foods, needed constant replenishing, and the Virginia leaders understandably would not permit the British to send men ashore to make pur-

43. Woodford to Pendleton, Dec. 10, 1775, "The Woodford, Howe, and Lee Letters," Richmond College Hist. Papers, I, 118.
44. John Page to Thomas Jefferson, Nov. 11, 1775, Papers of Thomas Jefferson, ed. Boyd, I, 257.
45. George Montague to Matthew Squire, July 20, 1775, Amer. Arch., 4th Ser., II, 1692.
46. Thomas Pierce and Thomas Smith to Edmund Pendleton, Dec. 17, 1775, "Miscellaneous Colonial Documents," Va. Mag. of Hist. and Biog., XIX (July 1911), 267.

chases. "Back settlers" who might have been willing to supply his lordship with provisions had "no means of conveying them,"[47] and Dunmore was driven to a dependence upon the foraging abilities of his Negro recruits. Marauding parties of predominantly ex-slave composition preyed on the countryside, making a night descent upon a plantation and making off with the choice livestock. One foraging party, captured while on its way to the Eastern Shore, was made up of "one white and sixteen blacks."[48]

Allegedly one of the services of Negroes to Dunmore was germ spreading. That the charge of germ warfare was propaganda-laden did not make it less potent in arousing indignation. The accusation was that Dunmore had inoculated two Negroes and sent them ashore at Norfolk to spread the smallpox.[49] The charge was ironic in view of the fate of the Negroes who fled to the British. The majority of them were disease fatalities. Late in March the governor informed his superior in England that the recruiting of the black regiment "would have been in great forwardness had not a fever crept in amongst them, which carried off a great many very fine fellows." He added that on advice of "medical people here," he had concluded that the trouble came from the overcrowded condition on the ships and the lack of clothing, both of which "we have now provided against."[50]

But the plague persisted, killing off the Negroes and the hope of the governor alike. Writing to Germain in June, Dunmore confessed defeat. The fever, he explained, was malignant, and had "carried off an incredible number of our people, especially blacks." Had this not happened he would have enlisted two thousand Negro followers. He was, ran his letter, separating the sick from the well and would try to keep the two groups from intermingling.[51] The governor's

47. "Extract of a letter to a gentleman in Scotland, dated Norfolk, Virginia, February 17, 1776," Amer. Arch., 4th Ser., IV, 1166.

48. Archibald Cary to R. H. Lee, Dec. 24, 1775, in Robert K. Brock, Archibald Cary of Ampthill (Richmond, 1937), p. 161.

49. Va. Gaz., June 15, 1776.

50. Dunmore to George Germain, Mar. 30, 1776, Amer. Arch., 5th Ser. (Washington, 1848–53), II, 159–160.

51. Dunmore to Germain, Mar. 30, 1776, Amer. Arch., 5th Ser., II, 162. Dunmore's policy of isolation appears to have prevented the smallpox from decimating the white troops. The monthly return of the 14th Regiment of

efforts were unavailing; by early June 1776 there were not more than "150 effective Negro men," although each day the black corps was augmented by from six to eight arrivals.[52]

The failure to arrest the smallpox, and the harassment by the Virginia and Maryland militia, finally brought an end to his lordship's stay in Chesapeake waters. In May 1776, faced with the likelihood "of a great reduction of our force" due to disease,[53] the fleet moved from their exposed quarters at Tucker's Mills near Portsmouth and took shelter on Gwynn's Island near the mouth of the Rappahannock. Nowhere were Dunmore and his "floating Town"[54] allowed peace; "we no sooner appear off the land, than signals are made from it," wrote Dunmore to Whitehall, "and if we come to anchor within cannonshot of either shore, guns are immediately brought to bear upon us...."[55]

Early in July the British, after suffering an attack on their shipping, took refuge on St. George's Island in the Potomac. By the end of the month the disease-ridden corps, lacking suitable drinking water, and despairing of re-enforcements, prepared to make their exit. Dismantling, burning, or running aground sixty-three out of their 103 vessels, they sailed out of the Potomac on August 6, seven of the ships bound for Sandy Hook and the others setting a southward course for St. Augustine and the Bermudas.[56] With the departing

---

Infantry, signed by Capt. Sam Leslie, lists a total of 128 men (with breakdowns as to rank) for Mar. 1, 1776, a total of 126 men for Apr. 1, 1776, and a total of 122 for May 1, 1776. "Monthly Return of a Detachment of His Majesty's 14th Regiment of Infantry, off Norfolk, Virginia, 1 March 1776," Clinton Papers; *ibid.*, for Apr. 1, 1776, and for May 1, 1776. In addition to the factor of isolation, the mortality of the Negro soldiers may have been due to their performing most of the garrison and fatigue duties; at Gwynn's Island the entrenchments were guarded "chiefly by the black regiment," Va. Gaz., June 1, 1776.

52. Entry of June 10, 1776, A. S. Hamond Diaries, 1775–77, U. Va. library. Andrew Snape Hamond, captain of the *Roebuck*, was the commanding officer in Virginia waters.

53. *Ibid.*, May 19, 1776.

54. The descriptive phrase is Hamond's. Letter to Hans Stanley, Aug. 5, 1776, *ibid.*

55. Dunmore to George Germain, July 31, 1776, Amer. Arch., 5th Ser., II, 166.

56. Hamond Diaries, Aug. 6, 1776. Dunmore himself went to New York, arriving on Aug. 14. *Journals of Lieut.-Col. Stephen Kemble*, New-York Historical Society, *Collections* (1883–84), I, 84.

fleet went some three hundred Negroes, the healthiest going north-ward, destined for further military service, and Dunmore's schemes came to an inglorious end.[57]

Perhaps not more than a total of eight hundred slaves had suc-ceeded in reaching the British,[58] and perhaps one eighth of these had been brought by loyalist masters. But Dunmore's proclamation un-doubtedly had an indirect effect on thousands of additional slaves, quickening their hopes for freedom. Perhaps the imagination of colo-nial editors was behind such stories as that of a colored mother in New York naming her child after his lordship,[59] and that of a Negro in Philadelphia jostling whites on the streets and telling them to wait until "lord Dunmore and his black regiment come, and then we will see who is to take the wall."[60] But whether fact or fabrication, such reports reflect the attitude of expectation that Dunmore en-gendered among persons of color along the Chesapeake. It made no difference that he had offered freedom to the bondmen of his enemies only,[61] and that as governor he had withheld his signature from a bill against the slave trade; to those who whispered his name in slave quarters he was in truth the "African Hero" he was derisively dubbed by a Virginia patriot.[62]

If Dunmore was viewed by one group as a tyrant and by another as a liberator, this was but another paradox in a war that abounded in paradox, and another illustration of the war as a social revolution.

57. Dunmore remained convinced of the soundness of his plan to arm Negroes in large numbers, reviving it even after Yorktown. See Percy Burdelle Caley, "Dunmore: Colonial Governor of New York and Virginia, 1770–1782," unpubl. diss., University of Pittsburgh, 1939, pp. 887–893.

58. Dunmore's Negro followers were computed in general terms; e.g., ". . . came in a great number of Black men from the Rebels." Logs of *Roebuck* and *Fowey*, in Greenwich Museum, England, entry of June 27, 1776. Photostat in A. S. Hamond MSS., U. Va. library.

59. Taking due note, the *New York Journal* carried an occasional poem, copied in the Va. Gaz., May 25, 1776:
> Hail! doughty Ethiopian Chief!
> Though ignominious Negro Thief!
> This BLACK shall prop thy sinking name,
> and damn thee to perpetual fame.

60. Va. Gaz., Supplement, Dec. 29, 1775.

61. John King, runaway slave of a loyalist, was ordered discharged from the *King's Fisher*. Logs of *Roebuck* and *Fowey*, Feb. 23, 1776.

62. R. H. Lee to Thomas Jefferson, July 21, 1776, in *The Letters of Richard Henry Lee*, ed. James C. Ballagh (New York, 1912–14), I, 210.

The Negro who fled to the governor was actuated by the same love of freedom for which the colonists avowedly broke with the mother country. Dunmore's invitation to the slaves was to prefigure the thousands of runaways below the Mason-Dixon line who served as military laborers to His Majesty's forces during the Revolution and who, when peace came, sailed with them from Savannah, Charleston, and New York.

Reginald Horsman,
*"American Indian Policy
in the Old Northwest, 1783–1812"*

The territorial settlement provided by the Treaty of Paris (1783)
which ended the American Revolution awarded the United States
not only the former thirteen colonies but also British holdings
between the Allegheny Mountains and the Mississippi River.
British policy which attempted to prevent American settlement
beyond the Alleghenies, mainly to keep peace between whites
and Indians, had long constituted a major colonial grievance. The
government and citizens of the new nation were well pleased
with the territorial settlement and eager to exploit the new lands.
But the Indians, who occupied the new territory and did not
recognize the claim of the United States government to it, presented
a barrier to the westward flow of white population. In "American
Indian Policy in the Old Northwest, 1783–1812," Reginald
Horsman analyzes the ways in which the United States attempted
to wrest the lands between the Ohio and Mississippi Rivers from
Indian control. Although the American government rapidly developed
a policy designed to minimize warfare between whites and
Indians, it is clear that it never deviated from its intention to
acquire most of the lands for white settlers.

American Indian Policy in the Old Northwest, 1783–1812

Reginald Horsman

In the years from 1783 to 1812 the one consistent element in American Indian policy in the Old Northwest was the desire to acquire the land between the Ohio and the Mississippi. The host of subsidiary objectives were all subordinated to this end. In theory, its attainment was simply a matter of telling the Indian inhabitants of the region that England had ceded it to the United States in 1783 and that the Indians could live only on lands allotted to them by the American government. In practice, it soon became apparent that the Indians were not prepared to acknowledge the English right to give away Indian land, and the Americans were obliged to obtain their objective in other ways. Between 1783 and 1812 the American government developed a policy that would secure land in the simplest and least expensive manner. Not only did it thus secure land, it also succeeded in convincing itself that what it was doing was in the best interests of the Indians. What had started out in 1783 as naked desire for land had, by 1812, been transmuted into lofty moral purpose. By 1812 American leaders were not only trying to convince

Abridged from Reginald Horsman, "American Indian Policy in the Old Northwest, 1783–1812," William and Mary Quarterly, XVIII (1961), pp. 35–53. Reprinted by permission of the author. Some footnotes have been renumbered.

others, but apparently had also convinced themselves that they were working for the ultimate benefit of the Indian. The manner in which national interest and moral purpose became entangled is a key to the history of nineteenth century expansion.

The first phase of post-Revolutionary American Indian policy in the Old Northwest lasted from 1783 to 1787. In the Treaty of Paris which ended the Revolution the British ignored their Indian allies. The Indians were left to make their own peace with the Americans, and their position was complicated by the fact that the Americans desired more than the cessation of hostilities in the Northwest. American frontiersmen had long since pushed into western Pennsylvania and down the Ohio to Kentucky. They were now anxious to settle the rich lands northwest of the Ohio. Moreover, the government of the Confederation had a financial interest in the movement of settlers into that region. By the sale of lands the Confederation hoped to solve its acute financial problems. It had already been agreed that the states with claims north of the Ohio would cede them to the central government, and by 1786 these cessions were accomplished. On October 10, 1780, Congress had promised that lands ceded to the United States would be disposed of for the common good, "and be settled and formed into distinct republican states."[1] Thus, in establishing peace with the Indians of the Northwest, the Confederation wished to begin the process of acquiring the lands between the Ohio and the Mississippi.

The document on which the Confederation based its Northwestern Indian policy from 1783 to 1787 was the report presented to Congress by James Duane, chairman of the committee on Indian affairs, on October 15, 1783. This resolved that a convention should be held with the Indians to make peace and establish boundary lines. The Indians were to be told that the land on which they lived had been ceded by Great Britain in the Treaty of Paris, and that as they had fought on the side of the British during the Revolution, they could justly be expelled to the north of the Great Lakes along with their allies. However, it was argued that America was prepared to forgive what was past and to draw a boundary line between the Americans and the Indians. As the United States needed land, both for her

1. Worthington C. Ford and others, eds., *Journals of the Continental Congress, 1774–1789* (Washington, 1904–37), XVIII, 915.

expanding population and for extinguishing her national debt, the Indians would have to cede a portion of their territory. This was justified as reparations for Indian hostility during the war. A boundary line was suggested that would have given most of the modern state of Ohio to the United States.[2] Though these suggestions were to be modified in detail, they formed the basis of policy until 1787.

The reasoning behind this report can best be understood by a consideration of letters sent to the committee on Indian affairs during the previous summer. The suggestions that most obviously influenced the committee were those made by George Washington and by General Philip Schuyler. Washington had twice written to express his views. In June 1783 he had supported the plan for establishing settlements of ex-soldiers in the west, arguing that the appearance of such formidable settlements in the vicinity of the Indian towns "would be the most likely means to enable us to purchase upon equitable terms of the Aborigines their right of preoccupancy; and to induce them to relinquish our Territories; and to remove into the illimitable regions of the West."[3] A far more comprehensive plan was submitted by Schuyler on July 29. He argued that America would be ill-advised to continue the war with the Indians to expel them from the country—it would cost a great deal, and the Indians would return if the force that expelled them should retire. Moreover, if driven to reside in British territory, the Indians would add strength to Great Britain. Even if America could expel the Indians at moderate cost, Schuyler argued, it would not be worth while. America should merely take the land she needed for present purposes: "It will be little or no obstacle to our in future improving the very country they may retain, whenever we shall want it. For as our settlements approach their country, they must from the scarcity of game, which that approach will induce to, retire farther back, and dispose of their lands, unless they dwindle comparatively to nothing, as all savages have done, who gain their sustenance by the chace, when compelled

2. *Ibid.*, XXV, 680–694. The boundary suggested was from the mouth of the Great Miami northward to its confluence with the Mad River, thence by a direct line to Fort Miami on the Maumee, and along the Maumee to Lake Erie. The committee that made this report consisted of James Duane, Richard Peters, Daniel Carroll, Benjamin Hawkins, and Arthur Lee.

3. To the President of Congress, June 17, 1783, John C. Fitzpatrick, ed., *The Writings of George Washington* (Washington, 1931–44), XXVII, 16–18.

to live in the vicinity of civilized people, and thus leave us the country without the expence of a purchase, trifling as that will probably be."[4] . . .

The committee on Indian affairs . . . paid close attention to the advice of Washington and Schuyler in its report of October 15, 1783, though needless to say the report did not mention that the drawing of a boundary line was intended as the prelude to the gradual extermination or expulsion of the Indians. In carrying out this policy in the following years, the Confederation stressed the idea that the Northwest had been ceded by the British, but it paid little attention to Washington's suggestion that the Indians should be conciliated in order to facilitate future land acquisition. Between 1783 and 1786 land northwest of the Ohio was acquired by three treaties—Fort Stanwix in 1784, Fort McIntosh in 1785, and Fort Finney in 1786. They were all dictated treaties. Though the extent of the land treated for was not as large as that envisioned by Congress originally, these negotiations resulted in the cession to the United States of what is now eastern and southern Ohio. . . .

Despite its apparent success, the Indian policy from 1783 to 1786 was disastrous. The United States not only proceeded on the assumption that the Indians should cede some of their land as retribution for their part in the Revolution, but also assumed that the territorial sovereignty granted by England in 1783 completely eliminated any Indian right to the soil of the Northwest. The Indians who inhabited the region naturally would not accept this interpretation of the Treaty of Paris. They could not conceive that the lands upon which they lived and hunted were not their own, and, moreover, during the colonial period they had become accustomed to the idea that the whites would purchase the Indian right to the soil in formal treaty. The American post-Revolutionary policy quickly produced Indian opposition. By 1786 hostilities were breaking out on the Northwest frontier, and the Indians were ready to fight to prevent American settlement northwest of the Ohio. The Shawnee almost immediately disavowed Fort Finney, and the Mohawk Joseph Brant was, with

4. To the President of Congress, July 29, 1783, Papers of the Continental Congress, No. 153, Letters of Schuyler, III, 601–607, National Archives, Washington, D. C.

British assistance, striving to unite the Northwestern tribes.[5] America had treaties to show her ownership of lands northwest of the Ohio, but in her straitened financial position she could not occupy and defend them.

An indication that force might soon be tempered by diplomacy came in the famous Northwest Ordinance of July 13, 1787. In regard to the intended acquisition of land from the Ohio to the Mississippi, the ordinance was perfectly in accord with previous policy. It laid down the system by which the land between those two rivers would come into the Union, and provided for not less than three nor more than five states in that area. This plan of course included the land allotted to the Indians between 1783 and 1786, in addition to Indian lands farther to the west. It was Article Three that foreshadowed a change in American thinking. "The utmost good faith shall always be observed towards the Indians," it stated; "their lands and property shall never be taken from them without their consent; and in their property, rights and liberty, they never shall be invaded or disturbed, unless in just and lawful wars authorised by Congress; but laws founded in justice and humanity shall from time to time be made, for preventing wrongs being done to them, and for preserving peace and friendship with them."[6]

Though the language of the ordinance seems so incongruous in view of what had gone before, the United States was in fact changing her policy in the summer of 1787. The objective of land acquisition remained the same, but the methods were to be modified. The change had been forced upon the United States by the extent of Indian resistance. On July 10, 1787, Secretary of War Henry Knox reported to Congress that there was neither sufficient money nor an adequate army to carry on an Indian war, Peace was essential.[7] Within two weeks Knox again told Congress of the precarious position and argued that it was better to spend a small sum on the

5. The growth of Indian resistance, and the encouragement given by the British is discussed in Randolph C. Downes, *Council Fires on the Upper Ohio: A Narrative of Indian Affairs in the Upper Ohio Valley until 1795* (Pittsburgh, 1940), 279 ff.

6. Clarence E. Carter, ed., *The Territorial Papers of the United States* (Washington, 1934—), II, 47, 39–50.

7. *Ibid.*, 31–35.

purchase of land than to fight an expensive Indian war.[8] Knox's report was referred to a congressional committee on Indian affairs, headed by Nathan Dane....

In accord with the suggestions of Knox and the committee, the United States moved toward a more diplomatic policy. On October 5 Congress acted on the committee report and recommended a general treaty. Later in the month it appropriated twenty thousand dollars for holding Indian treaties wherever Congress thought it necessary.[9] This sum was added to in the following years, and the United States attempted to follow a policy of purchase rather than conquest. However, the object of acquiring all the land to the Mississippi had not been abandoned—far from it. The instructions sent at the end of October 1787 to the governor of the Northwest Territory, Arthur St. Clair, told him: "You will not neglect any opportunity that may offer of extinguishing the Indian rights to the westward as far as the river Mississippi."[10]

The general treaty with the Indians, which was suggested as desirable in the summer of 1787, took a long time to accomplish. Neither the federation nor the Indians were noted for speed in negotiation, and it was not until the close of 1788 that Governor St. Clair met with the Indians at Fort Harmar on the Ohio in an attempt to bring peace to the Northwest. The council lasted into January 1789, and eventually St. Clair accomplished two treaties—one with the Six Nations and the other with the Wyandots, Delawares, Ottawas, and Chippewas. It was found impossible to obtain the boundaries suggested in St. Clair's instructions, but at least the new American policy was partially put into effect. In essence, St. Clair told the Indians that though the United States claimed the land by conquest she was prepared to pay for it as well....

Thus in the spring of 1789, when the Federal government came to

8. W. C. Ford, ed., *Journals of the Continental Congress*, XXXIII, 388–391.

9. *Ibid.*, 611–612, 665-666 (Oct. 12).

10. Secretary of Congress to St. Clair, Oct. 26, 1787, Carter, ed., *Territorial Papers*, II, 78–79. It was suggested that a suitable line might be one by which the Indians ceded everything south of a line drawn from the southern boundary of Pennsylvania to the Mississippi. On July 2, 1788, it was recommended that a better line might be the 41st degree of north latitude—this would have given considerably more to the United States all the way to the Mississippi; *ibid.*, 117. St. Clair realized that Indian resistance would make it impossible to obtain either line; *ibid.*, 130–132.

power, American policy was already changing in regard to the manner of acquiring lands. This change was to be accentuated by the new government. An immediate problem, however, was that the heavy-handed policy since 1783 had produced a crisis in the Northwest. The Fort Harmar treaty pleased the Indians no more than the treaties of Stanwix and McIntosh had done. It did nothing to solve the basic Indian dissatisfaction at losing their lands. Encouraged by the British, the Northwestern tribes were ready to insist once again upon an Ohio River boundary. They demanded that American settlers advance no farther.[11]

Henry Knox, who continued as Secretary of War, now made a determined effort to develop the new tendencies in American Indian policy. From this time forward the element of national honor played an increasingly important part in determining the methods of land acquisition. In a report of June 15, 1789, Knox urged negotiation rather than war. Even if the necessary force were available, he argued, it was debatable from the point of view of justice whether it would be wise to use it. In addition, he maintained that America did not have sufficient money to expel the Indians. Justice and expediency made negotiation essential. Knox estimated that to attach the Indians north and south of the Ohio to the United States for the next fifty years might cost $15,000 annually, whereas to coerce them would not only cost more money, but would also stain the character of the nation "beyond all pecuniary calculation." After these praiseworthy sentiments a rather more realistic calculation, reminiscent of Philip Schuyler's suggestion of July 29, 1783, entered into Knox's report: "As the settlements of the whites shall approach near to the Indian boundaries established by treaties, the game will be diminished, and the lands being valuable to the Indians only as hunting grounds, they will be willing to sell further tracts for small considerations. By the expiration, therefore, of the above period [fifty years], it is most probable that the Indians will, by the invariable operation of the causes which have hitherto existed in their intercourse with the whites, be reduced to a very small number."[12]

Several weeks later, in a report mainly concerned with the southern

11. At the Fort Harmar council the first Indian proposal had been for a boundary along the Ohio; see Draper MSS., 23U115–123.

12. *American State Papers, Indian Affairs,* I (Washington, 1832), 13–14.

Indians, Knox moved a step further in suggesting an acceptable Indian policy. He pointed out that in time there would probably be no Indians east of the Mississippi and he asked whether, instead of extermination, there should not be civilization of the Indians. He suggested the possibility of the use of missionaries and argued that even if this did not fully civilize the Indians, it would at least attach them to the American interest. To accomplish this, he also urged fair purchase from the Indians, the recognition of the Indian right of soil, the treatment of the Indian tribes as foreign nations, and the regulation of white emigration.[13] Knox was moving toward the idea that the acquisition of Indian land could be accomplished more easily, and with fewer pangs of conscience, if accompanied by a spreading of American civilization among the Indians and the protection of the Indians from brazen insult.

In the following years America was to pass various laws designed to protect the Indians from overt acts of violence and from exploitation. Regulations concerning the mode of white settlement, the encroachment on Indian land, the selling of liquor, and fair trading practices toward the Indians were all put into effect. These often did not work, owing to the problem of controlling the frontiersmen, but the American government was sincere in its effort to make them work. Everything possible was to be done to keep the Indians at peace. If fixed boundaries were established and peace were maintained, the land of the Northwest would eventually be absorbed by the American government at a small cost. Moreover, it would be absorbed in a manner that, it was presumed, would cast least discredit on the government.[14]

The irony of the situation was that the United States, though moving rapidly in 1789 toward a policy of peace and absorption, found it necessary to wage a five-year Indian war for which she had not the slightest desire. The Indians by 1789 were actively resisting the American advance—they did not want to yield any land beyond the Ohio either by war or purchase, and America would have to wage a successful campaign before she could put her desired policy into effect. General Josiah Harmar's defeat in 1790 made another campaign essential,

13. *Ibid.*, 52–54 (July 7, 1789).
14. A brief account of the governmental measures to prevent exploitation and injury of the Indians can be found in George D. Harmon, *Sixty Years of Indian Affairs . . . 1789–1850* (Chapel Hill, 1941), 18–19, 94–123.

and in 1791 St. Clair was sent into the Indian country. Secretary of State Thomas Jefferson expressed the position clearly in April 1791 when he said before St. Clair's expedition that "I hope we shall drub the Indians well this summer & then change our plan from war to bribery."[15] Unfortunately for the United States it was St. Clair who was drubbed, and this necessitated another three years of crisis before Anthony Wayne defeated the Indians at Fallen Timbers in August 1794. While these hostilities were proceeding, the American government advanced its plans to avoid such conflicts in the future.

In his messages to Congress, Washington advocated fair dealing with the Indians, impartial justice, reasonable trading practices, and strict regulation of the manner in which Indian lands might be obtained.[16] He also moved further in desiring the Americanization of the Indian. By 1792 the idea of teaching the Indians how to farm, to keep domesticated animals, and to build comfortable homes was entering into the instructions of American envoys to the Northwest. . . .

The military victory of Anthony Wayne in August 1794 allowed the government to put into effect its desired Indian policy. Already, in April 1794, instructions in regard to the peace had been sent to Wayne. He was to obtain the boundaries of the Treaty of Fort Harmar and could confirm to the Indians their right of soil in the remainder of the Northwest. However, and this was vital, the United States must have the right of preemption.[17] According to the prevalent theories the Indians would inevitably want to sell more lands, and all the United States needed was the exclusive right to purchase them. This had been a *sine qua non* of peace with the Northwest Indians since the start of the new national government in 1789.[18]

15. To James Monroe, Apr. 17, 1791, Paul L. Ford, ed., *The Works of Thomas Jefferson* (New York, 1904–05), VI, 242.

16. See James D. Richardson, ed., *A Compilation of the Messages and Papers of the Presidents, 1789–1897* (Washington, 1896–99), I, 59, 104–105, 125–127, 141, 167, 185.

17. Knox to Wayne, Apr. 4, 1794, Northwest Territory Collection, William Henry Smith Library, Indianapolis, Indiana.

18. Though the United States was so anxious for peace, the Senate did not ratify the treaty made by Rufus Putnam with the Wabash tribes in Sept. 1792 on the grounds that it did not contain a clause guaranteeing the American right of preemption. See *American State Papers, Indian Affairs*, I, 338; *Journal of the Executive Proceedings of the Senate of the United States of America* (Washington, 1828—), I, 128, 134–135, 144–146.

Given the right of pre-emption, America inevitably would advance to the Mississippi.

When, in the spring of 1795, Wayne was near to the conclusion of a treaty with the Northwestern Indians, the new Secretary of War, Timothy Pickering, sent additional instructions for his guidance. Pickering explicitly renounced the policy pursued by the Confederation government in the post-1783 period—that is, the policy of claiming the Northwest by conquest—and said that the land belonged to the Indians. He stressed that peace and the satisfaction of the Indians were the most important considerations in the treaty. As a result the United States would claim little more land than had been obtained in 1789 at Fort Harmar.[19] This seems most reasonable unless another statement made by Pickering to Wayne is taken into consideration. "When a peace shall once be established," he wrote, "and we also take possession of the posts now held by the British, we can obtain every thing we shall want with a tenth part of the trouble and difficulty which you would now have to encounter."[20] He was paying his respects to the now well-established idea that if a boundary and peace were established Indian lands would soon fall into the hands of the Americans. . . .

The resounding phrases of the famous Treaty of Greenville thus meant very little. Though only eastern and southern Ohio, together with a strip of what is now southeastern Indiana, were granted to the United States, and though the United States relinquished her claims to all lands beyond these boundaries, it was quite evident to the American government that this was not a permanent division. Article Five gave the right of pre-emption in the remaining land of the Northwest to the United States—it was put in because it was quite obvious that it was going to be used. Moreover, by the treaty, the United States was given sixteen reservations of land on the Indian side of the boundary line to use as posts and was also granted free communication between them.[21] Indians throughout the Northwest were to have

19. Pickering to Wayne, Apr. 8, 1795, Richard C. Knopf, ed., *Campaign into the Wilderness: The Wayne-Knox-Pickering-McHenry Correspondence* (Columbus, Ohio, 1955), IV, 19–32.

20. Apr. 15, 1795, *ibid.*, 34.

21. *Statutes at Large of the United States of America*, VII (Boston, 1853), VII, 49–54.

the contact with white civilization that would result in their withdrawal or diminution in numbers. The Indians thought the Greenville line was to last forever, the Americans knew better. The territorial organization of the Northwest proceeded in spite of the Greenville line; in 1796 Wayne County was organized, stretching westward to Lake Michigan, and in 1800 the organization of the Indiana Territory also ignored the division made at Greenville.[22] The peace that reigned after Greenville allowed American settlers to pour into the ceded areas.

The period of calm lasted little longer than the administration of John Adams, for American settlers soon looked beyond the land ceded at Greenville. From 1801 to 1809 President Thomas Jefferson sought the land between the Ohio and the Mississippi rivers with all the eagerness of the Confederation. With the ambivalence that is so characteristic of Jefferson, he was able to combine an apparent genuine interest in the welfare of the Indian with a voracious appetite for Indian land. In his public utterances Jefferson viewed the harsh realities of American-Indian relations through a roseate mist. His first annual message, December 1801, expressed happiness that the Indians were becoming "more and more sensible" of the advantages of farming and "the household arts" over hunting and fishing.[23] The wish was apparently father to the thought. In the following month he told a visiting delegation of Miamis, Potawatomis, and Weas that the United States would "with great pleasure see your people become disposed to cultivate the earth, to raise heards of the useful animals and to spin and weave, for their food and clothing, these resources are certain, they will never disappoint you, while those of hunting may fail, and expose your women and children to the miseries of hunger and cold."[24] This became the rallying call of Jefferson throughout his presidency. He was convinced that the United States should take every opportunity to persuade the Indians to abandon their old modes of life. His motives were not entirely altruistic.

In January 1803 Jefferson submitted a message to Congress recom-

22. Carter, ed., *Territorial Papers*, II, 567–568, III, 86–88.

23. Richardson, ed., *Messages and Papers of the Presidents*, I, 326.

24. Jan. 7, 1802, War Department, Secretary's Office, Letters Sent, Indian Affairs, A, 143, National Archives, Washington, D. C.

mending the continuance of the system of American trading factories among the Indians.[25] He went on to comment upon American-Indian relations and told Congress that the Indian tribes had been growing increasingly uneasy at the diminution of their land, and that the policy of refusing to contract any further sales had been growing among them. To counteract this policy, "and to provide an extension of territory which the rapid increase of our numbers will call for," Jefferson recommended two measures. The first suggestion was to encourage the Indian tribes to abandon hunting and to engage instead in stock raising, agriculture, and domestic manufacture. He argued that it would be possible to show the Indians that by following this new way of life they could live better with less land and less labor. Their extensive forests would thus become useless to them, and they would see the advantage of exchanging these lands for the means of improving their farms and increasing their domestic comforts. His second suggestion was to multiply trading-houses among the Indians, "and place within their reach those things which will contribute more to their domestic comfort than the possession of extensive but uncultivated wilds." These measures would, he argued, prepare the Indians to share ultimately in the benefits of American government and civilization. "I trust and believe," stated Jefferson, "we are acting for their greatest good."[26] ...

The transformation of the Indian into an American farmer, and the resulting surplus of land that would be happily yielded to the United States, was a vision which beset Jefferson throughout his two terms as president. Time and time again he told visiting delegations of Indians that the United States wanted them to abandon the difficulties of the chase and engage in the pleasures of farming. As game became increasingly scarce, he warned them, their families would starve.[27] Jefferson did not merely want the Indians to live in the

25. The Indian factory system had been established in 1796 to protect the Indians from unscrupulous traders, attach them to the United States, and counteract British and Spanish influence; see Ora K. Peake, *A History of the United States Indian Factory System, 1795–1822* (Denver, 1954), passim.

26. Jan. 18, 1803, Richardson, ed., *Messages and Papers of the Presidents*, I, 352–353.

27. See messages from Jefferson to the various Indian tribes, War Dept., Secretary's Office, Letters Sent, Indian Affairs, A, 315, 413–415; B, 147–148, 279–282, 369–373, 394–397, 400–402, 410–413.

American manner, eventually he wanted them to be absorbed into the American population. He spoke of the ultimate point of rest and happiness for the Indians as being when the two races would become one people and when the Indians would become American citizens.[28] The Indians would throw off their own traditions and would assume those of the United States. The original aim of appropriating Indian land was now becoming inextricably entwined with the moralistic aim of bringing civilization to the Indians.

Thus Jefferson conjured up a dreamland in which the Indians would agree that the white man's civilization was superior and would be eager to yield their surplus lands to the expanding Americans. The fact is, of course, that Governor Harrison of Indiana, acting on instructions from Jefferson, pressed the Indians into selling a goodly portion of the modern states of Indiana and Illinois between 1802 and 1809....

While Jefferson spoke in his messages to Congress as though all this met with the approbation of the Northwestern Indians,[29] the intensity of their resistance was becoming increasingly obvious in the years after 1802. Rather than rushing forward to sell their surplus lands to taste the delights of agriculture, spinning, and weaving, the Indians were in these years becoming infuriated at the flouting of promises made at Greenville. By 1805 Tecumseh and the Prophet were beginning to organize resistance in the Northwest, and by the time Jefferson left office in 1809 the area was on the verge of war. In spite of this, Harrison in September 1809 secured yet another tract of land in Indiana.[30] This American pressure for land in the first decade of the nineteenth century greatly simplified the British task of preparing for the war that was to come in 1812. Though the British had deserted the Northwestern Indians in 1783 and in 1794, Indian anger at the American land policy insured that the Indians would once again be in the British camp.

Meanwhile Jefferson continued his policy of peace, civilization, and land appropriation. For a time, after the purchase of Louisiana in

28. To Benjamin Hawkins, Feb. 18, 1803, P. L. Ford, ed., *Works of Jefferson*, IX, 445–449.

29. Richardson, ed., *Messages and Papers of the Presidents*, I, 343–344, 359, 371–372, 386–387.

30. *Statutes at Large*, VII, 113–116.

1803, he toyed with the possibility of removal west of the Mississippi as a solution to the Indian problem, but his interest in this project soon faded.[31] To the end of his second term, his desire for land, and the linked desire of civilizing the Indians, continued unassuaged. . . .

In December 1808 he told the Miami chief, Little Turtle, of the advantage of agriculture over hunting, and then continued by saying that "I have therefore always believed it an act of friendship to our red brethren whenever they wished to sell a portion of their lands, to be ready to buy whether we wanted them or not—because the price enables them to improve the lands they retain and turning their industry from hunting to agriculture the same exertions will support them more plentifully."[32] It would seem that Jefferson had come to believe that not only was the civilization of the Indian convenient for acquisition of land, but that he was also acquiring land in order to civilize the Indian.

Shortly before he left office he spoke with conviction, and with an eloquent peroration, when he told an assembled gathering of Northwestern Indians: "I repeat that we will never do an unjust act towards you. On the contrary we wish you to live in peace, to increase in numbers, to learn to labor as we do and furnish food for your ever encreasing numbers, when the game shall have left you. We wish to see you possessed of property and protecting it by regular laws. In time you will be as we are: you will become one people with us: your blood will mix with ours: and will spread with ours over this great island. Hold fast then my children, the chain of friendship which binds us together: and join us in keeping it forever bright and unbroken."[33]

American Indian policy in the Northwest during these hectic years revolved around the problem of the acquisition of land. The Confederation government first tried the simple methods of force, and discovered there was no surer way of producing Indian war. Anxious to avoid war, from financial as well as humanitarian motives, the Confederation turned to a policy of purchase, which involved the

31. See Annie H. Abel, "The History of Events Resulting in Indian Consolidation West of the Mississippi," American Historical Association, Annual Report . . . 1906 (Washington, 1908), I, 241 ff.

32. War Dept., Secretary's Office, Letters Sent, Indian Affairs, B, 400–401.

33. To chiefs of the Wyandots, Ottawas, Chippewas, Potawatomis, and Shawnee, Jan. 1809, ibid., B, 412–413.

recognition of Indian rights to land beyond certain boundary lines. Recognition of this right did not mean that America expected any difficulty in acquiring further areas of land. The government acted on the assumption that the pressure of white population up to the demarcation line would produce a diminution in game, a reduction in the Indian population, and a desire to sell land cheaply. The new federal government inherited this policy from the Confederation and added to it. The most important addition was a more acute awareness that the national honor was involved. An attempt was made to give the Indians as much justice as was compatible with the wholesale acquisition of land. In fact, the government was prepared to defend the Indian against everyone except itself. In the 1790's there was a growing governmental interest in the possibility of bringing civilization to the Indian—that is, in transforming him into an American farmer. There seems to have been little realization that the Indian might not consider this an advantage. From the American point of view it was an ideal solution, for the Indian would cede his vast lands, and what was left of the Indian population would be absorbed into American civilization. This concept received far greater development after 1800 during the presidency of Thomas Jefferson. Though comparatively little progress was made in this direction, Jefferson acted as if the whole program was taking tremendous strides and proceeded to support William Henry Harrison in the acquisition of considerable areas of land. He never seemed to realize the wide discrepancy between the lofty nature of his aims and the rather sordid land-grabbing that was taking place in the Northwest.

The basic object of American Indian policy in this period—the acquisition of land—was a striking success. The subsidiary aims of peace, friendship, and the eventual absorption of the Indian into the American way of life resulted in failure. This failure was to be repeated throughout American history, for wholesale land acquisition and friendship with the Indians were incompatible. However much members of the government might desire to win the friendship of the Indians, they could only do so by establishing a permanent barrier to the expansion of the American population over the North American continent. This would have meant leaving the area to the Indians, who were considered savages by the majority of the American people. While Indians roamed freely over the rich Mississippi Valley, the United States would have confined its rapidly increasing population to the eastern portion of its internationally recognized boundaries. Even if the government had desired such a policy, it could hardly have enforced it. Thus the American government was forced into the dilemma of trying to reconcile wholesale land acquisition and justice to the Indians. The dilemma was never solved—probably because it was insoluble—and America discovered very early in her history that the lot of a colonizer with a conscience is not a happy one.

During the early nineteenth century, the white citizens of Florida lived surrounded by two hostile nonwhite groups—blacks, both free and slave, and Seminole Indians. The white nightmare of a red and black coalition against Caucasian domination became a reality during the Seminole War. Kenneth Porter, in "Florida Slaves and Free Negroes in the Seminole War, 1835–1842," describes the nonwhite resistance to the United States government which blossomed into the most protracted Indian War in American history. He demonstrates that the Seminole revolt against the policy of Indian removal was significantly strengthened by the cooperation of slaves seeking freedom and free blacks who feared enslavement. Although the military power and duplicity of the government ultimately prevailed, many blacks secured their freedom by their spirited resistance.

Florida Slaves and Free Negroes in the Seminole War, 1835–1842

Kenneth W. Porter

At the outbreak of the Seminole War, the Negroes of Florida were divided into three categories: slaves to the whites, principally on the sugar plantations of the St. John's valley; free Negroes, the result of the lenity of the Spanish law which required the emancipation of any slave offering his master $300, principally in St. Augustine and vicinity; and "Indian Negroes," living among the Seminole, either as legal slaves, through purchases from Spaniards, English, or Americans, or, in a greater number of cases, runaways and their descendants, but all thoroughly identified in customs and interests with the Indians, at the worst as their favored dependents, at the best as advisers to the chief men of the tribe, and in no case treated as chattels.

The Seminole War, ostensibly caused by the insistence of the United States government on the removal of the Seminole to the Indian Territory, along with most of the other Indian tribes east of the Mississippi, in order to make room for white settlers and prevent border difficulties, was in large measure also urged on by the desire of slave traders and slave owners to gain possession of the

Abridged from Kenneth W. Porter, "Florida Slaves and Free Negroes in the Seminole War, 1835–1842," pp. 390–421. Copyright © by The Association for the Study of Negro Life and History, Inc. Published in *The Journal of Negro History*, XXVIII (January 1943). Some footnotes have been renumbered.

Negroes living among the Seminole; on the other hand, the unwill-
ingness of the Indians to leave the country in which they had established themselves was reinforced by the fear of the Seminole Negroes
lest, emerging from their fastnesses for transportation to the west,
they should be seized and enslaved.

All the parties to the controversy were well acquainted with one
another. There had been peace between the whites and the Seminole
ever since the annexation of Florida to the United States. The Indians and their Negroes had been accustomed to come frequently
into St. Augustine and other towns to trade, and were familiar with
the city and its inhabitants. Racial ties made the relations among the
various categories of Florida Negroes particularly close. Many of
the slave-men "had wives among the Indian negroes, and the Indian
negroes had wives among them."[1] . . .

As 1835 drew to a close it became evident that arrival at a state of
open hostilities was only a matter of time. Military preparations for
the forcible removal of the Indians were countered by sporadic raids
and murders on the part of the Seminole. The white people of
Florida did not, in general, however, regard the future very seriously.
They considered the Seminole an essentially peaceful, even rather
cowardly people, whose resistance could be abated in a few weeks; the
war actually lasted for nearly seven years and proved to be the most
protracted and expensive "Indian war," both in lives and money,
which the United States has ever undergone. The Floridians, and the
people of the United States in general, had overlooked or under-
estimated the Negroes—Indian Negroes, plantation slaves, free Negroes—as a factor of resistance. They were to be speedily disillusioned
and enlightened. . . .

When, late in December, 1835, hostilities broke out on a large
scale, it was evident that they had been carefully prepared and coordinated by the savage enemy. The St. John's River Indians, under
their chief Emathla, or King Philip as the whites called him, ably
seconded by his Negro associate and subordinate John Caesar, fell
upon the plantations of that region on the night of Dec. 26-27,
plundering and burning,[2] while on the morning of Dec. 28, Maj.

1. Douglas, Thomas, Autobiography of, N. Y. 1856, pp. 120–123.
2. Niles Register, vol. xlix, p. 369; "A Lieutenant of the Left Wing," Sketch of
the Seminole War, Charleston, 1836, pp. 19–20.

Dade's company of over one hundred men was annihilated on the march from Ft. Brooke (Tampa) to Ft. King (Ocala) by the Seminole of the Tampa and Withlacoochee region, led by head chief Micanopy, his war leader and nephew Alligator, his chief counsellor and brother-in-law Jumper, and his Negro adviser Abraham; Louis Pacheco ne Fatio, the slave who had been hired as a guide for the expedition, is generally said to have been in communication with the hostiles and to have assisted in the destruction of the troops, although in his old age, fifty-seven years later, he stoutly denied the charge.

The horror caused by the almost complete destruction of an entire command, including many well-known and popular officers, paled beside that inspired by the enthusiasm with which the plantation slaves rallied to the insurgent Seminole. From plantation after plantation came the menacing word. "Depeyster's negroes were traitors, and must have been in league with the Indians; they assisted them with a boat to cross over to Dummett's . . . the whole of Major Heriot's and Depeyster's negroes . . . moved off with the Indians." "Upwards of two hundred and fifty negroes . . . have joined the Indians and are more desperate than the Indians." Some of the Depeyster Negroes had painted their faces in symbol of their new allegiance. It was cold comfort even to learn that "Anderson's negroes behaved with the utmost prudence and fidelity," concealing as much as possible of their master's property before fleeing, for the reporter went on to announce gloomily that even this loyalty would be of little ultimate value, since the Negroes of neighboring plantations would, of course, readily discover this cache and reveal it to the foe. That the plantation Negroes were joining the Indians, Gen. Hernandez understandably declared, "is the very worst feature of the whole of this war."[3] . . .

The situation appeared serious enough to the St. Augustinians, into whose city were crowding the frightened or sullen refugees, white and black, from the devastated plantations to the south. But westwardly, where more than one serious action had already been

3. *The Charleston Courier*, Jan. 12, 21, 22, 1836; National Archives, War Department, Adjutant General's Office, Maj. Benjamin A. Putnam, Cantonment Rosetta, Dec. 29, 1835, to Brig. Gen. J. M. Hernandez, St. Augustine (316), Putnam, Bulowville, Jan. 4, 1836, to Hernandez (25), Hernandez, Dec. 30, 1835, to Lewis Cass (H129/316).

fought by the beginning of 1836, and where the United States posts were closely invested, it was really critical. The commander at Ft. Brooke, from which the Dade command had marched so confidently, announced, a week after its wiping out: "This place is invested by all the Florida Indians in the field, with a large accession of Negroes, particularly from the plantations of Tomoka & Smyrna, as appears from the examination of a prisoner just taken."[4] ...

In St. Augustine, where the planters, together with such of their Negroes as had not the desire or ability to "move off" with the Seminole, had taken refuge, they, and their fellows in the immediate vicinity, were still exposed to the dangers presented by the Negro-Indian alliance, actual or potential. With several hundred Negroes concentrated within the walls of the city, most of whom "had ... for years lived on the frontier in the neighborhood of the Indians" and "spoke their language," "strong apprehensions were felt ... that they would fire the town, and that, during the confusion resulting ...; the Indians might rush in." Patrols were organized to cope with this menace, but arms of any sort were almost non-existent and it was discovered that during the few weeks preceding the outbreak the Indians had purchased nearly all the powder and lead available in the local shops.[5]

In addition to an actual attack by the Seminole, in cooperation with Negro sympathizers in the town, the whites of St. Augustine had to guard against communications between the hostile Indians and Negroes without and potential allies among the Negroes within. Emissaries of the enemy endeavored to enter the town to induce Negroes to join them and to obtain information, and Negroes within the town endeavored to escape through the lines to join the Seminole, carrying with them knowledge of the plans of the whites, and sometimes supplies. In recognition of this Negro-Indian alliance the Territory of Florida passed an act, "respecting hostile negroes & mulattoes in the Seminole nation," providing that any free persons belonging to those categories who should be captured should be sold into slavery as a punishment....

It cannot, of course, be claimed that all the plantation slaves, even

4. National Archives, War Department, AGO, Capt. F. S. Belton, Ft. Brooke, Jan. 5, 1836, to the Adjt. Gen. (23).

5. Douglas, loc. cit.

those who had the opportunity, aligned themselves with the Seminole. A considerable number of the Indians themselves were, from the first, supporters of the United States government rather than of the cause of their own people. The same cannot be said of the Seminole Negroes, who, apparently to a man, maintained the cause of liberty until the background of resistance was broken and the principal chiefs had begun to surrender. The Negroes who were living among the whites had no such freedom of decision, and reacted according to circumstances and individual differences....

In the meantime, while the citizens of St. Augustine were endeavoring to deal with the "enemy within their gates," the first year of the Seminole War was drawing to a close, a year during which neither party had won a decisive advantage but in which, nevertheless, the Negro-Indian allies had at least held their own and perhaps maintained a slight superiority. It was a year, too, in which the Negroes, particularly, of course, the Indian Negroes but not neglecting the recent runaways, had borne their full share of the burden and heat of the day. "Micanopy, Philip, and Cooper ... are about a day's march from each other, each with from one hundred and twenty to two hundred Indian and negro warriors—the latter perhaps the more numerous," wrote on Dec. 9, 1836, Gen. Thomas Sidney Jesup, the newly appointed commander. "This, you may be assured," he continued, "is a negro, not an Indian war; and if it be not speedily put down, the south will feel the effects of it on their slave population before the end of the next season."[6] ...

But early in 1837, under Gen. Jesup's vigorous leadership, the United States troops and state militia struck a series of staggering blows at the Indian-Negro enemy, Osceola's force, in particular, being completely disrupted. It was at this time that John Caesar, the Indian Negro partisan leader, operating in the St. John's region, began a diversion which might well have been important—a series of guerrilla raids on plantations which extended almost up to the very gates of St. Augustine....

... That a band composed almost entirely of Negroes should have the temerity to attempt a raid in the immediate vicinity of St. Augustine ... and that the hostile Negroes should be ... conclusively

6. *American State Papers, Military Affairs*, vol. vii, pp. 820–821; 25th cong., 2nd sess., 1837–38, h. ex. doc., vol. iii, no. 78, p. 52.

demonstrated to be in ... close and constant communication with the Negro population of the city, revived something of the panic of the early days of the war. The city council, Jan. 23, 1837, accordingly passed "An ordinance to prevent the selling of ammunition to Slaves, free Negroes & molattos," which it is rather surprising to learn had not already long since been forbidden.[7] Stephen Merritt *alias* Wright, ... and Randall Irving, free persons of color, were indicted at the Superior Court "for treason against the United States, in supplying the Seminole Indians with provisions and ammunition. They were arraigned and pleaded not guilty."[8] The fears of the citizenry were not perceptibly diminished by the capture, in March, of one of the principal malefactors.

Andrew Gue [Gay] ... belonging to Col. Gue of this city, who ran away from his master in June last, was captured on Thursday morning at 4 A.M. by a detachment of six men under Lieut. John Ferreira, of Capt. Hudson's company of Mounted Volunteers. Andrew is a young negro not exceeding 21 years of age, and active and enterprising. He went off, joined the Indians, and after being with them for some weeks, he returned clandestinely to town, and held a meeting with some of his friends and enticed some of them off. At this meeting he stated that he had become high in the confidence of the Indians and he only wanted a white man's scalp to make him a great man. On several occasions since he has made his appearance in the vicinity, and was with the gang of negroes when Capt. Hopson [Hanson?] killed John Caesar,[9] at which time he received three wounds. He says he bled considerable, and since

7. "Minutes of the City of St. Augustine, Nov. 18, 1836–Nov. 15, 1854," City Building, St. Augustine, Fla., p. 8.
8. *The Daily National Intelligencer* (Washington, D. C.), Apr. 17, 1837. There is no record of either of these cases in the above-mentioned *Inventory*.
9. This must refer to the episode of January, and John Caesar must have been one of the two Indian Negroes killed; Andrew doubtless identified him after his own capture. No other encounter corresponding to this description is known to have taken place. For a description of John Caesar's career prior to the final episode in his life, see the author's "John Caesar: A Forgotten Hero of the Seminole War," *The Journal of Negro History*, vol. xxviii (Jan., 1943), pp. 53–65. At the time of writing this article, the author was unaware of the circumstances of John Caesar's death, though, of the three possibilities advanced, one comes pretty close to the facts as now known.

that time he has not seen or spoken to any person whatever. He has remained in the neighborhood of the place where he was wounded, subsisting on roots, &c., until he was induced from hunger to come to our neighborhood for provisions, and which led to his capture.[10]

Andrew was duly committed to prison, but even the knowledge that this dangerous character was behind bars and that the formidable John Caesar would no longer trouble the country, seems to have been of little comfort, compared with the uneasiness produced by the knowledge that there were at large other runaway slaves,[11] who, like Andrew Gay, might be longing for a white man's scalp, and with the ability to penetrate into the midst of the town to plot insurrection with their fellows, and imbue them with a desire for similar trophies. The city council on May 2 passed a resolution that Capt. Hanson's company, which had done such good service in hunting down and breaking up John Caesar's band, should be recalled and "employed to scour the country in the neighborhood"—"from within our own community," a resolution of a month later declared, "we know not how soon firebrands may be thrown amongst us," and the necessity for all to join in the defense of the city was stressed.[12] Thus the fear of a slave insurrection operated to keep the militia companies near home, deprived Gen. Jesup of their assistance, and relieved the pressure on the Negroes and Indians actually in the field. To that extent John Caesar, [the free Negro] Joe Merritt, Andrew Gue or Gay, and their fellows had not shed their blood in vain.

From the last of January to the first of June, 1837, it had seemed probable that hostilities might be speedily and permanently terminated. The war had been going badly for the Seminole and to Gen. Jesup the time seemed ripe for peace negotiations. But he recognized that the terms could not be too onerous, since "in all the numerous battles and skirmishes that have taken place, not a single first-rate

10. *The Charleston Courier*, Mar. 21, 1837. I have been unable to find any record of this case elsewhere, or any information as to Andrew's fate; his case is not listed in the *Inventory*.

11. *Ibid.* One such runaway was named Smart, and belonged to the late Pablo Salvate, having gone off the previous summer. He was detected lurking in the vicinity and may have been a member of the disrupted John Caesar band.

12. St. Augustine minutes, pp. 11, 13.

warrior has been captured, and only two Indian men have surrendered. The warriors have fought as long as they had life, and such seems to be the determination of those who influence their councils —I mean the leading negroes." Accordingly he communicated through a captured Indian Negro, Ben, with the principal Negro leader, Abraham, and through him got in touch with other principal chiefs, Indian and Negro. On March 6, 1837, an agreement was signed providing that "the Seminoles and their allies, who come in and emigrate West, shall be secure in their lives and property; [and] that their negroes, their bona fide property, shall also accompany them West."[13] This was understood by the Seminole as protecting not only the Negroes to whom some of the Indians might have a more or less valid title, but also "their allies," the other Negroes who were then living among them and fighting with them, and at first Gen. Jesup had insisted on that interpretation. "The negroes," that is, the Indian Negroes, "rule the Indians," he wrote on March 26, 1837, "and it is important that they should feel themselves secure; if they should become alarmed and hold out, the war will be renewed."[14] Obviously, any attempt to meddle with any of the Negroes who had been fighting in the Seminole ranks for over a year would arouse apprehension among the others. But Gen. Jesup's decision that the runaway Negroes among the Seminole were "their allies" and protected by the terms of the capitulation, was inevitably greeted with violent protest by planters who had lost slaves during the war, and finally, yielding to their pressure, he was induced to make a clandestine arrangement on April 8 with certain Indian chiefs, notably Coi Hajo, second chief of the St. John's River Seminole, "to surrender the negroes taken during the war,"[15] thus endeavoring to

13. ASP, MA, vii, 825–828; Army and Navy Chronicle, iv, 80.

14. ASP, MA, vii, 835.

15. Niles Register, Apr. 29, 1837, p. 133. See: Giddings, Joshua, The Exiles of Florida, Columbus, O., 1858, ch. xi, for a detailed discussion of this agreement. Although Coi Hajo had participated in the Seminole resistance to removal, he had been looked on, prior to the outbreak of the war, as weak-kneed in his opposition—so much so that it is said that it had been intended to put him to death along with Chalo (Charley) Emathla, leader of the emigration party. National Archives, AGO, Bvt. Lieut. Col. A. C. W. Fanning, Ft. King, Nov. 28, 1835, to Brig. Gen. D. L. Clinch, St. Augustine (478). It is possible that jealousy of Philip, head chief of the St. John's River Seminole, may partially account for some of the divagations of the second chief.

introduce a division, based on the time of their escape, into the ranks of the Negroes among the Seminole....
What was in the wind could not be long kept from the nostrils of those principally concerned. Not all the Negroes with the Indians had, of course, joined them entirely of their own free will, and many of those who had been eager enough at first had by this time no doubt become tired of the bargain. The Indians themselves had suffered severely from lack of food and clothing, and the less-experienced plantation Negroes had not, of course, been any better off, probably a good deal worse. Those who had not displayed any particular enthusiasm for defending their newly acquired liberty with arms in their hands had been sent off, with the women, old men, and children, to secluded islands and hammocks, and put to raising corn; they may well have felt that they had merely exchanged one slavery for another, almost as arduous and even less rewarding in physical comforts. Those who felt thus did not need to be "brought in"; they eagerly surrendered themselves whenever the approach of a body of troops gave them the opportunity, hoping that the excuse of having been "captured" would save them from punishment. A dozen Negroes who surrendered in May were clad only in ragged muddy breech cloths and complained that they had been forced to live entirely on koonti-roots, from which the Indians made a sort of bread, and on alligator tails, and that when things were going badly for the Indians they had sometimes vented their ill-temper on the Negroes by beating them.[16]

Other Negroes prized their freedom higher than considerations of immediate comfort. Lt. Col. W. S. Harney wrote on May 16 that "there was a party [of Negroes] on Cedar Creek who were all runaways and [when they learned that they were to be returned to their masters] resisted telling the Indians that they [the Indians] had not taken them & that they [the Negroes] would not give up."[17] Negroes of this mind and spirit received support from the more militant Indians, such as Osceola. Some of the Negroes who surrendered reported that Coi Hajo had announced in council that the runaway Negroes were to be returned, whereupon Osceola, rising in a rage,

16. Motte, Capt. J. Rhett, "Life in Camp and Field," St. Augustine Historical Society (ms.), p. 161.
17. Florida Historical Society (photostat).

declared that so long as he was in the nation it should never be done.[18] ...

The determined opposition of Osceola and other militant chiefs, and the resistance of freedom-loving Negroes who had gotten wind of Coi Hajo's plot with Gen. Jesup, naturally checked or diminished the movement toward Tampa Bay, particularly of Negroes, whether "Indian" Negroes or "captured." Even the Indian Negroes already assembled at Tampa Bay became uneasy as persons owning, or claiming to own, slaves who had taken refuge among the Indians, began to appear at the emigration camp. Many of the Indian Negroes were themselves runaways, though of long standing, or the children of runaways, and thus legally slaves, whatever the terms or interpretation of Gen. Jesup's already once-broken agreement. Finally, early in June, under the instigation and leadership of Osceola, Wild Cat, and the young Indian Negro chief John Cavallo, most of the Indian Negroes and many Indians fled the camp, taking with them, for good measure, the principal hostages they had given for the fulfillment of the Ft. Dade capitulation.[19]

Too late Gen. Jesup recognized his error. Most of the Indians and Negroes would probably have eventually surrendered to be sent out of the country had he not spoiled everything by trying to force the surrender of recent runaways. He had secured by this policy about a hundred each of Indian Negroes and runaways, but now the war was revived, with a greater danger than ever, in the general's opinion, of spreading to the plantations. "The two races," he wrote in June, "the negro and the Indians, are rapidly approximating; they are identified in interests and feelings"—and it is evident that Gen. Jesup is here speaking of the slave Negro, not the Indian Negro, whose "identity" with the Indian was too self evident to require comment....

Only a sense of humiliation, resulting from the failure of his carefully worked out plans of early 1837, and driving him nearly to desperation, can explain—it cannot justify—several of Gen. Jesup's actions in the autumn of that year and early in the following. The fortunate capture in September of Philip (Emathla), the St. John's

18. 1st Lieut. R. H. Peyton, May 24, 1837, to Harney, Florida Historical Society (photostat).
19. ASP, MA, vii, 371.

River head chief, made it possible to use him as a bait to attract, for conversation with his father, his favorite son Wild Cat, who was then employed as an emissary to draw in about a hundred Negroes and Indians, including several chiefs and sub-chiefs, among them those irreconcilables Osceola and John Cavallo, supposedly for a conference. Instead they were surrounded and captured. About twenty, including Wild Cat and John Cavallo, escaped the next month, but it was nonetheless a serious blow. Over a hundred others, including the head chief Micanopy, were seized by a similar device early in December and, discouraged by this, still others surrendered. But there were still enough hostiles in the field, under Wild Cat, Alligator, Sam Jones, and John Cavallo, to fight the most seriously contested action of the war, on Christmas Day, at Lake Okeechobee, against Col. Zachary Taylor. Gen. Jesup himself took the field next month and fought an action on the Laxahatchie west of Okeechobee—a battle in which an officer said there were as many Negroes as Indians among the Seminole warriors.[20]

Jesup now considered the time ripe to re-open peace negotiations. He had learned wisdom in the months since the previous June. He suggested to the Indians that they might be allowed to remain on a reservation in southern Florida, but said nothing about returning runaway slaves. He was becoming more and more convinced of the inadvisability of returning captured Negroes to servitude. He had hired a considerable number of Creek mercenaries, promising them as plunder all the Negroes they could capture, but when, in September, 1837, they succeeded in capturing eighty, he wrote: "It is highly important to the slaveholding States that these negroes be sent out of the country, and I would strongly recommend that they be sent to one of our colonies in Africa," i.e., Liberia. These Negroes were accordingly taken from the Creeks, and a "reward" of $20 per head substituted, much to the latter's dissatisfaction.[21] The Negroes were eventually sent not to Liberia but to the Indian Territory; in either case their freedom was assured.

Jesup also addressed himself directly to the Seminole Negroes, endeavoring to drive a wedge between them and the Indians, as he had previously striven to separate the Seminole, both Indian and

20. Motte, op. cit., p. 255.
21. ASP, MA, vii, 882.

Negro, from the recently escaped slaves. He issued an order "that all the property of the Seminole Indians in Florida at war with the United States who separated themselves from the Indians, and delivered themselves up to the Commanding officer of the troops, should be free"—an early and oddly-placed Emancipation Proclamation. Gen. Jesup's idea was now to send the Seminole Negroes to the Indian Territory with those who had already been transported, and put the Indians on a reservation in a remote part of the peninsula, trusting that its inaccessibility to the plantation region, and the absence of Negroes therein, would prevent its becoming a haven for runaways. He explained that "Separating the negros from the Indians weaken[s] the latter more than they would be weakened by the loss of the same number of their own people"[22]—evidence that Jesup still held to his original opinion that the Seminole Indian War might more appropriately be entitled the Negro War. Slavery among the Seminole was not so onerous that this offer in itself was probably of much effect; its importance lay in the suggestion that Jesup was now willing to make a special effort to conciliate the Negro element among the Seminole. In response to Jesup's invitation nearly 700 Seminole, about a fourth Negroes, assembled at Ft. Jupiter for a conference, but in the meantime the Secretary of War had refused to consider any peace except on the basis of emigration, so the general, probably against his real inclinations, accomplished another master-piece of treachery by arresting the entire lot. This discouraged the others so that 450 more, one-third of them Negroes, surrendered shortly after. On March 13 Jesup announced that "nearly all the blacks have left the field, by capture or surrender."[23] The only Negro chief who had not surrendered or been captured was John Cavallo, and he, with Alligator, the Indian chief with whom he was most closely associated, came in early in April, at the general's special invitation and promise of freedom.[24] Again it seemed that the war was over, and in May, Gen. Jesup was retired and was replaced by Zachary Taylor.

But, though nearly all the principal chiefs were dead or prisoners,

22. National Archives, Department of the Interior, Indian Bureau, Florida (Emigration) File A1282-1842, Statement of Brig. Gen. Zachary Taylor, Ft. Brooke, Apr. 30, 1840; ibid., Seminole File W244-1848, T. S. Jesup, near Ft. Jupiter, Feb. 28, 1838, to Brig. Gen. R. Jones, Washington.

23. A. & N. C., vi, 190.

24. N. R., May 5, 1838; A. & N. C., vi, 300, 315.

several minor chiefs, now, if only for want of competition, become of major importance, were left to carry on the fight—including one, who, for over a year, had been steadily increasing in stature until he could be recognized without qualification as of the first rank—Wild Cat or Coacoochee. After the Battle of Lake Okeechobee he had moved north to his old stamping-ground on the St. John's. Included in his band were a number of recent runaways from that region, and his expert utilization of their services as spies was known and commented upon by his adversaries.[25] He also, as before, found willing allies among the Negro population, slave or free, within the lines of the forces of slavery....

During William J. Worth's command the war was finally, in August, 1842, brought to an official and, this time, permanent conclusion—if thirteen years, the time elapsing between the end of the Second Seminole War and the outbreak of the Third, suffice for permanency. This was accomplished partly by the capture—sometimes through methods strongly reminiscent of Gen. Jesup—of the more militant chiefs still at large—Wild Cat, Hospitaka, Halleck Tustenuggee—and writing off the problem of corralling the patriarchal Apiaca, or Sam Jones, and the more youthful Holata Micco, or Billy Bowlegs, as the rather futile job it had long been demonstrated to be. The Seminole now living in Florida are descended from the members of these two bands, mostly of the former, since a part of Billy Bowlegs' band, including Billy himself, were rounded up and shipped west as a result of the Third Seminole War, 1855–1858.

But another contribution to the liquidation of the war was a definitely changed policy toward the Negro element, including not only the Negroes of long standing in the tribe but the recent runaways, or "captured" Negroes, as well, foreshadowed by Jesup's prevention of the sale of captured Negroes by their Creek captors. Jesup's successors devoted themselves exclusively to getting the Indians and Negroes out of the everglades, out of the peninsula, and safely west of the Mississippi, and would on the whole rather ship a Negro west than return him to his legal owner, with the latter process involving the danger of alarming other Negroes who would

25. Van Ness, Maj. W. P., "An incident of the Seminole War," *Journal of the Military Service Institute of the United States*, vol. 1 (1912), pp. 267–271.

not only refuse to surrender themselves, but also influence the Negroes in general, and Indians as well, to stay out. The sensible theory developed among army officers that if a Negro didn't really want to be returned to his master—if he did, they would, of course, be glad to be of service—the quicker he was put on a steamboat for New Orleans and the Indian Territory, the better. . . .

. . . The long struggle of the Negroes had not been entirely in vain. The Indian Negroes had again conclusively maintained the freedom which they or their ancestors had won first by flight and had then defended by force of arms against raids by Georgia borderers and in the First Seminole War; had they not thus demonstrated their mettle, but come passively in for transportation to the west, there is little doubt that many of them would have been enslaved. The slave raids against Negroes living among the Indians in West Florida, shortly before the outbreak of the Seminole War, are an indication of what the others might have expected, once they were made accessible to white aggression. Many, probably most, of the slaves who joined the Seminole at the outbreak of the war had been captured, through the double-dealing and treachery of Gen. Jesup and the perfidy of a few of the Indian chiefs, but those Negroes with both the initiative to join the Seminole in the first place and the courage, intelligence, tenacity, and good fortune to hold out until the third year of the war, i.e., about the middle of 1838, won their freedom, through being classified as "slaves" of the Indians, and were shipped to the Indian Territory along with the refugees of longer standing.

The participation of the Florida slaves in the Seminole War cannot, therefore, properly be disregarded. Hundreds, it is now known, seized the opportunity presented by the outbreak of the war to join the hostile Seminole Indians and Negroes. Those properly qualified by age and sex, strength and spirit, fought bravely and desperately at the side of Indian and Indian Negro, sometimes rising to positions of leadership. Others did good service behind the lines, collecting information and obtaining supplies for transmission to the hostiles. Free Negroes, with less to gain and more to lose than any others, nevertheless participated, both in the field and behind the lines. Particularly noteworthy were those Indian Negroes and runaways who operated as spies and secret agents, stealthily passing from Seminole camp to plantation or city slave-quarters and back again, to obtain recruits, information, and supplies. The general atmosphere of discontent and brooding hostility produced by all these operations and prevailing behind the lines held by the supporters of the slave system was such that it kept a large part of the militia at home, to guard against any sudden outbreak, thus relieving the pressure against the Indians and Negroes actually in the field and contributing to the prevention of their utter defeat.

Thus a close tie of common resistance to exploitation and oppression united the Indian chief, Wild Cat, the Indian Negro, John Caesar, the runaway slave, Andrew Gay, and the free Negro, Joe Merritt, who may stand as representatives of many other less known or entirely unknown figures in a fight for freedom of a century ago.

Part IV
Nonwhites in a Volatile Nation, 1840–1865

Nonwhites in a Volatile Nation, 1840–1865

Violence, territorial expansion, and a burgeoning nonwhite population marked the twenty-five-year period from 1840 to 1865 and created racial antagonisms which were not abated by the Civil War. Perhaps the key to understanding the era is the incessant craving of whites for new land, much of which was occupied by nonwhites.

Numerous Mexicans were annexed along with their lands as a result of the war which the United States waged against them. The Treaty of Guadalupe Hidalgo (1848) stipulated that the United States must grant the rights of citizenship to the new inhabitants. However, white Americans were selective in honoring the terms of the treaty, and many Mexican-Americans were deprived of both land and civil rights. Soon Spanish was no longer accepted in the southwest as an official language. Even in New Mexico where they outnumbered white immigrants, Mexican-Americans were unable to resist the decline because whites controlled the appointed territorial government.

Most blacks in the United States were enslaved and white southerners wanted to expand their "peculiar institution" to new land. This longing for land had led to war with Mexico, and southern zeal for carving new states out of the conquered territory became a major cause of the Civil War when northern abolitionists, both white and black, resisted the extension of slavery into the territories. Once the Civil War began, free blacks readily joined the union forces in an effort to end slavery, and those in bondage flocked to the lines of the union armies as they advanced southward. When the Civil War ended and the Thirteenth Amendment abolished legal slavery, blacks commenced their struggle for political, economic, and social equality.

Shortly after 1848 when the Chinese first entered the United States in response to dreams of wealth, discriminatory legislation was enacted to restrict their economic and legal rights and to deny them citizenship. The cultural heritage of the Chinese was attacked as well. For example, in 1855 San Franciscans enacted a "Pig Tail Ordinance" which provided that any Chinese man convicted of a crime should have his queue cut off. By the late 1850's, Chinese immigrants who entered the country as contract laborers frequently were forced to take jobs with western industries at miserly wages which kept them in debt bondage.

Although the southeastern Indians had already been removed from their lands by 1840, many of the Old Northwest tribes still suffered through the process of relocation. The Winnebagos, for example, were resettled seven different times in the thirty-five years before 1866, and other tribes also found the terms of treaties to be meaningless in defining their rights. Indians west of the Mississippi were relatively free from interference until the end of the Civil War when United States military power was turned against them, but even these tribes were not exempt from the intrusions of the landhungry Americans. When Stephen A. Douglas and other speculators wanted Kansas they pushed the Indians out, and in California, the Native American population was reduced by white-introduced disease and warfare from one hundred thousand in 1846 to thirty thousand in 1870. The Indians did not acquiesce in such depredations. Portents of the Plains Indian resistance which would plague western settlers for decades to come appeared when the Sioux of Minnesota revolted in 1862.

The westward movement, bringing with it the addition of the Mexican-American population, the issue of extending slavery into the territories, the importation of Chinese labor, and the dispossession and slaughter of the Indians created racial strife and left in its wake a residue of unsolved problems.

John C. Ewers,
"Blackfoot Camp Life"

Among the Indian nations populating the Great Plains as whites
pushed westward were the Blackfeet, who actually comprised
three tribes—the Piegan, the Kainah or Blood, and the Siksika or
Northern Blackfeet. The dominant military power of the
northwestern plains, Blackfeet roamed much of what is now the
state of Montana and the southern portions of the Canadian
provinces of Saskatchewan and Alberta. As did other Plains Indians,
the Blackfeet borrowed from the white invaders those devices
which could be readily adapted to their nomadic culture. For
example, the substitution of the horse for the dog enabled them
to transport more possessions and travel greater distances. It
also increased their effectiveness as hunters and fighters. To the
Plains Indians, the buffalo was of especial importance since most
of their food, clothing, shelter, and implements were derived
from that animal. In the following selection from The Blackfeet:
Raiders On the Northwestern Plains, John C. Ewers examines
various aspects of Blackfoot camp life.

Blackfoot Camp Life

John C. Ewers

In the middle of the nineteenth century Blackfoot life was a remarkable blend of traditional Indian customs modified by white influences. It was a way of life that would have been impossible without the European horse and the white man's trade goods. Nevertheless, Blackfoot economy was still based primarily upon buffalo hunting, as it had been in prehistoric times. Indeed, after American traders began to accept buffalo robes in trade, Blackfoot hunters had a greater incentive for killing buffalo than ever before. Then the buffalo not only furnished the Indians' subsistence but indirectly enabled them to obtain luxuries they never dreamed of before the coming of Napikwan [the white man]. Fortunately, buffalo were still very plentiful in the Blackfoot country....

...Blackfoot hunting bands roamed over a vast area nearly twice the size of New England, extending from the North Saskatchewan River southward to the headwaters of the Missouri and from the Bearpaw Mountains westward to the Rockies.

The Blackfoot Indians' year was divided into four seasons of un-

Abridged from "Camp Life," pp. 72, 88–106. From The Blackfeet: Raiders on the Northwestern Plains, by John C. Ewers. Copyright © 1958 by the University of Oklahoma Press. Some footnotes have been renumbered.

equal length. The longest period was the one spent in winter camp. Each band wintered separately. In late October or early November the band chief selected a winter campsite in a broad river valley sheltered from winds and snow by the high, natural walls of the valley itself. The valley floor afforded grass for the horses. The river itself offered clear, cold drinking water, and the cottonwood groves bordering the stream provided firewood. As colder weather arrived in late November or early December men and women cut out the underbrush and some of the trees and moved their lodges into the timber. The standing trees served as windbreak and snow fence. Unless food became scarce or the wild grass for the horses was exhausted they remained in this locality throughout the winter.

Blackfoot winter dress was designed for comfort rather than for beauty. It bore little resemblance to the elaborately decorated costume we usually have in mind when we think of Plains Indians. When out-of-doors, men and boys wore buffalo-hide caps with ear flaps, buffalo robes with the hair next to the body or Hudson's Bay blanket coats, and hair-lined mittens and moccasins. Women and girls wore the same kind of moccasins, mittens, and headgear. Trade blankets or buffalo robes covered their undecorated dresses.

The Indians obtained their drinking water from holes chopped in the river ice. At these water holes the horses were watered three times daily. The horses were left to rustle for their food by pawing away the snow to the grass below. Some men fed their best horses the inner bark of cottonwood, which the Indians considered "better than oats." Others employed this supplemental feed only when the snow was too deep for the horses to rustle their own food. In some winters deep snows combined with very cold weather killed off many horses. In spite of everything their owners could do for them, the animals froze to death.

Throughout the winter beaver bundle owners kept primitive calendars of notched sticks, one notch representing each day, by which they could predict the approach of spring. The band chief carefully examined the development of embryos taken from buffalo cows killed in late winter hunts. When he saw that the unborn calves were beginning to develop hair, he knew spring was near. Before the river ice broke up, the beaver men held their ceremonies. When geese were seen flying north, all knew it was time to leave their winter camp. This was usually in late March or early April. After five or more months in one location the people were restless. They were glad to roam the plains again.

March was a difficult month during which the buffalo began to drift away from the sheltered river valleys. Unless the bands packed and followed the buffalo, they would have to subsist on small game or go hungry. Each band went its separate way in pursuit of buffalo. Buffalo calves were born in spring, between the breakup of winter camp and the annual May storm, a sudden and in some years heavy fall of snow which melted and disappeared almost overnight. The Indians killed calves for children's robes and soft skin sacks. The medicine pipe ceremony was performed after the first thunder was heard in spring, usually in April or May. Spring was also the season for making willow backrests to furnish tipis, constructing and repairing riding gear, and fashioning warm-weather clothing. Horses, thinned and weakened during the winter months, fattened and grew strong on the rich spring grasses. Toward the end of spring women dug bulbs, which provided a welcome change in diet after the long winter of eating meat and dried foods.

When buffalo bulls became prime in June, the scattered hunting bands began to gather for the tribal summer hunt. It required several weeks for these bands to assemble and for each to occupy its assigned segment of the tribal camp circle. Then began the organized summer hunt under the leadership of the tribal chief and the strict regulation of men's societies chosen to police the camp and hunt. This summer hunt provided cowhides for new tipi covers, meat, and most important of all, the sacrificial food for the sun dance—buffalo tongues. Only bull tongues were collected, and as many as three hundred might be needed. After the tongues were prepared and scouts had selected the site for the sun dance encampment, the entire tribe moved toward the site in four daily marches. These were dress parades on which the people wore their finest clothes, decorated their horses with their most elaborate trappings, and the men displayed their weapons and shields. Sarvis berries were ripe when the sun dance began, usually in August. Some eight or ten days were spent in the sun dance encampment. At the end of that period the tipis were taken down, the camp circle was dissolved, and the bands separated for their fall hunt. This summer season was the only time of year when all the bands of the tribe camped together in one great village. In this tribal encampment friendships between individuals of the different bands were formed, renewed, and strengthened, the men's societies held their ceremonies and competed against one another in games and races, young men courted girls of other bands, horses were bartered, painted lodges and sacred bundles were ceremonially transferred, successful warriors were honored, visitors from friendly tribes were feasted and showered with gifts, and the chiefs and headmen of the tribe met in council to discuss the economic, political, and military problems of the entire tribe and to make plans for the future. All these varied activities helped to strengthen feelings of tribal unity and solidarity among members of hunting bands who might not even see each other from one summer until the next.

Fall, when cows were prime, was the great buffalo-hunting season. Berries also were collected, dried, and mixed with meat to make pemmican. Each family tried to put up as much dried meat, berries, and pemmican as their winter needs required or their means of transportation would permit. The number of camp moves during this autumn season depended largely upon the availability of buffalo. The more plentiful the buffalo in the vicinity of a band camp, the less frequent were its movements. Even though this mobile period ended with the establishment of winter camp, men continued to hunt in the vicinity of the camp and women continued to prepare stores of food for winter and to dress buffalo robes for the trade until heavy snows and bitter cold weather restricted their activity.[1]

As the weather permitted, and when an accumulation of buffalo robes was available, the bands visited the trading posts. This trading season generally lasted from about the middle of November until the middle of April. In mid-April the traders began to press their winter's receipts in robes and furs into bales. By the end of the month they were ready to start loading their boats, and early in May their cargoes of robes and furs started on the long journey downriver to market.[2]

Thus the annual cycle of camp movements varied with the seasons. It was influenced not only by the availability of game and the ripening of wild plant foods, but also by the severity of the winter weather and the demands of the Indians' own ceremonial calendar. Through the cold months the bands were settled in their winter

1. Ewers, "Horse in Blackfoot Indian Culture," B.A.E. Bull. 159, 123–29.
2. McDonnell, "Fort Benton Journal," MHSC, Vol. X, 7–30.

camps. At that season they were no more nomadic than many tribes of the eastern forests who did not rely upon wandering buffalo herds for their subsistence. In their tribal sun dance encampment they obtained a brief rest between the most active hunting seasons in summer and fall.

Frequent camp movements during spring, summer, and fall required that Blackfoot Indian homes be portable and that their household furnishings and ceremonial equipment be easily and efficiently packaged. The head chief, with the advice of the band chiefs, determined the movements of the great tribal camp in summer. He sent his herald around the camp circle the night before a move was to be made to tell the people to be ready to get under way early the next morning. In the much smaller band camps during spring and fall the band chief consulted with other prominent men of his band before announcing a move.

On the morning camp movement was to get under way women were up and bustling around at dawn. They prepared the family breakfast, finished packing, and were on the move before eight o'clock. Most of the family belongings were packed the night before. They needed only to be tied in their assigned places on horses or travois. The principal task was that of taking down the lodge. Two or more experienced women could accomplish this in a few minutes. The buffalo-hide cover of an average-sized lodge weighed about one hundred pounds. It was carefully folded and tied in place between the horns of a pack saddle. The poles of such a lodge numbered nineteen. Each was about eighteen to twenty-two feet long and weighed a little less than twenty pounds. Women divided the lodge poles into bundles of about five poles each. They tied the poles of each bundle together by a rawhide cord threaded through a hole burned in each pole near its upper end and tied one bundle of poles on each side of a pack horse. Thus two horses were needed to drag the poles of an average-sized lodge.

Buffalo-robe bedding and willow backrests, the principal lodge furnishings, were packed on a horse travois. Dried meat, tallow, and pemmican were placed in rectangular, rawhide parfleches which were suspended over the horns of a saddle, one on each side of the pack horse. Berries and tobacco were packed in sacks made from the skins of unborn buffalo calves and placed in the side pockets of buffalo-hide saddlebags. Kettles were put into skin sacks and tied on top of the pack horses' loads. Tools and utensils were placed in rectangular rawhide cases, which usually were carried on the horse travois. Ceremonial equipment was carried in bundles on the travois or in fringed rawhide containers over the horns of the favorite wife's saddle.

Scouts rode well in advance of the moving caravan, on constant lookout for signs of game or enemies. The other active warriors rode on the flanks and in the rear of the moving camp, carrying their weapons. The medicine pipe owner and the chief or chiefs and their families led the main body. Other camp members fell in behind the chiefs in family groups with their travois, pack animals, riding horses, and loose horses. Older boys drove the loose horses. Babies rode on their mothers' backs in the folds of their mothers' buffalo robes. Toddlers often rode on the travois. When they tired of riding, they got off and ran for a while. Older children usually rode horseback, sometimes two or three of them on a horse.

At noon the chief halted the caravan for a short rest and lunch. This was a cold meal of prepared meat, pemmican, or dried plant foods, and water. Usually the day's march ended in the middle or late afternoon so there was ample time for the women to erect the lodges, unpack the horses, and prepare the evening meal before dark. The chief chose the campsite and selected the spot for his lodge. Only during tribal movements in summer was the camp circle formed. At the end of a day's march by a separate hunting band the families pitched their lodges around that of their chief in an uneven cluster. They did not scatter widely because of the danger of enemy attack.

Usually the Indians knew in advance if their night camp was to be made without wood or water. If wood was lacking, dried buffalo chips were collected. Dried grass was used for tinder. The grass was ignited by sparks made by striking a curved fire-steel against a piece of flint. Water was brought along in buffalo paunches to supply a dry camp. Horses and dogs were watered in basin-shaped troughs of rawhide. There was little difficulty in obtaining water in spring. At that season the water from melting snows collected in many depressions which dried out by summer time.

When the Indians had to cross deep streams or rivers on the march, they rolled up the sides of their lodge covers to form rude boats in which baggage and children were placed. Horse travois poles and tipi poles were lashed together to form crude rafts on which other baggage was ferried. Horses towed these improvised craft while men swam ahead with tow lines, guiding the way, and women pushed from behind. Horses whinnied, dogs yelped, and people shouted as the crossing was made. When the Indians reached the far side of the stream, they generally stopped for the day to dry their clothes and gear.

On a rainy morning the Indians usually did not try to move camp. If a heavy rain fell while the band was on the march, they generally stopped for the day. Other factors helped to determine both the speed of movement and the distance covered. Among them were the character of the terrain traversed (whether level or hilly, the number and sizes of the water courses to be crossed), the availability of game, fear of enemy raiding parties in the vicinity, and the desire to reach a trading post or a particular camping spot before nightfall.

A normal day's march was about ten to fifteen miles. This was fully twice the distance the prehistoric ancestors of the Blackfeet could have made on foot carrying their meager possessions on dog travois and the backs of their women. A horse packing two hundred pounds on its back or hauling three hundred pounds on the travois could move four times the load of a heavily burdened dog twice as far on a day's march. So, animal for animal, the horse was eight times more efficient than the dog as a burden bearer. The application of horse power to camp movement thus enabled the Blackfeet to accumulate more property and to move it faster and farther as well.

An average family of eight persons (including two grown males, three women, and three children) needed ten horses to move camp efficiently. They needed a horse to carry the lodge cover and its accessories; two horses to drag the lodge poles; two for packing meat, other food, and equipment; three horses to carry the women (at least two of which would drag travois); and two riding horses for the men. Each of the men would also need a buffalo horse. A young married couple with a baby or no children needed no more than five horses. However, a large family of more than five adults required fifteen to twenty or more horses.[3]

Nevertheless, there were many poor families among the Blackfeet who owned only one or two horses. Their poverty in horses caused

3. Ewers, "Horse in Blackfoot Indian Culture," B.A.E. *Bull. 159*, 129–39.

their standard of living to be well below that of the average family in their tribe at the time. Their possessions more nearly resembled those of the pre-horse Indians in quantity. Their lodges were small, covered with no more than six or seven buffalo hides, with short, light foundation poles. Their clothing, household utensils, and weapons were few and poor in quality. They owned no fancy dress clothes, no handsome riding gear. Their guns, if they owned any, were worn, broken, and repaired with rawhide cord. They had few if any buffalo robes to offer the traders.

At the other end of the Blackfoot economic and social ladder were the relatively few wealthy families—the owners of large horse herds. The fur trader, Charles Larpenteur, writing in 1860, aptly characterized the rich Indian:

> It is a fine sight to see one of these big men among the Blackfeet, who has two or three lodges, five or six wives, twenty or thirty children, and fifty to a hundred horses; for his trade amounts to upward of $2,000 a year.[4]

The man of wealth and the members of his family dressed well. They owned several changes of clothing, including elaborately decorated garments to wear in dress parades, ceremonies, and feasts in honor of important visitors and on their own visits to other Indian camps or to the trading posts. They obtained the most attractive ornaments and best weapons from the traders' stock. They owned important and costly medicine bundles and showy and well-made riding gear. Their tipis were both large and handsomely furnished. As Larpenteur stated, some of them owned more than one tipi.

Wealth brought both opportunity and responsibility to the man who possessed it. The stingy rich man was despised by his less fortunate fellows. The generous man of wealth was beloved by them. If he was liberal in feasting and in giving away food and horses to the needy, if he lent horses to the poor for their use in hunting and moving camp, his fellow band members would want him for their chief—provided he also possessed a fine war record. James Doty described the Blackfoot chieftaincy thus in 1854:

4. *Forty Years a Fur Trader*, II, 401.

Every man who can acquire a large herd of horses, keep a good Lodge and make a large trade in Buffalo Robes is a chief, and he will maintain a persuasive influence over his people just so long as he continues wealthy, and ministers to the popular voice in directing the movements of the camp, leading war parties etc. Whenever he opposes his wishes to those of his band, it will desert him and turn to some chief more pliable.[5]

The hunting band, which was still the basic political unit among the Blackfeet, was probably a much more fluid unit than it had been in prehistoric times. In early times, when everyone stood literally and figuratively on an equal footing, the chiefs had no property to dispense. But in the middle of the nineteenth century poor families looked to their chief for charity. They changed their band allegiance if they believed they might better their economic condition as followers of a more liberal chief. Some of the larger bands had more than one chief. New bands were created when a rising leader and his followers broke away from an existing band. An older band might dissolve after the death of a prominent chief if there was no one who could take his place in the hearts of his followers. Even the names of bands were changed in honor of particular chiefs or in memory of some unusual happening to the band. As a result, contemporary and later estimates of the number of hunting bands in each of the three Blackfoot tribes in the middle of the nineteenth century vary widely. The tendency of later students was to list every band encountered as·a separate one, whether or not they were all contemporaneous. It seems most probable that in mid-century the Piegans comprised about thirteen bands, averaging about twenty-five lodges and about two hundred souls per band. In the winter of 1869–70 General Sully listed fifteen Piegan bands and nine bands each in the Blood and North Blackfoot tribes. These bands ranged from ten to thirty-six lodges each. Their average size was twenty-four lodges.[6]

The most influential band chief became recognized as the head chief of his tribe. However, his rank was of little significance except during the period of the tribal encampment in summer. Even then

---

5. Doty to Isaac I. Stevens, December 20, 1854. Indian Office Records.
6. General Alfred Sully, Census of Blackfoot Indians, 1870, Indian Office Records.

his role was more that of chairman of the council of chiefs than of ruler of his people. Important decisions were reached by agreement in council after each chief had an opportunity to speak his mind. The chiefs exercised little disciplinary power over their followers. In the summer tribal encampment, selected men's societies policed the camp. But throughout the greater part of the year, when the tribe was divided into separate hunting bands, tribal discipline simply did not exist. The individual who was wronged was expected to exact such punishment of the wrongdoer as he or his family was able to inflict. Not uncommonly, the criminal fled to another Blackfoot band or to a neighboring tribe. Theft customarily was followed by reclaiming of the stolen property. Murder was punished by the dead man's relatives, who usually took the life of the murderer. But if the murdered man was poor and the killer rich and powerful the matter might be ended by a payment of horses to the family of the deceased. Thus it was possible for a wealthy man literally to get away with murder, although he would not enhance his popularity by doing so....

Young men enjoyed remarkable freedom in their sexual life. They accosted girls while they were alone gathering wood or water on the outskirts of camp. They bragged of their conquests, particularly if they had had an affair with a married woman. Chastity before marriage was more an ideal than a reality for many girls. Yet a girl who earned a reputation for being too free with her favors might have to be satisfied with marrying a poor boy whose future prospects were equally poor....

Polygamy was common among the Blackfeet because it was a practical means of caring for the excess of women created by heavy war losses. Women outnumbered men by two or three to one. Possession of several wives was one of the distinguishing marks of the successful man. A few of the leading chiefs had ten or more wives. Probably more than half of the men had at least two. In these polygamous households the husband's favorite, his "sits-beside-me-wife," accompanied him to feasts and ceremonies and supervised the work of the other women in her husband's home. Cautious men tried to minimize the dangers of jealousy and friction at home by marrying sisters. A husband of an eldest sister could expect the younger ones to be offered to him as they reached marriageable age, although he did not have to accept them. Double-Victory-Calf-Robe had two elder sisters, both of them married to Iron Horn. One day her father said to her, "My son-in-law, Iron Horn, is very kind and good to us. You had better marry him and be with your sisters." Her family outfitted a travois, helped her mount the travois horse, and she rode over to Iron Horn's lodge. He accepted her as his third wife and gave horses to her father . . . .

In their late teens a group of young men banded together to purchase membership in the lowest of the graded men's societies at the tribal sun dance encampment. They selected a leader, who presented a pipe to the leader of the society. Each of the other youths gave pipes to other members of the society. If the pipes were accepted, the petitioners were expected to make other gifts of horses and valuable goods to those who relinquished their society membership to them and who taught them the ceremonial procedures of the organization. It was usual for societies to sell out to a group of younger men every four years.

There were seven of these age-graded men's societies among the Blackfeet in 1833. The youngest group was then the Mosquitos, the oldest the Buffalo Bulls. Two decades later the Bulls Society among the Piegans had become inactive on account of the death of many of its older members, but a new society, the Pigeons, or Doves, had been added to the bottom of the series.[7]

Because members of these societies belonged to different hunting bands, they were only active during the summer season when the tribal camp was organized. At that time the head chief called upon one or two of the societies, usually the younger of the mature groups, to police the camp and the tribal hunt. In the sun dance camp each society performed its peculiar ceremony. Collectively, the men's societies were known as the All-Comrades.[8]

There was a women's society among the Blood and Northern Blackfoot tribes which was unknown among the Piegans. Its members were wives of the most highly respected men in their tribes. Prior to the sun dance in summer, members of this Matoki society built a ceremonial lodge which resembled a buffalo corral, and on the final

---

7. Maximilian, *Travels*, II, 112–17.

8. Clark Wissler, "Societies and Dance Associations of the Blackfoot Indians." *American Museum of Natural History Anthropological Papers*, Vol. XI, Part 4, .361–450. Includes detailed description of specialized paraphernalia and ceremonies of each society.

day of their four-day ritual re-enacted the drive of buffalo into the corral. Some of the members wore buffalo headdresses and mimicked the actions of buffalo.[9]

The aged were no longer abandoned on the plains as had been the common lot of enfeebled old people before the Blackfeet acquired horses. If an old man or woman was too feeble to ride alone, he or she was carried on the A-shaped horse travois. If the head of a family knew he was about to die, he called his relatives together and told them how he wished his horses and other property divided among them. If he died without having made such a verbal will, the other people in camp made a run for his property as soon as they heard his relatives weeping and wailing. Men ran for his horses; women went for his household equipment. The men might take all his best horses and leave the poorest ones for his widow. Close relatives of the deceased, preoccupied with mourning his loss, made no attempt to prevent this raid on his property. Custom decreed that they should not do so. These raids were made with particular relish upon the property of a man of wealth who had had a reputation for miserliness during his lifetime. . . .

9. *Ibid.*, 430–35.

Raymond A. Bauer and Alice H. Bauer,
"Day to Day Resistance to Slavery"

Slavery's apologists justified the "peculiar institution" by claiming
that blacks were contented in bondage and inherently unable
to cope with the intricacies of life in the United States without
direction from their white superiors. The whites' duty was
to use the paternalistic auspices of slavery to educate, civilize,
uplift, and Christianize the black slaves. However, as most astute
plantation owners knew, blacks hated slavery and demonstrated
their dislike by participating in revolts, running away from
plantations, murdering whites, and seizing any opportunities for
freedom. Hatred for the institution was also illustrated in more subtle
ways. Masking emotions with a smiling countenance, a bow, or
a "yes sir," slaves worked as slowly as possible, ruined implements,
set buildings on fire, and plotted vengeance against the slaveowner.
In the following article, Raymond Bauer and Alice Bauer
catalogue some of the many forms of "day to day resistance"
to the institution of slavery. Slaves were, as another historian
asserted, "a troublesome property."

Day to Day Resistance to Slavery[1]

Raymond A. Bauer and Alice H. Bauer

The tradition that has grown up about Negro slavery is that the slaves were docile, well adapted to slavery, and reasonably content with their lot. . . .

This concept is gradually being changed as the study of slave revolts, and of the social tension caused by the constant threat of revolt progresses.[2] In answer to the question, " 'Are the masters afraid of insurrection?' (a slave) says, 'They live in constant fear upon this subject. The least unusual noise at night alarms them greatly. They cry out, 'What is that?' 'Are the boys all in'?"[3]

Abridged from Raymond A. Bauer and Alice H. Bauer, "Day to Day Resistance to Slavery," pp. 388–419. Copyright © by The Association for the Study of Negro Life and History, Inc. Published in *The Journal of Negro History*, XXVII (October 1942). Some footnotes have been renumbered.

1. We wish to express our appreciation to Professor M. J. Herskovits, under whose direction this research has been carried on.

2. Cf. Aptheker, Herbert, "American Negro Slave Revolts," *Science and Society*, 1:512–538, 1937; Wish, Harvey, "American Slave Insurrections before 1861," *Journal of Negro History*, 23:435–450, 1928; Wish, Harvey, "The Slave Insurrection Panic of 1856," *Journal of Southern History*, 5:206–222, 1939; see also Herskovits, M. J., *The Myth of the Negro Past*, pp. 99–105.

3. Clarke, Lewis, *Narratives of the Sufferings of Lewis and Milton Clarke*, Boston, 1846, p. 123.

Raymond A. Bauer and Alice H. Bauer

The purpose of this paper is to study a less spectacular aspect of slavery—the day to day resistance to slavery, since it is felt that such a study will throw some further light on the nature of the Negro's reaction to slavery. Our investigation has made it apparent that the Negroes not only were very discontented, but that they developed effective protest techniques in the form of indirect retaliation for their enslavement. . . .

The picture of the docile, contented Negro slave grew out of two lines of argument used in ante-bellum times. The pro-slavery faction contended that the slaves came of an inferior race, that they were happy and contented in their subordinate position, and that the dancing and singing Negro exemplified their assumption. Abolitionists, on the other hand, tended to depict the Negro slave as a passive instrument, a good and faithful worker exploited and beaten by a cruel master. As one reads the controversial literature on the slavery question, it soon becomes apparent that both sides presented the Negro as a docile creature; one side because it wished to prove that he was contented, the other because it wished to prove that he was grossly mistreated. Both conceptions have persisted to the present time. Writers who romanticize the "Old South" idealize the condition of the slaves, and make of them happy, willing servitors, while those who are concerned with furthering the interests of the Negroes are careful to avoid mention of any aggressive tendencies which might be used as a pretext for further suppressing the Negroes. . . .

The conceptual framework within which this paper is written is that the Negro slaves were forced into certain outward forms of compliance to slavery; that, except for the few who were able to escape to the North, the Negroes had to accept the institution of slavery and make their adjustments to that institution. The patterns of adjustment which we have found operative are: slowing up of work, destruction of property, malingering and self-mutilation. . . .

The Negroes were well aware that the work they did benefited only the master. "The slaves work and the planter gets the benefit of it."[4] "The conversation among the slaves was that they worked

4. Wm. Brown, an escaped slave; in: Benjamin Drew, *The Refugee*, Boston, 1856, p. 281.

hard and got no benefit, that the masters got it all."[5] It is thus not surprising that one finds many recurring comments that a slave did not do half a good day's work in a day. A northerner whom Lyell met in the South said:

"Half the population of the south is employed in seeing that the other half do their work, and they who do work, accomplish half what they might do under a better system."[6]

An English visitor, with a very strong pro-slavery bias corroborates this:

"The amount of work expected by the field hand will not be more than one half of what would be demanded of a white man; and even that will not be properly done unless he be constantly overlooked."[7] ...

Just how much of this was due to indifference and how much due to deliberate slowing up is hard to determine. Both factors most probably entered. A worker who has to devote himself to a dull task from which he can hope to gain nothing by exercising initiative soon slips into such a frame of mind that he does nothing more than go through the motions. His chief concern is to escape from the realities of his task and put it in the back of his mind as much as possible.

There is, indeed, a strong possibility that this behavior was a form of indirect aggression. ...

Certainly description after description emphasizes the mechanical plodding of the slave workers.

"John Lamar wrote, 'My man Ned the carpenter is idle or nearly so at the plantation. He is fixing gates and, like the idle groom in Pickwick, trying to fool himself into the belief that he is doing something—He is an eye servant.'"[8] ...

5. Thomas Hedgebeth, a free Negro; in: Benjamin Drew, *The Refugee*, Boston, 1856, p. 276.
6. Lyell, Sir Charles, *A Second Visit to the United States of America*, New York, 1849, II, 72.
7. Ozanne, T. D., *The South as It Is*, London, 1863, pp. 165, 166.
8. Phillips, U. B., *American Negro Slavery*, New York, 1918, p. 192.

To what extent this reluctant labor was the rule may be appreciated when it is pointed out that a southern doctor classified it under the name *Dysaethesia Aethiopica* as a mental disease peculiar to Negroes. Olmsted quotes this Dr. Cartwright as follows:

"'From the careless movements of the individual affected with this complaint, they are apt to do much mischief, which appears as if intentional, but it is mostly owing to the stupidness of mind and insensibility of the nerves induced by the disease. Thus, they break, waste, and destroy everything they handle—abuse horses and cattle—tear, burn, or rend their own clothing, and, paying no attention to the rights of property, steal others to replace what they have destroyed. They wander about at night, and keep in a half nodding state by day. They slight their work—cut up corn, cotton and tobacco, when hoeing it, as if for pure mischief. They raise disturbances with their overseers, and among their fellow servants, without cause or motive, and seem to be insensible to pain when subjected to punishment.

"'...The term "rascality" given to this disease by overseers, is founded on an erroneous hypothesis, and leads to an incorrect empirical treatment, which seldom or never cures it.'"[9]

There are only two possible interpretations of the doctor's statement. Either the slaves were so extraordinarily lazy that they gave the appearance of being mentally diseased, or the doctor was describing cases of hebephrenic schizophrenia. Either situation is startling. The phenomenon was obviously widespread, and if it was actually a mental disease it certainly would indicate that Negroes did not become "easily adjusted to slavery."

Whatever the case, it is certain that the slaves consciously saved their energy. Olmsted, who always had his eye open for such incidents, reported:

"The overseer rode among them, on a horse, carrying in his hand a raw-hide whip, constantly directing and encouraging them; but, as my companion and I, both, several times noticed, as often as he visited one line of the operations, the hands at the other end

9. Olmsted, F. L., *A Journey in the Seaboard Slave States*, New York, 1863, pp. 192, 193.

would discontinue their labor, until he turned to ride toward them again."[10]

The few statements on this point we have by ex-slaves seem to indicate that the slaves as a group made a general policy of not letting the master get the upper hand. . . . Writer after writer, describing incidents in which slaves were compelled to assist in punishing other slaves states that they did so with the greatest of reluctance.

"The hands stood still;—they knew Randall—and they knew him also to be a powerful man, and were afraid to grapple with him. As soon as Cook had ordered the men to seize him, Randall turned to them, and said—'Boys, you all know me; you know that I can handle any three of you, and the man that lays hands on me shall die. This white man can't whip me himself, and therefore he has called you to help him.' The overseer was unable to prevail upon them to seize and secure Randall, and finally ordered them all to go to their work together."[11]

In some cases it was noted that the slave resisting punishment took pains not to treat his fellows with any more than the absolute minimum of violence.

With such demonstrations of solidarity among the slaves it is not surprising to find a slave telling of how he and his fellows "captured" the institution of the driver. The slave Solomon Northrup was such a driver. His task was to whip the other slaves in order to make them work.

" 'Practice makes perfect,' truly; and during eight years' experience as a driver I learned to handle the whip with marvelous dexterity and precision, throwing the lash within a hair's breadth of the back, the ear, the nose without, however, touching either of them. If Epps was observed at a distance, or we had reason to apprehend

10. *Ibid.*, p. 388.
11. Brown, W. W., *Life of Williams Welles Brown, A Fugitive Slave*, Boston, 1848, p. 18. See also Williams, James, *Narratives of James Williams*, Boston, 1838, pp. 56, 62, 65.

he was sneaking somewhere in the vicinity, I would commence plying the lash vigorously, when, according to arrangement, they would squirm and screech as if in agony, although not one of them had in fact been grazed. Patsey would take occasion, if he made his appearance presently, to mumble in his hearing some complaints that Platt was whipping them the whole time, and Uncle Abram, with an appearance of honesty peculiar to himself would declare roundly I had just whipped them worse than General Jackson whipped the enemy at New Orleans."[12]

The amount of slowing up of labor by the slaves must, in the aggregate, have caused a tremendous financial loss to plantation owners. The only way we have of estimating it quantitatively is through comparison of the work done in different plantations and under different systems of labor. The statement is frequently made that production on a plantation varied more than 100% from time to time. Comparison in the output of slaves in different parts of the South also showed variations of over 100%. Most significant is the improvement in output obtained under the task, whereby the slaves were given a specific task to fulfill for their day's work, any time left over being their own....

The slaves were well aware of their economic value, and used it to good advantage. The skilled laborers among the slaves knew their worth, and frequently rebelled against unsatisfactory work situations. Slaves who were hired out would run away from the masters who had hired them, and then either return home, or remain in hiding until they felt like returning to work.

"The slave, if he is indisposed to work, and especially if he is not treated well, or does not like the master who has hired him, will sham sickness—even make himself sick or lame—that he need not work. But a more serious loss frequently arises, when the slave, thinking he is worked too hard, or being angered by punishment or unkind treatment, 'getting the sulks,' takes to 'the swamp,' and comes back when he has a mind to. Often this will not be till the year is up for which he is engaged, when he will return to his owner, who, glad to find his property safe, and that it has not died

12. Northrup, Solomon, *Twelve Years a Slave*, 1853, pp. 226, 227.

in the swamp, or gone to Canada, forgets to punish him, and immediately sends him for another year to a new master."[13] ...

Even the threat of a whipping did not deter such slaves from running off for a time when they were displeased.... Some of the resistance took on the aspects of organized strikes.

"Occasionally, however, a squad would strike in a body as a protest against severities. An episode of this sort was recounted in a letter of a Georgia overseer to his absent employer: 'Sir: I write you a few lines in order to let you know that six of your hands has left the plantation—every man but Jack. They displeased me with their work and I give some of them a few lashes, Tom with the rest. On Wednesday morning they were missing. I think they are lying out until they can see you or your Uncle Jack.' The slaves could not negotiate directly at such a time, but while they lay in the woods they might make overtures to the overseer through slaves on a neighboring plantation as to terms upon which they would return to work, or they might await their master's posthaste arrival and appeal to him for a redress of grievances. Humble as their demeanor might be, their power of renewing the pressure by repeating their act could not be ignored."[14] ...

The indifference of the slaves to the welfare of the masters extended itself to a complete contempt for property values. The slaves were so careless with tools that they were equipped with special tools, more clumsy than ordinary ones.

"The 'nigger hoe' was first introduced into Virginia as a substitute for the plow, in breaking up the soil. The law fixes its weight at four pounds,—as heavy as the woodman's axe. It is still used, not only in Virginia, but in Georgia and the Carolinas. The planters tell us, as the reason for its use, that the negroes would break a Yankee hoe in pieces on the first root, or stone that might be in their way. An instructive commentary on the difference between free and slave labor!"[15]

13. Olmsted, op. cit., pp. 100, 101.
14. Phillips, U. B., American Negro Slavery, pp. 303, 304.
15. Parson, C. G., Inside View of Slavery, Boston, 1853, p. 94.

Not only tools but livestock suffered from the mistreatment by the slaves. Olmsted found not only the "nigger hoe" but even discovered that mules were substituted for horses because horses could not stand up under the treatment of the slaves. . . .

Redpath verifies Olmsted's statement—by telling how he saw slaves treat stock. It is important to note that Redpath was a strong abolitionist and most sympathetic toward the slaves.

"He rode the near horse, and held a heavy cowhide in his hand, with which from time to time he lashed the leaders, as barbarous drivers lash oxen when at work. Whenever we came to a hill, especially if it was very steep, he dismounted, lashed the horses with all his strength, varying his performances by picking up stones, none of them smaller than half a brick, and throwing them with all his force, at the horses' legs. He seldom missed.

"The wagon was laden with two tons of plaster in sacks.

"This is a fair specimen of the style in which Negroes treat stocks."[16] . . .

In the Sea Islands off the coast of Georgia, Kemble reported that the slaves started immense fires, destroying large sections of woods through carelessness or maliciousness. . . .

The slaves on Lewis' West Indies plantation let cattle get into one of his best cane-pieces because they neglected to guard them, being more interested in a dance which was going on. They were fully aware that the cattle were ruining the sugar cane, but kept right on singing and dancing. Lewis was able to get only a handful of house servants to drive the cattle out of the cane, and that not until the cane-piece was ruined.[17]

One tobacco planter complained that his slaves would cut the young plants indiscriminately unless they were watched. When it became late in the season and there was need of haste to avoid frost they would work only the thickest, leaving the sparser ones untouched.[18] Another planter said that he could cultivate only the

16. Redpath, James, *The Roving Editor: or, Talks with Slaves in the Southern States*, New York, 1859, p. 241.

17. Lewis, M. G., *Journal of a West Indian Proprietor, 1815–1817*, London, 1929, p. 267.

18. Phillips, U. B., *Plantation and Frontier Documents, 1649–1863*, Cleveland, 1909, p. 34.

poorer grades of tobacco because the slaves would not give necessary attention to the finer sort of plants.[19] An English visitor said:

"The kitchens and out-offices are always at the distance of several yards from the principal dwelling. This is done as well to guard against the house-Negroes through carelessness setting the houses on fire, for they generally sit over it half the night, as to keep out their noise." (sic.)[20] . . .

But not only did the Negro slaves refuse to work, and not only did they destroy property, but they even made it impossible for planters to introduce new work techniques by feigning clumsiness. They prevented the introduction of the plow in this way on many plantations.[21] . . .

Malingering was a well-known phenomenon throughout the slave states.[22] The purpose of feigning illness was generally to avoid work, although occasionally a slave who was being sold would feign a disability either to avoid being sold to an undesirable master, or to lower his purchase price so as to obtain revenge on a former master. The women occasionally pretended to be pregnant, because pregnant women were given lighter work assignments and were allowed extra rations of food.

In a situation such as this in which physical disability was an advantage, one would expect much malingering. One might also expect to find functional mental disorders, hysterical disorders which would get one out of work. . . .

Of the extent to which illness was feigned there can, however, be

---

19. Olmsted, F. L., A Journey in the Seaboard Slave States, p. 91.

20. Hanson, C. W., The Stranger in America, London, 1807, p. 357.

21. Olmsted, op. cit., pp. 481–484.

22. Since this paper was written a significant contribution has appeared which throws a new light on the subject of slave illness. (Felice Swados, "Negro Health on the Ante Bellum Plantations," Bulletin of the History of Medicine, vol. x, no. 3, October, 1941.) Though Swados demonstrated that the rate of actual sickness among the Negroes was very high, she leaves some doubt as to what proportion of sickness was feigned. For instance, in a footnote (p. 472) she refers to Sydnor's compilations of the records of sickness on several plantations as indications of the extent of actual sickness, even going so far as to note that on one plantation most of the sickness occurred during the picking season. Sydnor, himself, indicates that he believes that these records demonstrate that a great deal of the sickness was feigned.

little doubt. Some of the feigning was quite obvious, and one might wonder why such flagrant abuses were tolerated. The important thing to remember is that a slave was an important economic investment. Most slave owners sooner or later found out that it was more profitable to give the slave the benefit of the doubt. A sick slave driven to work might very well die.

... The masters were always suspicious of the sick slaves, so that slaves who were moderately sick accentuated their symptoms in order to make out a convincing case. ...

Fortunately in this field we have some quantitative estimates which enable us to appreciate fully the extent of these practices. Sydnor has digested the records of sickness on various plantations. From the Wheeles plantation records he found that of 1,429 working days 179 were lost on account of sickness, a ratio of almost one to seven. On the Bowles' plantation, in one year 159½ days were missed on account of sickness but only five days were on Sundays. This is a recurrent pattern, everybody sick on Saturday, and scarcely anybody sick on Sunday. On the Leigh plantation, where thirty persons were working there were 398 days of sickness. In examining this record Sydnor discovered that the rate of sickness was greatest at the times of the year when there was the most work to be done.[23] Olmsted says that he never visited a plantation on which twenty Negroes were employed where he did not find one or more not at work on some trivial pretext.[24] ...

Pretending to be pregnant was a type of escape in a class by itself, since the fraud must inevitably have been discovered. This in itself may give us some insight into the Negroes' attitude toward the relative advantages of escaping work and of escaping punishment. Just as the slave who ran off into the woods for a temporary relief from work, the pseudo-pregnant woman must have realized in advance that she would inevitably be punished. ...

One woman sought to escape from the consequences of her fraud. The results were quite tragic.

"A young slave woman, Becky by name, had given pregnancy as the reason for a continued slackness in her work. Her master became skeptical and gave notice that she was to be examined and

23. Sydnor, C. S., *Slavery in Mississippi*, New York, 1933. pp. 45 ff.
24. Olmsted, F. L., *A Journey in the Seaboard Slave States*, p. 187.

might expect the whip in case her excuse were not substantiated. Two days afterwards a Negro midwife announced that Becky's baby had been born; but at the same time a neighboring planter began a search for a child nine months old which was missing from his quarter. This child was found in Becky's cabin, with its two teeth pulled and the tip of its navel cut off. It died; and Becky was convicted only of manslaughter."[25] . . .

The most effective means of retaliation against an unpopular master which the slave had at his command was by feigning disability on the auction block. How often this was done we do not know, but Phillips accepts it as a recognized pattern.

"Those on the block often times praised their own strength and talents, for it was a matter of pride to fetch high prices. On the other hand if a slave should bear a grudge against his seller, or should hope to be bought only by someone who would expect but light service he might pretend a disability though he had it not."[26] . . .

The strength of Negro resistance to slavery becomes apparent in the extent to which the slaves mutilated themselves in their efforts to escape work. A girl on Lewis' plantation who had been injured tied pack thread around her wounds when they started to heal and then rubbed dirt in them. In her anxiety to avoid work she gave herself a very serious infection.[27] But this action was mild compared to that of others.

"General Leslie Coombs, of Lexington, owned a man named Ennis, a house carpenter. He had bargained with a slave-trader to take him and carry him down the river. Ennis was determined not to go. He took a broadaxe and cut one hand off; then contrived to lift the axe, with his arm pressing it to his body, and let it fall upon the other, cutting off the ends of the fingers.[28]

25. Phillips, U. B., *American Negro Slavery*, p. 436.
26. Phillips, U. B., *American Negro Slavery*, p. 199.
27. Lewis, *op. cit.*, p. 168.
28. Clarke, *op. cit.*, p. 125.

" 'But some on 'em would rather be shot then be took, sir,' he added simply.

"A farmer living near a swamp confirmed this account, and said he knew of three or four being shot on one day."[29]

Planters had much trouble with slaves fresh from Africa, the new slaves committing suicide in great numbers. Ebo landing in the Sea Islands was the site of the mass suicide of Ebo slaves who simply walked in a body into the ocean and drowned themselves. A planter writing on the handling of slaves mentions the difficulty of adjusting the Africans to slavery. He advocates mixing them in with seasoned slaves.

"It too often happens that poor masters, who have no other slaves or are too greedy, require hard labor of these fresh negroes, exhaust them quickly, lose them by sickness and more often by grief. Often they hasten their own death; some wound themselves, others stifle themselves by drawing in the tongue so as to close the breathing passage, others take poison, or flee and perish of misery and hunger."[30]

The one problem of Negro resistance to slavery which is most enticing is that of the attitude of slave mothers toward their children. There are frequent references in the literature to Negro women who boasted about the number of "niggers they hade for the massah," but breeding was probably quite secondary to sex activity. It would be interesting to discover the motives behind this apparent pleasure in presenting babies to the master. Some of the women may have been sincere in their pride. What makes this problem peculiarly important is the presence of much indirect evidence that, the Negro mothers either had no affection for their children, or did not want them to be raised as slaves.

We know quite well that African Negroes are (at least reasonably) able to take care of their children, and that the slave women efficiently tended the children of the plantation mistress. Yet one runs across comment after comment that the Negro mothers were ignorant, and

29. Olmsted, F. L., A Journey in the Seaboard Slave States, p. 160.
30. Phillips, U. B., Plantation and Frontier Documents, II, p. 31.

careless, and did not know how to care for their own offspring. Typical of such statements is this:

"The Negro mothers are often so ignorant and indolent, that they cannot be trusted to keep awake and administer medicine to their own children; so that the mistress has often to sit up all night with a sick Negro child."[31]

Guion Johnson states that plantation owners in the Sea Islands offered the mothers rewards to take good care of their children. They were paid for those who survived the first year! This at least would indicate that there was something to be desired in their attitude toward their children.

Occasionally one runs across a reference to a slave mother killing her child, but the statements are almost invariably incomplete....

Several cases, where it was certain that parents killed their children to keep them from slavery, have been described. They are important enough to be given in detail.

"Of all the cases of slave rendition, the saddest and probably the most circulated at the time was that of Margaret Garner. Winter was the best time for flight across the Ohio River, for when it was frozen over the difficulties of crossing were fewer. Simeon Garner, with his wife Margaret and two children, fled from slavery in Kentucky during the cold winter of 1856 and, after crossing the frozen stream at night, made their ways to the house of a free Negro in Cincinnati.

"Quickly tracing the fugitive Negroes to their hideout in Cincinnati, the armed pursuers, after some resistance, broke down the door and entered the house. There they found Margaret, the mother, who, preferring death to slavery for her children, had striven to take their lives, and one child lay dead on the floor. The case was immediately brought into court, where despite the efforts made by sympathetic whites, rendition was ordered. On their return to slavery, Margaret in despair attempted to drown herself and child by jumping into the river but even the deliverance of death was denied her, for she was recovered and soon thereafter

31. Lyell, op. cit., p. 264.

sold to a trader who took her to the cotton fields of the Far South."[32]

"Not only were slaves known to take the lives of their masters or overseers, but they were now and then charged with the murder of their own children, sometimes to prevent them from growing up in bondage. In Covington a father and mother, shut up in a slave barracoon and doomed to the southern market, 'when there was no eye to pity them and no arm to save,' did by mutual agreement 'send the souls of their children to Heaven rather than have them descend to the hell of slavery,' and then both parents committed suicide."[33]

" 'Take off your shoes, Sylva,' said Mrs. A., 'and let this gentleman see your feet.'
" 'I don't want to,' said Sylva.
" 'But I want you to,' said her mistress.
" 'I don't care if you do,' replied Sylva sullenly.
" 'You must,' said the mistress firmly.
"The fear of punishment impelled her to remove the shoes. Four toes on one foot, and two on the other were wanting! 'There!' said the mistress, 'my husband, who learned the blacksmith's trade for the purpose of teaching it to the slaves, to increase their market value, has, with his own hands, pounded off and wrung off all those toes, when insane with passion. And it was only last week that he thought Sylva was saucy to me, and he gave her thirty lashes with the horse whip. She was so old that I could not bear to see it, and I left the house.
" 'Sylva says,' Mrs. A. continued, 'that she has been the mother of thirteen children, every one of whom she has destroyed with her own hands, in their infancy, rather than have them suffer slavery'!"[34]

The patterns of resistance to slavery studied in this paper are: (1) deliberate slowing up of work; (2) destruction of property, and indifferent work; (3) feigning illness and pregnancy; (4) injuring one's

32. Coleman, J. W., *Slavery Times in Kentucky*, Chapel Hill, N. C., 1940, p. 208.
33. *Ibid.*, p. 269.
34. Parson, C. G., *op. cit.*, p. 212.

self; (5) suicide; (6) a possibility that a significant number of slave mothers killed their children. . . .

The material presented here suggests the need for a reconsideration of the concept of the Negro's easy adjustment to slavery. He was not a cheerful, efficient worker, as has been assumed. Rather, he was frequently rebellious, and almost always sullen, as any person faced with a disagreeable situation from which he cannot escape will normally be. Nor, can the belief that racial inferiority is responsible for inefficient workmanship on his part be supported. For such deficiencies of his workmanship as he manifested, or, indeed, may still be manifested, are seen to be explainable in terms that are in no sense to be couched in the conventional mold of inherent racial differences.

Although Mexican-Americans today constitute a population in the
southwestern United States of something over four million, they
are still considered by the Anglo majority to be an inconsequential
and exploitable element of society. Carey McWilliams, in " 'Not
Counting Mexicans,' " points out that this attitude is rooted in well
over a century of racial and cultural conflict. White Americans,
pursuing the spirit of "manifest destiny," forged relentlessly
westward during the eighteenth and nineteenth centuries and in the
process clashed with any peoples who impeded their march.
By the 1830s, a rupture was imminent with Mexico as Anglo
settlers gained numerical supremacy in Texas. Racial and cultural
differences helped to promote the rift. The Anglos were white, Protestant, English-speaking proponents of slavery. The Mexican
inhabitants were darker-skinned, Catholic, Spanish-speaking
opponents of slavery. McWilliams describes the events which
followed—the Texas Revolution, the Mexican-American War,
the disputes over slavery, and the Cortina Affair—as the genesis for
the tense and bitter feelings of today.

'Not Counting Mexicans'

Carey McWilliams

When asked how many notches he had on his gun, King Fisher, the famous Texas gunman, once replied: "Thirty-seven—not counting Mexicans." This casual phrase, with its drawling understatement, epitomizes a large chapter in Anglo-Hispano relations in the Southwest. People fail to count the non-essential, the things and persons that exist only on sufferance; whose life tenure is easily revocable. The notion that Mexicans are interlopers who are never to be counted in any reckoning dies but slowly in the Southwest. To this day Mexicans do not figure in the social calculations of those who rule the border states. As I write these lines [1948], the Mexican consul-general in Los Angeles has just entered a vigorous protest against the insulting behavior of custom inspectors at the municipal airport.

A majority of the present-day residents of the Southwest are not familiar with the malignant conflict of cultures which has raged in the borderlands for more than a century. Blinded by cultural myths, they have failed to correlate the major events in a pattern of conflict which has prevailed from Brownsville to Los Angeles since 1846. Once this correlation is made, it becomes quite apparent that the Mexican-

American War was merely an incident in a conflict which arose some years before and survived long after the Treaty of Guadalupe Hidalgo. It is only within the framework of this age-old conflict that it is possible to understand the pattern of Anglo-Hispano cultural relations in the Southwest today. In summarizing the history of this conflict, one necessarily starts with Texas, for there the first blood was shed.

1. Los Diablos Tejanos

In Texas the Spanish-Mexican settlements were directly in the path of Anglo-American expansion. Unlike the rest of the borderlands, Texas was not separated from the centers of Anglo-American population by mountain ranges and desert wastes; geographically it invited invasion. In a series of belts or strips, its rich alluvial plains stretched from the plateaus to the gulf. The rivers that marked these belts could be crossed, at all seasons, at almost any point, without much trouble. On the other hand, between the most southerly settlements in Texas and those in Mexico, there was, as Dr. Samuel Harman Lowrie has pointed out, "a great expanse of semi-arid land which at that time served as a more or less natural, though temporary barrier to the effective extension of Mexican influence and control." Texas was 1,200 miles removed from its capital, Mexico City.

By 1834 the Anglo-Americans outnumbered the Mexicans in Texas: thirty thousand to five thousand. Most of the Mexicans were concentrated in the old Spanish towns or along the border, while the Anglo-Americans were to be found on the farms and ranches. Mexican townspeople had few opportunities for acculturation for they saw very little of the Anglo-Americans. From the outset, moreover, relations between the two peoples were clouded by the fear of war. The Anglo-Americans bore the brunt of Mexico's hostile distrust of the United States and were, in turn, encouraged to take an unfriendly attitude toward the natives by the unconcealed, aggressive designs of the jingoes in Washington.

As might have been expected, each group formed a highly unfavorable initial impression of the other. To the early American settlers, the Mexicans were lazy, shiftless, jealous, cowardly, bigoted, superstitious, backward, and immoral. To the Mexicans, on the other hand, the Texans were "*los diablos Tejanos*": arrogant, overbearing, aggressive, conniving, rude, unreliable, and dishonest. The first

Mexican ambassador to the United States had complained . . . of the "haughtiness of these republicans who will not allow themselves to look upon us as equals but merely as inferiors." Still another Mexican official had charged that the Americans in Texas considered themselves "superior to the rest of mankind, and look upon their republic as the only establishment upon earth founded upon a grand and solid basis." Full of brag, bluster, and spreadeagle chauvinism, the Americans of the 1800's were hardly the most tactful ambassadors of goodwill. The truth of the matter is that the border residents were not a credit to either group.

Under the most favorable circumstances, a reconciliation of the two cultures would have been difficult. The language barrier was, of course, a constant source of misunderstanding; neither group could communicate, for all practical purposes, with the other. The Mexicans knew almost nothing of local self-government, while the Americans, it was said, travelled with "their political constitutions in their pockets" and were forever "demanding their rights." Although tolerant of peonage, the Mexicans were strongly opposed to slavery. The Anglo-Americans, most of whom were from the Southern states, were vigorously pro-slavery. The Anglo-Americans were Protestants; the Mexicans were Catholic. Speaking of a Mexican, a Protestant missionary is said to have remarked: "He was a Catholic, but clean and honest." Both groups lacked familiarity with the existing Mexican laws, for there was no settled government in Texas. Anglo-Americans found it extremely difficult to respect the laws of Mexico in the absence of law-interpreting and law-enforcing agencies. Thus it was, as Dr. Lowrie writes, that "cultural differences gave rise to misconceptions and misunderstandings, misunderstandings to distrust, distrust to antagonism, and antagonism on a very considerable number of points made open conflict inevitable."

The first Anglo-Americans literally fought their way into Texas. While most of these early filibustering expeditions were defeated, they succeeded in laying waste to the country east and north of San Antonio. Both Mexicans and Americans were killed by these invading private armies. No sooner had the Mexicans driven out the filibusters, than the Comanches raided the entire stretch of country between the Nueces and the Rio Grande. According to one observer, the whole region was "depopulated, great numbers of stock were driven off, and the people took refuge in the towns on the Rio Grande." Preoccupied with revolutionary events in Spain and Mexico, the government could give little attention to the Texas settlements. After 1821, however, a measure of protection was provided against the devastating raids of the Comanches and many of the settlers moved back across the Rio Grande.

2. Alas! The Alamo

With the Texas Revolution came the embittering memories, for the Texans, of the slaughter of Anglo-Americans at the Alamo and Goliad; and, for the Mexicans, of the humiliating rout and massacre at San Jacinto. Prior bitternesses were now intensified a thousandfold. "Towards the Mexicans remaining within the limits of the Republic," writes Dr. Garrison, "the feeling of the Texans was scarcely better than towards the Indians." Memories dating from this period still poison relationships between Anglos and Hispanos in Texas. Some years ago a district judge told of how, as a child, he had heard an old man give an eye-witness account of the slaughter at the Alamo. "I never see a Mexican," he confessed, "without thinking of that." José Vasconcellos, the well-known Mexican educator and philosopher, tells in his autobiography of how these same memories poisoned his boyhood in Eagle Pass. After the Texas Revolution, as Erna Fergusson has pointed out, "Texans could not get it out of their heads that their manifest destiny was to kill Mexicans and take over Mexico."

Throughout the decade of the Texas Republic (1836–1846), the shooting war continued in "the Spanish country" south of the Nueces. Murder was matched by murder; raids by Texans were countered by raids from Mexico. Since a peace treaty was never negotiated, no boundaries could be fixed. Texas claimed to the Rio Grande, while Mexico insisted that its boundary rested on the Nueces. In the bloody zone between the two rivers an uninterrupted guerrilla warfare continued throughout the life of the Texas Republic. In 1839 General Don Antonio Canales launched a revolution on Texas soil against Santa Anna and raised the banner of the Republic of Rio Grande. Of the 600 men who rallied to his standard, 180 were Texans. Awakening to the fact that Texans were using his insurrection as a cover for an attack on Mexico, General Canales finally surrendered but not until his troops had fought several engagements along the border. At the head of a raiding party of five hundred men, General

Vásquez captured San Antonio in 1842 and held it for two days. These are but two of many similar episodes that occurred during the hectic life of the new republic.

Throughout the period of this border warfare, the Texas-Mexicans were caught between opposing forces. "When the Americans have gone there," explained a delegate at the Texas constitutional convention, "they have preyed upon the Mexicans; they have been necessarily compelled by force or otherwise to give up such property as they had. So vice versa, when the Mexicans have come in, they have been necessarily compelled to furnish them the means of support. . . . Since 1837 they [the Texas-Mexicans] have been preyed upon by their own countrymen as well as by ours." The Texans constantly suspected the Mexicans of inciting the Indians against them and every Indian raid provoked retaliation against the *Tejanos*. The Mexicans naturally regarded the Texas Revolution as American-inspired and the prelude to the conquest of Mexico.

However all Mexicans were not equally affected by this complex warfare. A sizable number of the upper-class settlers quickly became identified with the Texans. These Texanized Mexicans or "the good Mexicans" were called *Tejanos* and were invariably of the *rico* class. Two of the fifty signers of the Texas Declaration of Independence were native Mexicans and a third, born in Mexico, became the first vice-president of the republic. At a later date, Captain Refugio Benavides commanded a company of Texas-Mexicans which operated along the border against Mexican raiders and marauders.

3. The Mexican-American War

Provoked by the annexation of Texas in 1846, the Mexican-American War represented the culmination of three decades of cultural conflict in Texas. To the Mexicans, every incident in Texas from the filibustering raids to the Revolution of 1836 was regarded, in retrospect, as part of a deliberately planned scheme of conquest. To the Anglo-Americans, the war was "inevitable," having been provoked, in their eyes, by the stupidity and backwardness of the Mexican officials. Not only did Mexico forfeit an empire to the United States, but, ironically, none of the signers of the Treaty of Guadalupe Hidalgo realized that, nine days before the treaty was signed, gold had been discovered in California. That they had unknowingly ceded to the United States territories unbelievably rich in gold and silver—the hope of finding which had lured Coronado and De Oñate into the Southwest—must have added to the Mexicans' sense of bitterness and defeat. Furthermore the way in which the United States fought the Mexican-American War added greatly to the heritage of hatred. A large part of our invading army was made up of volunteers who, by all accounts, were a disgrace to the American flag. General Winfield Scott readily admitted that they had "committed atrocities to make Heaven weep and every American of Christian morals blush for his country. Murder, robbery and rape of mothers and daughters in the presence of tied-up males of the families have been common all along the Rio Grande." Lieutenant George C. Meade, of later Civil War fame, said that the volunteers were "driving husbands out of houses and raping their wives.... They will fight as gallantly as any men, but they are a set of Goths and Vandals without discipline, making us a terror to innocent people."

How bitterly these outrages were resented is shown by a passage which Lloyd Lewis has culled from one of the Mexican newspapers of the period: "the horde of banditti, of drunkards, of fornicators... vandals vomited from hell, monsters who bid defiance to the laws of nature... shameless, daring, ignorant, ragged, bad-smelling, long-bearded men with hats turned up at the brim, thirsty with the desire to appropriate our riches and our beautiful damsels." The year 1844 had seen the rise of a Native American Party in the states and much anti-Catholic feeling found expression during the war. Mexicans charged that the volunteers had desecrated their churches, "sleeping in the niches devoted to the sacred dead... drinking out of holy vessels." Two hundred and fifty American troops, mostly of Catholic background, deserted and joined the Mexican army to form the San Patricio battalion. The barbarous manner in which eighty of these deserters were executed in San Angel, a suburb of Mexico City, was long cited by the Mexicans as further proof of Yankee cruelty.

Nothing was more galling to the Mexican officials who negotiated the treaty than the fact that they were compelled to assign, as it were, a large number of their countrymen to the Yankees. With great bitterness they protested that it was "not permissible to sell, as a flock of sheep, those deserving Mexicans." For many years after 1846, the Spanish-Americans left in the United States were known in Mexico as "our brothers who were sold." As late as 1943 maps were still used in Mexican schools which designated the old Spanish borderlands as "territory temporarily in the hands of the United States." It is to the great credit of the Mexican negotiators that the treaty contained the most explicit guarantees to protect the rights of these people, provisions for which they were more deeply concerned than they were over boundaries or indemnities. It should never be forgotten that, with the exception of the Indians, Mexicans are the only minority in the United States who were annexed by conquest; the only minority, Indians again excepted, whose rights were specifically safeguarded by treaty provision.

Just as the end of the Texas Revolution did not terminate hostilities in Texas, so the Treaty of Guadalupe Hidalgo failed to bring peace to the borderlands. Under the terms of the treaty, it became the obligation of the United States to police 180,000 Indians living in the territories which we acquired from Mexico. This obligation the United States failed to discharge for many years. Taking advantage of the confusion which prevailed, the Indians launched fierce raids on both Anglo and Hispano settlements, conducted marauding expeditions deep in Mexican territory, and cunningly exploited the hatred that had been engendered between Anglo and Hispano. The Anglos promptly attributed these raids to Mexican duplicity and instigation; the Hispanos as promptly charged them up to the malice or carelessness of the Americans. Hard-pressed on all sides, the Indians had come to live off the plunder seized in these raids which, with the confusion and demoralization which prevailed in Mexico, were conducted on a larger scale than ever before. It was not until about 1880 that the United States finally managed to bring the Indians of the Southwest under close police surveillance.

Nor were Indians the only troublemakers in the post-war decades. Between 1848 and 1853, various American filibustering expeditions violated Mexican territory in Sonora, Lower California, and at various points along the border. When word of the discovery of gold reached the Eastern states, swarms of emigrant gold-seekers passed along the southern routes to California, often travelling in Mexican territory without passports, and not infrequently helping themselves to Mexican food and livestock en route.

In 1850 José M. Carvajal organized a revolution in Mexico, sponsored by American merchants, which aimed at converting the State of

Tamaulipas into the Sierra Madre Republic. Carvajal was a Texan by birth who had been educated in Kentucky and Virginia. Backed by Richard King and Mifflin Kennedy, two of the great cattle-barons of south Texas, the Carvajal revolution was supported by bands of armed Texans who crossed the Rio Grande. The American ambassador reported that these raids, in which as many as five hundred Texans participated, had "awakened a feeling of intense prejudice against everything connected with American interest."

The fateful strip of territory between the Nueces and the Rio Grande once again became the home of numerous outlaw bands who preyed indiscriminately upon both Mexican and American settlers. In the face of these staggering blows,—filibustering expeditions, Indian raids, revolution, war, and constant guerrilla fighting,—the Mexicans in Texas constantly retreated and their retreat, of course, gave rise to the notion that their conquerors were pursuing a mandate of destiny. Major Emery, writing in 1859, said that the "white race" was "exterminating or crushing out the inferior race"; and an American soldier wrote home that "the Mexican, like the poor Indian, is doomed to retire before the more enterprising Anglo-Americans."

4. Slaves and Peons

As early as 1839 fairly large numbers of Negro slaves had escaped from their Texas owners by crossing the Rio Grande and a sizable colony of ex-slaves had sprung up in Matamoros. During the Civil War, the Texans suspected that native Mexicans were implicated in the flight of fugitive slaves, an accusation that found circumstantial confirmation in the known opposition of Mexicans to slavery (Mexico had sought to insert a provision in the treaty barring slavery forever from the territory ceded to the United States). "The possession of slaves in Western Texas," wrote Colonel Ford, "was rendered insecure owing to the contiguity of Mexico, and to the efforts of the Mexicans to induce them to run away. They assisted them in every way they could."

To some extent, the movement of Negro slaves across the border was matched by the flight of Mexican peons into Texas. According to Dr. Paul S. Taylor, some 2,812 servants with families numbering an additional 2,572 persons, escaped to Texas from Nuevo Leon and Coahuila in the period from 1848 to 1873. The loss in unpaid debts, which the flight of these peons represented, was estimated by the Mexican government to be in excess of $400,000.

In 1856 a Negro insurrectionary plot was uncovered in Colorado County. According to the Texans, the Negroes had planned to rebel, kill their masters, and, with the aid of native Mexicans, fight their way across the border. Without exception every Mexican in the county was "implicated" and over two hundred slaves were arrested and punished (two were whipped to death). Mexicans were ordered to leave Matagorda and Colorado counties immediately and in Uvalde they were forbidden to travel the roads without passes. "Anti-Mexican sentiment," writes Dr. Taylor, "based on the belief that the peons imperilled the institution of slavery, broke out in meetings which in Austin, Gonzales, and other towns, passed resolutions protesting against their employment. At Goliad the resolution declared that 'the continuance of the greaser or peon Mexicans as citizens among us is an intolerable nuisance and a grievance which calls loudly for redress'." As always, the circumstance that Mexicans were concentrated in the strip of territory immediately north of the border aroused the most dire forebodings.

The Negro insurrection was quickly followed by the Cart War which broke out in 1857. Prior to this time, Mexican ox-cart freighters had been hauling—between San Antonio and the coast and from San Antonio to Chihuahua—an annual cargo of goods and merchandise valued at several million dollars. The Cart War involved a systematic campaign on the part of Anglo-Americans to force Mexican freighters out of this lucrative business. For over a year, organized bands of Texans preyed on the Mexican freight trains, killing the drivers, stealing the merchandise, and generally disrupting the traffic. So tense did the situation become, with the Mexican ambassador filing one vigorous protest after the other, that federal troops were finally dispatched to protect the cartmen.

5. "Red Robber of the Rio Grande"

In the wake of the Cart War came the highly significant Cortina episode. Juan Nepomuceno Cortina—"the red robber of the Rio Grande"—was born near Brownsville. A blocky, powerfully built, red-bearded Mexican, Cortina came from a prominent and well-to-do family. Like so many Mexicans in Texas, he was a magnificent horseman. The Cortina War, which was to last a decade, started on July 13, 1859, when a deputy sheriff arrested a Mexican who had been a servant of the Cortina family. Contending that the arrest was merely another example of gringo arrogance, Cortina shot the deputy and freed the prisoner. On the morning of September twenty-eighth, Brownsville awoke to the cry of "Viva Cortina! Viva Mexico! Maten los Gringos!" as Cortina, at the head of an armed force, swept into the town, killed five Americans, released the pelado culprits from the jail, and plundered stores and shops. By 1860 Cortina had laid waste to the country from Brownsville to Rio Grande City—a distance of a hundred and fifty miles—and inland as far as Arroyo Colorado. Fifteen Americans and eight "friendly" Mexicans were killed in these raids, while Cortina is said to have lost a hundred or more of his men.

For fifteen years, Cortina was the scourge of the Lower Rio Grande Valley, defying capture, constantly eluding his pursuers. At one point in the Cortina War, Captain McNelly of the Texas Rangers crossed the Rio Grande, in defiance of orders, and gave Cortina's forces a severe defeat in a pitched battle at Las Cuevas. Incensed by these continued raids, the Texans burned the homes of all Mexicans suspected of being implicated or of giving aid and comfort to Cortina's forces. On his part, Cortina terrorized the Mexican residents and made short shrift of ... informers. This continued terror naturally silenced the Mexicans—a circumstance which only confirmed the Texans' belief in their innate duplicity and treacherousness.

A real expert in border warfare, Cortina hoisted the Mexican flag in Texas, and, so it was said, often raised the American flag in Mexico. Both Texas Rangers and Mexican troops from Matamoros on more than one occasion met defeat at his hands. Although he was a bandit and a cattle-thief, there was unquestionably something of the Robin Hood about Cortina. He had become a desperado, so he said, because the Anglo-Americans had tried "to blacken, depreciate, and load with insults" the Mexican residents of Texas. In one of numerous manifestoes, he pointed out that "a multitude of lawyers" in Texas sought to rob the Mexicans of their lands. In particular, he charged that one Adolph Glavecke, a deputy sheriff, acting in collusion with certain lawyers, had spread terror among the Mexicans, threatening to hang them and to burn their homes unless they abandoned the country. "Our personal enemies," he said, "shall not possess our lands until they have fattened it with their gore." Major Heintzelman, on the border at the time, stated that after the Brownsville raid Cortina was a great hero in the eyes of the people. "He had defeated the gringo and his position was impregnable. He had the Mexican flag flying in his camp and numbers were flocking to his standard. He was the champion of his race—the man who would right the wrongs of the Mexicans and drive the hated Americans to the Nueces."

While some Mexicans undoubtedly sympathized with Cortina and gave him aid, it is also a matter of record that others, at great personal peril, joined in the fight to defeat him. Despite this fact, however, the Anglo-Texans believed that every Mexican along the border was in league with Cortina and would, if given a chance, "murder every white inhabitant." At the request of the American government, Díaz finally brought the Cortina War to a close in 1873 by making Cortina his prisoner; but, as Walter Prescott Webb has written, "the evil consequences lived on." . . .

Gunther Barth,
"Chinese Sojourners in the West: The Coming"

Beginning in 1848 the first Chinese immigrants to California
settled in the northern portion of the state at San Francisco
and near the gold fields. Gunther Barth describes the newcomers as
"Chinese Sojourners in the West," and indicates that these
were men who hoped to return to their homeland as wealthy and
respected individuals. He recounts the means by which Chinese
laborers were contracted, the types of the agreements which
were made for their labor, and the perils of the voyage to the
United States. Only a handful succeeded in returning to their
homeland; yet, immigration to the west coast increased, and within
a few years the Chinese comprised about 10 percent of the population
of California. The influx alarmed white Californians, who
feared the competition of Chinese labor and used threats, violence,
and legislation to bar the Orientals from the mines and other
potentially lucrative endeavors.

Chinese Sojourners in the West: The Coming

Gunther Barth

In the 1850's and 1860's, a wave of Chinese surged into California in pursuit of a dream. The newcomers envisioned making money to return to China with their savings for a life of ease, surrounded and honored by the families which their drudgery had sustained.[1] Their pursuit of this limited goal influenced their reception in America, excluded them from the privileges and obligations of other newcomers, and kept them apart from the flood of immigrants who entered the United States permanently. In America these Oriental sojourners became the docile subjects of bosses and headmen, still directed by the dictates of the Chinese world.

The Chinese overseas emigration to Southeast Asia provided the pattern for the Cantonese traffic to California. Unable to pay for their passage, the impoverished mass of travelers to the plantations, mines, and godowns of Malaysia relied on the credit-ticket system. They obtained their tickets on credit from Chinese merchants who furnished the transportation. In some cases, the creditors worked their debtors in any way that guaranteed a profitable return for their in-

Gunther Barth, "Chinese Sojourners in the West: The Coming," *Southern California Quarterly*, XLVI (1964), pp. 55–67. Reprinted by permission of the author. Notes appear at the end of the article.

vestment. In others, relatives of the travelers or their future employers, reimbursed the merchants for the passage. In return the newcomers labored until their debts were paid off and then were free to accumulate the modest fortune which had lured them across the sea. Only the completion of this task assured a return to their villages as respected men.[2]

The steady demand for docile laborers in Southeast Asia perpetuated the credit-ticket system. Dutch, English, and Spanish officials, realizing its immediate value for colonial development, tolerated its operation. At first sight, the arrangement by which passage money was advanced to laborers in Chinese ports and repaid by them out of their earnings overseas appeared an expedient and harmless device. In reality, the credit-ticket system camouflaged a world of debt bondage that turned indentured emigrants into slaves of their countrymen.

The extension of the credit-ticket system to the passage between Hongkong and San Francisco transplanted certain oppressive elements of the Chinese social structure to the United States. Although Californians opposed debt bondage, Chinese merchants successfully adjusted and masked the institution by utilizing district companies and kinship organizations as instruments of extra-legal control. The sojourners' loyalty to their families in the villages of the Pearl River Delta served to enforce the creditors' hold over the indentured emigrants. A review of the mode of coming discloses the outlines of a world of suppression and points to a source of future strife between Chinese and Americans. The details of the passage reveal the incipient control system: its transfer to the United States through the transport of indentured emigrants to California.

In addition to indentured emigrants, two other types of emigrants stood out among Chinese sojourners to Southeast Asia: contract laborers and coolies. In the contract system, foreign importers and Chinese middlemen played the principal role. They hired laborers to fill the specific demand for Chinese workers in Malaysia and America. In contrast to the credit-ticket system upheld by debt bondage, this labor system was based on a service contract. The coolie traffic to the West Indies, Latin America, and the Indian Archipelago produced the extreme form of the contract system in the middle of the nineteenth century.[3] Force alone sustained it. Kidnapped or decoyed into barracoons, the coolie was virtually sold into service. The term which originally designated a hired laborer soon came to describe any cheap worker who was pressed into and kept in service by coercion.

Indentured emigrants and contract laborers endured the hardships of coolies although they fell into their creditors' or contractors' clutches at their own volition. They were but one step removed from the despotism of the coolie trade. The nefarious traffic stimulated compassion for its victims and an increasing urge for control by western powers. The oppressive nature of the contract labor system and the subtle tyranny of the credit-ticket system escaped observers whose awareness was already blunted by the coolie trade's cruelty.[4] The three different types of labor represented mere variations on the basic theme of all these modes of Chinese emigration. They disguised the enslaved nature of the indentured emigrants, contract laborers, and coolies.

The adoption of the system of indentured emigrants to the western scene required modifications. These changes resulted from the dictates of geography, the conditions of California, and the objections of Americans to forms of labor resembling bondage or slavery. In March, 1852, the San Francisco *Alta California* referred to the movement of Chinese indentured emigrants into the Indian Archipelago as the prototype for the traffic to California. The newcomers at San Francisco, the paper explained, "had either contracted with wealthy Chinese at home to labor at the mines ..., or had agreed on certain rates per month with the foreigners who brought them." But the ease with which "all contracts could be set aside, the temptation of the mines, and the impossibility of coercion, caused ... these contracts to be broken with severe loss to the holders."[5] One year earlier, six Chinese laborers "who were under contract in consideration of a free passage," had demonstrated the weakness of the contract system in the United States. When they ran away to the mines, the contractor failed to get warrants for their arrest. Since the "offence was not cognizable by a criminal tribunal," the court recommended that he "obtain his remedy in a civil suit."[6]

The bulk of the Chinese emigration to California consequently depended on the credit-ticket system and its instruments of debtor control. Chinese brokers, merchants at San Francisco or at Hongkong, paid the expenses of the travelers. The emigrants remained under their supervision until these debts were paid off. To facilitate a speedy repayment, the Chinese merchants in California employed the laborers in their own enterprises or sold the lien on the emigrants' services to other employers.[7] Western sailing vessels substituted for Chinese junks, while district companies and kinship organizations functioned as extra-legal controls over the indentured emigrants in a country where courts and customs failed to support contract labor. During their sojourn, the majority of the emigrants rarely left the narrow confines of the Chinese world which had commanded their allegiance since they set out from their villages.

The value of the system for the merchant-creditors impressed an editorial writer of the *Alta California* in 1855. Wealthy Chinese traders, he observed, paid for the sojourners' transportation and took them "into the mines and derived the entire profit of their labor." These indentured emigrants were "in fact little better than slaves, and their own countrymen were their master." They "have laws of their own," the editor emphasized, "and they enforce their contracts not only without, but in defiance of our State laws."[8] In May, 1859, a reporter of the Stockton *Argus* described the arrival of Chinese miners at Stockton who were "bundled on board the boat like so many cattle." Their countrymen, engaged in mining operations, had traveled in the cabin and "brought them from China for the purpose of speculating in their labor."[9] One year later the Stockton *Republican* lamented that Chinese agents forwarded "load after load" of indentured emigrants "in the same manner as other freight."[10]

Western vessels had linked Kwangtung with California after the discovery of gold attracted the shipping fleets. Hastily unloaded at San Francisco, the craft were dispatched to China, where they "either competed successfully with English ships for return cargoes to the Atlantic, or were profitably employed" in carrying emigrants to California.[11] Chinese merchants, recently established in San Francisco and without lines of communication to Hongkong equal to those of the traditional junk routes in Southeast Asia, came to rely on western sailing vessels for transporting their countrymen. As charterers or owners of an ill-assorted fleet, these traders, with the aid of such San Francisco commission merchants as Cornelius Koopmanschap, controlled the flow of Chinese emigrants to California as effectively as to Malaysia.[12]

The transport of sojourners employed shipping at a time of great demand for freight. It relieved the depression in one aspect of an overexpanded trading economy. High freight rates made the traffic so lucrative that ships frequently did not wait for additional cargo, but took passengers aboard and sailed in ballast. Contemporary observers speculated about the profits of ship owners or charterers. Chinese merchant-creditors earned no quick return whether they owned or chartered ships to transport the emigrants whose passage they furnished. For a profitable return on their considerable investment they speculated not on the shipping venture but on the labor potential of their countrymen in California.[13] Western ship owners, on the other hand, reaped their money as soon as the Chinese paid for the vessels they chartered.

The fare, at the lowest estimate, amounted to forty dollars for the voyage to San Francisco and twenty dollars for the return trip. Most observers considered fifty dollars as average fee.[14] The easy profits attracted a multitude of vessels. Their owners represented most nations trading with China. American craft soon overcame the numerical superiority which British bottoms originally enjoyed. Size and type of the ships varied as larger boats came to dominate the shipping business and were utilized in the human traffic. In the 1840's, a sailing vessel of five hundred tons burden still represented a respectable ship; in the first quarter of the 1860's, nearly half the craft at Hongkong registered over a thousand tons.[15]

Isolated news items, merchant circulars, and Chinese notes furnish a composite picture of the passage.[16] With minor exceptions, Hongkong served as point of departure.[17] The chaotic state of the Pearl River Delta, foreign wars, internal unrest, and rebellion drove Western shipping into the British colony. Hongkong also freed sea captains and Chinese brokers from the clutches of avaricious officials at Whampoa or the barracoons of coolie traders at Macao. Proclaimed a free port in 1841, Hongkong required no duties, not even bills of health since, according to the bon mot of a United States consul, no new disease could be imported.[18]

The regulations of Western powers hardly affected Chinese emigration before the 1880's.[19] In the United States, inadequate legislation went hand in hand with a lack of information about the nature of the traffic. The regimentation, the squalor of the crowded quarters, and the "fearful mortality" among the passengers, from time to time directed the compassion of Americans to conditions that threw "the most indefatigable slaver which ever sailed on the African coast completely in the shade."[20] However, court actions failed to awaken the conscience of ship owners who counted upon the confiscation of worthless hulks as a matter of course and calculated their possible loss into the expenses of the ventures. The merchant community's credo of the destiny of American commerce in China and the clamor for the trade's undisturbed development, lent quasi-sanction to the traffic. Its oppressive elements were accepted as a matter of course, perhaps because they seemed to resemble the stern shipboard discipline which many Californians had experienced in the not-too-distant past. Incapable of recognizing the sojourners as human beings through the barrier of the Chinese world, San Franciscans came to view the traffic's seedier sides as symptomatic of Chinese emigration.[21]

While the credit-ticket system was the dominant mode of traveling from Hongkong to San Francisco, the passage was made at times under conditions similar to the thinly-veiled slave traffic of the coolie system. The credit-ticket system became partly a disguised slave trade, managed chiefly by Chinese crimps and compradors. Middlemen lured artisans, peasants, and laborers into barracoons and sold them to ticket agents. At the Chinese ports and at San Francisco, the sojourners were confined, watched, and terrorized by the thugs of Chinese societies who acted in the creditors' interest.[22]

The travelers, waiting for the day of departure, were induced to gamble and lost money. Additional costs were added to the passage fee. Skippers frequently charged the emigrants for fitting up bunks or water tanks in the steerage. Harry Parkes, the Chinese interpreter of the Superintendent of British Trade in China, noted that the merchant-creditors paid fifty dollars for the passage and twenty dollars as additional expenses of the emigrants, on "the condition of receiving" in return "the sum of two hundred dollars." Most of the travelers accepted any arrangement that promised their transportation to the Golden Hills without realizing their financial obligations. The prospect of returning to China with two or three hundred dollars was inducement enough for men whose total annual income at home rarely amounted to one-tenth that sum; no venture for such princely gain was deemed too arduous.[23]

The emigrants to California traveled in junks, lorchas, or sampans over the waterways of the Pearl River Delta from their villages to Hongkong.[24] Messages from Chinese in California circulating through the hamlets, reports of returned sojourners reminiscing on their success, broadsides and open letters for and against emigration, and the rumors about the distant riches radiating from the shipping centers of South China filled the imagination of the travelers.[25] In company with other sojourners, the emigrants cast off before daybreak to avoid an encounter with fellow villagers and the possibility of hearing unlucky words which might endanger their enterprise. A roll of bedding and a bamboo basket with netting on the top, containing shoes, hat, and provisions, represented their worldly possessions.[26] At Hongkong, passage brokers provided a bunk in a dormitory, or friends and relatives furnished a domicile until the day of departure arrived.

The emigrants' limited contact with the strange environment of a Western sailing vessel served as an indicator of their relationship with the barbarian world for their entire sojourn. The travelers lined up on deck for inspection. After a mate had counted noses and tickets, to see that the charterers kept the bargain, the emigrants descended to their quarters below. With the exception of the cooks, few came up on deck during the voyage. Several bills of lading suggest that there might not have been room on the upper deck.[27] But even when ships sailed with a clear deck, the steerage was the easiest place to control large numbers of emigrants. It was one of the surest ways to avoid fights between the Chinese and the crew.

The length and course of the voyage varied with the season.[28] Between 1848 and 1867, a vast number of Chinese emigrants lived for an average of two months at the mercy of the ocean, their bosses and comrades, and the ships' crews. Calm days presented their particular problems. While the ship drifted idly on the smooth sea, and the sailors amused themselves by fishing, the emigrants gambled in their quarters or lay in their bunks, vainly listening for the yells, creaks, and gongs of their junks. Such tension-filled days brought fights between sailors and travelers and quarrels among the Chinese. In addition, the quality of the provisions and the neglect of the quarters caused friction between the emigrants and their countrymen who represented contractors or charterers.

During the course of the voyage, the dark, dank depths of the sailing vessels grew increasingly oppressive to men who were there under compulsion and afflicted by superstition, apprehension, and dreams of their destination. When barrel after barrel of rotten pork had to be thrown overboard; when rough seas prevented the travelers from using the badly constructed cooking places, arranged with an eye to maximum economy on the crowded main deck; when cheaply-built bunks continued to break down to the risk of heads and limbs, the strain-charged air could explode at any moment. While the Chinese insisted on settling their disturbances in their own way, the sailors liked to put down unrest by force. In the event of a clash with the crew, the Chinese swarmed up from the lower decks, hurling pieces of lumber and brickbats from the cooking places. Forced to retreat, the emigrants usually smeared blood over the faces of their wounded comrades and left them on the upper deck as if dead. Such moments tested the ability of captain and officers to prevent an open battle.[29]

The average captain handled the difficult task capably. His name disappeared behind the stories of the few who bungled their job or earned the praise of their Chinese passengers. There were few disturbances on Chinese emigrant ships "in which the commanders have not been blameworthy in a very high degree," Dr. John Bowring, Superintendent of British Trade in China, commented.[30] On other occasions the travelers presented their skippers with rings and flags as expressions of their gratitude for a safe voyage and friendly treatment.[31] Only in these instances did the emigrants break through the invisible barrier of the Chinese world, which confined them, and appeared more as a group of human beings than mere figures in the ships' papers and the registers of harbor masters. Generally the complete isolation of the sojourners from the world of Western shipping was one of the characteristics of the traffic.

When the emigrants' eager eyes finally caught the first glimmer of the Golden Gate, they strained every sense to catch the golden hues with which their imagination had invested the gateway to California. However, nothing but rock formations crowned with fog gratified their gaze. The stream of Western travelers who approached San Francisco by sea in the 1840's and 1850's, sensed the raw, cold, and disagreeable scene. To the Chinese, however, the barren shoreline, as far as it was visible through the mist, much resembled the bleak islands of the Pearl River's estuary and presaged an equally familiar world of unrewarding work.

Noise and confusion accompanied the disembarkation on the wharves of San Francisco. Baskets, matting, hats, and bamboo poles covered the pier that was crowded with boatmen, agents of Chinese merchants, draymen, custom officials, and spectators. Suddenly, as a traveler remembered, "out of the general babble some one called out in our local dialect, and, like sheep recognizing the voice only, we blindly followed and soon were piling into one of the waiting wagons." Everything appeared so "strange and exciting," he confessed, that his memory of the landing was "just a big blur." The Chinese quarter was the destination of other groups who marched in single file through the streets, carrying their luggage suspended from the ends of bamboo poles slung across their shoulders. The first night in the strange country the newcomers slept in the dormitories owned by the companies under whose management they had made the long sea voyage, safely confined within the narrow limits of a Chinese world that had harbored them ever since they departed from their villages.[32]

The adaptation of the credit-ticket system to the passage between Hongkong and San Francisco extended the physical and social framework of the Chinese world to California. The maintenance of this world within the United States required further modifications to sustain the pattern of indenture without the aid of American courts and customs. The basic sentiments of Californians, derived from their experience with the Indians and with Negro slavery, and influenced by their exalted vision of the state's future, ran counter to an extension to California of the Chinese concept of debt bondage. Chinese merchants utilized district companies and kinship organizations as instruments of extra-legal control and secured the continuation of the pattern. The application of the traditional mode of Chinese emigration to the passage facilitated transplanting the system of oppression. Characterized in terms not of liberty but of survival, a Chinese California emerged, isolated from, yet part of, Western development.

Notes

1. William Speer and Augustus W. Loomis, missionaries of the Presbyterian Board of Foreign Missions to the Chinese in California, in their reports to the Secretary of the Presbyterian Board of Foreign Missions in New York between 1853 and 1865, frequently refer to this goal of the Chinese emigrants. *Correspondence of the Presbyterian Board of Foreign Missions*, Presbyterian Historical Society, Philadelphia. See also *Hsia-Erh Kuan-Chen* [Gathered Gems from Far and Near] (Hongkong), II (January 1, 1854), 5b–7b; "Letter from Fou Sin to his Father & Brothers," printed in a pamphlet, *Murder of M[artin]* V. B. Griswold, *By Five Chinese Assassins* . . . (Jackson, Calif., 1858), pp. 25–26.

2. E[lihu] Doty and W[illiam] J. Pohlman, "Journal of a Tour on the Island of Borneo [in the Districts of Sambas and Pontianak], November, 1838"; W[illiam] Youngblood and E[lbert] Nevius, "Journal [of Travels in Western Borneo in March, 1840]"; [Elbert Nevius and William Youngblood], "Journal of a Tour to Mandoor and Sandak [April, 1840]," Papers of the American Board of Commissioners for Foreign Missions, Borneo Mission, 1838–1844, I–II, Houghton Library, Harvard University; John Crawford, History of the Indian Archipelago . . . (3 vols., Edinburgh, 1820), I, 135, III, 183; Charles Gutzlaff, Journal of Three Voyages Along the Coast of China, in 1831, 1832 & 1833 . . . (London, 1834), pp. 165–168; [Siah U Chin], "Remittances by Chinese Immigrants in Singapore to Their Families in China," Journal of the Indian Archipelago and Eastern Asia (Singapore), I ([January–February], 1847), 35–37; C[oenrad] J. Temminck, Coup-D'Oeil Général sur Les Possessions Néerlandaises dans L'Inde Archipélagique (3 vols., Leiden, 1847), II, 169; Siah U Chin, "The Chinese in Singapore; General Sketch of the Numbers, Tribes, and Avocations of the Chinese in Singapore," Journal of the Indian Archipelago and Eastern Asia, II ([May], 1848), 285–287; G. F. Davidson, Trade and Travel in the Far East; or Recollections of the Twenty-one Years Passed in Java, Singapore, Australia, and China (London, 1848), p. 46; [Johan Hendrick Croockewitcz], "De Tinmijnen van Malaka," Tijdschrift voor Nederlandsch Indie (Zaltbommel, Netherlands), XIII (November, 1851), 301–302; "Notes on the Chinese of Pinang," Journal of the Indian Archipelago and Eastern Asia, VIII ([January–February], 1854), 2–3.

3. Persia Crawford Campbell, Chinese Coolie Emigration to Countries within the British Empire (London, 1923); Watt Stewart, Chinese Bondage in Peru, 1849–1874 (Durham, North Carolina, 1951).

4. For an example, see William Speer, China and California; Their Relations, Past and Present. A Lecture in Conclusion of a Series in Relation to the Chinese People, Delivered in the Stockton Street Presbyterian Church, San Francisco, June 28, 1853 (San Francisco, 1853), pp. 13–16; "What are Coolies?" San Francisco Oriental, or Tung-Ngai San-Luk, January 11, 1855; An Humble Plea addressed to the Legislature of California, In Behalf of the Immigrants from the Empire of China to this State (San Francisco, 1856); "Democracy of the Chinese," Harper's New Monthly Magazine, XXXVII (November, 1868), 839–848; The Oldest and the Newest Empire: China and the United States (Hartford, Conn., 1870), pp. 462–492; San Francisco Alta California, April 2, 1857; San Francisco Herald, July 14, 1853; December 8, 1855.

5. San Francisco Alta California, March 8, 1852.

6. Ibid., March 23, 1851; San Francisco Herald, March 25, 1851.

7. Speer to Walter Lowrie, December 18, 1852; Loomis to Lowrie, March 1, 9; June 25, September 19, 1860; April 17, 1862; June 29, 1863; March 5, 1864; Correspondence of the Presbyterian Board for Foreign Missions; San Francisco Alta California, September 20, October 1, 1849; May 11, 1850; March 31, 1851; March 1, August 28, October 1, 18, 1852; March 24, 28, April 25, May 20, September 28, 1853; February 2, March 25, 1854; August 26, September 16, 1856; October 15, 1857; May 30, July 17, 23, August 13, 1858; June 16, October 29, November 2, 3, December 13, 1859; February 9, 26, May 24, July 7, October 20, 1860; January 14, 28, March 1, 5, 16, 17, 19, April 16, August 22, 1861; March 12, May 7, October 17, November 14, 1862; May 5, July 28, December 9, 1864; March 2, 14, June 6, 1865; January 14, April 1, 5, July 26, September 16, 1866; May 12, June 9, September 29, 1867; May 9, 1868; June 24, 1869;

San Francisco Herald, April 12, August 29, 1852; May 16, 23, 1853; January 11, 1854; October 27, 1855; July 2, 18, 24, August 13, 1858; July 6, 1859; May 12, June 16, 1860.

8. San Francisco Alta California, February 21, 1855.

9. Ibid., quoting Stockton Argus, May 16, 21, 1859.

10. Ibid., quoting Stockton Republican, September 2, December 5, 1860. For additional descriptions see San Francisco Alta California, June 12, November 26, 1861; May 8, 24, 1862; January 15, July 6, 1863; April 26, 27, July 11, 1864; July 26, August 14, 15, 16, 18, 23, 1866; May 27, June 30, September 2, 1867; July 15, 1869; San Francisco Herald, May 20, 1852; May 29, August 4, 1853; February 14, August 22, 1854; February 4, 1855; April 20, 1858; May 20, 1859; July 23, 1861; San Francisco California Police Gazette, May 25, June 8, 1867; May 29, 1869; Sacramento Placer Times, March 2, 1850.

11. Frank Soulé, John H. Gihon, and James Nisbet, The Annals of San Francisco ... (New York, 1855), p. 419.

12. San Francisco Alta California, June 3, September 18, 19, October 30, 1853; June 27, 29, July 1, August 22, 1854; San Francisco Herald, September 17, 1853; October 18, 1855. For the leading position among Western firms which Cornelius Koopmanschap gained in the traffic of Chinese emigrants during the 1860's see San Francisco Alta California, January 15, 1863; July 15, 30, 1869; New York World, July 20, 21, 1869; New York Evening Post, July 15, 20, 1869; New Orleans Daily Picayune, July 14, 15, 28, August 6, October 2, 4, 14, 1869; January 6, 8, 9, 1870; St. Louis Republican, July 15, 1869 (Bancroft Scraps, Chinese Clippings, VI, 144–148, Bancroft Library, University of California); "The Chinese Again," Hunt's Merchants' Magazine, LXI (September 1869), 214; U.S. Senate Report 689, 44 Cong., 2 Sess., p. 76.

13. San Francisco Herald, August 17, 1852; May 9, 1854; May 7, 1856; San Francisco Alta California, May 16, June 27, August 22, 1854; San Francisco Daily Evening News and Evening Picayune, January 28, 1854. The circulars of the house of King & Co. at Canton and the firm of Rawle, Brinker & Co. at Hongkong readily documented the possibility of the traffic with detailed lists of the ships carrying Chinese passengers. San Francisco Herald, June 12, August 17, 1852. Eldon Griffin, Clippers and Consuls; American Consular and Commercial Relations with Eastern Asia, 1845–1860 (Ann Arbor, Mich., 1938), reviewed in detail the American commerce with China during the period.

14. Peter Parker to Daniel Webster, March 27, 1852. U.S. Senate Ex. Doc. 99, 34 Cong., 1 Sess., pp. 119–120; San Francisco Alta California, April 25, 1852; San Francisco Herald, February 11, 14, 1856; Speer, Humble Plea, p. 7; E[rnest] J. Eitel, Europe in China; The History of Hongkong from the Beginning to the Year 1882 (London, 1882), p. 259.

15. San Francisco Herald, March 13, August 17, 1852; March 29, 1853; Hongkong China Mail, April 3, 1860.

16. The mode of coming received no attention in the secondary accounts discussing the Chinese in the United States. Russell H. Conwell, Why and How. Why the Chinese Emigrate, and the Means They Adopt for the Purpose of Reaching America. With Sketches of Travels, Amusing Incidents, Social Customs, &c. (Boston, 1871), pp. 212–213, formed the exception and gave a sketch of Chinese life on one of "those palace steamships owned by the Pacific Mail Steamship Company."

17. San Francisco *Herald*, June 7, 1853; San Francisco *Alta California*, January 3, 1857; January 3, 1860.

18. *U.S. Senate Ex. Doc. 107*, 4 vols., 34 Cong., 1 Sess., III, 638; Hosea Ballou Morse, *The International Relations of the Chinese Empire* (3 vols., New York, 1910–18), I, 292.

19. San Francisco *Herald*, September 9, 1854, quoting *China Mail*; Harley F. McNair, *The Chinese Abroad, Their Position and Protection; A Study in International Law and Relations* (Shanghai, 1926), pp. 1–27, gives details of the legal aspects of Chinese emigration.

20. San Francisco *Herald*, August 12, 1854.

21. *Ibid.*, October 27, December 29, 1851; February 18, March 22, July 23, November 1, 1853; July 20, 21, 22, 23, 24, 25, 26, 27, August 8, 12, 13, 15, 17, 19, 21, 22, 24, 26, 27, September 4, 16, 22, 23, 28, 30, October 9, December 29, 1854; December 18, 1855; March 16, May 7, 1856; January 28, 1857; April 20, 1858; San Francisco *Alta California*, June 29, October 19, 1852; July 19, 21, 22, 27, 28, 29, August 1, 4, 12, 15, 17, 18, 19, 24, 26, September 1, 11, 20, 21, 22, 23, 24, 27, 28, October 7, 8, 1854; September 10, 13, 1855; May 22, July 11, 1857; February 19, 1858; February 20, March 1, 5, 1862; August 3, 16, September 18, 1866; July 15, 1869; San Francisco *Occidental and Vanguard*, July 5, 1867.

22. Speer to Lowrie, November 15, December 16, 1852; Loomis to Lowrie, November 18, 1859; March 1, June 25, 1860; April 17, 1862; June 29, 1863; *Correspondence of the Presbyterian Board for Foreign Missions*; San Francisco *Oriental*, January 11, April 28, May 26, 1855; San Francisco *Alta California*, July 8, August 11, 1851; June 16, October 1, 3, 1852; January 14, 16, 21, May 31, June 7, November 17, 18, 1853; August 22, October 14, 1854; April 5, 1856; June 19, 1859; January 24, August 16, 1860; August 23, 1864; August 17, 1867, and quoting Sonora *Union Democrat*, December 10, 1856; San Francisco *Herald*, July 28, October 9, 1851; June 9, 1852; January 13, May 28, 29, 1853; August 27, September 24, 1854; January 10, 1857; "Chinese Mercantile Operations [in San Francisco]," *Hunt's Merchants' Magazine*, XXXI (September, 1854), 391; Rev. J. C. Holbrook, "Chinadom in California. In Two Papers—Paper the First," *Hutchings' Illustrated California Magazine*, IV (September, 1859), 130; Frank Marryat, *Mountains and Molehills; or Recollections of a Burnt Journal* (New York, 1855), pp. 172, 299–300; Speer, *Oldest and Newest Empire*, pp. 554–557; Hemman Hoffmann, *Californien, Nevada und Mexico. Wanderungen* [March, 1864–June, 1867] *eines Polytechnikers* (Basel, 1879), p. 49; J[ames] O'Meara, "The Chinese in Early Days," *Overland Monthly*, III (2nd ser., May 1884), 480.

23. Harry Parkes, "General Remarks on Chinese Emigration," *British Parliamentary Papers, 1852–53*, LXVIII [263], 26.

24. Yan Pou Lee, *When I Was A Boy in China* (Boston, [1887]), pp. 96–97.

25. Russell & Co. to William Appleton, April 22, 1849; June 19, 1850, *Dexter MSS*; Appleton to George D. Carter, February 5, 1849, *Appleton MSS*, Baker Library, Harvard University; *U.S. House of Rep. Ex. Doc. 123*, 33 Cong., 1 Sess., pp. 83–85; *U.S. Senate Ex. Doc. 99*, 34 Cong., 1 Sess., pp. 102–103, 178–179; Adam W. Elmslie [British Consul at Canton] to Dr. John Bowring, August 25, 1852, *British Parliamentary Papers, 1852–53*, LXVIII [263], 7–8; "Journal of Occurrences: . . . emigration of Chinese to America . . ," *Chinese Repository* (Can-

ton), XIX (September, 1850), 510–511; San Francisco *Alta California*, February 17, March 29, June 12, 1852; September 8, 1856.

26. Kin Huie, *Reminiscences* (Peking, 1932), p. 12.

27. San Francisco *Alta California*, June 10, 14, 1850; June 29, 1852; San Francisco *Herald*, June 30, 1852; March 29, 1853.

28. For the shortest and the longest voyages of Chinese immigrants between Hong-kong and San Francisco, see San Francisco *Herald*, April 29, 30, 1853; San Francisco *Alta*, September 11, 1854; January 3, 1857. For the course turn to Thomas G. Cary, "Chinese in California—Clipper Ships," MS, Houghton Library, Harvard University, p. 14; San Francisco *Alta*, April 9, 1858; February 25, 1865; M[atthew] F. Maury, *Explanations and Sailing Instructions to Accompany the Wind and Current Charts* (Washington, D.C., 1851), p. 309; [Pacific Mail Steamship Co.], *A Sketch of the Route to California, China and Japan, via the Isthmus of Panama* (San Francisco, 1867), p. 95.

29. *China Mail*, April 29, 1852; October 14, 1854; July 2, 1857; August 23, 1864. Andrew Wilson, in the latter 1850's editor of the Hongkong *China Mail*, described his experiences with Chinese emigrants on a trip to California in a letter published in the *China Mail*, July 11, 1861. See also John Haskell Kemble (ed.), "Andrew Wilson's 'Jottings' on Civil War California," *California Historical Society Quarterly*, XXXII (September, 1953), 213–214.

30. Dr. John Bowring to the Earl of Malmesbury, May 17, 1852, *British Parliamentary Papers, 1852–53*, LXVIII [263], 2. For the disaster on the American ship *Robert Bowne*, to which Dr. Bowring referred, see *U.S. Senate Ex. Doc. 99*, 34 Cong., 1 Sess., pp. 119–165; Hongkong *Friend of China*, April 28, 1852; *China Mail*, April 29, 1852; *Hongkong Overland Register*, May 18, 1852; San Francisco *Herald*, June 28, 30, July 1, 20, August 15, October 19, 1852; San Francisco *Alta California*, June 29, July 20, 1852; Earl Swisher (ed.), *China's Management of the American Barbarians; A Study of Sino-American Relations, 1841–1861, with Documents* (New Haven, Conn., [1953]), pp. 199–203.

31. San Francisco *Alta California*, June 12, 1852; August 1, 1854; February 26, 1856; July 4, 1857; May 21, 1860; San Francisco *Herald*, July 4, 1854.

32. Loomis to Walter Lowrie, March 1, 1860, *Correspondence of the Presbyterian Board of Foreign Missions*; San Francisco *Alta California*, April 27, July 24, August 20, 22, 1851; February 26, March 14, 28, June 12, September 25, 1852; April 20, October 14, 1854; May 6, 1857; August 3, 1860; October 17, 1861; San Francisco *Herald*, May 17, June 26, August 20, 1851; April 11, 12, June 27, 1852; March 2, November 1, 1853; July 2, 6, 1857; San Francisco *Daily Evening News and Evening Picayune*, February 16, 1854; Huie, *Reminiscences*, p. 24.

Part V
Divided We Stand,
1865–1900

Divided We Stand, 1865–1900

During the decades following the Civil War, white Americans sought to mend the nation's sectional wounds. White reunion was accomplished, at least on a political level, and the country enjoyed a spectacular growth of industrialism accompanied by the rapid development of cities, urban problems, and strife between capital and labor. The advances in the quality of life which were secured by at least a part of the white society were withheld from the nonwhite minorities. In a capitalist society which found its theoretical justification in the doctrine of "survival of the fittest," nonwhites were ruthlessly exploited and cast aside as unfit for economic competition. An age dedicated to "hard-headed" notions of progress had little sympathy for underdogs and scorned proposals for social reform as "sentimentality." White racism was dignified by a cult of Anglo-Saxonism which assumed the inferiority of nonwhite peoples. For America's nonwhites these were bitter years which brought a new form of servitude to blacks, exclusion to the Chinese, and loss of land and culture to the Indians and Mexican-Americans.

The harsh realities of the postwar years made a mockery of the promise of freedom and equality to black Americans. The "radical reconstruction" of southern society proved to be superficial and ephemeral. The guarantees of equality in civil rights, including that of the ballot, were systematically eroded by the aggressive opposition of white southerners and the growing indifference of the federal government as epitomized by the withdrawal of federal troops from the South in 1877. State governments controlled by white "conservatives" enacted legislation which insured that blacks would remain politically and economically powerless. Most southern blacks became sharecroppers, enslaved in a new kind of debt bondage which tied them to the land. Even those who escaped to the cities were relegated to the least skilled and lowest paying jobs by a system of racially biased economic competition.

Competition between the races for jobs and wealth also helped to determine the fate of the Chinese-American in the late nineteenth century. The Burlingame Treaty of 1868 between the United States and China guaranteed the right of free migration between the two countries, but as larger numbers of Orientals entered the United States, prejudice against them grew among whites. Excoriation of their contract labor system as a new form of slavery, bitterness toward their strikebreaking activities, envy of their economic success, and contempt for their culture made the Chinese the target of racist politics in California which soon spread to the rest of the nation. By 1876, both national parties had taken a stand against the Orientals, and in 1882 the political agitation produced the first of a series of laws which effectively excluded further Chinese immigration until 1943.

Following the Civil War, the United States army turned its attention from the defeated South to the Great Plains where the American Indian was making his last stand in defense of his traditional way of life. During the 1870s scattered tribes of Kiowas, Comanches, Arapahoes, Cheyennes, Sioux, Utes, Nez-Percés, and Modocs resisted the attempts of the government to confine them to reservations, but the cavalry, assisted by such technological aids as railroads and Gatling guns, eventually eliminated all opposition. Indian submission constituted a surrender of land and culture. The government's Indian program envisoned the "civilizing" of the red man, a concept which involved the substitution of Christianity for native religions, of private property for communal life, and of white values for red heritage. Idealistic in its conception, white America's program was a disaster for the red man. Under the Dawes Severalty Act of 1887, Indians were forced to accept the allotment of small farms from the government, a process which brought forth an amazing display of white chicanery and resulted in the red man's loss of almost all his useful land. Programs of education and Christianization accomplished little more than the degradation of Indian culture. In effect, white victory over the American Indian presaged the virtual destruction of a people.

Mexican-Americans also found themselves struggling against overwhelming odds for their survival as a people. The inhabitants of the lands taken from Mexico in 1848 were the victims of white progress. In the years after the Civil War, white Americans poured westward into the states of Texas and California and the Colorado, New Mexico, and Arizona territories. Vicious racial hatred and armed conflict marked the relationship between whites and Mexican-Americans as the latter struggled, often unsuccessfully, to preserve their land, culture, and political rights. Even in New Mexico, where the Mexican-Americans remained a majority during the nineteenth century, the white newcomers successfully manipulated the political machinery of the territory for their own advantage.

At the end of the nineteenth century, Theodore Roosevelt sang the praises of Anglo-Saxon Americans for their victory over Spain, noting that "in every instance ... expansion has taken place because the race was a great race," while popular novelist Jack London wrote disparagingly of, "dark pigmented things, the half castes, the mongrel bloods, and the dregs of long conquered races." The jubilation over the nation's coming of age as an international power was a celebration of white power. The nation's nonwhite minorities, routed and despised, were barred from the hopeful exultation with which white America looked to the new century.

Ralph K. Andrist,
"Ghost Dance and Gatling Guns"

The end of the Civil War signaled the closing chapter in the history
of intermittent warfare which marked the relationship between
whites and Indians in the United States. The last Indian resistance
to the steady loss of land and the ravaging of their culture transpired
during the 1880s on the Great Plains. In "Ghost Dance and
Gatling Guns," Ralph K. Andrist recounts the final Indian uprising,
that of the Sioux in the Dakota Territory. Driven to desperation
by the deceitful practices of the United States government, some
of the Sioux sought to renew their strength through the mystical
ghost dance religion. Attempts to prohibit ghost dancing led to
a series of minor hostilities between Sioux warriors and the United
States cavalry. The shameful episode ended with the massacre of
almost three hundred Indians, the majority of them women
and children, at Wounded Knee in 1890. The "battle" of Wounded
Knee, which occurred in the same year that the Census Bureau
announced the disappearance of the frontier, stands as a tragic
symbol of the final Indian capitulation to the superior armed
force of the white society.

Ghost Dance and Gatling Guns
Ralph K. Andrist

...Civilization was blotting out the last remnants of the old ways of life everywhere in the West, and in few places more thoroughly than on the Great Plains. There were still great spaces where a man could raise his eyes and still see nothing but grass and horizon— there are even today, although one must search well to find them— but with each passing year the open plain was giving way to cattle herds, sod shanties, plowed fields, and the sky-pointing towers of windmills.

Nothing did more to break up the open character of the plains than barbed wire. Fencing had been one of the unsolvable problems of living in a treeless country until Joseph F. Glidden of De Kalb, Illinois devised a wire fence with barbs for use around his own farm. It worked so well he started a small factory in 1874 with five boys stringing barbs on wires; by 1880 he had a huge factory in De Kalb with 202 machines turning out 600 miles of fencing every ten hours. As fast as it was produced, this barbed wire was being strung over land where herds of buffalo had grazed less than ten years before....

Abridged from "Ghost Dance and Gatling Guns," pp. 330–354. Reprinted with permission of the Macmillan Company from *The Long Death: The Last Days of the Plains Indians* by Ralph K. Andrist. Copyright © 1964 by Ralph K. Andrist.

The last remnant of the great, brown living blanket that had once grazed the plains from Canada to Texas was now concentrated in Montana, and, to a lesser extent, in northwestern Dakota Territory. And there the professional hunters went to work with a skill that had been drawn fine with several years of practice. The grass to the north of the herd was burned over to discourage the beasts from migrating northward into Canada. The buffalo, surrounded on all sides, were helpless before the hunters, whose equipment now included telescopic sights. A hunter could lie, with his gun on a good rest, and wipe out a small herd from a distance; all he had to do was to keep knocking down the animal that became nervous and tried to lead the herd away.

The northern herd was much smaller than the huge masses of buffalo that had ranged in the south. It melted away under the guns of experts who seldom wasted a shot or spoiled a hide; the clumsy amateurs of the early days in Kansas who wasted more than they marketed were missing. "I saw buffaloes lying dead on the prairie so thick that one could hardly see the ground," a hunter described the scene created by the industrious killers along the Little Missouri in the winter of 1881–82. "A man could have walked for twenty miles upon their carcasses." ...

There had been a time when it was an article of faith that the civilizing of the Plains Indians would follow close on the annihilation of the buffalo—and a civilized Indian was universally understood to mean one who had given up everything of his own culture and had become an imitation white man. Once the buffalo were gone, it had been believed, the Indian would be forced to give up his roaming ways and settle down to feed and clothe himself by the sweat of his brow as a farmer, a herdsman, or a laborer. There were a couple of things wrong with this theory. One was that the former nomadic tribes had no experience in farming, and although the government promised implements, seeds, and instruction every time a treaty was made, it produced precious little that was tangible.

What was even more to the point was that almost all tribes, former farming peoples from the east and from the tall-grass prairie as well as the one-time horse-and-buffalo tribes, had been put on land that could by no means be called the best. Dohesan, a Kiowa chief, remarked acidly that if the President was so eager to have Indians raise corn, he should have given them land that would grow corn.

But even yet the land greed of the settlers was not satisfied. The biggest prize remaining was Indian Territory, the last piece of the old and forgotten permanent Indian Country. In the beginning, it had been the land of the Five Civilized Tribes until the government had taken the western half away from them on the thin pretext that it was punishing them for treason during the Civil War; the vacated western part was used as a dumping ground for unwanted tribes that were in the way of the tide of settlement elsewhere.... However, after the other tribes had been brought in, a large tract of land in the center of Indian Territory remained empty. These "Unassigned Lands" began to be irresistible to settlers as early as 1879, and organizations of land-seekers, who came to be called "Boomers," persistently moved in and were ejected by troops. When they transferred their efforts to Washington and began speaking the loud, clear language of votes, Congress listened and soon opened the Unassigned Lands to white settlement. The result was one of the most fantastic episodes in American history, when a pistol shot at high noon on April 22, 1889 set off tens of thousands of men and a good number of women from the Kansas border by wagon, horseback, railroad train (a line ran south through the lands), and even on foot to stake out claims.

Before night, the entire Unassigned Lands, almost two million acres, had been claimed and entire cities had been platted. Once the camel's head was in the tent, the rest of the beast quickly followed. The next year, the entire western half of Indian Territory, along with the Panhandle to the west, which was part of no state or territory, was organized into the Territory of Oklahoma. The Indian reservations were sold during the next several years and the land opened to settlers some of it by land rushes, some by lotteries. The eastern half of the former Indian Territory, the lands of the Five Civilized Tribes, continued to bear the old name for a few years more. Then the tribes, although they were operating as strong, effective nations with their laws and governments, were coerced into giving up their free existence. The result was the extinguishment of the last part of Indian Territory, which was merged with Oklahoma Territory.

...A great deal of other Indian land was taken in smaller bites, a nibbling away by "adjusting" reservation boundaries. Scores of such changes were made during the decade of the 1880's by simple presidential decree. Some of these adjustments, let the truth be said, were for increased efficiency in administration and two or three did correct minor injustices, but most of them seemed to end up leaving the Indians with less territory, or edging them onto land that was more rocky, sandy, or hilly.

There were few ways in which these were good years for Indians. Hunger was often with them; deprived of most ways of obtaining their own food, they had to depend overmuch on the annuities that were usually late in arriving and short in amount. Children were often virtually kidnaped to be sent away to boarding school, or sometimes rations were withheld from parents who refused to let their youngsters be taken. Disease was prevalent, fostered by malnutrition and exposure. Even the fact of being an Indian was a cause for shame as both agents and missionaries often tried to root out symbols of the old culture: tribal dances, Indian clothing, even the traditional way the men wore their hair.

In a time of misery and hopelessness, people who can see no way out of their troubles and woes are prone to look to some higher power for help, and the voice that now spoke to the unhappy Indians came from Nevada, from a messiah named Wovoka. This young man—he was about thirty-five—was a Paiute; he had never been outside the narrow limits of mountain-girt Mason Valley (about fifty miles southeast of Reno). When his father died when he was a young boy, he had been taken in by the family of a rancher named Dave Wilson, and so had come to be called Jack Wilson by all the whites in the valley (he had, several years before becoming famous, adopted the name of his grandfather, Kwohitsauq or "Big Rumbling Belly," which is undoubtedly a perfectly good Paiute name, but mercifully did not replace his boyhood name, Wovoka or "Cutter," in general use).

Wovoka received his inspiration from on high in 1888 during an eclipse which occurred while he was ill with a severe fever. The event, which he considered supernatural—"the sun died"—had a powerful effect on a mind disordered by fever. He was taken up into heaven where he not only saw God in a long white robe but all the people who had died in the past, now forever young and happy and engaged in their old sports and pursuits. God directed Wovoka to go back and teach his people to put aside war and love each other, and that they must also live in peace with the white men.

But the heart of the revelations was that the earth was to be regenerated and returned to the Indians, including all the dead of the past who would come back in all the beauty and strength of their youth. The Indians were given a special ceremonial dance, which required five successive nights to complete; the oftener they performed the dance, the more they would hasten the coming of the millennial future.

Wovoka, whose beliefs were a strange blend of Indian religion and the Christian theology he had learned from the Wilson family, apparently never claimed to be other than a prophet, although he had received certain small powers from God, such as songs by which he could produce fog, snow, a shower or a hard rain, or sunshine (once he had offered, for an annual fee, to keep Nevada supplied with rain but was ignored, a short-sighted act by a state which can use a great deal more precipitation). But rain-making and such were minor matters; it was the vision of the return of the Indians' old days of glory that won him his following as soon as he began preaching his doctrine. His own people, the Paiutes, danced, and soon Paiutes went out as missionaries to spread the new gospel to the tribes beyond the mountain valleys.

And the tribes, in their unhappiness, listened eagerly, because here was exactly what they wanted to hear. The Arapahoes and Cheyennes, both northern and southern, the Bannocks, Sioux, Shoshones, Utes and other tribes sent delegates to talk to the messiah; they returned full of wonders to start the dance—which the whites had named the Ghost Dance because it was to help bring back the dead—among their own tribesmen.

The Ghost Dance religion spread over most of the West, with the exception of the Columbia River country and much of the Southwest. Each tribe practiced it with its own variations, just as there are differences of liturgy among Christian denominations, but all believed in the same basic thing: the world made young again and returned to the Indians, with the dead come back to enjoy the good life. As they danced to bring the new day nearer, the excess of their emotions sent many of them into trances in which they saw visions—and this appears to be much of the hold it had over many of them, almost like a narcotic—and from their visions they built most of the simple, chanting songs which they used in subsequent dances....

There was one place where the Ghost Dance did take on a slight martial note. Among the Sioux, where the new religion happened to coincide with a number of causes of unrest, "Ghost shirts" magically impervious to white men's bullets were worn, at first only in the dance, but later beneath the outer garments at other times.

The catalogue of misery and despair of the Sioux had grown very long by 1890. There was of course, the passing of the buffalo and the growing scarcity of deer and other game which deprived them of food and clothing, and except for what the poor land of their reservation would produce, put them at the mercy of government annuities. Then, only the year before, they had been separated from more of their land. About one-third of the Great Sioux Reservation had been lost when the Black Hills and adjacent regions were taken from the Indians during the Sioux War. A few years later, settlers in the Black Hills were demanding a corridor to eastern Dakota so they would not have to cross the reservation. They finally got their passage in 1889; it carved out the heart of the remaining reservation, cutting it in two and taking half its area, an opening sixty miles wide—no danger of rubbing elbows against Indian land on either side as they went down that alleyway. The remaining land was divided into five reservations.

The Sioux had been assured they would continue to receive the same rations after giving up so much of their lands, but immediately after the agreement had been approved, Congress cut the beef ration by 2,000,000 pounds at Rosebud Reservation, by 1,000,000 pounds at Pine Ridge, and by lesser amounts at the other three reservations. When the agent at Pine Ridge informed the Indian Bureau in April, 1890 that the monthly beef issue was only 205,000 pounds when agreements with the Sioux called for 470,400, he received the helpful answer that it was better to give half rations all year than to give three-quarters or full rations for a few months and none for the rest of the year. However, this was one case where the Indian Office was not much to blame. The fault rested with Congress which then, as ever, economized in the wrong places.

In both 1889 and 1890, severe outbreaks of measles, influenza, and whooping cough caused many deaths. Agency physicians blamed the high death rate on the poor physical condition of the Indians due to hunger. Whatever the cause, it greatly increased the mood of gloom and hopelessness affecting the Sioux. So did poor harvests and drought.

Into this unhappy situation, in March of 1890, came a group of returning Sioux who had been sent the previous autumn to visit the messiah and learn about the new religion. The stories they brought back were wonderful indeed. Wovoka had come to earth in a cloud of smoke to talk to them, and had shown them nail marks on his hands and feet; the very next spring he was going to wipe out the white men for being so wicked to him at his first coming to earth. When they were returning home, they had come on an encampment of the dead of their tribe and had visited with old friends for some time. On continuing their journey, they found a herd of buffalo (these buffalo had apparently returned from the dead for the occasion, too), and had killed one and feasted on its meat; head, hoofs, and tail were left lying as Wovoka had instructed them, and as they walked off, had reassembled into a new buffalo. This appears to be the most outrageous kind of fabrication, but many visitors to Wovoka came back with tales no less fantastic; apparently in their extremely suggestible state of mind the difference between reality and illusion all but disappeared....

But while the Ghost Dance religion was promising a glorious hereafter, the present was looking more and more grim. Agent Gallagher, who had earlier written the Indian Bureau that his charges at Pine Ridge were getting less than half the beef they were supposed to, was writing more letters as the summer wore on, reporting that the Indians were suffering from hunger. The Bureau received warnings from other sources as well that the Sioux were becoming increasingly restive, but no more food arrived, and in the summer the Pine Ridge Indians rebelled and refused to accept the half-ration. They eventually took it—they had not much choice—but Gallagher decided his job was a hopeless one and resigned.

He was replaced in early October by one D. F. Royer. Few men less qualified have held the post, even in a service known for the general sorry level of its appointees. He was described as "destitute of any of those qualities by which he could justly lay claim to the position— experience, force of character, courage and sound judgment." The Indians quickly took his measure and dubbed him Lakota Kokipa-Koshkala, "Young-man-afraid-of-the-Sioux." From the first he had no control over his Indians; before he had been there a week he had stood by helplessly while a handful of them had released a prisoner from the jail. Before two weeks were up he was reporting that more than half his six thousand Indians were dancing, and that he was afraid troops would be needed because the situation was entirely beyond the control of the Indian police at his disposal.

The Sioux were dancing at the other four reservations, too, but the agents there, better endowed than Royer with judgment and courage, remained calm and tried to stop the dancing, though with only partial success. The fervor with which the Sioux were accepting the Ghost Dance religion was a measure of their need of it.

Agent Royer became more and more frightened by the strange chanting and dancing going on a few miles from his agency. He wrote to the Indian Bureau on October 30, saying that the situation could be saved only by the arrival of six hundred or seven hundred troops; within a week he was sending daily telegrams asking for permission to come to Washington to explain, but was told that the place of an agent during a crisis was at his post. At last, on November 15, he was directed to report the situation to the commander of Fort Robinson in northern Nebraska, the nearest Army post. Royer, by now in a state of near-panic, had sent off a message saying that the Sioux were wild and out of their heads, and that at least a thousand soldiers were needed to cope with the situation. But Royer was not speaking completely from hysteria, for the agent at adjoining Rosebud Reservation reported that his Indians were so engrossed in their dancing as to be beyond the control of himself and his police.

The old formality was observed, of transferring jurisdiction over the Sioux from the Interior to the War Department. The Army at once began moving units into the region, most of them into the area around the Pine Ridge agency, until within a matter of days it had almost three thousand men in the field. On the appearance of the troops, a large number of the Sioux, almost two thousand, living on Pine Ridge and Rosebud reservations fled to an area called the Bad Lands on the western edge of Pine Ridge, a place of hills, canyons, and weirdly eroded tablelands which provided a hiding place where an army might not find them. Within a short time, as more refugees joined them, their numbers increased to at least three thousand. The escaped Indians, some of them rebellious but most only frightened, were declared to be hostiles, although the last thing most of them wanted was to engage in hostilities with Army forces. The movement to the Bad Lands had been almost entirely a stampede caused by panic at the appearance of the soldiers.

Things became quieter on the reservations with so many troops around. Most of the Ghost Dancing ended or was reduced to a much smaller scale; the main centers where it continued were at the camp of Sitting Bull on Grand River in Standing Rock reservation, northernmost of the five reserves, and at the camp of a chief named Big Foot on the Cheyenne River. The Indian Bureau, feeling that it should get some use out of all the troops on hand, asked its agents to submit lists of trouble-makers who should be arrested and removed, with the help of the military if necessary. Among them, four of the agents produced a total of about fifteen names. The fifth agent was Royer; all by himself he came up with a list of sixty-four which was a "conservative estimate" and to which no one paid any attention.

As it turned out, most of the men honored by being included on the list were in the Bad Lands at the moment, but the one considered the most potentially dangerous of them all, Sitting Bull, was within easy reach. There is not much doubt that the great medicine man was a center of mischief during most of the time since he had reached the agreement with the government that had let him return from Canada in 1881. Except for joining Buffalo Bill Cody's Wild West show for a season and touring the country, he had remained on or near the reservation, brooding on the past and feeding his hate of white men. Toward the last he refused even to come in to the agency. He was a matter of concern to the authorities because he was a rallying point for all conservative and dissident elements among the Sioux. When the Army took control of the Sioux reservations, it moved quickly to arrest the famous medicine man, and as its deputy it called on William F. Cody. It was believed that Cody had a great deal of influence over Sitting Bull, supposedly the result of friendship engendered by shared experiences in show business, and he was given authority to reach surrender terms with the Sioux leader or, failing that, to arrest him and bring him in by force. Cody arrived at Fort Yates on November 28, but the scheme was called off when Agent James McLaughlin of Standing Rock heard of it and urgently protested.

Wait until the weather got colder, said McLaughlin. Then Sitting Bull and his band would not be so likely to bolt and join the hostiles in the Bad Lands. McLaughlin also felt that the arrest should be made by his own Indian police, who were trained, dependable men, and not as liable to arouse opposition as white soldiers. The agent got his way; the arrest was deferred until December 12 when orders came to Colonel Drum commanding Fort Yates to make arrangements with

McLaughlin to take Sitting Bull in. The two decided to arrest the famous chief on the twentieth, when most of the Indians would be at the agency collecting their annuities and Sitting Bull would have few potential defenders.

But on the afternoon of the fourteenth, a messenger came from the Indian school near Sitting Bull's camp, saying that Sitting Bull had just received an invitation to come to Pine Ridge because God was about to appear there. The medicine man was even then making preparations for the trip, the informant said.

It was then sundown, but McLaughlin and Colonel Drum made plans to arrest Sitting Bull the next morning. The agent already had police watching the Sioux leader's camp; more were assembled by hard-riding couriers until forty-three men, under the command of Lieutenant Bull Head, approached the camp at daybreak. Two troops of cavalry, about one hundred men, with a Hotchkiss gun (a rapid-fire gun that shot two-inch explosive shells), rode more than thirty miles from the fort during the night to be within supporting distance of the police.

Indian police had been first authorized by Congress in 1878, and eventually they were used on a majority of reservations, although to varying extents. Those on the Sioux reservation were, in general, well-trained men with excellent morale. But Agent McLaughlin had miscalculated in thinking that an arrest by them would be less offensive to Sitting Bull than one by white soldiers. For the police represented the most progressive element among the Sioux, those who had accepted the white man's way completely. Sitting Bull and those around him were the most conservative element; the medicine man himself was an apostle of the good old days and looked with scorn on all Indians who cooperated with the white authorities.

At dawn on December 15, these two opposed forces confronted each other. The police surrounded Sitting Bull's house; then Lieutenant Bull Head and several others entered to find the prophet asleep on the floor. When he was awakened and told he was a prisoner, Sitting Bull agreed rather mildly to go with them to the agency, but as his followers began to gather outside, calling on him to resist, he started to berate the police for breaking into his house and waking him. When his seventeen-year-old son, Crow Foot, taunted him as a coward, he abruptly refused to go, and called on his people to rescue him.

By that time, the police outside had been backed up against the house wall by more than a hundred threatening men, and as Sitting Bull was brought outside and the police attempted to clear a path, one of the followers shot Bull Head in the side. The police lieutenant was walking beside Sitting Bull; as he sagged, mortally wounded, he turned and shot the Sioux Chief in the side as another policeman, Red Tomahawk, behind Sitting Bull, shot the leader through the head. The entire situation exploded into a deadly, close-quarter combat, in which the training of the police more than made up for the difference in numbers. They drove their attackers off and held the house until the cavalry came up to their relief about two hours later.

Six policemen were killed or fatally wounded, while their assailants lost eight, including Sitting Bull and his son, Crow Foot. Sitting Bull died in his fifty-sixth year, a great man, not only a valiant fighting leader, but a famous prophet and medicine man. In the end, however, the gift of prophesy faded; during his last years his visions were increasingly of the past. . . .

Except for the few military units engaged in controlling potential trouble-makers in the north, the great body of troops was operating against the Indians in the Bad Lands. Almost three thousand of them were there, under the immediate command of General John R. Brooke, although General Miles was in over-all command. It was the general strategy of the two men to avoid bloodshed if at all possible, and Brooke had thrown a strong wall of troops to the north and west of the hostiles' stronghold. With these he maintained a steady pressure which gradually forced the Indians toward the east and Pine Ridge agency.

Most of the Indians were weary and cold and ready to give up anyway; some of them never had had any real chip on their shoulder but had fled only from fear. Along with military pressure, General Brooke got word to the Indians that he would protect their rights as far as he was able, and this helped swing the balance toward surrender, even though the Sioux had scant faith left in the government. The hostiles began moving in, and on December 27, the entire body left the Bad Lands to go to the agency. There had not been a single battle except for a fight between hostiles and Cheyenne scouts; the only engagements between troops and Sioux were two or three very minor skirmishes. But the book had not yet been closed on the uprising, if such it can be called.

Big Foot and his people, fleeing south, had nothing on their minds except to get away from soldiers. They passed very near several ranches without committing any depredations, and once went directly through a pasture without taking even one of the horses or cattle there. At the edge of the Bad Lands, they sent scouts to make contact with the Indians camped in the stronghold, but no answers were received to their signals for the hostiles had already gone and were on their way to the agency. It was then, on December 28, as the band was proceeding along the edge of the Bad Lands, that it was intercepted by Major S. M. Whitside with four troops of the 7th Cavalry, about two hundred men.

Big foot was ill, too sick with pneumonia to ride on a horse, and was being carried on a travois. He got to his feet, had a white flag raised, and asked for a parley. Whitside refused, insisting on nothing other than unconditional surrender, and the Sioux chief, with only about one hundred cold and hungry warriors, was in no position to resist even if he had been of a mind to. The band was conducted by the cavalry to a place called Wounded Knee which was only a post office and a few scattered Indian houses near Wounded Knee Creek. There they went into camp as directed by Major Whitside, while the cavalry set up its tents nearby.

General Brooke, when informed of the capture, sent Colonel George A. Forsyth, commander of the 7th Cavalry, with four more troops of the regiment to reinforce the guard around the Sioux. A company of scouts also joined the guard, and a battery of four Hotchkiss guns, making a total of 470 men to keep a watch over about 340 Indians, of whom only 106 were warriors. . . .

The next morning, December 29, Forsyth made ready to disarm the Sioux. Their lodges had been set up on a flat piece of ground a short distance west of Wounded Knee Creek, which there flows approximately north. Just south of the tepees, a dry ravine running from west to east opens into the creek; to the north of the camp was a slight hill on which the four Hotchkiss guns were posted, and trained directly on the camp. On all sides of the camp, soldiers were stationed, both mounted and on foot. The Sioux had hoisted a white flag in the center of their camp as an indication of their peaceful intentions and a guarantee of safety.

At about eight o'clock the warriors came out of their lodges and sat on the ground in a semicircle. They were instructed to go, about a score at a time, into their tepees, and return with their weapons. The first twenty went, and came back with only two guns. The officers conferred. It was plain that this method was not going to produce the guns. Troops stationed by the council ring were ordered to move up to within ten yards of the seated warriors, and other enlisted men were detailed to search the tepees. It is exactly at this point that the situation began to get out of hand—and it is hard not to blame Forsyth, who approved the action, for letting it get out of control.

The soldiers acted like bully-boys, overturning beds and other lodge furnishings, shoving aside the women who protested loudly and tried to bar their way. The Sioux men were becoming greatly agitated at the sounds of strife from their tepees and the voices of their women, especially since they did not know what was going on. Most of them had knives under their blankets, and were approaching a state of mind when they were ready to use them. In the midst of this tense situation, a medicine man, Yellow Bird, walked about, blowing an eagle-bone whistle, and calling on the men to resist because, as he reminded them, they were invulnerable to bullets because of the Ghost shirts they wore. The officers did not understand Sioux; the dangerous trend of Yellow Bird's exhortations passed them by.

The search was completed and produced about forty guns, most of them antiquated and worn pieces. But one weapon they did not find, for the good reason that it was being carried under his blanket by a young Indian, name unknown but probably Black Fox, who was described by a Sioux witness to the event, later testifying in Washington, as "a crazy man, a young man of very bad influence and in fact a nobody. . . ." But for a brief moment he was a very important somebody as he pulled out the gun and fired into the line of soldiers, killing one of them.

The line of troops replied instantly with a volley at point-blank range, killing possibly as many as half the warriors. The rest of the Sioux men threw off their blankets and drew their knives or, in some cases, pulled out old-fashioned war clubs, and grappled with the soldiers in hand-to-hand fighting. At almost the same instant, the Hotchkiss guns on the hills opened fire on the camp, pouring their two-inch explosive shells at the rate of nearly fifty a minute into the women and children gathered there. This, too, must be weighed when the question of whether Forsyth showed good judgment is considered.

Afterward, it was pointed out in his defense that he had separated women and children from warriors during the search for arms, to prevent just such a thing as did occur. Nevertheless, the Hotchkiss guns on the hill were trained from the beginning on the camp where there were women and children only, and if Forsyth did not know this, he should have.

The murderous fire was augmented by the weapons of the outer cordon of troops who surrounded the entire camp; they began shooting, killing many Indians who attempted to flee. Within a matter of minutes, some two hundred Indians and sixty soldiers lay dead or wounded, and many of the tepees had been ripped apart by explosive shells and were burning above helpless wounded. A good number of the soldier casualties appear to have been victims of their own comrades' bullets since troops were firing from four sides with rather blind enthusiasm.

The 7th Cavalry had a splendid record, but all witnesses agree that from the moment it opened fire, it ceased to be a military unit and became a mass of infuriated men intent only on butchery. Women and children attempted to escape by running up the dry ravine, but were pursued and slaughtered—there is no other word—by hundreds of maddened soldiers, while shells from the Hotchkiss guns, which had been moved to permit them to sweep the ravine, continued to burst among them. The line of bodies was afterward found to extend for more than two miles from the camp—and they were all women and children. A few survivors eventually found shelter in brushy gullies here and there, and their pursuers had scouts call out that women and children could come out of their hiding place because they had nothing to fear (one wonders how these Sioux scouts could have found the stomach to stay at their work); some small boys crept out and were surrounded by soldiers who then butchered them. Nothing Indian that lived was safe; the four-year-old son of Yellow Bird, the medicine man, was playing with his pony when the shooting began. "My father ran and fell down and the blood came out of his mouth," he said, "and then a soldier put his gun up to my white pony's nose and shot him, and then I ran and a policeman got me." . . .

No one knows how many Indians died on that miserable field, because by the time anyone could count the bodies, some had already been removed. But the number was very close to three hundred, about two-thirds of them women and children. The sound of the firing had been heard very clearly at Pine Ridge agency, almost twenty miles away, and in time survivors reached the agency with their stories and their wounds. Some of the Indians who had come in from the Bad Lands to surrender rode out to Wounded Knee, where they found the troops scattered about the field, hunting down the few refugees. The Sioux attacked the cavalrymen, driving them in toward the center, where the troopers collected their dead and wounded, as well as about fifty Indian prisoners, almost all wounded, and then marched through to the agency....

The effect of the massacre on other Indians was immediate. Those camped at Pine Ridge agency, who had just come in from the Bad Lands to surrender, went hostile again. They attacked the agency itself, they attacked small troop detachments and wagon trains, and they killed one unfortunate herder near the agency who thereby gained the distinction of being the one white civilian slain in all the uprising. These Indians, even with the provocations they had, had somehow lost the will to fight after so many years of going down bloody for lost causes. Their attacks were half-hearted, and after their first anger had burned out, many of them began looking for ways to break away from the main hostile band.

General Miles moved his headquarters to Pine Ridge agency, and followed his former strategy of trying to avoid armed clashes; a cordon of troops was thrown around the hostiles again, and they were nudged and pushed toward the agency. It was over, for good and all, on January 16, 1891, when the hostiles surrendered. General Miles had them set up their tepees, 724 in all, just west of the agency, and from the Army's commissary supplies he issued beef, coffee, and sugar. It was their first full meal in several weeks.

So, abruptly, the history of the Indian wars of the West ends around cooking fires with hungry Sioux gnawing on ribs of grass-fed beef. There is very little epilogue. The Ghost Dance died at Wounded Knee, as far as the Sioux were concerned. When the Ghost shirts proved as impotent as everything else they had ever put their faith in, they quickly dropped the entire religion of the Ghost Dance. Skepticism proved to be as contagious as the first enthusiasm, and other tribes throughout the West soon followed suit. Although some tribes continued to dance for a year or two, final disillusionment set in when the bright world peopled by friends from the past and covered with restored buffalo herds did not appear as Wovoka had promised. The dance became a game for children, where it was remembered at all. There was never any more fighting by Indians after the uprising on the Sioux reservations. The strength of the tribes everywhere was gone. They were broken up; apathy, hopelessness, hunger, and disease became their constant companions. Nor had the rapacity of their white neighbors lessened, for they have since lost three-fifths of the land they still possessed shortly before Wounded Knee—and what they have managed to keep is largely sand or rock that no white man has considered worth taking from them.

It is not completely coincidence that the Sioux who fell at Wounded Knee died at the close of the same year in which the Superintendent of the Census announced that the frontier, until then a dominant fact of American life, had ceased to exist. The Indian of the Old West was a creature of the other side of the frontier, the dwindling side, and when it finally pinched out, there was no place left for him. He became in truth the Vanishing American, and it was a long time before any bright spots began to appear on his future. There still are not anywhere near enough of them.

But that is another story entirely. This one began on the Great Plains, when uncounted buffalo grazed over grass that had never been marked by wagon wheels, where the great tribes fought and hunted, secure in their own strength. It has ended, after many years, broken promises, and tragedies, at the edge of a mass grave in Dakota. Indians have gone down many paths to defeat, along many ways filled with pain and heartbreak, but none so much so as this long, last trail.

John Hope Franklin,
"History of Racial Segregation in the United States"

The Civil War brought a legal end to the institution of slavery in the United States. The Emancipation Proclamation, the Thirteenth, Fourteenth, and Fifteenth Amendments, and the Civil Rights Act of 1875 seemed to promise a status of equality under the law to all Americans. Yet the steady refusal of the white majority to recognize the principle of legal equality made a hollow mockery of the constitutional protections provided for black Americans. Supreme Court decisions, economic pressures, and violence were used by the white majority to relegate the black minority to second class citizenship. State legislation enforcing discriminatory treatment of black citizens, particularly in the South, was also an important part of the process. In the following article, John Hope Franklin, a distinguished black historian, traces the "History of Racial Segregation in the United States." He demonstrates that during the late nineteenth and early twentieth centuries, southern state legislatures borrowed from practices defining the status of free blacks in the antebellum period and created a system of racial apartheid which prohibited contact between blacks and whites.

208

History of Racial Segregation in the United States

John Hope Franklin

The enactment of state segregation statutes is a relatively recent phenomenon in the history of race relations in the United States. Of course there had been numerous segregation practices and some segregation statutes for many years, even before the nineteenth century. But it was not until the final quarter of the nineteenth century that states began to evolve a systematic program of legally separating whites and Negroes in every possible area of activity. And it was not until the twentieth century that these laws became a major apparatus for keeping the Negro "in his place." They were both comprehensive and generally acceptable, because they received their inspiration from a persistent and tenacious assumption of the innate inferiority of the Negro and because they had their roots deep in the ante-bellum period.[1]

Abridged from John Hope Franklin, "History of Racial Segregation in the United States," *The Annals*, CCCIV (1956), pp. 1–9. Reprinted by permission of the author and The American Academy of Political and Social Science. Some footnotes have been renumbered.

1. For an illuminating discussion of the assumptions of the inferiority of the Negro see Guion Griffis Johnson, "The Ideology of White Supremacy, 1876–1910," in Fletcher M. Green (Ed.), *Essays in Southern History Presented to Joseph Grégoire de Roulhac Hamilton* (Chapel Hill: University of North Carolina Press, 1949), pp. 124–56.

For centuries many Northerners and Southerners subscribed to the view that Negroes were of a permanently inferior type. As slavery came to be concentrated in the Southern states and as that section became conspicuous by the tenacity with which it held on to slavery, it built its defenses of the institution along lines of the inferiority of the Negro. A whole body of thought was set forth to demonstrate that "the faculties of the Negro, as compared with those of the Saxon, qualified him for a state of servitude and made him unfit for the enjoyment of freedom."[2] Slavery was, therefore, the natural lot of the Negro; and any efforts to elevate him to the status of freedom and equality were manifestly in opposition to the laws of nature and of God.

The slaveholder's task of keeping the Negro slave in his place was complicated by the presence of several hundred thousand Negroes who were not slaves, although they can hardly be described as wholly free. So that they would not constitute a threat to the slave regime, free Negroes were denied the full rights and privileges of citizens. They enjoyed no equality in the courts, their right to assemble was denied, their movements were circumscribed, and education was withheld. Their miserable plight caused them to be unfavorably compared with slaves and confirmed the views of many that Negroes could not profit by freedom. They were regarded as the "very drones and pests of society," pariahs of the land, and an incubus on the body politic.

Outside the South free Negroes fared only slightly better. White Christians began to segregate them in the churches in the first decade of the national period, and Negroes in Philadelphia and New York City withdrew rather than accept this humiliation. As early as 1787 a white philanthropic organization opened a separate school for Negroes in New York City. In 1820 the city of Boston established a Negro elementary school. Separate schools became the practice throughout the North. When Charles Sumner challenged the constitutionality of segregated schools in Massachusetts in 1849, his posi-

2. William S. Jenkins, Pro-Slavery Thought in the Old South (Chapel Hill: University of North Carolina Press, 1935), p. 243. See also Albert T. Bledsoe, "Liberty and Slavery, or Slavery in the Light of Moral and Political Philosophy," and Samuel C. Cartwright, "Slavery in the Light of Ethnology," in E. N. Elliott, Cotton is King, and Pro-Slavery Arguments (Augusta, Ga.: Pritchard, Abbott and Loomis, 1860), pp. 271–458, 691–728.

tion was bitterly opposed; and it was not until 1855 that the legislature of that state abolished them. Meanwhile numerous acts of violence in urban communities underscored Northern hostility to free Negroes. Between 1830 and 1840 anti-Negro riots occurred in Utica, Palmyra, New York City, and Philadelphia.

These ante-bellum experiences with free Negroes proved invaluable in the period following the close of the Civil War. In 1865 white Southerners were not "caught short" in facing the problem of the freedmen. From their point of view the former slaves simply augmented the group of free Negroes that they already regarded as "the most ignorant . . . vicious, impoverished, and degraded population of this country."[3] Thus, the whites merely applied to the former slaves the principles and practices that had guided them in their relations with ante-bellum free Negroes. The latter had subsisted somewhere in the hazy zone between slavery and freedom. To concede the freedmen this "place" was regarded by white Southerners as generous, the Emancipation Proclamation and the Reconstruction amendments to the contrary notwithstanding. . . .

As the ex-Confederates proceeded to restore order in their war-torn communities, they took little cognizance of the implications of the Emancipation Proclamation and the proposed Thirteenth Amendment. The major assumptions of the slave regime, the cornerstone of which was the permanent inferiority of the Negro, were still so powerful as to be controlling in most matters involving Negroes. While making some concessions, such as the competency of Negroes to testify in the courts, they nullified almost every semblance of freedom with numerous proscriptive laws. Mississippi legislators passed laws forbidding Negroes to rent or lease lands except in incorporated towns. They also enacted a law requiring every Negro, after January 1, 1866, to carry on his person written evidence that he had a home and an occupation. Louisiana forbade Negroes to move about in certain parishes or to be out at night without special permits. North Carolina extended to the freedmen the same privileges, burdens, and disabilities that had previously applied to free persons of color.

That the races should be kept apart, except where the whites were clearly in a superior role, was an important feature of most codes.

3. From a statement by Howell Cobb, quoted in Jenkins, *ibid.* (note 2 supra), p. 246.

Louisiana required that every Negro be in the regular service of some white person who was held responsible for his conduct. Mississippi forbade employees of railroads to permit Negroes to ride in first-class cars with white persons, except in the case of Negroes or mulattoes, "traveling with their mistress, in the capacity of maids." Many states provided that if Negro offenders could not pay their fines they were to be hired out to "any white person" who would pay the fines and costs and take the convicts for the shortest period of time.

Negroes were not indifferent to the process by which their former masters and their associates were nullifying the gains of the war. While they displayed no spirit of vindictiveness against those who had held them in slavery, they manifested a firm determination to secure the rights to which they, as free men, were entitled.[4] The better educated and the more articulate among them assumed the leadership in expressing apprehension regarding the developments that were pushing them back toward slavery. They were especially concerned about the numerous acts of violence perpetrated against the freedmen, the burning of their schools and churches, and the economic proscriptions to which they were subjected. In Harrisburg, Pittsburgh, Indianapolis, and Cleveland they met in conventions and solicited the support of their Northern fellows in the effort to attain first-class citizenship. In Alexandria, Norfolk, Raleigh, Charleston, and other Southern communities they met, exchanged views, and addressed appeals to Southerners, Northerners, and federal officials. These supplications fell on deaf ears in the South, but they contributed to the increasing awareness elsewhere that the victory at Appomattox was empty.

The ex-Confederates looked upon the lenient Reconstruction policies of Lincoln and Johnson, which gave them virtual autonomy in every phase of life, as a normal concession to a section which was right on all the basic points in the dispute that led to the war. In the North, however, many people viewed the policy of leniency with skepticism from the outset; and congressional leaders made no secret of the fact that they regarded the resultant Presidential actions as unwise and improper, if not actually illegal. The first significant asser-

---

4. On the point of the absence of vindictiveness among Negroes see Francis B. Simkins, "New Viewpoints of Southern Reconstruction," *Journal of Southern History*, Vol. 5 (February 1939), pp. 49–61.

tion of their own prerogatives was the passage of the Freedmen's Bureau Bill in March 1865, which called for an extensive program of relief and rehabilitation in the South.

The Bureau's establishment of schools for the former slaves and its attempt to protect them in their relations with white employers were especially obnoxious to the white Southerners. They were loud in their condemnation of both these features of the Bureau's program, calling them incendiary, radical, and political. They realized all too well the adverse effect that a successful prosecution of the program would have on the continued subordination of Negroes. The attempts of whites to drive out teachers of Negroes and to assert their authority over their employees were well calculated to subvert the program of complete emancipation and to preserve the old relationships between Negroes and whites.

The findings of the Joint Committee on Reconstruction, established by Congress in 1865, convinced a majority of congressional members that federal intervention was necessary to salvage the victory over the South. The committee was of the opinion that there was in the South "no general disposition to place the colored race ... upon terms even of civil equality" and that no semblance of order could be maintained without the interposition of federal authority.[5] In accordance with the recommendation of the Joint Committee, Congress proceeded to enact a civil rights measure, to submit the Fourteenth Amendment to the states, and to pass a series of laws placing the reconstruction of the former Confederate states under congressional control.

The Civil Rights Act that became law on April 9, 1866, defined citizenship so as to include Negroes. Senator Lyman Trumbull of Illinois said that the purpose of the bill was to destroy the discrimination against the Negro in the laws of Southern states and to make effective the Thirteenth Amendment.[6] White Southerners were, of course, outraged that Congress should undertake to guarantee the equality of Negroes, especially since the law had been enacted in the absence of representatives from the former Confederate states. As

5. *Report of the Joint Committee on Reconstruction, at the First Session Thirtyninth Congress* (Washington: Government Printing Office, 1866), p. xvii.

6. Horace Edgar Flack, *The Adoption of the Fourteenth Amendment* (Baltimore, Md.: The Johns Hopkins Press, 1908), p. 21.

a matter of fact, fear that at some later date a majority of Congress or a federal court would strike down the Civil Rights Act was an important motivation for writing the provisions of the act into the Fourteenth Amendment.[7]

During the debates on the resolution that was to become the Fourteenth Amendment the question arose as to whether the proposed amendment protected Negroes against discrimination and segregation. There was no agreement, but proponents of the amendment were optimistic regarding its effect. In supporting the amendment, Senator Jacob M. Howard of Michigan said that the equal protection clause "abolishes all class legislation in the states and does away with the injustice of subjecting one caste of persons to a code not applicable to another." Representative John Bingham of Ohio declared that the amendment would protect "by national law the privileges and immunities of all the citizens of the Republic and the inborn rights of every person within its jurisdiction whenever the same shall be abridged or denied by the unconstitutional acts of any state."[8]

Neither the Fourteenth Amendment nor the radical legislation embodied in congressional Reconstruction was sufficient to protect the Negro in his political and civil rights. Southern resistance was stiff and effective, while efforts at enforcement left much to be desired. Once they recovered from the initial staggering blow of Radical Reconstruction legislation the ex-Confederates grimly went about the task of nullifying it in every possible way. By violence, intimidation, and ingenious schemes of economic pressure, by increased participation in political affairs, they began to "redeem" their state governments. Neither the Fifteenth Amendment nor the Ku Klux Klan Acts could stem the tide. In one state after another, between 1870 and 1877, they were successful; and as they took over the Southern state governments, they began to enact laws to separate Negroes and whites.

Congress, against the bitter opposition of the ex-Confederates who were taking over the seats the Radicals had occupied, made one final

7. Ibid., pp. 75–87, and Benjamin B. Kendrick, The Journal of the Joint Committee of Fifteen on Reconstruction (New York: Columbia University Press, 1914), pp. 267–69.

8. Congressional Globe, Thirty-ninth Congress, First Session (Washington: F. and J. Rivas, 1866), pp. 2459, 2766.

effort to prevent the destruction of the rights of Negroes. Between 1871 and 1875 it devoted much attention to various proposals for a comprehensive national civil rights bill. While the act that was passed in 1875 omitted the provision of earlier drafts requiring the admission of persons regardless of race to all public schools, it declared that all persons, regardless of race or color, should be entitled to the full and equal enjoyment of the accommodations, advantages, facilities, and privileges of inns, public conveyances, theaters, and other places of public amusement. In its scope and in its provisions for enforcement it far surpassed anything that had ever been done in the area of protecting the civil rights of Negroes.

Although the Southern whites viewed the Act of 1875 with utter contempt and violated it with impunity, they were not entirely comfortable so long as it was on the statute books. They found it impossible, therefore, to restrain their elation when the Supreme Court declared the act unconstitutional in 1883. When the decision was announced during a performance at the Atlanta Opera House, the audience broke into "such a thunder of applause . . . as was never before heard within the walls of the opera house."[9] An Arkansas newspaper expressed hearty agreement with the majority of the Court when it said, "Society is a law unto itself, which in matters social in their nature overrides the statutes. Against its decrees the written law is powerless."[10]

Before the momentous decision in the Civil Rights Cases in 1883 segregation by statutes was confined to a relatively few but highly important areas. In many states, for example, the laws against intermarriage preceded the Civil War by many years.[11] Although they were omitted from some state codes during Reconstruction, there was no wholesale repeal of them, and they remained in effect in many parts of the North as well as in the South.[12] The practice of maintaining separate schools for white and Negro children was well established in the North before the Civil War; and in the South if

9. Atlanta *Constitution*, October 16, 1883.

10. Little Rock *Daily Arkansas Gazette*, October 19, 1883.

11. Intermarriage was prohibited in Arkansas in 1838; in Louisiana in 1810. For a discussion of these statutes see Charles S. Mangum, *The Legal Status of the Negro* (Chapel Hill: University of North Carolina Press, 1940), pp. 236–73.

12. Gilbert Thomas Stephenson, *Race Distinctions in American Law* (New York: D. Appleton and Company, 1910), pp. 78–101.

ex-Confederates provided schools for Negro children at all they were of course separate. Although the Radicals made some attempts to break down segregated schools during their brief period of control, they met with little success.[13] In the military services Negroes had almost always been segregated, and the Civil War did much to strengthen the practice.

The decision in the Civil Rights Cases was an important stimulus to the enactment of segregation statutes. It gave the assurance the South wanted that the federal government would not intervene to protect the civil rights of Negroes. The decision coincided, moreover, with a series of political and intellectual developments that greatly accelerated the program of segregation. In the eighties several Southern governments were embarrassed by financial scandals, and some of them outstripped the Reconstruction governments in defalcations and pilfering.[14] Meanwhile, the agrarian unrest induced by widespread economic distress frightened the conservatives and forced them to adopt extreme measures in order to regain the leadership which in some states they had temporarily lost to white and Negro Populists. Distressed by the possibility of a strong new party composed of white and Negro farmers and workers, they dominated the Negro vote where they could and expressed grave fears of "Negro domination" where they could not. Thus, the magical formula of white supremacy, "applied without stint and without any of the old reservations of paternalism, without deference to any lingering resistance of Northern Liberalism, or any fear of further check from a defunct Southern Populism," gained ascendancy in the final decade of the nineteenth century.[15]

These were the years that witnessed the effective constitutional disfranchisement of Negroes by such devices as understanding clauses, grandfather clauses, and good conduct clauses. They also saw the

13. Francis B. Simkins and Robert H. Woody, *South Carolina During Reconstruction* (Chapel Hill: University of North Carolina Press, 1932), pp. 439–42, and T. Harry Williams, "The Louisiana Unification Movement of 1873," *Journal of Southern History*, Vol. 11 (August 1945), p. 362.

14. C. Vann Woodward, *Origins of the New South, 1877–1914* (Baton Rouge: Louisiana State University Press, 1951), pp. 67–70.

15. C. Vann Woodward, *The Strange Career of Jim Crow* (New York: Oxford University Press, 1955), p. 65.

launching of an intensive propaganda campaign of white supremacy, negrophobia, and race chauvinism, supported by a sensational and irresponsible press that carried lurid stories of alleged Negro bestiality. New waves of violence broke out, with increased lynchings of Negroes, unspeakable atrocities against them, and race riots. Concurrently, and at a "higher level," the literary and scientific leaders of the South wrote numerous tracts and books designed to "prove" the inhumanity of the Negro.[16] In this climate segregation took a giant step toward a fully developed white supremacy apparatus.

In the decade after the Civil War few laws were enacted demanding segregation. The first state segregation statutes were those of Mississippi and Florida in 1865, requiring segregation on public carriers. Texas followed in 1866, but five years later repealed the act. The Tennessee law of 1881, sometimes referred to as the first Jim Crow law, directed railroad companies to provide separate cars or portions of cars for first-class Negro passengers, instead of relegating them to second-class accommodations as had been the custom. There were only two votes against the measure in the House and one in the Senate.

In the ensuing twenty years separation of Negroes and whites on public carriers became a favorite preoccupation of Southern legislators. By 1892 six other Southern states had joined the ranks—Texas, Louisiana, Alabama, Arkansas, Georgia, and Kentucky. In some states, however, opposition had been bitter. In Louisiana, for example, a Negro representative declared that the law would humiliate Negroes and "make them appear before the world as a treacherous and a dangerous class of people."[17] In Arkansas a Negro member of the House sought to ridicule the bill's supporters by insisting that if whites did not want to associate with Negroes there should be laws to divide the streets and sidewalks so that Negroes could go on one side and white people on the other. "He would like to see an end put to

16. See the books by Thomas Dixon, notably *The Leopard's Spots: A Romance of the White Man's Burden—1865–1900* (New York: Doubleday, Page & Company, 1902); Charles Carroll, *"The Negro a Beast,"* or, *"In the Image of God"* ... (St. Louis, Mo.: American Book and Bible House, 1900); and Robert W. Shufeldt, *The Negro, A Menace to American Civilization* (Boston: R. G. Badger, 1907).

17. *Louisiana House Journal, Second Session, 1890,* pp. 202–203.

all intercourse between white and colored people by day, and especially by night."[18]

With the pattern firmly established in a number of Southern states and the pressure for segregation growing, the other Southern states followed before the end of the century. South Carolina passed its law segregating Negroes and whites on railroads in 1898; North Carolina, Virginia, and Maryland soon after. When Oklahoma entered the Union in 1907 segregation had already been provided for.

By this time laws were being extended to cover all activities related to transportation. In 1888 the railroad commission of Mississippi was authorized to designate separate waiting rooms for Negroes and whites. By 1893 the railroad companies, on their own initiative, were doing the same thing in South Carolina, and in 1906 the state required separation of the races in all station restaurants and eating houses. Ultimately, legislation covered steamboats, buses, and other forms of transportation.

The first decade of the twentieth century witnessed the enactment of a wide variety of segregation statutes. Georgia had required separation of the races on streetcars as early as 1891. It was between 1901 and 1907, however, that North Carolina, Virginia, Louisiana, Arkansas, South Carolina, Tennessee, Mississippi, Maryland, Florida, and Oklahoma followed suit. Ordinances in Southern cities were even more specific than state laws. In 1906, for example, the city of Montgomery, Alabama, went so far as to insist that Negroes and whites use separate streetcars.

As the states assumed greater responsibility for the various wards of society they were careful to provide separate facilities for whites and Negroes. In 1875 Alabama made it unlawful for any jailer or sheriff to imprison white and Negro prisoners before conviction in the same apartments of the jail, if there were sufficient separate apartments, and ten years later prohibited the chaining of white and Negro convicts together or housing them together. In 1903 Arkansas directed that in the state penitentiary and in county jails, stockades, convict camps, and all other places where prisoners were confined, separate apartments should be provided and maintained for white and Negro prisoners. Within the next ten years most of the other Southern states had similar legislation. During the same period segre-

18. Little Rock Arkansas Gazette, February 14, 1891.

gation of white and Negro insane, feeble-minded, blind and deaf, paupers, tubercular patients, and juvenile delinquents was provided for.

In rounding out the system of legal segregation some states provided for the separation of whites and Negroes at work, at play, and at home. In 1915 South Carolina forbade textile factories to permit employees of different races to work together in the same room, or to use the same entrances, pay windows, exits, doorways, stairways, or windows at the same time, or the same lavatories, toilets, drinking-water buckets, pails, cups, dippers, or glasses at any time. In 1905 Georgia passed a law making illegal the use by Negroes and whites of the same park facilities; individuals were permitted to donate land for playground use only if they specified which race alone was to make use of it. Until 1940 Negroes and whites in Atlanta, Georgia, were not permitted to visit the municipal zoo at the same time. In 1929 Oklahoma authorized the Conservation Commission to segregate the races in the use of fishing, boating, and bathing facilities on lakes and streams under the supervision of the state. Arkansas enacted a law in 1935 requiring the separation of Negroes and whites at all race tracks and gaming establishments. Beginning in 1910 several cities, among them Baltimore, Atlanta, and Louisville, passed ordinances designating certain blocks, territories, and districts as Negro or white and forbidding members of one race to live in the area assigned to the other. Such zoning laws, however, were declared unconstitutional in 1917.

The supply of ideas for new ways to segregate whites and Negroes seemed inexhaustible. In 1915 Oklahoma authorized the Corporation Commission to order telephone companies to maintain separate booths for white and Negro patrons. North Carolina and Florida provided that textbooks used by the children of one race be kept separate from those used by children of the other race, despite the fact that both states have stringent rules covering fumigation of textbooks. In 1922 Mississippi forbade members of both races to ride in taxicabs at the same time unless the vehicle held more than seven passengers and was traveling from one city to another. New Orleans deemed it in the interest of the public welfare to enact an ordinance separating Negro and white prostitutes.

The law had created two worlds, so separate that communication between them was almost impossible. Separation bred suspicion and hatred, fostered rumors and misunderstanding, and created conditions that made extremely difficult any steps toward its reduction. Legal segregation was so complete that a Southern white minister was moved to remark that it "made of our eating and drinking, our buying and selling, our labor and housing, our rents, our railroads, our orphanages and prisons, our recreations, our very institutions of religion a problem of race as well as a problem of maintenance."[19]

Yet law was only one part of the mechanism keeping the races segregated. Numerous devices were employed to perpetuate segregation in housing, education, and places of public accommodation even in communities where civil rights statutes forbade such practices. Patriotic, labor, and business organizations kept alive the "Lost Cause" and all that it stood for, including the subordination of the Negro. Separate Bibles for oath taking in courts of law, separate doors for whites and Negroes, separate elevators and stairways, separate drinking fountains, and separate toilets existed even where the law did not require them. Finally, there was the individual assumption of responsibility for keeping Negroes in their place, such as the white man who placed a rod across the boat to segregate his Negro fishing companion while they ate lunch, and the archivist of a Southern state who cleared a room of manuscripts, ordered a special key, and assigned an attendant to serve a visiting Negro scholar who would otherwise have had to use the regular search room, from which he was not barred by law.[20]

By the middle of the twentieth century the pattern of segregation was as irregular as it was complex. Every conceivable form of segregation had been evolved, although one would have to visit many places to observe all the variations. The wall of segregation had become so formidable, so impenetrable, apparently, that the entire weight of the American tradition of equality and all the strength of the American constitutional system had to be brought to bear in order to make even the slightest crack in it.

19. Edgar Gardner Murphy, The Basis of Ascendancy (New York: Longmans, Green & Company, 1909), p. 138.

20. For numerous examples of the informal but tenacious practices of segregation see Charles S. Johnson, Patterns of Negro Segregation (New York: Harper and Brothers, 1943).

Leonard Pitt,
"Decline of the Californios:
The Second Generation, 1865–1890"

American society underwent a series of major changes after the
Civil War which included rapid industrialization, urbanization,
and westward migration. Leonard Pitt, in "Decline of the Californios:
The Second Generation, 1865–1890," analyzes the effect of these
changes on the descendents of the Mexicans who were incorporated
into the United States as a result of the Treaty of Guadalupe
Hidalgo. While many of the first generation maintained their
traditional culture under American rule, the second generation
saw their heritage succumb to the steady stream of Yankee
immigration to California. The Yankee invasion brought railroads,
cities, the imposition of alien laws, and the introduction of new
agricultural patterns; as a result, the Californios suffered loss of land,
decline in status, and eventual elimination from political influence.
By the end of the nineteenth century, the Californios were disappearing as a distinct group within society. A few men of Caucasian
lineage and inherited wealth were absorbed into the dominant
white society. The rest were relegated, along with more recent
Mexican immigrants, to the status of a despised minority.

Decline of the Californios:
The Second Generation, 1865–1890
Leonard Pitt

When the first railroad started running in southern California in November, 1869, shuttling back and forth from Los Angeles to San Pedro, vaqueros would gleefully race their horses against the locomotive. They won the short sprint, but of course lost in the long haul.[1] The results were symbolically quite meaningful, for the civilization represented by the locomotive was bearing down on them slowly but with irresistible force. In September, 1876, the Southern Pacific arrived from the north and in March, 1887, the first Santa Fe Railroad train snaked through the San Bernardino Mountains into Los Angeles. Thereafter, as many as three and four coach trains descended on the city each day, depositing in 1887 alone more than 120,000 tourists, health seekers, farmers, artisans, and businessmen.

These developments inaugurated southern California's first major

Abridged from Leonard Pitt, "The Second Generation, 1865–1890," *The Decline of the Californios: A History of the Spanish-Speaking Californians, 1846–1890*, pp. 249–276. Originally published by the University of California Press; reprinted by permission of The Regents of the University of California. Some footnotes have been renumbered.

1. Remi Nadeau, *The City Makers* (New York, 1948), p. 30.

land boom—"the most extravagant in American frontier experience"[2] —which sealed the coffin of the old California culture. Until the advent of the boom of the eighties, the embattled Californios were still fighting a desperate holding action in the south—forty years after the Mexican War, a generation removed from the gold rush, fifteen years beyond the Civil War and the great drought of the 1860's. Spanish conversation, adobe architecture, and traditional clothing, manners, and recreations had told the newest or most refractory gringo that, like it or not, he was in "foreign" territory and could not completely brush the "natives" aside. To all this the boom put an effective end.

Between 1865 and 1890 the second generation of Californios came to maturity: those persons who were only vaguely aware of the Arcadian period and the revolutions and wars that had engrossed their parents, but acutely conscious of the consolidation of the new order. The wellbeing of this generation greatly depended on the amount of land it might inherit. In the north, where the original estates had been checkered with settlers, alienated from their owners, or greatly reduced in size, the transmission of a viable rancho holding from father to son was a rare event indeed. And yet in the south, islands of rancho land remained intact, at least until the 1870's. They were sometimes large and contiguous, creating the effect of a vast chain or archipelago of rangeland stretching from the Tehachapis to the Mexican border.

By 1875, however, the southern rancho islands had shrunk and had lost their common boundaries. Family farms increased noticeably in their midst, and rails were approaching them from the north with the promise of commercial and real estate developments that would interfere with rancho supremacy.

From 1865 to 1885, miscellaneous ills beset the southern rancheros. At Santa Barbara their vaqueros had to crash through fences to secure access to grazing land, in a struggle reminiscent of the nester-cattle-man conflict on the Great Plains.[3] In the San Fernando Valley, a ferocious Basque squatter, Miguel Leonis, armed a hundred fellow countrymen and Mexicans at Calabasas and clung to land by brute force, staving off both Yankees and Californians with better claims

2. Blake McKelvey, *The Urbanization of America, 1860–1915* (New Brunswick, 1963), p. 28. This chapter relies considerably on Glenn S. Dumke, *The Boom of the Eighties in Southern California* (San Marino, Calif., 1944).

3. Annie L. Morrison and John H. Haydon, *History of San Luis Obispo County and Environs* . . . (Los Angeles, 1917), pp. 81–85.

than his.[4] At Stockton, Major José Pico was arrested for alleged land-sale fraud concerning property in Baja California.[5] But the most chronic and incurable ills still concerned finances—high mortgage interest, costly litigation, low beef prices, and out-of-state competition for stockmen—and were compounded by the high living expenses of the more aristocratic rancheros. The financial troubles were severe enough to ruin Yankees, too—men with lower expenses, more flexible social values, and a keener sense of business tactics than the Californios'. For example, Abel Stearns, the south's wealthiest landowner, whose personal empire had incorporated the defunct Bandini estate, in turn was unable to prevent creditors from eating up his property after the drought.[6] ...

The post-Civil War Yankee immigrants who acquired the sub-divided ranchos ... significantly altered the uses of the soil. For one thing, they introduced sheep in a big way, generally renting vacant rancho land for grazing purposes and simultaneously managing the ranchero's own stock; some land they bought outright. While the sheep craze lasted, it helped the Californios recoup their cattle losses.

The Americans also promoted agriculture, particularly wheat farming. Rancheros irrevocably wedded to pastoral agriculture could scarcely comprehend, much less use, the new farm techniques and never got into the swim of things. When Antonio María Lugo first saw a mowing machine, he lifted a bony finger and exclaimed in Spanish: "The Yankee is but one finger shy of the devil!"[7] The rancheros' sons and grandsons, however, did wield the devil's instruments. José M. Ramirez experimented with wheat as early as 1872; Rómulo Pico raised a crop near former Mission San Fernando in 1880; and in the same year C. Castro of Santa Clara shipped to San Francisco 400 tons of hay which he had grown on his 250-acre farm. Two years later Señores Olivera, Machado, Higuera, and M. Coronel planted the grain near La Ballona. Truck gardening also increased

4. Horace Bell, *On the Old West Coast: Being Further Reminiscences of a Ranger* (New York, 1930), p. 181ff.

5. *San Jose Pioneer and Historical Review*, Dec. 1, 1877.

6. John C. Hough, "Abel Stearns, 1848–1871," unpublished MS, ed. by John Caughey, p. 450.

7. Henry D. Barrows, "Don Antonio Maria Lugo: A Picturesque Character of California," *Historical Society of Southern California Annual Publications*, III (1893–1896), 32.

among the Spanish-speaking.[8] At Los Nietos, east of Los Angeles, more than 120 men ran farms in 1880, including scores of men with Spanish surnames who called themselves "farmer," "small farmer," or "farm laborer," depending on whether they had sons as helpers, worked for a Yankee, or worked for themselves. Few of the 120 owned much land, and several rented parcels or sharecropped on plots of from 15 to 75 acres.[9]

Rancheros and vaqueros uprooted by the drought or by poor finances had to take work they would ordinarily disdain. Able-bodied gentry of the lower and middle ranks went on a sheep-shearing circuit in the 1870's. Fifty or sixty strong—with silver trimmed bridles and stirrups, tooled leather saddles, broadcloth suits, ruffled shirts, dark sombreros—they rode from one sheep ranch to another looking for work. When hired, these original migratory laborers put away their finery and reappeared in brown overalls and red bandanas, ready for action. They supplied their own bedding and meals and stayed for a month or so at each stop.

The conversion to sheep provided only seasonal labor, however, lasting three to eight months in the year, and it generally made the vaquero a supernumerary. Majordomo Juan Canedo of Rancho Los Cerritos, a dignified person who understood but never deigned to speak English, grew melancholy as the cattle died and the place changed hands and became a sheep pasture. Yet he claimed that he "belonged" to the property when Jonathan Bixby bought it, and refused to leave. To Bixby's daughter he "looked like a bronze statue, with brown face, brown clothes, brown horse and infinite repose." Bixby's son comforted Juan on his deathbed and supported Juan's widow—to repay the old man, as the boy said, for having taught him horsemanship.[10]

Apart from agricultural work, California's Spanish-speaking lower class performed only one other main semiskilled job, mining. "By far the larger portion of work-people in California mines are Mexicans,"

8. El Demócrata (Los Angeles), Oct. 1882; H. S. Foote, Pen Pictures from the Garden of the World, or, Santa Clara County, California (Chicago, 1888), pp. 350, 488–489, La Crónica (Los Angeles), May 25, 1872.
9. United States Bureau of the Census, Tenth Census, 1880, Enumerator's Roll Book, Los Angeles County (microfilm).
10. Sarah Bixby-Smith, Adobe Days . . . (Cedar Rapids, Iowa, 1926), pp. 113–114, 126–127.

an expert observed in 1867.[11] Several hundred Mexican gold miners worked in Soledad Canyon in 1880. More important, until 1887 more than half of the world's mercury supply came from California, the greater proportion from the New Almadén Quicksilver Mine near Santa Clara. For this tedious and deadly work, employers rated the Mexicans "more adventurous than Cornishmen," who were generally reputed to be the world's best miners. Using techniques reminiscent of their ancestors three hundred years earlier, the 1,500 Mexicans at New Almadén clambered upward hundreds of feet, on groaning ladders, supporting 200-pound sacks of ore strapped to their foreheads and resting precariously on their backs. Above ground the smelters were often exposed to the fatal mercury fumes and died violently from it. Drinking, gambling, whoring, and murderous brawls erupted every payday, because, as one lady observer explained, New Almadén had "no advantages of church or school." A paternalistic management later organized a model company town, lining the streets with flowers and whitewashing the miners' cottages, until it became a sightseer's "must."[12] For some unaccountable reason, fashionably attired wedding parties came from San Jose to gape at the men emerging from the pithead.

The Spanish-speaking did not readily gravitate into newer industries. The oil refinery at Newhall had not a single Mexican hand in 1880. By then, Chinese hands harvested the fruit crops and did other menial jobs the Spanish-speaking might have hired out for previously. Southern California's most important new employer, the Southern Pacific Railroad, used Chinese gangs to bore the mammoth tunnel through the mountains and into the San Fernando Valley in 1875. Only on the last leg of the construction, from the valley to Los Angeles, did Mexicans and Indians join the work gangs, but the hundred railroad hands permanently employed at the downtown switching yard, a stone's throw from Sonoratown, came mainly from the eastern United States, not from Mexico or California.[13]

For many Spanish-American youths, California represented a place

11. J. Ross Browne, "Down in the Cinnabar Mines: A Visit to New Almadén in 1865," *Harper's Magazine*, XXI (Oct. 1865), 549.

12. Carrie Stevens Walter, quoted in Eugene T. Sawyer, *History of Santa Clara County, California* . . . (Los Angeles, 1922), pp. 86–87.

13. U. S. Bureau of the Census, *op. cit.*

that had robbed them of their birthright, but had meanwhile provided innumerable opportunities to steal back parts of it. In any event, many of the disaffected still turned badmen. From 16 to 20 percent of San Quentin inmates from 1854 to 1865 were Mexicans or Californians[14]—a high figure in view of the relative numerical decline of the Spanish-speaking, even when correcting for Yankee prejudice in law enforcement. Mexicans engaged in numerous and brutal individual crimes, but their forte was highway robbery, stage holdups, and rustling, activities in which they continued to surpass all other nationalities, even after the gold rush. As late as 1875 the most notorious characters in the state still wore sombreros. . . .

Probably the last old-fashioned mob lynching in California of a person of Spanish-American background occurred in San Jose in 1877, when a pair of confessed murderers and robbers were snatched from the jail and strung from the Upper San Lorenzo Bridge.[15] As popular tribunals gave way to regular law enforcement, banditry in the old manner also declined; gold and livestock were now shipped more securely by railroad, and sheriffs' telegrams flashing up and down the state made a badman's escape more difficult.

A sheriff now could succeed without vigilante aid, particularly if, like Alameda Sheriff Harry Morse, archenemy of bandidos, he possessed perseverance to match their bravado. So closely did Morse hound bandidos that they took him for a demon. Between 1864 and 1874 he trailed Borjorques mercilessly (but never laid eyes on him); killed Norrate Ponce (although killing was not his specialty); captured Tejada; and simply strode up to Procopio in a San Francisco dance hall, laid a hand on the bandido's shoulder, calmly declared, "Procopio, you're my man," and took him to jail.[16] For sheer drama nothing surpassed his single-handed showdown with Juan Soto, whom he began tracking after the badman had robbed and killed a Suñol shopkeeper in January, 1871. With customary aplomb Morse hiked directly into Soto's mountain fastness south of Gilroy, masquerading as a weary and lost traveler. His disguise gained Morse easy entry into

14. California State Prison Directors, "Annual Report," in California Legislature, Journals of 1860 Assembly (Sacramento, 1861), App. 13, pp. 18–19; 1865–1866 Senate and Assembly (Sacramento, 1866), App., p. 66.

15. Pioneer and Historical Review, May 5, 1877.

16. Charles Howard Shinn, Graphic Description of Pacific Coast Outlaws (Los Angeles, 1958), p. 64.

Soto's casa for "a rest." When the bandit and his crew discovered the ruse, they began shooting it out with the sheriff. A Mexican amazon momentarily pinioned Morse's arms, but he broke her grip and got safely outside. Finally the wounded Soto burst from the shack, "bareheaded, his long black hair streaming behind him, a cocked revolver in each hand," and flying suicidally at Morse. At this, the sheriff raised his rifle and shot Soto in the head.[17] . . .

After Juan Soto's death, only one important bandido remained at large—Tiburcio Vasquez, a Californio. A long and checkered career as cattle rustler, stage robber, and jailbird lay behind him when he engineered his final spree against the shopkeepers of Tres Pinos. A wanton killing aroused the authorities of several counties to weave a net around him. In a scenario-like episode appropriately played out near present-day Hollywood, a brigade of sheriffs and deputies tightened the net and caught Vasquez. Bound in irons, he seemed at close range as vicious and gallant as the Yankees had expected. When asked for the motives for his crimes, he recalled a boyhood scene in which he bade his mother good-bye and set out to avenge Yankee injustice— a touching and believable explanation, but altogether irrelevant to the judge and the jury that had him executed.[18] Bandido depredations soon subsided in California, partly as a function of Mexico's subsiding political turmoil. The archetypal California badman of the 1880's, Black Bart, wore a dark bowler instead of a sombrero.

Bandido Vasquez personified a major motif among the Spanish Americans in California—alienation of the second generation. Nevertheless, a good many of his contemporaries responded altogether differently to recent events by picking themselves up, resettling in the towns, and making a new life for themselves. In the town environment, the younger generation came in contact with new cultural influences and adjusted accordingly. Submergence of the Spanish-speaking thus entailed various possibilities: for some, an irrational armed resistance through crime; for a few, assimilation into the mainstream of Yankee culture; and for still others, assimilation into the Mexican community.

In the rural hamlets of Los Angeles County, a quarter of the in-

17. Joseph Henry Jackson, *Bad Company* (New York, 1949), pp. 264–267.
18. Ernest May, "Tiburcio Vasquez," *Historical Society of Southern California Quarterly*, XXIX (1947), 123–134.

habitants had Spanish surnames as late as 1880. Of course, in some townships Yankees reigned supreme. At Pasadena not one of the 392 occupants was Spanish American (the Chinese did all the menial labor); at Santa Ana only 4 of the 714 were Spanish-speaking; and at the beach suburb of Santa Monica, 7 of the 418. Elsewhere, on the other hand, Spanish Americans clustered so thickly as to alienate gringos. New Mexicans were still entrenched at isolated, self-contained, culturally preserved San Jose township. Also, near former mission San Juan Capistrano, there were 345 Spanish-speaking residents, as indigenous as the famous sparrows, born in California of California parents (some perhaps of neophyte Indian background); the remaining 31 residents were Europeans. . . .

When a hamlet acquires a railroad, cheap labor, and slums, it is well launched toward cityhood. These requisites for maturity Los Angeles had attained by 1876. Nigger Alley, north of the plaza, had undergone the most striking change since epidemic smallpox had killed off so many Spanish Americans a decade earlier; excepting some French traders, every inhabitant was Chinese. This area was one of two slums. As the town updated itself, the neighborhood east and south of the plaza, as far east as the river and as far south as the railroad, remained a Mexican village and thus, by comparison, a slum. There the shops, saloons, brothels, and gambling dens crowded one another in overwhelming disarray. "Sonoratown" provided all the amusements, comforts, and vices of a ghetto except work, which lay in the better parts of town. The underworld of all nationalities gravitated to Sonoratown, and axe murders, shootings, beatings, and knifings commonly occurred there. Should the police seek an out-of-town villain, they knew where to look, perhaps at Francisco Carmona's disorderly house on Buena Vista Street. Gringo citizens once tried to close the place, but a judge dismissed their case as legally weak although morally sound.[19] Suddenly, about the time of the boom, Sonoratown became Chinatown and the Spanish-speaking went to live in other neighborhoods.

The Spanish-American town dwellers made a living chiefly as laborers, but also as farmers, broom makers, barbers, gamblers, butchers, zanjeros, miners, and shepherds. Women, too, worked. Those from better families often had had girlhood training in sewing and thus

19. Los Angeles *Times*, March 6, 10, 25, 1883. See also W. W. Robinson, *Los Angeles, from the Days of the Pueblo* . . . (San Francisco, 1959), pp. 63–64.

became seamstresses; others became domestics; and some, prostitutes. Brothels sprang up even outside Sonoratown, as at the docks at Wilmington, where the Mexican-born Señora Paredez lived with two children and three women of Baja California and California; the census taker jotted her down as "Keeping House," and as an afterthought wryly added "of Ill Fame."[20] Indeed, the Spanish-speaking worked at anything to bring in "poco dinero"; they rated higher wages than the Chinese but lower than the Anglos.

The relative impersonality of town life was partly offset by the enveloping warmth of the family. The older the family and the longer its stay in California, the larger it was apt to be; small households denoted recent arrivals, sometimes of single Mexican men living in boarding houses. Californio families ran large in both town and country. Fifty-four-year-old Joaquín Sepúlveda and his wife had nine children, ranging in age from twenty to five years. Tomás Palomares, also in his fifties, lived at suburban San José township with his wife and ten children, the eldest twenty-two years and the youngest six months. Dwellings tended to be overcrowded with aged parents, grown and infant children, grandchildren, in-laws, nieces and nephews, boarders, and adopted orphans—all living under one roof, or next door, or down the street. Fifteen Reyeses stuck close together in two Main Street homes. In the household of Mr. and Mrs. Mott and their five children (a branch of the Sepúlveda family), eleven people lived under one roof, including Mrs. Mott's septuagenarian mother, a California-born servant, two sisters-in-law, and Mott's sister. . . .

As Californio influence waned in Los Angeles, immigrant Mexicans assured the continuance of Spanish-American culture, which therefore never died. In San Francisco and other northern localities the Mexican community evolved independently of the native-born, but in Los Angeles it merged gradually and imperceptibly with them. The number of Mexicans slowly increased until they were ready to overtake the Californios, probably by the turn of the century. The Mexican community, moreover, attained a sense of respectability it formerly had lacked. As the memories of Manifest Destiny waned, Yankees thought better of Mexico and, at least for the record, had some good words for the sister republic—perhaps that it was finally "waking up" and "uniting with our country [in] the spread of civiliza-

20. U. S. Bureau of the Census, op. cit.

tion in the West."[21] Respectable Mexican patriotic organizations formed, disbanded, and re-formed, such as the Hispano-Americano Society of Los Angeles, dedicated to combating the "decadent" state of the community, the Mexican Progressive Society; the Juarez Patriotic Society (with a branch in San Juan Capistrano in 1872); and Botello's Cavalry and the Mexican Lancers, which appeared on festive occasions.[22] . . .

As part of the old-line community blended imperceptibly with the Mexicans, however, another merged into the dominant gringo culture. Thus, in a sense, the Californios were ground down between the upper and nether millstones of two immigrant groups.

The old upper class, particularly the Californios of Caucasian origin, continued to mingle with the new. . . .

If in olden days the dominant Mexican culture had transformed some Yankees into "Mexicanized gringos," now the new culture created a class of "gringoized Mexicans." This did not, however, represent a true blending of two cultures, but rather a triumph of the most aggressive and a defeat of the most recessive cultural characteristics. The socially prominent del Valle family of Los Angeles aspired toward, and in most respects attained, the status of the new "better classes." For all their old-fashioned fiestas at Camulos, their values looked to the present. Their personal mementos give this impression unmistakably. The family photograph album captures handsome dark faces, racially indistinguishable from most Anglo-Saxon ones. The album also contains the ordinary minutiae of the Gilded Age—society column notices, dance invitations, travel brochures, pressed flowers, flowered stationery, wedding and funeral notices, calling cards, school graduation programs, and illustrations of home furnishings and women's fashions. Except that many of the items relate to church or parochial-school functions, one can find scarcely any attributes of the older culture.[23]

Of all the battlefields on which the Spanish Americans fought a holding action to preserve their influence, they succeeded best on the

21. Los Angeles *Times*, Sept. 18, 1883.
22. Broadside in Coronel Collection, items 1563, 1568F, PC9, Los Angeles County Museum; *La Crónica* (Los Angeles), June 10, Nov. 2, 1872; Aug. 23, 1873.
23. Del Valle Collection, Los Angeles County Museum.

political one. A prestigious Spanish surname (especially when combined with a Caucasian face) remained a good entreé into public office, and many Spanish Americans used it successfully. Estevan Castro became a Monterey constable and later an assemblyman, although Don José Castro's other sons remained "without social standing"; Martin Aguirre became Los Angeles sheriff in 1885; Andrés Pico's son Ramon ran for state treasurer in 1875 (but lost); Andronico Sepúlveda served as Los Angeles county treasurer in 1873; Andrés Castillero sat in Congress in 1880; José G. Estudillo was state treasurer from 1875 to 1880; Santa Barbara's Angel G. Escandon served in the legislature from 1869 to 1874; and, following in the footsteps of his father, Manuel Coronel entered politics and served one term in the state legislature.[24]

Of all Spanish-speaking Californians, Romualdo Pacheco accomplished the most brilliant and unusual political stroke, by seating himself in the governor's chair. Born the son of a Santa Barbara army officer in 1831, young Romualdo received a superior Yankee schooling in the Sandwich Islands and came back with a head for figures; then he hired out as a supercargo on various trading vessels plying the California coast. After the Mexican War he managed his mother's rancho in San Luis Obispo and at the age of twenty-two (1853) won an assembly seat. He became state senator as a Democrat in 1858, and as a Union Democrat in 1862. After a stint in the Union Army in 1863, he changed party affiliation and gained election as Republican state treasurer, serving four years (and yielding that post to his kinsman, Ramón Pacheco). Except for Unionism, no particular political views clung to Romualdo's name, but his background made good press notices—he was an aristocratic native son, a ranchero, a bear fighter, a vigilante, a soldier, a sometime stockbroker, and the husband of an Anglo-Saxon woman. His popularity, the modest importance of the "Spanish" vote, and a desire to balance the ticket between two rival factions encouraged the Republican Party to nominate him for lieutenant governor in 1871. He came in during the Republican sweep of that year, serving routinely until 1875. In February, Governor Booth took an interim seat in the United States Senate and handed Pacheco the governorship for the balance of that year. Pacheco was

24. La Crónica (Los Angeles), March 12, 1873; El Demócrata (Los Angeles), Nov. 1, 1882.

little more than a figurehead in a caretaker government, but even so it gave the Spanish-speaking particular satisfaction to see their man in so exalted a position. The party managers thought better of re-nominating Pacheco, however, and upon leaving office he turned to selling stocks in San Francisco. Meanwhile, from 1878 to 1882, he served two terms in Washington as Santa Clara's congressman, and spent some of his declining years in Mexico and Texas.[25] . . .

The Spanish-speaking leaders staved off complete annihilation for a remarkably long time, considering their early economic and numerical losses. Perhaps they could have accomplished more had they not iso-lated themselves from their own people as they entered "society" and abandoned their traditional ways. Perhaps, too, the ethos of the Gilded Age, which resisted social reform and encouraged political cynicism, prevented them from coping with the real social ills that beset the Spanish Americans. The greatest problem of the Spanish-speaking stemmed, however, from their loss of numbers, for which none of their leaders could provide a remedy. Although about 12,000 strong in Los Angeles by 1887, the Spanish-speaking constituted less than 10 percent of the total population, and too many of them were newcomers—ignorant, indifferent, or hostile to Yankee politics.

More or less suddenly, in the 1880's the Californians' political hold-ing action ceased. When Ignacio Sepúlveda retired from the bench, Romualdo Pacheco from Congress, and Antonio Coronel and Regi-naldo del Valle from active local politics, gringos replaced them. No younger brothers or sons duplicated the old Californios' prestige. The native-born leaders were left holding honorary chairmanships in this or that committee, but little else, and their community went leader-less.

In 1885 Los Angeles awaited the railroad spike-driving ceremony at Cajon Pass, promised for November, which would greatly promote the direct rail linkup with the East. The completion on September 16 of an intermediary rail hookup with Pasadena created only minor excitement; yet, because it coincided with Mexican Independence Day, it had symbolic meaning and called for a speech by a Spanish-American orator.[26] Not a Mexican, however, but Reginaldo del Valle,

25. Hubert Howe Bancroft, "Pioneer Register and Index," in *History of California* (San Francisco, 1886), IV, 764.

26. Los Angeles *Times*, Sept. 17, 1885.

was given the honor. In his own and his father's time, the San Gabriel Valley had burgeoned from an Indian hunting ground to a mission pasturage, then to a rancho empire, and was now sprouting farms, orchards, and towns. It turned out to be a notable September Sixteenth, although symbolically confusing; a Californian born in the American period paid tribute to Mexican liberty by speaking in English to a gringo crowd about Yankee progress. As expected, "The Little One" peppered his remarks with humorous anecdotes of the past thirty years, but the unfunny fact was that the same railroad he was commemorating would soon obliterate practically everything connected with the pastoral era, even his own political career.

The boom of the eighties contributed vastly to the ongoing process of "Americanization." The sheer volume of immigration brought to southern California the very transformations the northerners had witnessed a generation earlier. In two years or so the population of Los Angeles jumped 500 percent, automatically transforming the electorate into an Anglo-American one. The mores changed equally radically. The type of consumer goods advertised for sale, the tastes in food and dress, the prevalence of English over Spanish in daily and official conversation, the Gilded Age recreations, and the style of commerce—all changed rapidly and irreversibly. While describing the changing ethos of real estate promotion and commerce, Professor Glenn S. Dumke notes that "from 1888 onward, the southern counties were imbued with Anglo-American aggressiveness."[27] What started out as a "semigringo" town and a cultural backwash became practically overnight a booming Yankee commercial center and the best-known place in the entire West.

From the vantage point of the Californios, the most elemental change lay in the chopping up of the ranchos into farms and towns, a process long under way but now dramatically speeded up. Although the economic boom converged on the city of Los Angeles, the chief activity concerned the rancho-blanketed suburbs. In 1887 Los Angeles real estate men and buyers daily engaged in thirty to seventy transactions and exchanged as much as $100,000. The evolution of the ranchos involved a variety of legal and business transformations, all of them well tested in California in previous years. Among the most common were forfeiture of loans, conveyance of mortgages to new

27. Op. cit., p. 226.

owners, tax delinquency, family litigation, legitimate sales, division of undivided interest by court order, and bankruptcy proceedings or sheriff's sales. No set pattern emerges in these transformations, but the eroded claims of the original claimants washed away steadily and flowed into the hands of the newcomers—financiers, railroad developers, town promoters, cooperative colonizers, and irrigation companies.

Some of the larger southern California ranchos, it is true, seemingly impervious to the usual ravages of death and taxes, acquired a kind of immortality of their own. The Irvine Ranch and Dominguez Estates are two venerable properties whose twentieth-century boundaries correspond closely to those of the original Spanish and Mexican grants. More than 24,000 acres remained with Don Manuel Dominguez at his death in 1882, and his will divided them up among his six daughters in 1885.[28] In turn, Dominguez' grandchildren also kept a good hold on their property and were able to lease and develop the estates without selling outright. These durable properties have, however, changed internally with the times. Recent aerial photographs show the sprawling Dominguez properties dotted with oil fields, airports, factories, freeways, shopping centers, and suburban homes, as the city now totally surrounds the rancho that once was set apart by 20 miles of open range. The Yankee-owned Irvine Ranch was operated as a cattle ranch until a decade ago and is only now slowly being urbanized, through carefully controlled regional planning.

More than a hundred towns and thousands of orchards and farms were platted out in southern California before the boom of the eighties collapsed in 1888. But even those evanescent communities, which disappeared as quickly as they arose, had gone through financial and legal gyrations which permanently disrupted the legal basis of most ranchos, much as the drought of the sixties had disrupted the way of life and the economy of those same estates.

28. Robert Cameron Gillingham, *The Rancho San Pedro* (Los Angeles, 1961), p. 271. See also Robert Glass Cleland, *The Irvine Ranch of Orange County, 1810–1950* (San Marino, Calif., 1952), pp. 148–150.

William R. Locklear,
"The Celestials and the Angels:
A Study of the Anti-Chinese Movement
in Los Angeles to 1882"

President Chester A. Arthur signed a bill in 1882 prohibiting further
Chinese immigration to the United States for a period of ten
years, the first of a series of such exclusion acts which remained
in force until 1943. Although the most virulent and unremitting
exhibitions of anti-Chinese sentiment came from citizens of San
Francisco, prejudice against the new immigrants was not confined to
that city. The willingness of Chinese-Americans to work for low
wages, and particularly their use as strikebreakers, created animosity
throughout the country. William R. Locklear, in "The Celestials
and the Angels," examines the growth of anti-Chinese feeling in
Los Angeles. Although the Chinese population of Los Angeles
was not large, the success of the newcomers in the laundry and
vegetable businesses generated a jealous hostility from the whites.
Fanned by inflammatory orators from San Francisco, anti-Chinese
prejudice soon became politically expedient in Los Angeles and led
to the passage of local ordinances aimed at forcing Orientals from
the city. Los Angeles and the rest of California played a role in
making Chinese exclusion a national political issue and bringing
about the passage of the Act of 1882.

The Celestials and the Angels:
A Study of the Anti-Chinese
Movement in Los Angeles to 1882

William R. Locklear

The anti-Chinese movement in California which led to the Chinese exclusion act of 1882 was essentially a product of agitation in San Francisco and Northern California. It was here that the population of the state, both Chinese and non-Chinese, was concentrated, and it was here that agitation against the Chinese originated and developed.[1] Yet, one event in Southern California history—the massacre of nineteen Chinese at Los Angeles in 1871—brought nation-wide attention to the California movement, and this event has come to represent, or rather to misrepresent, the character of Los Angeles' role in the campaign to restrict Chinese immigration. The facts are, however, that agitation in Los Angeles developed far later than it did in San Francisco, was more difficult to arouse and sustain, and was, on the whole, less passionate and less violent.

California's resentment to the "Celestials"[2] was first manifested among the miners of Northern California when the Chinese became numerically ominous in 1852. As large Chinese populations congregated in northern cities agitation spread among the urban laborers,

Abridged from William R. Locklear, "The Celestials and the Angels: A Study of the Anti-Chinese Movement in Los Angeles to 1882," *Southern California Quarterly*, XLII (1960), pp. 239–256. Reprinted by permission of the author. Some notes have been renumbered; they appear at the end of the article.

who feared the results of competing with them. Over the years, sympathetic and ambitious officeholders produced a mass of state and local legislation designed to stem the tide of immigration and to drive the Chinese away, but the courts declared most of the acts unconstitutional. The pulse of this agitation seems to have quickened during depression years or years in which immigration was particularly high, and it subsided to dormancy only when some relief from either "evil" was obtained.[3]

In justification of the agitation a series of objections to the Chinese was voiced, of which the validity of several is still open to debate. But whether factually true or not the Californians responded to them as if they were, and, thus, they became a semiconscious part of almost every citizen's perspective. The Chinese immigrant was characterized as merely a slave of another color—an intolerable situation after 1865. Moreover, because his needs were few, he could work at a very low rate of pay, thereby underselling white labor, throwing Americans out of jobs and causing their destitute families to turn to crime and prostitution. He was further described as a heathen and inveterate liar who had no respect for American social, religious or political institutions. He lived in "herds" amid squalor, gambled, smoked opium and forced Chinese women into prostitution, thus endangering the health and morality of the community. An ironic complaint was added that he—this "immoral, filthy heathen"—refused to assimilate with the white population![4]

Underlying these objections, many of which were applicable to the white community as well, was a deep-seated racial prejudice among the Caucasians which had previously been vented against the Indian, the Negro and the dark-skinned Frenchman and Latin-American. The refusal of the Chinese to adopt American dress and customs tended to intensify this basic animosity. But the critical element seems to have been the great numbers of Chinese who immigrated. To many Californians there was a very real threat of a Mongolian invasion that would extend the frontiers of the Chinese empire into California. As late as 1882 there was published "A Short and Truthful History of the Taking of California and Oregon by the Chinese, in the year A.D. 1899," written by a "survivor." At one time or another all of these elements found expression in Los Angeles, but usually on a very reduced scale.[5]

Popular sentiment against the Chinese did not appear in Los

Angeles until 1876, the massacre of 1871 notwithstanding. This was almost two full decades after organized labor opposition expressed itself in San Francisco. Of the several factors which account for this delay the lack [of] a sizeable Chinese population is paramount. In 1850 only two Chinese resided among 1,610 Angelenos. Ten years later, while the city's population had risen to 4,385, there were just nine Chinese present. The Chinese community grew considerably during the sixties, totaling 172 in 1870, but this was still only three per cent of the city's population. In contrast, San Francisco housed over 2,700 Chinese in 1860 and more than 12,000 in 1870. Railroad construction around Los Angeles after 1875 drew "carloads" of Chinese into the area and set the stage for local agitation.[6]

A second factor in Los Angeles' delayed reaction derives from the local economy. Southern California was "cow country" in the fifties and sixties. Most of the town's business enterprise was devoted only to meeting the more immediate of local needs and was conducted by self-employed craftsmen. It was only after severe droughts decimated the herds in the sixties that agriculture and horticulture became serious endeavors. When they took hold in the seventies and gave Los Angeles new life, the population then increased rapidly and introduced a laboring force that could identify itself with state-wide labor opposition to the Chinese.[7]

The lack of economic opportunity partially explains the slow growth of a Chinese community as well. More significant, however, was the surplus of opportunity which existed, in spite of racial antagonism, in and around San Francisco, the port-of-entry for Chinese immigrants. Then, too, the early reputation of Los Angeles did little to attract visitors. A primitive and undeveloped town, it had a "larger percentage of bad characters than any other city" in the country....

If there was ever any direct competition between Chinese labor and white labor in early Los Angeles it must have been brief and of no serious proportion. By the seventies the Chinese were concentrated in a few occupational fields which, for all intents and purposes, had become their particular fortes. As domestic help they were well regarded and came to replace the Indians and Negroes who had formerly monopolized such endeavors. In 1872 eleven Chinese laundries employed nearly half of the city's "Celestial" population while only two "white" laundries were operating. During the seventies

Chinese gardeners undertook to supply Los Angeles homes with vegetables, and they came to dominate that field, too. Though individual Chinese appeared in other occupations their total number was never significant.[8]

During the sixties the clannish "Celestials" congregated in one area—along a short street which in the Mexican period had been known as *Calle de los Negros*, but since then called "Nigger Alley" by the race-conscious whites. Long before the arrival of the Chinese this vicinity had deteriorated into a slum and was the established center of gambling, drinking and prostitution in Los Angeles. The selection of this site seems to have been voluntary on the part of the Chinese rather than as a result of any restrictions against their lodging in other parts of town. It is likely that low rents were a major consideration in the selection. Negro Alley (as the name appeared most often in print) was about forty feet wide and 500 feet long and was bordered on either side by veranda-fronted adobes. Most of the Chinese living and business activities were stuffed into its narrow, multi-roomed apartments. (In the main only washhouses were located in other parts of town.) This became the nucleus of a gradually expanding Chinatown, and it was here that the Chinese set up their opium dens and houses of prostitution.[9]

With the introduction of the first Chinese woman in 1859 Angelenos became acutely aware of one facet of the objections to Chinese immigration. Within six weeks of her arrival this first "Celestial" lady tried to commit suicide. And though the chivalry of the *Star's* editor allowed, "Family squabbles seem to have driven her to the rash undertaking," it is more likely that her after-hours assignment was the motivation. In mid-1861 over a dozen other females arrived, and the Chinese community was immediately taken to task for its "unblushing conduct." Strangely enough, the Chinese merchants, who were also the owners of the prostitutes, enjoyed favorable reputations among the citizens of Los Angeles.[10]

There was, to be sure, a local awareness of the agitation being conducted in the north during this period, and in time the insulation of distance and difficult communication gave way before the mounting cries of the anti-Chinese. With the gradual influx of disappointed gold-seekers and "busted" businessmen from up-state, first-hand Chinese prejudices were introduced, for it was common practice among the northerners to attribute all their misfortunes to the "yellow-skinned" scapegoat. And though it took considerable time for these seeds to blossom, they had been planted in a fertile soil where racial animosity was currently being directed toward the Indian, Negro and a sizeable Mexican population.

As early as 1857 the topic discussed at a meeting of the local Mechanics' Institute was: "Is the importation of Chinamen into this State advantageous to the people thereof in its present and future results?" At that time there were only three Chinese living in the city. The word "importation" is indicative of the attitude most often expressed in Los Angeles throughout the next decade. There seems to have been real moral indignation which grew out of the belief that Chinese laborers were actually slaves. An 1867 editorial in the *Semi-Weekly News* analyzed Chinese "coolieism" and concluded that it possessed "more than all the evils of African slavery, without any one of its redeeming virtues."[11]

In the late sixties there is occasional evidence of changing attitudes. When Benjamin D. Wilson was campaigning for state senator in 1869 he was "slanderously" accused of employing Chinese while posing as a friend of labor, and in 1870 real concern arose over the possibility of Chinese being given the right of naturalization. Two new laundries began business in 1870, basing their advertising appeal on not employing Chinese. And in April 1871 a warning was posted in the Mexican section of town that no Chinese should try to settle there. However, these were isolated cases and did not reflect wholesale public resentment to the Chinese. There had been no local reaction to the signing of the Burlingame Treaty in 1868 in which the United States and China recognized "the inalienable right of man to change his home ... and the mutual advantage of the free migration and emigration of their citizens ... for purposes of curiosity, of trade or as permanent residents." Nor did Los Angeles send any representatives to the anti-Chinese convention held in San Francisco during August, 1870.[12]

Even from the vantage point of history, nothing occurred in the months immediately preceding the 1871 massacre that would have permitted its prediction. Nonetheless, on the evening of October 24 a mob of 500 "Angels," enraged over the killing of a white by some "Celestials," stormed through Negro Alley leaving eighteen dead Chinese in its wake—fifteen of them suspended from make-shift gallows. A nineteenth victim died from bullet wounds three days later. In addition to the slaughter the Chinese quarters were looted of over $30,000 in money and personal property.[13]

One cannot contest that this was a very real expression of anti-Chinese sentiment among a portion of the population. The mob did not seek out the guilty parties, but gave way to blind racism in taking revenge against the entire Chinese community. However, no evidence exists to suggest that this attitude was representative of Los Angeles as a whole. There is no way of knowing how many people swelled the ranks of the mob merely out of curiosity or from a compelling sense of horror. A heroic few actively opposed the onslaught, and through their efforts reduced the number of victims by perhaps as many as ten. Others tried less successfully to temper the crowd with words. Elsewhere in town whites were hiding Chinese in their homes in case the mob should enlarge its hunting ground. The following day, the newspapers agreed in blaming the "scum and dregs of the city" for the outrage, and though this smacks of civic white-wash, judging from Los Angeles' reputation, the figure of 500 may not have been large enough to embrace even the "bad" element in town. Moreover, the extensive pillage that took place and the fact that the Chinese settlement was located in the center of the local slum lessens much of the skepticism such a statement arouses. On October 26 a City Council member stated that some of the police, apparently seeking to share in hidden Chinese savings, offered bribes to incite the mob.[14]

Within the context of this study a most important point regarding the massacre of 1871 is that it was not a part of any anti-Chinese movement. It was not an attempt to drive the Chinese from town nor to discourage others from coming. At this time there was no anti-Chinese movement afoot in the city. The Chinese population was still quite small and was engaged in occupations which did not directly compete with any significant number of whites. And though 1869–71 were depression years economic pressures were easing by mid-1871, and just two weeks before the massacre the Star observed, "There are fewer idlers and men out of employment in Los Angeles than in any other city of its size on the Pacific Coast." The murdering and looting of October 24 seems to have been more the dying breath of a period of general lawlessness than an expression of any city-wide sentiment against the Chinese.[15]

Except for a single, insignificant meeting in 1873 the anti-Chinese movement did not gain expression in Los Angeles until 1876. Anti-coolie clubs in northern California revived agitation in 1873 when a new influx of immigrants intensified an already unfavorable employment situation, and Los Angeles responded in June with its own anti-Chinese meeting. But no enthusiasm could be generated among the Angelenos, and the agitation died out immediately. Actually Los Angeles took a critical view of the northern agitation. Of the anti-Chinese legislation being considered in San Francisco the *Star* editorialized, "To cut off the queues ('pigtails') of those who are here, and to awe away from us those who are in our midst by refusing to let them remove the bones of their dead to the sacred soil of their fathers, is a recourse unworthy of intelligent men." It also pointed out that "this kind of persecution will weaken the cause of the anti-Chinese, and make friends for the Mongolians," and suggested that the energy of the agitators be directed toward obtaining Congressional action.[16]

State-wide agitation reached new heights in 1876. Recent immigration had been greater than any time since 1852, while economic conditions had deteriorated measurably. By this time every political party in the state and nation included anti-Chinese planks in their platforms, and sufficient pressure was finally brought to bear in Congress that a Joint Special Committee was sent to San Francisco in late 1876 to investigate Chinese immigration.[17]

Even Los Angeles entered into the agitation and organized an Anti-Coolie Club in May. The club was favorably endorsed and initially grew rapidly. But though the meetings it sponsored during the summer were well attended, club membership never exceeded 300. In its platform the club sought abrogation of the Burlingame Treaty and Congressional action to restrict Chinese immigration. It denounced the use of illegal or violent measures and circulated anti-Chinese petitions which were forwarded to representatives in Congress with 2,500 signatures. The only concrete achievement of the club, however, was inducing the City Council to award no public works contracts to persons who employed Chinese. The insignificance of Los Angeles in the over-all movement is effectively implied in the *Report* of the Joint Special Committee—of over 1,200 pages of testimony recorded, only two referred to the local situation.[18]

Despite the meager immediate results of this agitation in Los Angeles, the short-lived Anti-Coolie Club left a legacy of some consequence. Local laborers now identified themselves closely with state-wide labor opposition to the Chinese. Furthermore, membership in the club had transcended class lines by enlisting some of the "wealthiest and most prominent men" of the community, and some of these influential sympathizers were later to lead the workingmen in their political attempts at correcting various social and economic evils. Local agitation in 1876 and subsequent years resulted from several factors. Construction of the Southern Pacific and other railroads brought large numbers of Chinese into the area after 1875, and the unemployed of Los Angeles saw in them the cause of all their misfortunes. In anticipation of the rail connection with San Francisco local business men overextended themselves. This was forcibly brought home when, instead of ushering in an era of prosperity, completion of the railroad in 1876 introduced an after effect to the Panic of 1873. Coupled with a serious drought in 1876–77 this brought on a depression which lasted to the end of the decade.[19]

For these ills the Chinese, the railroads and "big business" were variously blamed, but the larger part of the Los Angeles populace remained aloof from anti-Chinese activities. A visitor to the city in 1876 noted that while anti-Chinese sentiment was "highly developed" there was still a great demand for Oriental labor and domestic help. In this regard, annual attempts by workingmen after 1876 to organize boycotts against Chinese and Chinese-employing businesses, though heavily pledged to, failed miserably.[20] . . .

The Chinese had dominated the laundry business since the sixties, and in 1879 Chinese laundries probably outnumbered the non-Chinese by nearly ten to one, while employing close to 300 of their countrymen. As for the vegetable peddlers, 200 Chinese truckmen employed at least fifty wagons in carrying out their door-to-door trade. In 1876 Chinese vegetable peddlers had outnumbered non-Chinese forty-seven to two. To maintain their monopoly they gathered in Negro Alley each morning at dawn and exchanged particular items of produce to insure that each peddler had a full selection to offer his patrons. It was reported in 1879 that nine out of ten families relied upon the Chinese for their vegetable supplies.[21]

Under the tax ordinance proposed in January, 1879, "regular" laundries (as differentiated from "poor women who do washing") were to be taxed $25.00 per month, instead of $5.00 as formerly. The vegetable peddlers, who had been paying $3.00 per month per wagon since 1877, were now to pay $20.00 each month. For vegetable peddlers who walked, a monthly tax of $10.00 was to be levied. And so as not to miss the rest of the Chinese community, a tax of $5.00 per month was proposed for "all aliens ineligible to the privilege of becoming citizens of the United States, who were employed in any capacity in the city of Los Angeles."[22]

The simple economics of this tactic and the public conscience of the council proved to be stumbling blocks, however. In order to meet municipal expenses and to liquidate a part of the large city debt it would be necessary to recoup the revenue losses that would result from a Chinese exodus. To accomplish this no tax reduction was given to other businesses (one of the other Workingmen's [Party] campaign promises); it was, in fact, increased five-fold on some, and for the first time in Los Angeles a tax was to be made on professional pursuits.[23]

Thus, the ordinance drew criticism from many quarters. And an editorial in the Herald suggests that there was not unanimous agreement even over the Chinese provisions:

... The question as to whether a man of whatever color, race or previous condition of servitude, can be legislated out of his means of earning a livelihood, is a grave one, and it is by no means concluded when a City Council has announced its sovereign pleasure. The Chinese should go, but the place to secure this going is the National Capital.[24]

Under such an economic threat the myth of "docile John Chinaman" was quickly exploded. The Chinese vegetable peddlers taxed themselves $2.00 each to obtain legal aid in testing the constitutionality of the law. And to enlist public sympathy they gave two-days' notice and then went on strike, intending to remain out three weeks. However, some doubts apparently arose about the wisdom of this tactic, and they returned to their wagons after four days. The laundrymen, on the other hand, chose to adopt a wait-and-see attitude, but rumor soon had it that the "wily Mongolians" were plotting to establish an enormous laundry under one roof, thereby having to pay only one tax.[25]

With the very real possibility of expensive litigation facing the city, the Council reduced the fees to $6.00 and $12.00 per month on laundries and vegetable wagons, respectively, and withdrew the tax on employed persons not eligible for citizenship. Although the laundrymen quietly accepted the new tax, which was merely a 20% increase over the former, the vegetable vendors pushed a test case before the courts and won. A county court justice found the tax "oppressive, partial, unfair and in restraint of trade and therefore void." Encouraged by this success the vendors refused to pay even the revised fee of $5.00 and went on strike again in May. Available sources did not reveal the success or failure of this particular effort, but the vendors were soon back at work. In August they petitioned the Council for a reduction to $2.00 and enlisted enough sympathy among customers that several petitions from local housewives asked that the license tax on vegetable peddlers be completely abolished. These efforts, however, gained no further concessions.[26]

In conjunction with trying to tax the Chinese out of town the Workingmen had simultaneously organized a boycott against Chinese goods and labor. There was even established an "Anti-Chinese Vegetable and Produce Market." Though subscription to the boycott was heavy the pledges were most often observed in their neglect. The only pledge reported honored by the Star was the replacement of all Chinese help with whites by the United States Hotel in March.[27]

If there was any one aspect of the Chinese issue upon which public opinion was united it was the blight of Chinatown. Though a number of non-Chinese still lived along Negro Alley, the health menace caused by accumulated filth was attributed solely to the "Celestials." The Chinese themselves owned no real estate in Los Angeles, and their landlords had regularly refused to cooperate with earlier efforts to eliminate the eye-sore. In 1877 a frustrated City Council had to settle for merely changing the official name of Negro Alley by incorporating it into Los Angeles Street. When the Workingmen took office public hopes were high that at last some progress would be made, but the best the Workingmen could do was to prorate among the owners the cost of fumigating the area. Later attempts to improve the situation were equally unsuccessful, until 1888 when Los Angeles Street was physically extended, and the adobe apartments of Negro Alley were demolished.[28]

The Workingmen suffered one defeat after another in their campaign against the Chinese. The state "Lodging House Law of 1876," better remembered as the "Cubic Air" law, required that 500 cubic feet of air exist for each tenant of a building. That no effort was made to apply the law in Los Angeles before 1879 reflects the general lack of active resentment to the Chinese, and the conditions under which it failed in that year certainly suggest a continuation of public apathy. In January of 1879 the City Health Officer caused ten Chinese to be arrested for violation of the law. But the city was unable to get a conviction. With absolute evidence on the side of the prosecution, the jury disagreed nine to three for acquittal. Instead of ordering a retrial the judge dismissed the case, explaining that the city could lose a fortune in pursuing such a hopeless cause. Thereafter the law became a dead-letter in Los Angeles.[29]

Anti-Chinese sentiment in Los Angeles decreased rapidly during late 1879 and 1880. The failures of the Workingmen and their defeat in the next election, the improvement of economic conditions, and the departure of large numbers of Chinese for railroad construction in Arizona, all were factors. At the height of the Workingmen's agitation in 1879 the Chinese population may have exceeded 1,000, but the 1880 census recorded only 605 Orientals among more than 11,000 inhabitants. And by the end of the year that figure had been "substantially reduced." The temporary blossoming of agitation in early 1879 can best be attributed to the political advantage labor interests held during the year, although the size of the Chinese community should not be disregarded. That the campaign lasted as long as it did illustrates the determination of the Workingmen, rather than prolonged public endorsement.[30]

In November, 1880, a new treaty was negotiated with China in which the United States was permitted to "regulate, limit or suspend" the immigration of Chinese laborers. This was a major step toward achievement of the anti-Chinese movement's goal, but Los Angeles gave it no particular attention. Jobs were plentiful enough and sentiment against the Chinese was so reduced by July, 1881, that the Los Angeles Woolen Mills began replacing white laborers who refused to work a 15-hour day with Chinese, and no issue was made of the action.[31]

In the early months of 1882, when statewide agitation over the impending passage of a Chinese restriction bill was high, the Los Angeles Times put forth a distasteful and unsuccessful campaign to arouse the citizenry. A series of articles attributed the majority of major crimes in California to the Chinese, representing American hoodlums as "tame and insignificant" in comparison. Other articles purported that a "prominent physician" held Chinese wash-houses responsible for the appearance of cases of mysterious "syphilitic sores" among "moral persons." The *Times* supported these accusations with the "well known fact that so impure has become the Chinese nation as a whole that the custom of handshaking is unknown among them."[32]

Seated amid the snowballing excitement in Northern California, the governor set aside March 4, 1882, as a legal holiday for the purpose of each locality helping to demonstrate state-wide opposition to further immigration. The Los Angeles rally was well attended. The city band played, a cannon was fired which "smashed every window in the neighborhood," and a resolution was drawn up and sent on to Washington to encourage Congress. This jubilant holiday may have occasioned the half-hearted attempt in April to exclude the Chinese from the city, relying upon the 1879 state constitution and subsequent laws for the authority to do so. However, the matter was immediately dropped when the city attorney pointed out the obvious conflict of such an ordinance with the federal constitution.[33]

In 1882 local newspapers showed mixed reaction to President Arthur's veto of a twenty year restriction bill. The *Evening Express* called it an abuse of the veto power while the *Times* agreed with the president that such a long period of restriction amounted to exclusion and thereby constituted a spiritual breach of the new treaty with China. In other parts of the state the President was being hanged in effigy. Some localities organized anti-Chinese leagues with the express purpose of expelling the Chinese forcibly. However, no such reaction found expression among Angelenos. On May 6, 1882, President Arthur signed a bill which provided for suspension of the immigration of Chinese laborers for ten years. While most of California celebrated, Los Angeles accepted the news without any demonstration. The rabidly anti-Chinese *Times* extended a soft note of thanks to Pacific Coast congressmen without further comment. At the next meeting of the City Council the achievement was not even mentioned.[34]

Anti-Chinese agitation in Los Angeles did not die with the passage of this act in 1882. In a very real sense it had died in 1879 with the demise of the Workingmen. The indifference exhibited by Angelenos when restriction finally was achieved was representative of the local attitude throughout most of the pre-1882 campaign. The slaughter that occurred in 1871 is misleading when regarded as an episode of the anti-Chinese movement. The only relation that might be drawn is that the massacre tended to retard such a movement in Los Angeles and perhaps exerted a sobering influence on the character of the local campaign. Over most of the period covered here there were too few Chinese in the city to warrant concerted agitation. Nor was the laboring element of Los Angeles either large enough or well enough organized in these years to arouse and sustain popular sympathy for their cause, especially among a population that obviously found Chinese services and prices irresistible.

An enlarged laboring class resurrected anti-Chinese agitation from its grave in 1885-1886, but with results similar to those of 1879. The futility of the anti-Chinese movement in Los Angeles is well illustrated by the "death-bed" appeal of the 1886 campaign—that the City Council should at least compel Chinese launderers to write their tickets in English![35]

Notes

1. The standard works on the anti-Chinese movement are Mary Roberts Coolidge, *Chinese Immigration*, New York, 1909, and Elmer C. Sandmeyer, *The Anti-Chinese Movement in California*, Urbana, Ill., 1939. The former is the more exhaustive study, but the less objective.

2. This was one of several popular terms of reference to the Chinese and appears to have been second only to "John Chinaman" in usage. In California it was frequently used to ridicule the "obviously non-celestial" Chinese immigrant. The term probably derived from "Celestial Empire," an Occidental name for China.

3. Coolidge, *op. cit.*, 30–31. John Walton Caughey, *California*, Englewood Cliffs, N. J., 1957, 383. Sandmeyer, *op. cit.*, chap. 3, gives concise coverage of the early legislation. Lucile Eaves, *A History of California Labor Legislation*, Berkeley, 1910, 134–140. Grace Heilman Stimson, *Rise of the Labor Movement in Los Angeles*, Berkeley, 1955, 10.

4. Sandmeyer, *op. cit.*, chap. 2. Ira M. Condit, *The Chinaman as We See Him and Fifty Years of Work for Him*, New York, 1900, 21–22.

5. Caughey, *loc. cit.* Condit, *op. cit.*, 22. Sandmeyer, *op. cit.*, 109–110, 120.

6. Stimson, *op. cit.*, 10–11. Ira B. Cross, *A History of the Labor Movement in California*, Berkeley, 1935, 78. *Seventh Census of the United States, 1850*, 969. Maurice H. and Marco R. Newmark, *Census of the City and County of Los Angeles, California, for the Year 1850*, Los Angeles, 1929, 30–31, 67, 115, 117. *Eighth Census of the United States, 1860*, I, 29. *Ninth Census of the United States, 1870*, I, 90; the actual population of the city being 5,728. Sandmeyer, *op. cit.*, 17.

7. Stimson, op. cit., 3. Caughey, op. cit., 394.

8. Harris Newmark, Sixty Years in Southern California, Boston, 1930, 123. Star, March 22, 1872. All newspapers cited are of Los Angeles; City of Los Angeles, Register of Licenses, 1872; contains records of 1872–1873 and 1875–1877.

9. Marco R. Newmark, "Calle de los Negros and the Chinese Massacre of 1871," Historical Society of Southern California Quarterly, XXVI, Nos. 2 and 3 (June, September, 1944), 98. Harris Newmark, op. cit., 30–31. Edwin R. Bingham, The Saga of the Los Angeles Chinese. (Unpublished M. A. thesis, Occidental College, Los Angeles, 1942), 23. Evening Express, March 4, 1880.

10. Star, October 15, November 26, 1859; April 27, June 8, August 17, 1861; August 27, September 6, November 1, 1870; June 2, 1875.

11. Star, January 24, March 21, 1857. Semi-Weekly News, June 21, 1867.

12. Star, September 4, 1869; July 9, 16, 21, 24, August 16, 1870; April 27, 1871. Sandmeyer, op. cit., 78. Stimson, op. cit., 10.

13. Star, October 25, 26, 27, 1871. Chester P. Dorland, "Chinese Massacre at Los Angeles in 1871." Historical Society of Southern California, Annual, Vol. III (1894), 22–26. Remi A. Nadeau, City-Makers, Garden City, N. Y., 1948, 63–70. Hubert Howe Bancroft, "California Inter Pocula," The Works of Hubert Howe Bancroft, XXXV, San Francisco, 1888, 563–568. Paul M. De Falla, "Lantern in the Western Sky," Historical Society of Southern California Quarterly, XLII, No. 1 (March, 1960), 57–88, No. 2 (June, 1960), 161–185. For a much-questioned account see Horace Bell, On the Old West Coast, New York, 1930, 166–177.

14. Harris Newmark, op. cit., 434. Dorland, op. cit., 25–26. Star, October 25, 1871. City of Los Angeles, Records of the Common Council, VII, 387.

15. Cross, op. cit., 63–64, Star, October 9, 1871. Stimson, loc. cit. A story has been perpetuated that a "heavy indemnity" was paid to China by the United States government as a result of the Los Angeles riot. Available sources reveal no such payment. It is possible that payments in 1887 and 1889 for Chinese property losses in Wyoming and Washington riots have led to this misconception. Compare Marco R. Newmark, "Calle de Los Negros and Chinese Massacre of 1871," loc. cit. and Marco R. Newmark, Jottings in Southern California History, Los Angeles, 1955, 41.

16. Stimson, op. cit., 10–11. Cross, op. cit., 84. Star, May 30, June 5, 27, 1873. Evening Express, May 28, June 2, 1873.

17. Sandmeyer, op. cit., 57–58, 81–82. Cross, op. cit., 85. Stimson, op. cit., 11. U. S. Congress, Report of the Joint Special Committee to Investigate Chinese Immigration, 44th Congress, 2nd Session, Report No. 689, Washington, 1877, 1.

18. Evening Express, May 6, 10, 11, 17, 26, June 30, August 23, 1876. Star, May 9, 18, 25, August 24, 1876. Stimson, op. cit., 11–12. U. S. Congress, op. cit., 1140–1141.

19. Harris Newmark, op. cit., 504. Stimson, op. cit., 7, 9–12.

20. Ludwig Louis Salvator, Los Angeles in the Sunny Seventies [trans. by Marguerite Eyer Wilbur], Los Angeles, 1929, 41, 43.

21. The number of Chinese laundries in 1879 is estimated at 30, based upon a general trend found in compiling occupation totals from the Register of

Licenses, 1872 (see note 8); the figures are: 1875, 17; 1876, 24; 1877, 25. The Star, January 29, 1879, estimated that each Chinese laundry employed an average of 10 workers. *Tenth Census of the United States, 1880*, XIX, 781. Star, January 14, 1879. *Herald*, February 29, 1879.

22. Star, December 15, 1878. *Herald*, January 28, 29, 1879.

23. Herald, January 28, 29, 30, 1879. Stimson, *op. cit.*, 25.

24. Herald, January 29, 1879.

25. Herald, January 29, February 2, 1879. Star, February 2, 3, 6, 1879.

26. Records of the Los Angeles Common Council, XII, 759–767, XIII, 318, 434, 766. Star, February 6, 7, 10, 14, 21, May 14, 1879. *Herald*, January 29, February 2, 7, 9, 14, May 2, 4, August 8, September 26, 27, 1879. *Evening Express*, May 2, August 4, 1879. Stimson, *loc. cit.*

27. Star, January 14, 29, February 13, March 11, 27, 1879. *Herald*, February 19, 1879.

28. City of Los Angeles, *Deeds From the City of Los Angeles*, III. City of Los Angeles, *Assessment Roll*, 1862, 1867–1873, 1876, 1879, 1881. Marco R. Newmark, "Ordinances and Regulation of Los Angeles, 1832–1888," *Historical Society of Southern California Quarterly*, XXX, No. 2 (June, 1948), 105. Star, March 24, 1879; June 17, 1879. *Herald*, January 12, June 6, 13, 1879. William M. Caswell, compiler, *Revised Charter and Compiled Ordinances and Resolutions of the City of Los Angeles*, Los Angeles, 1878, 452. Records of the Los Angeles Common Council, XIII, 207.

29. Cross, *op. cit.*, 82. Sandmeyer, *op. cit.*, 63. *Herald*, January 31, February 4, 5, 1879.

30. Star, January 12, 1879. The speaker at a Workingmen's rally referred to the "herd of 1500" Chinese in Los Angeles. Carey McWilliams, *Southern California County*, New York, 1946, 84–85, shows a 1879 figure of 236 for Los Angeles, but he does not indicate his source. His 1880 figure is 1170, considerably higher than the census figure and the mayor's calculation at the end of the year. *Herald*, December 13, 1879. *Evening Express*, March 4, June 19, December 23, 1880. *Tenth Census of the United States, 1880*, I, 416. The total population reported for Los Angeles was 11,183.

31. Eaves, *op. cit.*, 172–173. Sandmeyer, *op. cit.*, 91–92. *Evening Express*, December 28, 31, 1880. *Herald*, May 15, July 27, August 19, 1881.

32. Times, January 26, 27, 28, 31, February 1, April 7, 8, 1882.

33. Times, March 5, April 9, May 2, 1882. Records of the Los Angeles Common Council, XV, 342, 343.

34. Times, April 5, 19, May 9, 1882. *Evening Express*, May 10, 1882. Records of the Los Angeles Common Council, XV, 381–392.

35. Stimson, *op. cit.*, 66; the 1885–1886 anti-Chinese campaign in Los Angeles is given excellent coverage in chap. 5, "Union Against the Chinese."

Part VI
Time of Transition, 1900–1940

Time of Transition, 1900–1940

Many United States citizens entered the twentieth century bent on reforming the political and economic structure of the nation. Partial success at reform by Progressives at home and abroad preceded a period of reaction and retrenchment in the twenties. The depression which followed spawned the New Deal and its wide-ranging efforts at social and economic planning. But these reform impulses offered little to the nation's burgeoning nonwhite population. In fact, white reformers frequently attacked minorities as obstructions to the national progress.

Only during the New Deal did a shift begin in the basic attitude of whites toward nonwhites. Even then, gains for these minorities failed to keep pace with the improved status of the remainder of the population. The experience of the various nonwhites was broadly similar in that all remained second-class citizens, but the circumstances of each group varied according to its economic and organizational resources, and, for Orientals and Chicanos, according to the nation's foreign policy.

Blacks, for example, confronted a rash of lynchings, segregation laws, and political restrictions by organizing associations such as the NAACP, Marcus Garvey's Back-to-Africa movement, and A. Philip Randolph's union, the Brotherhood of Sleeping Car Porters and

Maids. They also fought back, as exemplified by riots in St. Louis (1917) and Longview, Texas (1919). In search of better opportunities, other black Americans migrated from country to city and from the South to the North and West. Many blacks also switched their political allegiance from the Republican to the Democratic party, especially during the administrations of Franklin D. Roosevelt.

Dependent upon an often heedless national government, American Indians had few possible means of ameliorating their plight. Unarmed, stateless, poorly clothed, ill-fed, and decimated in population, they were vulnerable to the machinations of whites. The Indians were restricted to reservations or encouraged to take up farming on small, impoverished tracts of land as whites enforced acculturation on the red man. Government funds and supplies were siphoned off by unscrupulous Indian agents and other whites. Education provided by the boarding school plan separated youths from their families and sent them east in an effort to sunder them from parental authority as well as the body of Indian tradition. One response of the Indians was to withdraw, as evidenced by the Native American Church, a blend of Christianity and native religions emphasizing peyote-induced visions. Eventually, white policy began to change; in 1924 all Indians were granted citizenship, and in 1934 the Indian Reorganization Act enabled tribes once more to acquire land and allowed self-government on the reservations.

The Chinese fell victim to United States exclusionary tactics and their own pattern of immigration. Because of the series of exclusion acts in force from 1882 to 1943, few Chinese were able to come to the United States. Those who had immigrated were generally men who had the goal of working in order to send the proceeds back to the families they left behind or to return to their homeland themselves. Their return to China and the lack of females inhibited natural population increases, which, together with the exclusion policy, caused their population in California to decline from approximately 73,000 in 1890 to 36,000 in 1930.

Japanese, who increasingly immigrated to the United States, as demonstrated by their growth in the population of California from 10,000 in 1900 to 97,000 in 1930, soon encountered the tactics that were employed against the Chinese. The San Francisco School Board precipitated an international incident in 1906 when it segregated Japanese pupils. Shortly afterward, Theodore Roosevelt negotiated the infamous Gentlemen's Agreement in which Japan promised to limit immigration to the United States. By 1924 anti-Japanese forces dominated the political scene, and Congress closed off further immigration.

More Mexican nationals also entered the United States, partly as a result of political disturbances in Mexico and partly to take advantage of economic opportunities in the United States. But conditions were barely tolerable for the Mexican-American, whether he lived in ramshackle rural housing and toiled as a farmhand or inhabited a southwestern city barrio and worked as an industrial laborer. Enmity between Anglos and Mexicans, encouraged by United States military invasions of Mexico during Woodrow Wilson's administration, separated the latter from the white culture and legal system. In some areas, most notably south Texas during and after World War I, Anglos murdered Mexicans with impunity.

In some respects, the years between 1900 and 1940 modified the dismal conditions in which nonwhites lived. Overt discrimination decreased, employment opportunities improved, and the national government responded more vigorously to minority problems. But these gains were limited; significant improvements awaited the mid-century mark and a new spirit of militancy by nonwhites.

Randolph C. Downes,
"A Crusade for Indian Reform, 1922–1934"

For American Indians survival required contending with a federal government which vacillated in its policies according to the pressure by whites for Indian lands and which developed specious rationalizations to support the displacement of the tribes. For example, land speculators and their governmental allies proposed that Indians develop small farms to foster acculturation. The farm allotments were to come from the reservations, but any excess Indian land could be sold. Under this scheme approximately ninety million acres of the best remaining Indian land came into the possession of whites. Randolph C. Downes, in "A Crusade for Indian Reform, 1922–1934," details the efforts of reformers and administrators, culminating in the Indian Reorganization Act of 1934, to eradicate the more reprehensible aspects of the allotment system.

A Crusade for Indian Reform, 1922–1934

Randolph C. Downes

The 8th of February, 1887 "may be called the Indian emancipation day."[1] Thus spoke the reform-minded, government-sponsored Board of Indian Commissioners in 1887 in reporting to the Secretary of the Interior on the passage of the Dawes Act for the allotment of tribal land in individual farms to the American Indians. Forty-seven years later, on June 18, 1934, President Franklin D. Roosevelt signed the Wheeler-Howard Act which had for its aim the restoration and revival of Indian tribal life, and the stoppage of all further individual allotting of land. Said John Collier concerning this event: "Whether that date shall be known hereafter as the Independence Day of Indian history will be determined by the Indians themselves.... The Allotment law—the agony and ruin of the Indians—has been repealed."[2] Thus spoke the reform-minded, government-sponsored Commissioner of Indian Affairs as he set about the job of inaugurating a typically

Abridged from Randolph C. Downes, "A Crusade for Indian Reform, 1922–1934," *Mississippi Valley Historical Review*, XXXII (December 1945), pp. 331–334, 336–337, 339–345, 349–354. Reprinted by permission of the Organization of American Historians. Some footnotes have been renumbered.

1. "Annual Report of the Board of Indian Commissioners, 1887," in *Report of the Secretary of the Interior ... 1887* (Washington, 1887), 6.

2. *Indians at Work* (Office of Indian Affairs, Washington, D.C.), I, July 1, 1934, p. 1.

twentieth-century collectivistic reform to replace a typically nineteenth-century individualistic one....

"The allotment act," said Commissioner Collier in submitting his draft[3] of the reform bill to the Indian Affairs committees of Senator Burton K. Wheeler and Representative Edgar Howard, "contemplates total landlessness for the Indians of the third generation of each allotted tribe."[4] He pointed out that since 1887 the total Indian land holdings had decreased from 138,000,000 acres to 48,000,000 acres, 20,000,000 of which were arid or semi-arid. Three kinds of sales had accounted for this diminution: sales of "surplus" lands left over on a reservation after the members of the tribe had received their allotments; sales by Indians after they had received full title to their allotments; and sales of allotments divided into small pieces by parents who never increased the size of their holdings, but who either divided the land in their wills evenly among their children or who died intestate. The continuation of these sales, especially of the third type, for two more generations "mathematically insures and practically requires that the remaining Indian allotted lands shall pass to whites." This means that there was a gradually accelerating fragmentation of the Indian lands especially by division among the heirs of the original allottees and this fragmentation was reducing the size of the holdings to unworkable dimensions. The process usually took the form of a lease or sale of the small parcels of land to neighboring white farmers so that Indian lands were becoming "mere islands within a sea of white-owned property." "The Indians," concluded Collier, "are practically compelled to become absentee landlords with petty and fast-dwindling estates, living upon the always diminishing pittances of lease money."[5] . . .

3. A dispatch to the New York Times of February 14, 1934, p. 8, stated: "The bill was drafted in the Office of Indian Affairs with the help of Nathan R. Margold, Solicitor of the Interior Department." See also New York Herald Tribune, Feb. 14, 1934, p. 4.

4. "Readjustment of Indian Affairs," Hearings on H. R. 7902, House Committee on Indian Affairs, 73 Cong., 2 Sess., Part 1, p. 17.

5. For more detailed treatment of the allotment system see ibid., 15–21; D. S. Otis, "History of the Allotment Policy," ibid., Part 9, pp. 428–89; Lewis Meriam, et al., The Problem of Indian Administration (Baltimore, 1928), 469–72; John Collier, "A Lift for the Forgotten Red Man, Too," New York Times Magazine, May 6, 1934, pp. 10–11; and Felix S. Cohen, Handbook of Federal Indian Law (Washington, 1942), 206–236.

Before the administrators of Indian affairs could take hold of the job of reform, the problem had to go through the muckraking stage. Conditions had to be played up, even exaggerated, by those who could focus public attention on the problem through the publicity of episodes seemingly illustrative of particularly outrageous treatment of the Indians. And it would have been unusual if the scandal-ridden years of the early 1920's had not provided grist for reformers of Indian affairs. It is not surprising then that in 1922–1924 the fight against the so-called Bursum Pueblo Land bill provided an appropriate episode, and that the principal villain should be the ill-starred Secretary of Interior Albert B. Fall of Teapot Dome fame. It was this affair which gave birth to the dynamic, crusading American Indian Defense Association,[6] and it was this association, through its indefatigable executive secretary, John Collier, which sparked the reform movement that reached its climax in the adoption of the Wheeler-Howard Act. . . .

. . . The summer of 1923 saw the issuance by the newly-formed American Indian Defense Association of a statement of general principles drawn up by Dr. [Herbert J.] Spinden [of the Peabody Museum at Harvard] in collaboration with the Indian Welfare Committee of the General Federation of Women's Clubs. The program emphasized the need of developing Indian " 'group loyalties and communal responsibilities,' " including tribal landholding, self-government, and religious freedom, the creation of an organization to promote the sale of genuine products of Indian arts and craftsmanship, and a complete reorganization of the education, health, and irrigation services.[7] Not to be outdone, the 42-year-old Indian Rights Association revamped its services with the aid of a grant from John D. Rockefeller, Jr., and in February, 1924 began to issue a monthly bulletin known as *Indian Truth*.[8] The two associations collaborated in an exposé of the exploitation of Oklahoma's Indians, but eventually found themselves at var-

6. John Collier, "No Trespassing," *Sunset*, L (May, 1923), 60.

7. *The Survey*, L (Aug. 1, 1923), 501. In 1925 the Indian Defense Associations of California began the publication in San Francisco of a periodical called *American Indian Life*. In 1927 the publication was announced as being "issued on behalf of the American Defense Association." See *American Indian Life*, Bulletin 1, June, 1925; and Bulletin 8, May, 1927.

8. *Forty-Second Annual Report of the Board of Directors of the Indian Rights Association* (Philadelphia, 1924), 5.

iance because of the more radical aims and less quietistic policies of the Indian Defense Association of which the militant Collier was executive secretary.[9] . . .

An orgy of muckraking ensued. Alleged government maladministration in tribe after tribe was set before the public. Loudest and longest in the attack, though not first, was Sunset, "the West's Great National Magazine," which, from November, 1922 until June, 1924, had only six issues without at least one leading article denouncing the Indian Bureau.[10] Lead-off man was novelist Stewart Edward White, whose article "Our Treatment of the Indians," called the story of American Indian affairs American history's blackest page. White's article was accompanied by one written by Indian storyteller James Willard Schultz, entitled "America's Red Armenians," which accused the Indian Bureau of blocking private relief to the starving Blackfeet of Montana. . . .

The climax came early in 1924 with the publication by the Indian Rights Association of a pamphlet entitled "Oklahoma's Poor Rich Indians," and subtitled "An Orgy of Graft and Exploitation of the Five Civilized Tribes—Legalized Robbery." It was written by Gertrude Bonnin, Research Agent of the Indian Welfare Committee of the General Federation of Women's Clubs, Charles H. Fabens of the American Indian Defense Association, and Matthew K. Sniffen of the Indian Rights Association. It asserted that, as the result of the transfer in 1908 to the county probate courts in Oklahoma of all jurisdiction over the estates of Indian minors and incompetents, the Indians were being "shamelessly and openly robbed in a scientific and ruthless manner." It was claimed that in many counties the Indians were virtually at the mercy of groups or rings of judges, guardians, attorneys, bankers, merchants, and undertakers, all of whom regarded the Indian estates as "legitimate game."[11]

These charges made the Oklahoma tribes the leading Indian sensation in the press for the next two years. In the spring of 1924 the House of Representatives ordered an investigation by its Committee on Indian Affairs which in turn sent a subcommittee to Oklahoma to

9. Indian Truth, I (Feb., 1924), 1; (May, 1924), 2–3; (Aug.–Sept., 1924), 3.
10. Sunset, XLIX (Nov., 1922) to LII (June, 1924).
11. Gertrude Bonnin, Charles H. Fabens, and Matthew K. Sniffen, Oklahoma's Poor Rich Indians (Philadelphia, 1924), 11–17.

conduct hearings. On February 19, 1925 the subcommittee reported,[12] declaring that "the wholesale charges made against the judges, attorneys, business and professional men of Oklahoma are not sustained by any evidence," but that in the oil producing districts inhabited by the Osages there were some "reprehensible and indefensible practices carried on . . . by unconscionable attorneys and persons who make it a profession to obtain appointments as guardians." The result was the passage of the act of February 27, 1925, greatly increasing the guardianship powers of the Indian Bureau over wealthy Osages.[13]

The Pueblo Lands Board Act of 1924 and the Osage Guardianship Act of 1925 were signs of a new day. It was not long before administrators began to see that, in order to avoid the embarrassment of these pin-prick reforms, a general review of the entire Indian service would be a good thing. The occasion for this was the accession in 1923 of Hubert Work as Secretary of Interior in the place of Fall. With the air full of slurs on the quality of the Indian Service, Work sought to clarify the situation by inviting one hundred leaders in the field of Indian welfare to constitute a National Advisory Committee on Indian Affairs. A heterogeneous collection of seventy-five advisers thereupon assembled in Washington on December 11 and 12, 1923, and, after two days of futile wrangling and parliamentary ineptitude, passed a series of innocuous resolutions in which, save for a health proposal, "not one fundamental proposition . . . was put across," to use John Collier's words.[14]

Secretary Work was no radical reformer, but he could see, as Collier saw, the amateur quality of the report of the Advisory Com-

12. "Indian Affairs in Oklahoma," *House Report 1527*, 68 Cong., 2 Sess., 7, 8. See pamphlet of Indian Rights Association by M. K. Sniffen, " 'Out of Thine Own Mouth'—An Analysis of the House Subcommittee Report Denying and Confirming the Looting of Oklahoma's 'Poor Rich Indians'" (Philadelphia, March 10, 1925), 1–5.

13. *House Report 1527*, 68 Cong., 2 Sess., 10; *Statutes at Large*, XLIII, 1008.

14. John Collier, "The Red Slaves of Oklahoma," *Sunset*, LII (March, 1924), 100; O. G. V. [illard], "For the Indian's Sake," *Nation*, CXVII (Dec. 26, 1923), 734–5; Elizabeth Shepley Sergeant, "The Red Man's Burden," *New Republic*, XXXVII (Jan. 16, 1924), 199–201. For a summary of the resolutions passed, see letter by Arthur C. Parker, the committee's chairman, in *New York Times*, Jan. 20, 1924, Section 8, p. 8.

mittee. Therefore, on June 23, 1925, ignoring temporarily Collier's proposal to engage the fact-finding services of the institute for Government Research, he called upon the 55-year-old advisory Board of Indian Commissioners to investigate and make recommendations. "These reiterated charges and counter-charges," said Work, "give rise to a desire on my part to have a competent body of observers such as is to be found in the membership of your board, and unconnected with the Department of the Interior, formulate their views after proper inquiry."[15] The Board's unpublished report of January 26, 1926 was a whitewash. It said that all charges against Commissioner Burke were "puerile," and that those against Superintendent Wallen of the Five Civilized Tribes in Oklahoma were "politics." It recommended that the office of Superintendent of the Five Civilized Tribes be put under the Civil Service and that all Indians having annual incomes of over $5,000 be segregated for special aid in the administration of their estates.[16]

Just what Secretary Work thought of the Board's report he kept to himself. But it evidently soon became clear to him that the business of constructive Indian reform required something more than the attention of unendowed part-time committees. By 1926 he had come around to Collier's view that expert, unbiased, and full-time counsel should be consulted. The Board of Indian Commissioners was also of the same opinion in its annual report of June 30, 1926. It admitted the great complexity of the Oklahoma problem, its own inability to cope with it, and the need for outside, unbiased investigation. "We believe," said the Board, "there are organizations, amply financed and manned, which would undertake this task without expense to the Government.... [A] report from a non-Government,

15. New York Times, July 24, 1925, p. 12.
16. Ibid., Jan. 29, 1926, p. 10. The report is referred to in Annual Report of the Board of Indian Commissioners to the Secretary of the Interior, ... June 30, 1926 (Washington, 1926), 1, 17. The Board of Indian Commissioners had been created by Congress in 1869 to consist of nine presidentially-appointed philanthropists to serve as unpaid advisers to the Indian Bureau. Long before 1934, indeed long before 1887, "the Board had demonstrated its inability to effect vital improvements" and had thus turned the reform movement over to outside agencies. Loring Benson Priest, Uncle Sam's Stepchildren: The Reformation of United States Indian Policy, 1865–1887 (New Brunswick, N.J., 1942), 42–53.

disinterested organization, with a field force of experts, would carry great weight not only with Congress but also with the general public."[17]

Even before the official submission of this report Work had made up his mind, and, on June 12, 1926, had requested W. F. Willoughby, director of the Institute for Government Research, to make a survey of the economic and social conditions of the American Indians. Members of the staff of the Institute headed by Lewis Meriam, aided by nine specially selected experts, at once applied themselves to the job, and, after seven months intensive field work, prepared the monumental report which Willoughby submitted to Work on February 21, 1928.[18]

The Meriam Report was a masterpiece of reform propaganda in the best sense of the word. Its high-minded scientific accuracy was never seriously questioned. Its non-controversial tone commanded the respect of both supporters and critics of the Indian Bureau. Although highly critical of American Indian policy, it avoided personalities. Indeed, it won friends from the very Bureau which it criticized. "The object of the survey," said Willoughby in his letter of transmittal, "has not been to take sides for or against the Indian Office, but to endeavor through constructive criticism to aid insofar as possible in pointing the way toward marked improvement in this important activity of the national government. That was our understanding of your request."[19] Obviously Indian reform was now lifted from the field of controversy and placed in the realm of practical businesslike possibility.

A second piece of scientific research into the Indian service was the Preston-Engle Irrigation Report. This was the result of Secretary Work's request of March, 1927, that a survey be made of Indian irrigation projects with a view to the improvement of Indian farming conditions. . . .

But these investigations had very little effect on the Indian Service during the years of Secretary Work's incumbency. The Commissioner

17. *Annual Report of the Board of Indian Commissioners*, 1926, p. 13.

18. Meriam, vii–x.

19. *Idem*. The Report was widely applauded by the press throughout the country. See *New York Times*, May 23, 1928.

of Indian Affairs from 1921 to 1929 was Charles H. Burke, formerly Congressman from South Dakota, and author of the so-called Burke Act of 1906 speeding up the individual distribution of Indian land under the allotment system. Burke was an avowed rugged individualist. In 1923 he was quoted as saying: " 'I believe in making the Indian take his chance, just the same as white folks do.... Don't fool yourself. The Indian makes good when he has the chance.' "[20] This attitude led the New York Times to say editorially that prior to 1929 the administration of the Bureau of Indian Affairs "never quite overcame the frontiersman's attitude" toward the Indians.[21] This last of the "frontier" Commissioners was quite contemptuous of reformers of the Collier type. Speaking of the Pueblo agitation he said: "It is like going to a lot of children and telling them they ought to start a row for more than they are getting.... Propagandists are touring part of the country with a company of dancing and singing Pueblos in full Indian regalia in order to awaken people to the 'crime' in New Mexico. There is no crime in New Mexico."[22] ...

The pre-New Deal phase of the Indian reform movement really got under way in 1929 when President Hoover appointed Ray Lyman Wilbur, educator, social worker, and president of Leland Stanford University, to be Secretary of the Interior. That Wilbur's appointment presaged progressive measures in the Indian Bureau was seen in the replacement of Burke and Meritt, the last of the "frontier" administrators, by two Quaker humanitarians, Charles J. Rhoads, wealthy Philadelphia banker, and president of the Indian Rights Association, and J. Henry Scattergood, treasurer of Haverford and Bryn Mawr Colleges, Pennsylvania Working Home for the Blind, and Christiansburg Industrial Institute.[23] Reformers rejoiced. John Collier declared the appointment "well nigh incredibly fortunate,"[24] and Ickes predicted: "Mr. Rhoads will write a new and fairer chapter in the terrible story of our treatment of the Indian.... He gives the im-

20. Herbert Corey, "He Carries the White Man's Burden," Colliers (May 12, 1923), p. 13.
21. New York Times, April 16, 1929, p. 28.
22. Ibid., March 16, 1924, section 9, p. 3.
23. Indian Truth, VI (May, 1929), 1–2.
24. American Indian Life, Bulletin 14, May, 1929, p. 6.

pression of sympathy and understanding, of justice and fair dealing."[25] ...

No aspect of the Indian reform problem illustrates the difficulty of preparing the red men for individualized farming better than that of Indian irrigation. Unaided by systematic education, the Indians were less able to compete with whites on irrigable land than on fertile land. As the Meriam Survey pointed out: "To win success from a small area of high cost irrigated land requires far better farming than is necessary on a similar area of low cost land watered by natural rainfall." The Preston-Engle report declared: "The development of an irrigated farm ... [requires] far more capital, ingenuity, and perseverance than most Indians possess.... If such a small proportion of our own race can make a success of irrigated farming ... how can it be expected that every Indian can succeed as an irrigation farmer?" And yet in arid country the allotment system of the Dawes Act had been carried out without regard to segregation and future irrigation projects so that, as the Preston-Engle report stated, there resulted "a condition that brought both Indian and white lands under the same irrigation system," and the Indian Service was frequently put "in the position of operating and maintaining irrigation systems more for white people than for the use of the few Indians under the system." The inevitable result had been that the "vast majority" had either leased or sold their lands and the net result was paradoxically enough "to encourage indolence and improvidence." It was estimated that as soon as "irrigated Indians" received unrestricted titles to their lands "70 to 90 per cent ... immediately sell their land."[26]

The proposed remedies were in effect a form of default. Implying that it was too late or too difficult for the Indian Bureau to assume its neglected duty of irrigation education, Preston and Engle recommended that the larger projects be turned over to the Bureau of Reclamation, that the remaining personnel in the Indian irrigation service be drastically improved in quality, and that some of the projects be abandoned.[27] About all that Rhoads seems to have been willing to

25. Ickes, quoted in Cong. Record, 71 Cong., 2 Sess., 2498.
26. Meriam, Problem of Indian Administration, 508; Preston-Engle Report, 2235, 2236, 2280.
27. Ibid., 2217, 2222, 2255, 2258–9, 2504, 2528.

do in this respect was to reorganize the irrigation service,[28] and for his failure to follow Preston and Engle in the other recommendations he was severely criticized by Senators William H. King of Utah and Lynn Frazier of North Dakota.[29] Perhaps the most outstanding reform was the cancellation of several million dollars of so-called "reimbursable debts," charged against Indians for various projects deemed no longer useful to the red men.[30] . . .

How much farther along the road to reform Rhoads would have gone if he had not been replaced by Collier in 1933 is, of course, impossible to say. It is true that Collier accelerated reform to a degree to which Rhoads was incapable. But the Collier administration was an acceleration, and not a break. . . .

. . . From 1933 on, as Collier groomed himself to strike down what Rhoads feared to attack, the Rhoads achievements in education, health, and other lines were carried on and supplemented. The transfer of Indian children from boarding schools to day schools near their homes was speeded up as boarding school enrollment dropped from 22,000 in 1933 to 17,500 in 1934, and plans were made for a decrease to 13,000 in 1935.[31] In the meantime the remaining boarding schools were being transformed into institutions for the care of special classes of children: orphans, those with poor home environments, those without local school facilities, and high school pupils needing vocational training not offered locally.[32] A new spirit came into the Indian Service as Collier issued an order based on the most progressive educational and psychological foundations: " 'No interference with Indian religious life or expression will hereafter be tolerated. The cultural history of Indians is in all respects to be considered equal to that of

28. *Annual Report of the Commissioner of Indian Affairs*, 1931, p. 22.
29. *Cong. Record*, 71 Cong., 3 Sess., 1375–6; "Survey of Conditions Among the Indians of the United States," *Senate Report 25 on Irrigation and Reclamation on Indian Lands*, part 4, 72 Cong., 2 Sess. (1932), 8–9.
30. *Statutes at Large*, XLVI, 1519; *ibid.*, XLVII, 564–5; *Annual Report of the Commissioners of Indian Affairs*, 1930, p. 32; *ibid.*, 1932, p. 19; *ibid.*, 1933, p. 103; *Annual Report of the Directors of the Indian Rights Association, 1932* (Philadelphia, 1933), 10; "Some Reimbursable Wrongs Corrected," *American Indian Life*, Bulletin 18, July, 1931, p. 22; "Pima Relief," *Indian Truth*, VIII (March, 1931), 1–2.
31. *Annual Report of the Secretary of the Interior . . . 1934*, pp. 84–5.
32. "Civilizing the Indian," *Nation*, CXXXVIII (Jan. 10, 1934), 33–4.

any non-Indian group. And it is desirable that Indians be bilingual. . . . The Indian arts are to be prized, nourished, and honored.' "³³ . . .

. . . The time of timorous testing was over, and Commissioner Collier was determined to give the new Indian policy a charter basis. Accordingly the Bureau drafted its own bill with great care and, in February, 1934, submitted it to the tender mercies of Senate and House consideration. Then, while the Congressional committees held their hearings,³⁴ the fighting Collier took to the hustings. Backed by the specific and outspoken endorsement of President Roosevelt,³⁵ Collier took the bill to the country at large and to the Indians in particular. The press and radio were enlisted to create public sentiment in its favor.³⁶ Under the auspices of Bureau employees, great Indian congresses were held throughout the West so as to give as many Indians as possible the chance to hear, discuss, and criticize the bill. Characteristically enough most Indians were more or less suspicious and preferred to return to their people and discuss the proposal at their leisure.³⁷ However, by May 9 fifty-eight tribes comprising a population of 146,194 Indians had voted in favor of the bill and thirteen tribes made up of 15,213 Indians had voted against it.³⁸

Although assailed as communistic, pagan, and Bureau-bought, the measure became law with little difficulty. The title itself is an adequate summary: "An Act to conserve and develop Indian lands and resources; to extend to Indians the right to form business and other

33. *Annual Report of the Secretary of the Interior . . . 1934*, p. 90.

34. "Readjustment of Indian Affairs," *Hearings on H. R. 7902*, House Committee on Indian Affairs, Parts 1–9, 73 Cong., 2 Sess. (1934); "To Grant to Indians Living under Federal Tutelage the Freedom to Organize for Purposes of Local Self-Government and Economic Enterprise . . . ," *Hearings on S. 2755 and S. 3645*, Senate Committee on Indian Affairs, 73 Cong., 2 Sess. (April 26, 28, 30, May 3, 4, 17, 1934).

35. *Hearings on H. R. 7902*, 233–4.

36. *Cong. Record*, 73 Cong., 2 Sess., 9265.

37. Congresses were held at Rapid City, South Dakota, March 2–5, 1934; at Santo Domingo Pueblo, New Mexico, March 15, 1934; at Phoenix, Arizona, March 15–16, 1934; at Riverside, California, March 17–18, 1934; and at Muskogee, Oklahoma, March 22, 1934. See Cohen, 84; Minutes of the Plains Congress (Rapid City Indian School, 1934); and Proceedings of the Conference for the Indians of Southern California held at Riverside, Calif., March 17 and 18, 1934, to discuss the Wheeler-Howard Indian Bill (mimeographed, n. p., n. d.).

38. *Hearings on H. R. 7902*, 399.

organizations; to establish a credit system for Indians; to grant certain rights of home rule to Indians; to provide for vocational education for Indians; and for other purposes."[39] Thus allotment in severalty was explicitly forbidden and any surplus lands still remaining were to be restored to tribal ownership. Sales of lands to, and inheritance by, non-Indians were most drastically restricted. The Secretary of the Interior was enabled to acquire land for incorporation into tribal estates and the expenditure of not over $2,000,000 a year for this purpose was authorized. The sum of $250,000 a year might be spent to defray the expenses of organizing Indian chartered corporations. A revolving fund of $10,000,000 was authorized to make loans to such corporations "for the purpose of promoting the economic development" of the tribes. Another sum of $250,000 a year was to be spent for tuition loans to Indians attending "recognized vocational and trade schools." Exemption of Indians from civil service rules was granted to promote an increase in the number of tribesmen in the staff of the Indian Service. Tribal constitutions were authorized to be created and ratified by the Indians themselves to give them extensive rights of political home rule. The act itself was not to apply to any tribe which should vote not to accept it.

And so we return to where we began. If the rugged individualism of the Dawes Act of 1887 and its subsequent administration were completely at variance with the sociological requirements of cultural amalgamation, the needed scientific adjustments were proposed, promoted, and in some measure adopted in the years before the enactment of the Wheeler-Howard Act of 1934. Indeed, in view of this pre-invasion of twentieth-century reform ideals into the anachronistic preserves of a nineteenth-century Indian administration, modernists might be pardoned their flight of fancy in suggesting that, had the Wheeler-Howard Act been passed in 1887, the American Indians might by 1934 have been ready for the Dawes Act.

39. *Statutes at Large*, XLVIII, 984. Two major parts of the bill as originally introduced were omitted, viz., the creation of a Court of Indian Claims and the application of the law to the Oklahoma Indians.

Elliott M. Rudwick,
"DuBois versus Garvey: Race Propagandists at War"

The early twentieth century gave birth to a series of virulent anti-black practices, including lynching, beating, segregation by law as well as in fact, denial of civil rights, and exclusion from politics. In response, black leaders emerged who voiced opposition to the racist behavior of the white majority and introduced programs for improving the lot of their race. Elliott M. Rudwick contrasts the methods of two prominent black leaders in "DuBois versus Garvey: Race Propagandists at War." Although both men were concerned with alleviating the condition of blacks in the United States, they differed in approach, technique, and personality. Marcus Garvey was outspoken, flamboyant, and emotional; he appealed to the masses of black people. William E. B. DuBois was soft-spoken, reasonable, and moderate; he spoke primarily to the well-educated members of the black race. Both leaders, however, emphasized black pride, confrontation with the white community, black nationalism, and the need for action to eradicate the ills of society.

DuBois versus Garvey:
Race Propagandists at War

Elliott M. Rudwick

After World War I, large numbers of Negroes were stirred by race pride and demanded a "spiritual emancipation." They were encouraged to seek improvement of their own living conditions and work for the betterment of the natives on the African continent. During this post-war decade two prominent leaders, W. E. B. DuBois and Marcus Garvey, clashed in their separate plans to establish an African state and an international organization of Negroes. Both men were propagandists. DuBois was editor of the *Crisis*, the official magazine of the N.A.A.C.P. and Garvey owned the *Negro World*. (The Jamaican regularly wrote articles for his newspaper and the editorial writers he hired adopted his tone.) The present article is based primarily on a study of these two publications and seeks to examine the DuBois-Garvey debate which—especially from Garveyite quarters —was abusive and acrimonious.

In 1917, DuBois favored the formation of a "great free central African state" (the amalgamation of German East Africa and the Belgian Congo); later, he declared that the state should be enlarged to include Uganda, French Equatorial Africa, German Southwest

Elliott M. Rudwick, "DuBois versus Garvey: Race Propagandists at War," *Journal of Negro Education*, XXVIII (1959), pp. 421–429. Reprinted by permission of the author and the publisher.

271

Africa, and the Portuguese territories of Angola and Mozambique.[1] In his conception, a "Brain Trust" of Negro administrators were to be responsible for the establishment of an "industrial democracy," *i.e.,* a socialized system of production and distribution.[2] In 1919, through the help of Blaise Diagne, a Negro Senegalese representative in the French Chamber of Deputies, DuBois received permission from Prime Minister Clemenceau to organize the First Pan-African Congress in Paris. The delegates (from the United States, West Indies, Europe, and Africa) asked the League of Nations to guarantee political, social, and economic rights to the African natives and set up a legal code for the "international protection" of these people. The League was requested to consider the Africans in "international labor legislation" and to provide for native representation within the organization.

According to the Pan-African Congress, "Negroes of the world demand" that the natives should hold title to all African land which they could "profitably" cultivate. The conclave petitioned for effective controls upon the white capitalists in order to prevent further economic exploitation. The conferees also maintained that the Africans should receive assurances that elementary, vocational, and college education would be available to them.[3] To create international racial unity, DuBois proposed to found the *Black Review* (with English, French, and perhaps Spanish and Portuguese editions). He hoped that American Negroes would learn to speak French and Spanish and he was certain that Negro literature and art would thereby gain momentum in all nations. He suggested that U.S. Negroes should travel to Europe on "*personal rencontres* for information and propaganda."[4] The League paid little attention to DuBois's Pan-African Congress, nor did any other group consider the conclave as "representative of the Negro race." The convention had no real grass roots organizational support; only on paper was the N.A.A.C.P. headquarters concerned and the N.A.A.C.P. branches simply ignored the Pan-African Congress. However, DuBois seemed undaunted and con-

1. *Crisis* XV (1917–1918), p. 114.
2. *Crisis* XVII (1918–1919), pp. 119–120.
3. *Crisis* XVII (1918–1919), pp. 271–274.
4. *Crisis* XVII (1918–1919), pp. 269–270.

tinued to grind out propaganda which was moderate in tone and intellectual in approach.

Unlike DuBois, Marcus Garvey was able to gain mass support and his propaganda had a tremendous emotional appeal. He established the Universal Negro Improvement Association in New York (with branches in many U.S. cities and several foreign countries). The aim of the organization was the liberation of Africa. By 1919, he set up the Black Star Line and the Negro Factories Corporation. In August, 1920, Garvey called a month-long convention of the U.N.I.A. in New York City. In the name of "400,000,000 Negros of the World," he declared that Africa must be free. He did not bother to display the restraint which characterized Pan-African leaders and many of his remarks were inflammatory. He warned that his race was prepared to shed its blood to remove the whites from the natives' rightful land in Africa.[5] His convention delegates and members paraded through Harlem. Tens of thousands of Negroes were excited by the massed units of the African Legion in blue and red uniforms and the white-attired contingents of the Black Cross Nurses. Garvey's followers sang the new U.N.I.A. anthem, "Ethiopa, Thou Land of Our Fathers" and they proudly waved the Association's flag (black for Negro skin, green for Negro hopes, and red for Negro blood). Never again was the race to have a leader who could produce such a wonderful show.

DuBois publicly ignored Garvey until December of 1920 and this tardiness of editorial recognition was probably due to the *Crisis* editor's ambivalence toward him. DuBois was profoundly impressed by "this extraordinary leader of men," and he acknowledged that Garvey was "essentially an honest and sincere man with a tremendous vision, great dynamic force, stubborn determination and unselfish desire to serve." However, the *Crisis* editor also considered him to be[6]

dictatorial, domineering, inordinately vain and very suspicious. . . . The great difficulty with him is that he has absolutely no business sense, no flair for real organization and his general objects are so shot through with bombast and exaggeration that it is difficult to pin them down for careful examination.

5. New York *Times*, August 3, 1920. See also *Negro World*, September 11, 1920.
6. *Crisis* XXI (1920–1921), pp. 58–60.

The following month, after DuBois had requested (and failed to receive) a financial statement from the Jamaican on the Negro Improvement Association and the Black Star Line, the *Crisis* editor wrote:[7]

> When it comes to Mr. Garvey's industrial and commercial enterprises there is more ground for doubt and misgiving than in the matter of his character.

Originally, DuBois believed that his own hopes for Africa's reclamation and an international black economy could be achieved through Garvey's mass appeal. He concluded that the failure of the Garvey Movement, which had generated so much "spiritual" potential, might seriously damage racial self-confidence. He was impressed by the "bold effort and some success" of the Jamaican, who, after all, had sent ships ("owned by black men") to sea. However, the editor of the *Crisis* announced that Garvey was expending funds for current expenses instead of using the money for capital improvements. (The flamboyant Garvey seemed more interested in public relations than in buying ships.)

Nevertheless, the *Crisis* editor saw a bright future if Garvey was willing to eschew certain tactics which had been employed in the past:

1. Garvey "introduced" the Jamaican black-mulatto schism to the U. S., where DuBois claimed it had no relevance and only bred disunity. (One of DuBois's own errors was that he minimized this conflict.)
2. Garvey alienated the British by his tactlessness, and the help of Great Britain was required in his international trade plans.
3. He did not seem interested in establishing a friendly relationship with the N.A.A.C.P. and went out of his way to antagonize its officials.
4. His relations with the Liberian Government were less than satisfactory, even though he hoped to establish headquarters there.
5. With inadequate material resources, he still made bellicose statements about conquering Africa.

7. *Crisis* XXI (1920–1921), pp. 112–115.

DuBois's comments showed remarkable temperateness in view of the fact that the Garvey Movement had been attacking him for more than a year. Just before the Pan-African Congress in 1919, Garvey alleged that DuBois talked so mildly and equivocally to French reporters about American race relations, that the Jamaican's "High Commissioner" abroad found his own work sabotaged.[8] DuBois denied the accusation. The *Negro World* instructed its readers that the *Crisis* was basically reactionary and was published from an "aristocratic Fifth Avenue" office.[9] After a *Crisis* editorial on Woodrow Wilson's faithlessness, and following a DuBois comment on the post-war imperialist resurgence in England, the *Negro World* reminded the N.A.A.C.P. propagandist that Garvey had foreseen these developments as early as 1918, when the editor was counseling cooperation with the United States Government. DuBois was pictured as a fallen old warrior whose contributions to the race were at an end. With relish the *Negro World* also took up the cry of A. Philip Randolph's *Messenger* that DuBois was "controlled" by white capitalists on the N.A.A.C.P. board.[10] When the *Crisis* editor was awarded the Spingarn Medal in 1920 for "founding" the First Pan-African Congress, Garvey's paper charged that the entire affair was "a discreditable fraud."[11] (The N.A.A.C.P. citation ignored a 1900 Pan-African conclave. By juggling words, DuBois had "founded" the first Congress because he argued that the 1900 organization was called the Pan-African "Conference.")[12] As far as Garvey was concerned, the 1919 Pan-African Congress had accomplished little and he asserted that William Monroe Trotter's National Equal Rights League had contributed more to the race when it presented its petition to the Peace Conference in Paris:[13]

But perhaps Mr. Villard [one-time N.A.A.C.P. board chairman] and the other gentlemen of the Committee on award regard Mr.

8. *Crisis* XXI (1920–1921), pp. 112–115.
9. *Negro World*, May 24, 1919.
10. *Negro World*, March 13, April 3, 1920.
11. *Negro World*, June 19, 1920.
12. *Crisis* XXI (1920–1921), p. 198.
13. *Negro World*, June 12, 1920.

Trotter as too radical, perhaps they do not regard him from a white man's point of view as safe and sane a leader as Dr. DuBois.

At the 1920 U.N.I.A. convention, Garvey called the *Crisis* editor "the associate of an alien race," and his remark received "the most enthusiastic applause" of the session. The *Negro World's* editorial reaction to DuBois's lengthy critique was typical: "subtle, shrewd, untruthful in its professed sincerity, cunning and adroit in its attempt to blow hot and cold at the same time." The N.A.A.C.P. propagandist was accused of petty jealousy and of being quite possibly "more of a white man than a Negro and [he] seems to be only a professional Negro at that." Garvey mounted the platform to chide DuBois for ignoring the masses and believing in a "bastard aristocracy." In contrast, the Jamaican recalled how he "always walked among [his own] ordinary humble people . . . (cheers)." Garvey proved his ability to write demagogic propaganda:[14]

Where did he [DuBois] get his aristocracy from? He picked it up on the streets of Great Barrington, Mass. He just got it into his head that he should be an aristocrat and ever since that time he has been keeping his very beard as an aristocrat; he has been trying to be everything else but a Negro. Sometimes we hear he is a Frenchman and another time he is Dutch and when it is convenient he is a Negro (Derisive cheers and laughter). Now I have no Dutch. I have no French, I have no Anglo-Saxon in me, but I am but a Negro now and always (thunderous applause). I have no Frenchmen to imitate, I have no Anglo-Saxon to imitate; I have but the ancient glories of Ethiopia to imitate. (Great applause.) The men who built the Pyramids looked like me, and I think the best thing I can do is to keep looking like them. Anyone you hear always talking about the kind of blood he has in him other than the blood you can see, he is dissatisfied with something, and I feel sure that many of the Negroes of the United States of America know that if there is a man who is most dissatisfied with himself, it is Dr. DuBois.

In order to demonstrate that displeasure with DuBois was mounting in various quarters of the race, the *Negro World* reprinted several

14. *Negro World*, January 8, 1921.

comments and editorials from other Negro papers. The Richmond *Planet* believed that DuBois was much out of his element for having the audacity to reproach Garvey, the "man of action." The Oakland *Sunshine* expressed similar sentiments: "DuBois is talking big things and Garvey is doing big things. We rather admire the man that does rather than talks." According to this newspaper, the N.A.A.C.P. propagandist was hurting the Association by his anti-Garvey campaign. The *Sunshine's* editor contended that the Garvey organization was larger and more powerful than the N.A.A.C.P. and was dedicated to DuBois's principles of improving the status of Negroes in the United States. The *National Review* took DuBois to task for editorializing on Pan-African movements and omitting the U.N.I.A. For this incompleteness, DuBois was dubbed, "king of journalistic jugglers."[15]

The *Negro World* was resentful because of the *Crisis's* tone of superiority and public omniscience. DuBois was castigated for thinking that Negroes who wanted to start race enterprises were obliged to appear before his inquisition.[16] A Garveyite published a pamphlet in 1921 entitled, "The Mistakes of Dr. W. E. B. DuBois," which was designed to show its victim's feet of clay:[17]

> Garvey's old, unseaworthy wooden ships are still plowing through the turbulent waters of old Father Neptune's salty domains. Unlike the wreck of the Niagara Movement, they are not lying high and dry upon the weather-beaten shores of Disaster.

Such remarks brought forth DuBoisian retaliation, and he blasted the Garveyites as "scoundrels and bubble-blowers" who were causing havoc within the race. He denounced them for damning all whites and exploiting the Negro masses. (He claimed that the white supremacists were retreating and that the N.A.A.C.P. would liberate the Negroes in another quarter of a century.[18] In the past, DuBois had also condemned whites in wholesale fashion, but in fighting Garvey, he undoubtedly tried to appear more optimistic about interracial relations than he actually was.)

15. Reprinted in *Negro World*, January 29, March 5, and May 21, 1921.

16. *Negro World*, May 14, 1921.

17. Wheeler Sheppard, *Mistakes of Dr. W. E. B. DuBois*, pamphlet, New York, 1921.

18. *Crisis* XXII (1921), p. 8.

During the early months of 1921, DuBois was preparing for the Second Pan-African Congress which he announced for the fall. He promised to invite not only the Negro Governments, but "all Negro organizations interested in the peoples of African descent." He also mentioned that colonial powers would be encouraged to send delegates to the conclave which was to be held in Europe again.[19] Realizing that his organization would be confused with and compared with the Garveyites, he stressed that the Second Pan-African Congress was not convening to prepare a "scheme of migration." Shortly before the Congress, the *Negro World* reminded DuBois that only about one-fourth of the delegates to his first Congress were from Africa, and since the ratio had been so small, the term "Pan-African" was unrealistic. The N.A.A.C.P. propagandist had only recently printed a letter from the Liberian President, and the note was intended to rebuke the Garveyites. (The Liberian chief of state warned that his country would not allow itself to serve as a base of operations from which the Garvey Movement could harass other governments in Africa.)[20]

DuBois found it necessary to make a public statement after it became known that Garvey had not been invited to the coming conclave, and the *Crisis* editor announced that the U.N.I.A. leader was ignored because his movement was "dangerous" and "impracticable."[21] The *Negro World* told its readers that such studied neglect was all that could be expected of DuBois, who directed his Pan-African Congress like "an exclusive college function."[22] The newspaper followed up this criticism with another entitled, "Is Dr. DuBois Misled or Is He Misleading?" In this piece, DuBois was advised to join forces against the "white beasts."[23] (Garvey predicted a race war, and he asserted that DuBois and the old-time leaders were not really preparing for it.) The *Crisis* editor was invited to attend the second convention of the U.N.I.A.[24]

Strategically, Garvey decided to call his own international con-

19. *Crisis* XXI (1920–1921), p. 101. *Crisis* XXII (1921), p. 5.
20. *Crisis* XXII (1921), p. 53.
21. New York *Age* note reprinted in *Negro World*, July 2, 1921.
22. *Negro World*, July 2, 1921.
23. *Negro World*, July 23, 1921.
24. *Negro World*, July 23, July 30, 1921.

clave in New York a few weeks before the Pan-African Congress. Unanimously, the U.N.I.A. delegates condemned DuBois's movement (and they dispatched their caustic comments to European newspapers). Garvey considered it an absurdity for the Pan-African Congress leaders to ask white representatives of the imperialists to attend their meetings:"[25]

> Just imagine that! It reminds me of the conference of rats endeavoring to legislate against the cats and the secretary of the rats convention invites the cat to preside over the convention.

The Jamaican tried to create the impression that DuBois represented "the antithesis" of the U.N.I.A.—on the alleged grounds that the *Crisis* editor's policy was racial amalgamation. Contending that the whites would always hold firmly to their racism, Garvey suggested that the Negro develop[26]

> a distinct racial type of civilization of his own and...work out his salvation in his motherland, all to be accomplished under the stimulus and influence of the slogan, 'Africa for the Africans, at home and abroad!'

His speech was delivered at a special meeting "called unexpectedly" after press dispatches of the Second Pan-African Congress (condemning the U.N.I.A.) arrived from Europe.

The Second Pan-African Congress met in London, Brussels, and Paris, in late August and early September of 1921. As in 1919, the conclave promulgated its belief in the physical, social, and political equality of all races. The Negroes were to be guaranteed "the ancient common ownership of the land and its natural fruits and defence against the unrestrained greed of invested capital." The League of Nations was asked to set up one agency to study Negro problems and another to insure that native labor was not exploited. England, Belgium, and France were accused of taking advantage of the natives. However, within the Pan-African movement itself there was a rupture between the American-British delegation who favored a critical ap-

25. *Negro World*, August 6, 1921.
26. *Negro World*, September 17, 1921.

proach to colonialism and the French-Belgian delegates, who desired an accommodation to the status quo.[27]

In Belgium, the Pan-African leaders were regarded as Garvey's henchmen, and white European newspapers continually asked if DuBois expected to eject the whites from Africa.[28] Repeatedly, the Pan-African Congress spokesmen asserted that they eschewed "any policy of war, conquest, or race hatred."[29] However, the moderate propaganda approach received the sympathy of some newspapers. The Paris *Humanite* stated:[30]

> The black and mulatto intelligentsia which the Congress revealed or permitted us to know better, showed by its very existence that the black race is not naturally or essentially an inferior race, and that it is not destined to remain so forever.

After the Second Pan-African Congress, Marcus Garvey challenged DuBois's group "to fight to a finish" (applause).[31] He laughed at those who argued that they owed their primary allegiance to the nations in which they lived. When one Pan-African leader said that he would "lose everything" if he returned permanently to Africa, Garvey jibed that "everything" meant Parisian white women. Garvey charged that the American whites were encouraging European immigration in order to replace the Negro "and cause him to die by starvation."[32] The Jamaican argued that it was only a matter of time before the whites would exile Negroes from all countries. However, he declared that some members of the race would remain in the United States for another hundred years; he announced that they would occupy a higher status because their welfare would be guaranteed by the prestige of the African Republic.

Although he excoriated N.A.A.C.P. leaders, Garvey denied that

27. *Crisis* XXIII (1921–1922), pp. 5–8. See also, Jesse Fauset, "Impressions of the Second Pan-African Congress," *Crisis* XXIII (1921–1922), p. 13.

28. *Negro World*, October 8, 1921.

29. W. E. B. DuBois, "A Second Journey to Pan-Africa," *New Republic* XXIX (1921–1922), p. 41.

30. Jesse Fauset, *op. cit.*, pp. 12–18.

31. *Negro World*, September 17, 1921.

32. *Ibid.*

he hoped for the demise of the organization. He announced that he would not "originate an attack" on the Association, but that he was prepared to defend the race against "our bitterest enemies [who] are not so much those from without as within; men who will continue to find faults where there are no faults." He asked the N.A.A.C.P. to send its representatives to the third convention of the U.N.I.A. and to permit "the real leadership" to assume command of the race.[33] The Jamaican wanted his followers to believe that DuBois lived in fear of being dropped by the Association—"the National Association for the Advancement of (Certain) Colored People."[34]

During all of this time, DuBois was still requesting the U.N.I.A. to issue a financial statement of its activities, and the Negro World's reply was that this interloper had no right "to say what people should do with their money and what other organizations should do." The Garveyites declared that their leader supplied jobs to twelve hundred Negroes, when one included such enterprises as the U.N.I.A., the Negro World, the Negro Times, a printing plant, the Negro Factories Corporation, a hotel, restaurant, steam laundry, and a doll factory.[35]

In sharp contrast to the Garveyite hysterics, DuBois's comments about the Jamaican's program were usually calmly delivered and based on objective data. Since he viewed the Black Star Line as crucial in a consideration of the leader's fame and influence, DuBois examined the development of this business venture. He proceeded to recount the history of Garvey's mismanagement of the enterprise. DuBois described the unseaworthy Yarmouth's voyage to the West Indies. The ship carried a cargo of whiskey, much of which was stolen; the American Government fined the vessel's owners. Since the ship was old, much money was spent on repair bills, and the Yarmouth was finally sold in order to pay off the creditors. Another vessel, the Antonio Maceo, was also lost to the Black Star Line after it was beached in Cuba because it required extensive repairs. A third ship, the Shadyside, suffered the same ignominious fate, after it served a short propaganda stint as an excursion boat up the Hudson. In

33. Negro World, October 29, 1921. Negro World, February 4, 1922.
34. Negro World, September 9, 1922. Negro World, November 4, 1922.
35. Negro World, July 8, 1922. Negro World, January 6, 1923.

early 1921, the Jamaican said he purchased the Phyllis Wheatley in order to handle the African trade, and later he stated that some of his associates had absconded with funds which had been designated as a deposit for the ship. Since Garvey had announced sailings and sold passage on the Phyllis Wheatley, he was indicted for fraud. In 1922, after the Black Star Line collapsed, DuBois wrote feelingly, "Here then is the collapse of the only thing in the Garvey Movement which was original or promising."[36]

The Crisis editor also attempted to learn how many members of the U.N.I.A. there actually were. Garvey claimed four million by August of 1920[37] and for 1921 he listed two figures. (During the early part of the year he stated that there were still four million members, but two years later, he recalled that there were six million members in 1921.)[38] The year after Garvey's indictment, DuBois estimated the membership in the U.N.I.A. for the period of September, 1920 to July, 1921. (He divided the annual dues into the total sum which was collected.) The Crisis editor calculated that there were fewer than ten thousand "paid up members," between ten and twenty thousand "active members," and very much less than a hundred thousand "nominal members."[39]

DuBois reached a white public when he analyzed the Garvey Movement in Century magazine, and while he made no attempt to mask his disapproval of the organization, he did try to account for it. He viewed Garvey as a disoriented victim of the color line:[40]

All his life whites have laughed and sneered at him, and torn his soul. All his life he has hated the half-whites, who rejecting their darker blood, have gloried in their pale shame.

DuBois referred to the Jamaican as a "little, fat, black man; ugly, but with intelligent eyes and a big head." Garvey made the most

---

36. Crisis XXIV (1922), pp. 210–214.

37. Marcus Garvey, "The Negro's Greatest Enemy," Current History XVIII (1923), p. 955.

38. Speech of Marcus Garvey to the Beulah Baptist Church of Cincinnati, Ohio. Typescript, February 19, 1921. (Located at Hampton Institute Library.) See also Garvey, "The Negro's Greatest Enemy," Current History XVIII (1923), p. 956.

39. Crisis XXV (1922–1923), p. 120.

40. W. E. B. DuBois, "Back to Africa," Century CV (1922–1923), p. 544.

of this description, replying that his physiognomy was "typical of the African":[41]

> Anything that is black, to him [DuBois] is ugly, is hideous, is monstrous, and this is why in 1917 he had but the lightest of colored people in his office, when one could hardly tell whether it was a white show or a colored vaudeville he was running at Fifth Avenue [the offices of the N.A.A.C.P.].

The Crisis editor was labeled as an apostle of "social equality," which in Garvey's thinking represented the kind of person who demanded to squire a white woman to a dance at the Waldorf-Astoria Hotel.[42] The Jamaican said that the U.N.I.A. was the only agency which was able to protect the darker-skinned Negro masses against the DuBois-led "caste aristocracy" of light mulattoes, many of whom were "intellectuals."[43] Paradoxically, Garvey denied that he was prejudiced against mulattoes, and he argued that all men had equal opportunity in the U.N.I.A.

In 1923, Garvey was convicted of mail fraud. After the trial, DuBois reprinted an editorial from a West Indies newspaper, wherein the U.N.I.A. leader was termed a "transparent charlatan."[44] Frustratedly, DuBois declared once again that his own attempt to settle the race problem on an international scale (through "cooperation" with the whites) was "harmed by the tragedy and comedy of Marcus Garvey."[45] The Jamaican refused to accept his defeat. In his prison cell, he continued to write diatribes, and DuBois angrily denounced him as "the most dangerous enemy of the Negro race in America and in the world. He is either a lunatic or a traitor."[46]

Since DuBois had been his chief critic, Garvey charged that the Crisis editor was responsible for his indictment and conviction. He blamed the N.A.A.C.P. propagandist for all of his difficulties and he asserted that the editor's malevolence had prevented the Black Star Line from sending "dozens" of ships to sea. During the summer

41. Negro World, February 10, 1923. Negro World, February 17, 1923.
42. Negro World, March 3, 1923.
43. Negro World, March 1, 1924.
44. Crisis XXVI (1923), p. 230. See also, Crisis XXVIII (1924), pp. 8–9.
45. Crisis XXVII (1923–1924), p. 9.
46. Crisis XXVIII (1924), pp. 8–9.

of 1924, the U.N.I.A. exiled DuBois from the Negro race.[47] However, such sentiments were only the last breaths of the movement. The Liberian Government announced that no members of the Garvey organization were welcome in the country. In January, 1925, President King remarked that his administration would not support any organization which dedicated itself to stirring up racial animosity. DuBois, who had recently been in Liberia as American Envoy Extraordinary and Minister Plenipotentiary, was identified by Garvey as the leader in the Liberian plot to destroy him.[48]

During the same years in which the Garvey Movement attracted thousands of average Negroes, DuBois's Pan-African Congress barely managed to survive. However, in 1923 and 1927, he was finally able to persuade the National Association of Colored Women to sponsor his conclaves.[49] These Congresses attracted few people and DuBois's large hopes to arouse the Negro were unrealized. In his leadership of the movement DuBois did not seem to understand that a truly effective propagandist related his work to a functioning organization. Since he did not build a real machine and did not have N.A.A.C.P. aid, his movement faded away.

This article has examined the intra-racial battles between DuBois and Garvey. During the 1920's, in the pages of the Crisis and the Negro World, they employed the same propaganda style and approach in their attacks on each other as they used in their organizational pronouncements on Africa. Garvey's expressions were explosive, irrational, and flamboyant. Their emotional appeal attracted large numbers of frustrated, uneducated blacks. DuBois's remarks were usually moderate, thoughtful, and analytical and were directed to a minority within the minority.

47. Negro World, April 10, 1924, New York Times, August 29, 1924.
48. Edmund D. Cronon, Black Moses (Madison, 1955), pp. 129–131.
49. Crisis XXVII (1923–1924), p. 122, 170. Crisis XXXIV (1927), p. 264.

Manuel P. Servín,
"The Pre-World War II Mexican-American:
An Interpretation"

Mexican nationals migrated to the United States in increasing numbers during the early twentieth century, a movement which added approximately one million legal and illegal immigrants to the population by 1930. Most of the new immigrants settled in the Southwest, which was enjoying an economic boom in industries such as oil, cotton, and railroads, but Mexican-Americans were seldom participants in the rising prosperity. They provided manual labor for the growing area, filling the need for unskilled workers created by whites who moved up the economic ladder. In addition, as whites left tenant farming for the cities and towns, many Mexican immigrants, working as migratory laborers paid by the piece rather than by the hour or day, were relegated to the fields of the Southwest. Manuel P. Servín, in "The Pre-World War II Mexican-American: An Interpretation," depicts the life styles of these immigrants, destroying in the process numerous white myths regarding them.

The Pre-World War II Mexican-American: An Interpretation

Manuel P. Servín

The Mexican-American resident in the United States constitutes this nation's most unique, if not mystifying, minority group. Descendant of the aboriginal American inhabitants and of the first European settlers in the New World, the Mexican-American, despite the fact that he preponderantly lived and still lives in areas that were wrested from him, has until the recent war years been considered not an American but a foreigner. This fact has been so evident that even European immigrants, whose accents patently reveal their very recent arrival in the United States, did not hesitate to regard the Mexican-American not as an American but as a Mexican, whom they considered less American than themselves.

That such an attitude should prevail is clearly understandable to those possessing an historical insight into early North American-Mexican relations. Incredible as it may seem, the Mexican became a minority group—a despised minority—not when he immigrated to the North American Republic, but rather when the North American migrated to Mexican Texas and California, finding on the whole a

Abridged from Manuel P. Servín, "The Pre-World War II Mexican-American: An Interpretation," California Historical Society Quarterly, XLV (1966), pp. 325–338. Reprinted by permission of the author and the California Historical Society. Notes have been renumbered and appear at the end of the article.

poor class of Hispanic settler. Consequently, despite his residence on his own national soil, it was the Mexican who became the backward, somewhat unassimilable foreigner.

This attitude toward the Mexican, particularly in Texas, was further intensified by the wars affecting the North Americans and Mexicans. With the few exceptions of the *ricos* (the few wealthy ones) who passed themselves off as Spaniards, the Mexican truly became a minority group in the worst sense of the word. Generally despised in Texas, dispossessed of his lands in California, and denying his racial heritage in New Mexico, he lacked an acknowledged Mexican aristocracy—social, economic, and clerical—which would visibly prove to him that he was capable of achieving success and status....

The decades that followed the 1880's North Americanization of the Southwest and preceded the early twentieth-century wave of Mexican immigration are in an historical sense extremely quiet concerning North American and Mexican-American relations. Perhaps it would not be too rash to surmise that the Mexican-American of this period generally resigned himself to a fate that previous historical events had cast upon him. He was, at least in the eyes of the North American, an inferior being, a half-breed, if not a *coyote*; he was unassimilable, especially if he was dark skinned; he was treacherous; he was cowardly; he was lazy; and thus he was not an American but a Mexican whose lot was to exist in poverty, subservience, and isolation.

That such was the fate of the Mexican after the 1880's is attested to by the treatment of the Mexican immigrant who arrived in the United States in the early twentieth century after the fall of Don Porfirio Díaz.

Unfortunately for this new Mexican immigrant, he was neither prepared for the treatment that he would receive nor would he be able to understand the reasons for it. Because of the great changes, relative progress, and social and political stability imposed upon Mexico by the benevolent dictator Porfirio Díaz, the twentieth-century Mexican immigrant was a different person from his early predecessor in the Borderlands. He was far from lawless—Díaz's *rurales* had created respect for law and order. He was not the idle, lazy Greaser so eloquently characterized by early American writers—he had been oppressed in peonage for much too lengthy a period. Generally speaking, he was a moral and religious man—he had emigrated generally from the highly religious areas of Mexico. Finally, he was meek and submissive—Díaz's policy of *pan ó palo* had been effective.

It was this humble and meek person who began arriving in 1901 in great numbers to reside permanently in the United States. His increasing immigration, as determined by the United States Census of 1930, reflected the chaotic condition of Revolutionary Mexico and the need of North American cheap labor. Thus in 1901-1910 over 93,000 Mexicans legally entered the United States and remained at least until 1930; in 1911–1914 approximately 77,000; in the War years of 1915–1919 about 137,000; in 1920–1924 over 135,000, and in 1925–1930 just under 109,000.[1] By 1930 there were about 617,000 legal Mexican immigrants residing in the United States, constituting almost one-half of the legal Mexican population in the nation.[2] Actually, however, it is quite safe to state that if the illegal entrants —the predecessors of the wetbacks and fence-climbers—were taken into account, the majority of the Mexicans then residing in the United States were foreign born.[3] And, perhaps even more significant than the rate of foreign born Mexicans are the sound indications that they were not predominantly a rural group, as is often asserted, but were perhaps in the majority emigrants from urban areas.

This wave of legal and illegal Mexican immigration, plus the birth rate of the early Spanish Borderlands' Mexican, swelled the total legal Mexican population in the United States in 1930 at least to just under one and one-half million.[4] Although Mexicans migrated in some numbers to such states as Michigan, Illinois, Kansas, and Indiana, it was in the Southwest, the former Mexican territory, that the overwhelming majority—some one and one-quarter million—settled.[5] By 1930, Texas, long reputed among Mexicans as the most racially bigoted state, had the largest Mexican population, some 683,000. California had approximately 368,000; New Mexico, possibly 200,000 (although only 59,000 of these descendants from the early colonizers confessed to being Mexican to the census taker); Arizona, just over 114,000; and Colorado, about 57,000.[6] . . .

The panoramic picture presented of the early twentieth-century Mexican, who was born before 1926 and who did not enjoy the social and economic opportunities resulting from World War II, is interesting. . . . Arriving in poverty, unable to speak English, and inheriting the anti-Mexican prejudice engendered decades before, the Mexican was definitely at a disadvantage and greatly in need of help. Unfortunately, such help was not given, particularly by the groups from which the Mexican expected aid. The Spanish-speaking aristocracy —old Mexicans who disguised their heritage under such euphemisms as Californios, Spanish-Americans, and Hispanos—generally not only ignored but apparently despised the immigrant.[7] The Roman Catholic Church, aside from building churches and stationing refugee Mexican priests in Spanish-speaking parishes, did little to aid materially or socially.[8] Paradoxically, it was certain Protestant churches, especially the Methodist, that appeared to be most cognizant of the plight of the immigrant.[9] It is, therefore, not strange that bitterness toward the Spanish-speaking aristocracy and some antipathy toward the Church should have developed—a bitterness characterizing the aristocracy in a most unprintable manner and an antipathy resulting in the conversion of many Mexicans to Protestantism.

Unaided by their own groups and unable to obtain work in their previous occupations, the Mexicans were forced to take the lowest paying jobs as well as the most difficult work. In the agricultural areas of Texas, Colorado, and California they became the neglected, underpaid, exploited migratory farm workers. In the north central areas of the nation they performed various forms of low-paid unskilled labor. In Chicago and the Calumet area, for example, they worked in the railroad sections and in the meat packing plants. In Minnesota they worked in the sugar beet industry. And, in the area of Bethlehem, Pennsylvania, they became unskilled steel workers. Thus, the Mexicans were consciously relegated to the lowest working positions.[10] Perhaps the classical example of this policy was best expressed to Dr. [Paul S.] Taylor by an executive in the Chicago and the Calumet area who bluntly stated the hiring policy found in the area:

We use no Mexicans. We have more refined work and have not had to resort to the greasers. They use them for rough work and around blast furnaces.[11]

But regardless of the demeaning work which they were assigned, the Mexicans, despite conflicting testimony, appear to have been good but not excellent workers. Preferred in California and Texas as farm laborers, the Mexicans did not merit this preference and achievement because they were built closer to the ground and possessed a physical advantage. The preference was simply economic: they were unorganized, apparently docile, and did not demand decent wages and living conditions.[12] In the industrial areas their record, as in the farming areas, was also respectable. They compared both favorably and unfavorably with the Slovaks, Wends, Negroes, and Irish.[13] Perhaps the most favorable report on the Mexicans' work occurred in Bethlehem when Dr. Taylor interviewed a number of executives, one of whom stated that he

> rated the Mexicans as equals or possibly the superior of the two important groups of Europeans available for the same work: 'The Mexicans are a good class of men as a whole; the majority are good steady workers. As a class their intelligence is above the Slavish [Slovaks] and Wendish. They are a bright, keen race, and good workers.' And in response to my observation [Dr. Taylor's] that in other localities some persons regard Mexicans as possessing low intelligence, he added, 'If some people think the Mexicans are dumb, they should see some of our Irish. . . .'[14]

Notwithstanding the Mexican's at least average work record, he, along with the Negro, was the lowest paid of the workers, both on the farms and in the plants. Unlike the Japanese who was disliked by his fellow workers because of his industriousness and efficiency, the Mexican was unacceptable to his co-workers for a number of reasons. The reasons generally cited were that he lowered wages and weakened union organization.[15] But the racial difference, the dark skin, unhygienic appearance, and quaint dress habits appear to be, at least to me, the more basic reasons. Following almost an identical pattern of the well-known segregation that existed in Arizona, California, and Texas, the Mexican had difficulty renting in better neighborhoods. . . .

The low wages received by the Mexicans, regardless of area, plus their own cultural and racial drawbacks, of course, had a very essential influence upon their living conditions. While Texas has always possessed among both Mexicans and dogmatic liberals the worst reputation for oppressing Mexicans and for retaining them in the lowest substandard living conditions, it is my judgment—as a person who has traveled in Texas, attended school in New Mexico, journeyed extensively through Arizona, and was reared in California—that the living conditions, with some very few exceptions in New Mexico, were equally as poor in utopian California as in Texas, Arizona, and other areas.[16]

Southern California, whose record for indiscriminate, hypocritical discrimination is difficult to excel, possessed perhaps the Southwest's most blatant opposing living conditions between the White North American and the Indian-Spanish Mexican. Few Mexican *barrios* could compete in poverty with that of Maravilla Park in Los Angeles County where two and sometimes three shacks built of scrap lumber, old boxes, and other salvage were erected in one small lot; where there were forty houses to a city block; where the average family income in 1928 was $795; where almost all workers were unskilled laborers; and where out of 317 houses only ten had cesspools connected with flush toilets.[17]

But in reality Maravilla Park was not an exception in California. Similar living conditions could be found in El Centro, San Fernando, and the outskirts of Montebello, Whittier, and El Monte—and, incidentally, in various cities of the San Joaquin Valley, even today.[18]

Actually, such poverty was not unknown to the Mexican in his home country, and would not be a great source of unhappiness. What did strike the Mexican was the irrational prejudice and disdain that he encountered. In many areas he could not eat in the same restaurant with the North American, nor could he swim in the same pools. In other areas he could not attend the same theatres, or if allowed to do so, he would have to sit in a segregated section; but this segregation, similar to his living among his own people, did not seem to bother him—perhaps he inwardly considered himself equal or even superior to the Americans in some areas.[19]

Yet despite all the disheartening and degrading conditions that he encountered, the Pre-World War II Mexican not only maintained a good record but made certain remarkable achievements.

Although he inherited the poor reputation for crime from the very early Mexican settlers, his crime record, basing it on random examples, was not outstandingly bad.[20] In the Chicago and the Calumet area, a two-year survey—1928–1929—revealed that 1.4 percent of all persons arrested were of Mexican nativity, while the Mexican population constituted only .57 percent of the total population.[21] In Los Angeles City the 1927–1928 percentage of Mexican arrests, revealing narcotics (probably marihuana), drunkenness, and vagrancy as the rising element, amounted to 17.5, while the Mexican population of the city was slightly over 10 percent.[22] In rural Imperial Valley, an important farming area, where the Mexican in 1925 was supposed to be responsible for 75 percent of all crimes, it was authoritatively found that he was responsible for only one-fourth of all crime, while he constituted approximately one-third of the population.[23] Thus, seeing that the rural crime rate was less in proportion to that of the urban, one might conjecture (perhaps somewhat dangerously) that since the Mexican population in the United States was almost equally divided between rural and urban, its crime rate was in proportion to, or even lower than, its total population.

A similar picture is found in California regarding juvenile delinquency—a reflection of family life. In Los Angeles County as of March of 1928, 19 percent of the Mexican boys and 28 percent of the Mexican girls were on probation—figures which were far above the estimated 11 percent total Mexican population.[24] Yet in Imperial Valley the picture was reversed. The percentage of Mexican children involved in juvenile court was proportionately much less than the total Mexican population, and incidentally less than that of old North American stock.[25]

Besides possessing a rather good work record and not a bad adult and juvenile crime rate, the Mexican also possessed fairly good records in marital relations and relief. Insofar as married life was concerned, there is little doubt that his divorce rate was less than either that of the Negroes or Whites.[26] His public relief record, based upon statistics of California—the nation's most magnanimous or perhaps most foolish state—was not quite as good, but it was apparently below his proportional maximum. Despite unfavorable relief records in Los Angeles, Orange, and Riverside counties, and despite the low and seasonal wages he was paid, it is evident from Governor C. C. Young's *Report* that the Mexican in California was not only not a burden on the state but that he received only a slight amount above his just proportion of relief funds.[27] That such a case seems to have been true throughout the nation appears most plausible from the *Report* of the Governor's Interracial Commission in Minnesota and from the Mexicans' practice of organizing societies such as the Cruz Azul for helping each other financially and otherwise.[28]

Undoubtedly the Mexican's area of least success and greatest failure was in obtaining an education. Coming from a culture failing to prize mass education, finding it necessary to put even his elementary-age children to work, and perhaps feeling frustrated that an education would not help him overcome the prejudices and disdainful treatment he received throughout the Southwest, the Mexican failed drastically to take advantage of the educational opportunities opened to him. Of all the groups listed in the Census of 1930, he had the lowest percentage of school attendance—a factor of course that in the long run militated and still militates against him and his future advancement.[29]

Yet despite the Pre-War Mexican's lack of educational interest, language barrier, and racial and cultural prejudice, he made some formidable breakthroughs in addition to gradually changing his portrait in the areas of work, crime, family life, and relief. Unlike some other persecuted minorities, he established a very good, cultural Spanish press, as exemplified by the Los Angeles La Opinión. He broke into the motion pictures and produced respectable and respected stars such as Ramón Novarro, Dolores del Río, and Gilbert Roland. In the East he gave such distinguished professional men as conquistador-descended Harold Medina, the jurist; Alonso E. Escalante, American Maryknoll missionary bishop for Mexico; and American-trained dancer-choreographer, José Limón. In crime, he at least showed some ability to think "big" as exemplified in the case of the fugitive Los Angeles police lieutenant, Peter Del Gado. In music he developed popular crooners such as Andy Russell and more serious singers as José Mojica and Tito Guízar. And, in higher education, in addition to the colonial-descended and highly distinguished Espinoza family, he came forth with such academic limelights as Carlos Eduardo Castañeda and George Isidore Sánchez, both from the University of Texas.[30]

Breakthroughs into North American life were not, however, the only achievement that the Pre-World War II Mexican attained. He also made some contributions to United States culture—and I do not mean just the adding of tacos, tamales, and margaritas to the North American diet. He contributed, as Henry Lopez's recent interview with Katherine Anne Porter in Harper's Magazine indicates, an incentive for enriching American letters.[31]

The period of [the] Pre-World War II Mexican in the United States came to an end with opening of hostilities late in 1941 and early in 1942. . . .

Notes

1. U. S. Bureau of Census, *Fifteenth Census of the United States, 1930: Population* (Washington, 1933), II, 498.

2. *Ibid.*, II, 25, 27, 405.

3. *Ibid.* For an estimate of illegal immigration see Emory S. Bogardus, *The Mexican in the United States* (Los Angeles, 1934), p. 15; also see Leo Grebler, *Mexican Immigration to the United States: The Record and Its Implications* (Los Angeles, 1965), pp. 7–11, 17–29.

4. *Ibid.*, II, 27; Enrique Santibañez, *Ensayo acerca de la inmigración Mexicana en los Estados Unidos* (San Antonio, 1930), pp. 47–48.

5. *Fifteenth Census of the United States, 1930: Population*, II, 35.

6. *Ibid.*

7. Interview with José Bravo, Los Angeles, September 11, 1965; interview with Dionisio Rodríguez, Los Angeles, September 11, 1965.

8. The Rev. Francis J. Weber, "His Excellency of Los Angeles: The Life and Times of the Most Reverend John J. Cantwell," MS, pp. 96–103, Archives of the Archdiocese of Los Angeles, Los Angeles, California; *Notes: Outline of Protestant Proselytism in the United States* (Los Angeles, 1945), pp. 1–8, 54–55, 66–82; *Notes: The Mexican Problem and its Latin American Background* (Los Angeles, 1942), *passim*, Kathryn Cramp et al., "A Study of the Mexican Population of Imperial Valley, California," MS, p. 23, Bancroft Library, Berkeley.

An example of the Catholic Church's neglect of the Mexican is graphically illustrated by the late date (1944) that the Bishop's Committee for the Spanish Speaking was formed. See Rosemary E. Smith, "The Work of Bishops' Committee for the Spanish Speaking on Behalf of the Migrant Worker" (master's thesis, The Catholic University of America, 1958), p. 4.

9. In order to obtain a true insight of the zeal and efforts of the Methodists in working with Mexicans of the period it is only necessary to read the *Minutes of the Southern California Conference of the Methodist Episcopal Church, 1879–1939*, Conference Headquarters, Los Angeles. For a very limited view into Methodist Church activities see Edward Drewry Jervey, *The History of Methodism in Southern California and Arizona* (Los Angeles, 1960), pp. 90–100. Also see *Notes: The Mexican Problem and its Latin American Background*, *passim*.

10. For the work the Mexican performed see Paul S. Taylor, *Mexican Labor in the United States*, published in the University of California Publications in Economics. Dr. Taylor's different studies utilized in this essay and cited individually are: *Mexican Labor in the United States: Imperial Valley* (Berkeley, 1928); *Mexican Labor in the United States: Valley of the South Platte, Colorado* (Berkeley, 1929); *Mexican Labor in the United States: Dimmit County, Winter Garden, South Texas* (Berkeley, 1930); *Mexican Labor in the United States: Bethlehem, Pennsylvania* (Berkeley, 1931); *Mexican Labor in the United States: Chicago and the Calumet Region* (Berkeley, 1932). Also see Kathryn Cramp et al., "A Study of the Mexican Population in Imperial Valley, California," MS, 1926, Bancroft Library; Santibañez, *Ensayo acerca de la inmigración Mexicana en los Estados Unidos*, especially p. 53; The Governor's Interracial Commission, *The Mexican in Minnesota* (Minneapolis, 1953); and Carey McWilliams, *North from Mexico* (Philadelphia, 1949).

11. Taylor, Mexican Labor in the United States: Chicago and the Calumet Region, p. 80.

12. For a summary of Mexicans' [efforts] to unionize agriculturally in the early 1900's see Federal Writers' Project, "Organization Efforts of Mexican Agricultural Workers," (Oakland, 1939), MS, Bancroft Library. For other areas see Cramp et al., "A Study of Mexican Population in Imperial Valley, California," pp. 1–2, 6–11; George L. Cady, Report of Commission on International and Interracial Factors in the Problem of the Mexicans in the United States (1926), pp. 11, 21; State of California, Mexicans in California: Report of Governor C. C. Young's Mexican Fact-Finding Committee (San Francisco, 1930), pp. 159–171, especially 171, and also pp. 123–150, 176–179.

13. Taylor, Mexican Labor in the United States: Chicago and the Calumet Region, pp. 81–87; Taylor, Mexican Labor in the United States: Bethlehem, pp. 13–14.

14. Taylor, Mexican Labor in the United States: Bethlehem, p. 13.

15. For examples of lowering wages see Taylor, Mexican Labor in United States: Chicago and the Calumet Region, pp. 77–80.

16. The information compiled by George L. Cady, Report of Commission on International and Interracial Factors in the Problem of the Mexicans in the United States, as well as Paul Taylor's studies on Mexican Labor in California, Texas, Colorado, Chicago and the Calumet, appear to bear out this writer's evaluation.

17. Mexicans in California: Report of Governor C. C. Young's Mexican Fact-Finding Committee, pp. 177–178. For an all enclosing view of the poverty of Mexican communities in Chicago, Colorado, Texas, New Mexico, Arizona, and California see W. Rex Crawford, "The Latin American in Wartime United States," The Annals of the American Academy of Political and Social Science, 223 (September, 1942), 127.

18. Mexicans in California: Report of Governor C. C. Young's Mexican Fact-Finding Committee, pp. 178–179.

19. A fine example of almost complete segregation is contained in Cramp et al., "A Study of the Mexican Population in Imperial Valley, California." A partial list of segregated living and school districts in California is found in Mexicans in California, pp. 176–177. Also see Bogardus, The Mexican in the United States, pp. 28–29, for an area in which the Mexican did not consider himself inferior to the North American.

20. George L. Cady in his Report of Commission on International and Interracial Factors in the Problem of Mexicans in the United States gives a fine example of this pre-World War II exaggeration, p. 10. A somewhat different interpretation, indicating "an unusually high rate of crime and delinquency," is found in Bogardus, The Mexicans in the United States, pp. 52–58.

21. Taylor, Mexican Labor in the United States: Chicago and the Calumet Region, p. 144.

22. Mexicans in California, pp. 175–176 and 203.

23. Cramp et al., "A Study of the Mexican Population in Imperial Valley, California," p. 11, also see p. 12.

24. *Mexicans in California*, p. 204.

25. Cramp *et al.*, "A Study of the Mexican Population in Imperial Valley, California, pp. 10 and 25.

26. *Fifteenth Census of the United States, 1930: Population*, II, 842.

27. *Mexicans in California*, pp. 190–191, 195–196.

28. *The Mexicans in Minnesota*, pp. 44–45; Taylor, *Mexican Labor in the United States, Bethlehem*, p. 17; Taylor, *Mexican Labor in the United States: Chicago and the Calumet Region*, pp. 124, 128–129, 132–133; Cramp *et al.*, "A Study of the Mexican Population in Imperial Valley, California," pp. 13–14; interview with José M. Bravo, Los Angeles, September 11, 1965.

29. *Fifteenth Census of the United States, 1930: Population*, II, 1094–1095; Pauline R. Kibbe, *Latin American in Texas* (Albuquerque, 1946), p. 92, presents a fine example of the frustration encountered by enthusiastic Mexican students.

30. For biographical data on Ramón Novarro, Dolores del Río, and Gilbert Roland see Langford Reed and Hetty Spiers, eds., *Who's Who in Filmland* (3rd ed.; London, 1931), pp. 84, 227, 259.
Judge Harold Medina's Mexican ancestry is discussed in *Time Magazine*, LIV (October 24, 1949), 23. Bishop Alonso E. Escalante's biographical data are found in the *Dictionary of the American Hierarchy, 1789–1964*, p. 84. Biographical data on José Limón are published in the *Celebrity Register* (New York, 1963), p. 375.
For Peter Del Gado's part in the Shaw administration in Los Angeles see *Time Magazine* XXXII (December 5, 1938), 14; interview with Mr. Richard Rodríguez, Los Angeles, September 29, 1965.
For the Mexican singers of the period only Tito Guízar is listed in Otto Mayer-Serra, *Música y Músicos de Latinoamerica* (Mexico, 1947), I, 459. For José Mojica, who entered the Franciscan Order, see *The Tidings* (Los Angeles), January 14, 1966. Andy Russell's biographical data are found in J. T. Mize (ed.), *The International Who Is Who in Music* (Chicago, 1951), pp. 359–360.
Professors Carlos Eduardo Castañeda and George I. Sánchez are listed in Jacques Cattell, *Directory of American Scholars: A Biographical Dictionary* (3rd ed.; New York, 1957), pp. 122, 653.

31. Katherine Anne Porter, "A Country and Some People I Love: An Interview by Hank López," *Harper's Magazine* 231 (September, 1965), 58–68.

Masakazu Iwata,
"*The Japanese Immigrants
in California Agriculture*"

Japanese immigrants to the United States arrived in the twentieth
century with expectations and backgrounds similar to those
of the Chinese who, beginning with the Exclusion Act of 1882,
had been barred from entering the United States. The Chinese
had worked in the gold mines, on the railroads, in agriculture, and in
their own small businesses. Most of the Japanese, on the other
hand, engaged in farming. As Masakazu Iwata indicates in "The
Japanese Immigrants in California Agriculture," they were
generally quite successful and became landowners. Japanese efficiency
and flair for reclaiming previously undesirable land fanned the wrath
of white Californians, who in most other instances, had emphasized
the need for immigrant settlers in the state but now enacted
legislation curtailing alien land ownership.

The Japanese Immigrants in California Agriculture

Masakazu Iwata

The noteworthy contributions made by the Japanese immigrants to California's agricultural development before World War II are undeniable. Indeed, a study of their history reveals that the realization of the agricultural potentialities of the State has been due in no small measure to their endeavors. The Japanese, as in the case of most European immigrants to this country, were induced to leave their homeland because of unfavorable economic conditions. Arriving in ever increasing numbers after the turn of the twentieth century, the Issei[1] settled in the Pacific Coast states where most of them worked as ordinary laborers in various industries. Spurred on by the desire for wealth which would enable them to return to and retire in Japan, the Japanese worked diligently under the most trying circumstances. Their vaulting ambitions soon enabled them to make successfully the

Abridged from Masakazu Iwata, "The Japanese Immigrants in California Agriculture," *Agricultural History*, XXXVI (1962), pp. 25–37. Reprinted by permission of the author and the Agricultural History Society. Some footnotes have been renumbered.

1. *Issei* literally means "first generation." The children of the first generation Japanese in the United States are called *Nisei*, or "second generation." The bulk of the Japanese-American students in high schools and colleges today are *Sansei*, or third generation Japanese.

transition from laborers to tenant farmers. As farm operators, the *Issei* continued a life of struggle not only against the elements but also against adverse social, economic, and political pressures. But despite such discriminatory legislation as the anti-alien land laws, the Japanese, many of whom sought protection in organization, made notable advances in agriculture. Hence by 1941, they, along with the *Nisei* who in the meantime had joined their parents in farming, were producing between thirty and thirty-five percent by value of all commercial truck crops grown in California as well as occupying a dominant position in the distribution system of fruits and vegetables, both wholesale and retail. Many of the immigrant farmers were also engaged in the production of fruits and nuts and in the raising of flowers and poultry. Although the significance of the *Issei* in agriculture was virtually terminated as a result of the Second World War,[2] it would be remiss if history should fail to recognize the vital part they have played in the growth of California agriculture.

In general, the history of Japanese immigration to the United States varies very little from that of other new immigrant groups who came to this country. The Japanese, like the Europeans, were motivated by a desire to better their economic situation. They were likewise compelled to engage in the more menial tasks in their initial efforts to earn a livelihood, and in time were to arouse hostility among groups within the economy. Finally, as in the case of other immigrants, the Japanese were to gain for themselves a foothold in limited fields of endeavor, predominantly agriculture.[3]

Japanese immigration to the United States prior to the turn of the twentieth century was insignificant. Before 1900 arrivals from Japan comprised less than one percent of the total annual volume of im-

2. At the beginning of World War II the average age of the *Issei* was already in the sixties. Consequently, after the evacuation interlude, only a small minority among them had the necessary energy, inclination, and capital to re-establish themselves in farming. The *Issei* are a fast disappearing generation. For statistics regarding their average age, see United States Bureau of the Census, *United States Census of Population: 1950*, Vol. IV, *Special Reports*, Part 3, Chapter 13, Nonwhite Population by Race (Washington: Government Printing Office, 1953), p. 86.
3. See United States Congress, *National Defense Migration*, Fourth Interim Report of the Select Committee Investigating National Defense Migration (House Report No. 2124), 77th Congress, 2nd Section, May, 1942 (Washington: Government Printing Office, 1942), p. 59. Hereafter cited as U. S. Congress, *National Defense Migration*.

migration to this country.[4] The earliest Japanese entrants were ship-wrecked seamen, the most famous of them being apprentice sailor Hikozo Hamada who in the 1850's was adopted and educated by the collector of customs in San Francisco.[5] In 1870 only fifty-five Japanese lived in the United States, but by 1890 two thousand more had reached the country.[6] An increasing number of Japanese aliens were admitted after 1900; during this one year alone more than 12,000 new arrivals were counted. The peak was reached in 1907 when more than 30,000 migrants reached the "land of promise." Thereafter the annual influx steadily declined as the result of the Gentlemen's Agreement of 1908 which curtailed the migration of Japanese nationals to the United States and Hawaii. By the eve of World War I, however, the migration figures had once more begun an upward trend with 10,168 Japanese admitted in 1918, a reflection of America's willingness to receive aliens to compensate for the dearth of laborers in the national emergency. Finally, after the passage of the Oriental Exclusion Act of 1924 the flow of immigrants became a mere trickle. In 1928, for example, only 522 Japanese were admitted to the United States.[7]

Figures indicate that among the Japanese entering the various Paci-

4. In 1899 the immigrant aliens admitted from Japan numbered 3,395 out of a total of 311,715 immigrant aliens who entered the United States. See United States Department of Labor, Bureau of Immigration, *Annual Report of the Commissioner General of Immigration: 1928–1929* (Washington: Government Printing Office, 1929), p. 194.

5. Yamato Ichihashi, *Japanese in the United States* (Stanford: Stanford University Press, 1932), pp. 19–21. It is said that members of the Japanese race came to California as early as 1610. Three years later a group of Japanese Catholics on its way to Rome landed here. See Tomatsu Murayama, "Tokyo Topics: First Japanese Landed in California Near Mendocino," *Pacific Citizen,* December 17, 1954, Sec. B, p. 9; James Murdoch, *A History of Japan* (London: Kegan Paul, Trench, Trubner and Co., Ltd., 1925), II, p. 595 ff. A San Francisco newspaper gives an account of "a party of refined Japanese gentlemen, one of whom had been the Governor of Jedo [sic]," who in 1868 were compelled to flee Japan and come to the United States because of their liberal ideas. These Japanese, who spoke English and French, leased a farm in Alameda County and hired a few intelligent white men to instruct them in farm methods. Their venture subsequently produced handsome profits. Editorial in the San Francisco *Chronicle,* June 17, 1869.

6. United States Bureau of the Census, *Fifteenth Census of the U. S.: 1930. Population,* Vol. II. General Report (Washington: Government Printing Office, 1933), p. 32.

7. United States Department of Labor, *Annual Report of the Commissioner General of Immigration: 1928–1929,* pp. 194–196.

fic Coast ports a large percentage of them drifted to and eventually settled in California. Hence the proportion of all Japanese in continental United States settled in California increased from 42 percent in 1900 to 57 percent in 1910 and 65 percent in 1920. The Chinese in contrast were in the beginning exclusively in California and later dispersed to other parts of the United States.[8] Obviously the Japanese were drawn to California by its climate and increasing agricultural and business opportunities.

The Japanese were motivated to come to America primarily by economic factors. To many of them emigration was a means by which they could escape the hardships of life in an impoverished homeland where, especially after the Russo-Japanese War of 1904–05, living conditions progressively worsened. Japan's population density had increased from 1,335 per square ri[9] in 1872 to 1,885 in 1903 which meant that with each successive year a country with limited resources and land area had to satisfy the needs of more and more people.[10] Intense competition among the working classes forced millions of them to live under great economic pressure. The workers, together

8. Varden Fuller, *The Supply of Agricultural Labor as a Factor in the Evolution of Farm Organization in California*, United States Congress, Senate, Committee on Education and Labor, *Violation of Free Speech and Rights of Labor*, Hearings before Subcommittee, 76th Congress, 3rd Session, on S. Res. 266, January 13, 1940, Pt. 54, *Agricultural Labor in California* (Washington: Government Printing Office, 1940), p. 19828. In 1900 out of the total of 24,326 Japanese residents in the country over 10,000 of them lived in California while by 1940 these figures had risen to 126,947 and 93,717, respectively. The following is a breakdown of figures of the California Japanese population into native and foreign-born elements covering the period 1900–1940:

Year	Foreign Born	Native Born	Total
1900	10,008	143	10,151
1910	38,184	3,172	41,356
1920	51,138	20,814	71,952
1930	48,477	48,979	97,456
1940	33,569	60,148	93,717

See United States Bureau of the Census, *Fifteenth Census of the United States: 1930. Population*, Vol. 11, p. 32; United States Bureau of the Census, *Sixteenth Census of the United States: 1940. Population*, Vol. 11, Characteristics of the Population, Pt. 1, U. S. Summary (Washington: Government Printing Office, 1943), pp. 21, 518.

9. A square ri equals 5.9552 square miles.

10. Yosaburo Yoshida, "Sources and Causes of Japanese Emigration," *The Annals of the American Academy of Political and Social Science*, Vol. XXXIV (September, 1909), p. 158.

with the farmers upon whom fell a disproportionate share of the tax load, eagerly came to the United States, hoping to make a quick fortune while at the same time avoiding military conscription. A smaller group of immigrants came specifically to attend American schools.[11] Once in America the immigrants themselves advertised the benefits of life in the new land and thereby induced other Japanese to venture across the Pacific. Like their European counterparts, the Japanese in America delineated in their letters to friends and relatives an often exaggerated picture of American opulence and opportunities. Such correspondence, as well as magazine and newspaper articles dealing with success stories among the Japanese residing in the United States, encouraged migration as did emigration societies which advertised for emigrants through newspapers and traveling solicitors.[12]

The early Japanese immigrants were mostly unmarried males, the majority of whom were under thirty-five years of age,[13] who began their careers in this country as common laborers. Most of them worked as railroad, cannery, and logging camp laborers while a smaller number were employed in the mining, meat-packing, and salt industries. Their willingness to accept even lower wages than laborers of other races enabled the Japanese to secure employment readily.[14] In a number of instances they were used as strike breakers in the mines of Colorado and Utah.[15] The Japanese, in contrast to the Chinese, were unable to enter manufacturing establishments in the cities, such as the cigar, shoe, and clothing factories, partly as a result of the earlier agitation against the Chinese who were employed in these industries and because there was an adequate supply of European immigrant labor for these jobs.[16]

Unable to enter the ranks of the more desirable occupations and unwilling to remain as laborers in non-agricultural employment, the

---

11. *Ibid.*, pp. 159–160.

12. *Ibid.*, pp. 163–164. See also Yamato Ichihashi, *op. cit.*, pp. 87–88; United States Immigration Commission, *Reports of the Immigration Commission* (Washington: Government Printing Office, 1911) I, p. 662. Hereafter cited as U. S. Immigration Commission, *Reports.*

13. U. S. Immigration Commission, *Reports,* XXIII, p. 8.

14. *Ibid.*, p. 58. For a comparison of the pay received by the Japanese and other races in the railroad, lumber, fishing, mining industries, see *ibid.*, pp. 37–41, 47, 48–49, 53, 56.

15. U. S. Immigration Commission *Reports,* I, p. 664.

16. U. S. Immigration Commission, *Reports,* XXIII, p. 33.

Japanese even prior to 1910 showed a strong inclination to leave their original work for employment in agriculture. This movement into farm work was motivated by a desire for higher earnings in an occupation that had always been looked upon with respect in Japan and for which the Japanese were better fitted through experience.[17] ... The predominance of Japanese immigrant labor in California agriculture by 1910 was due to several factors. During the nineties when there was a general abundance of agricultural laborers[18] the newly arrived Japanese resorted to wage-cutting to gain a foothold in the various farming districts.[19] After 1902 a labor vacuum drew heavily on the large number of incoming migrants from Japan.[20] Other characteristics of Japanese labor favored their employment in the intensive type of agriculture of the State. The localities in which intensive farming was carried on usually specialized extensively in one or only a few crops, a situation which required large forces of laborers for short seasons only. The Japanese, present in large numbers after 1900, had few family ties and property and were therefore less reluctant than the white men to engage in seasonal agricultural work which required migrating from one district to another.[21] The organization of *Issei* laborers in gangs under Japanese bosses, which was as much

17. *Ibid.*, p. 59. In the Japanese social structure under Tokugawa feudalism (1600–1867) the farmer ranked above the merchant and below the warrior class.

18. Although Chinese exclusion had cut off the source of Chinese labor by the nineties, the stagnation in non-agricultural industries beginning in 1889 and extending throughout the 1890's caused the release of a large number of white workers who drifted into farm work. Fuller, *op. cit.*, p. 19830.

19. *Ibid.* In one community where the Chinese were paid five dollars per week, the Japanese first worked for thirty-five cents per day in the early nineties. In another district the wages of the Japanese varied from sixty to ninety cents as against one dollar per day, including board, for white laborers. U. S. Immigration Commission, *Reports*, XXIII, p. 63. Although they at first worked for lower rates than either Chinese or whites, the Japanese received a progressively increasing amount of wages. By 1910 both Chinese and Japanese rates were approximately equal to those of the whites. Fuller, *op. cit.*, p. 19834.

20. The progressively decreasing number of Chinese farm laborers and the outflow of many white workers who, with the return of prosperity in the non-agricultural industries after 1900, created by 1902 a farm labor vacuum into which the Japanese stepped. Fuller argues that the Japanese, coming at a crucial period in California's labor history, enabled the perpetuation of the State's farm organizational pattern established during the period of Chinese labor dominance. Hence had the Japanese not come when they did the California farmers might have had to change their employment policy, i.e., giving laborers drawn from other ethnic groups better housing, etc. Fuller, *op. cit.*, pp. 19830.

21. U. S. Immigration Commission, *Reports*, XXIV, p. 15.

a boon to the laborer as it was to the employer, served also to secure the position of the Japanese as farm workers.[22] The Japanese labor agents located in various farming communities conducted boarding houses and stores where their men lived on a cooperative plan. The bosses not only obtained work for their gangs and carried on all the necessary wage negotiations with the employers but collected the wages for men and paid them their individual earnings. Under these conditions the employers could keep their bookkeeping at a minimum, having to pay only the labor agent the contracted sum, and be assured of a supply of reliable labor. Hence California ranchers made little effort to secure white laborers for whose services the employers had to negotiate individually, whose wages had to be paid to each personally, and whose reliability was doubtful because only those of an irregular, nomadic class were attracted to farm work.[23]

The Japanese contract labor system which prevailed in California, furthermore, helped to create conditions favorable for the transition of the Japanese from wage-earners to tenants or farm owners. In many instances California farmers resorted to leasing their holdings to the Japanese as a means of securing the nucleus of a labor supply and of transferring to the tenants the task of obtaining the other laborers needed. The Japanese, moreover, venturesome and ambitious to become independent producers, were sought as tenants by landowners because of their willingness to pay higher share or cash rents, to make improvements upon lands and to tolerate conditions not acceptable to white tenants in matters of housing.[24] Furthermore, their operations brought high yields and proportionately high profits to the landowners who rented on a share basis. Again the fact that the Japanese required little or no capital to begin with encouraged them to undertake independent farming. Competing packers and commission merchants financed the Japanese growers after taking liens upon the crops while storekeepers and landlords themselves made generous cash advances. Lastly, their willingness to form partnerships and pool their

22. Labor gangs were not peculiar to the Japanese. The Chinese were earlier organized in the same manner. For a discussion of the various tactics employed by Japanese labor contractors in obtaining work and bargaining for wages for their men, see Lloyd Fisher, *The Harvest Labor Market in California* (Cambridge: Harvard University Press, 1953), pp. 24–31.

23. U. S. Immigration Commission, *Reports*, XXIV, pp. 16–17.

24. U. S. Immigration Commission, *Reports*, XXIII, pp. 81–82.

money in leasing land was of considerable advantage to the *Issei*, a form of cooperation which the other races seldom undertook to better their economic position in agriculture.[25]

Thus by shrewd bargaining, industry, and the ability to tap credit sources the Japanese were able to climb the agricultural ladder from farm laborer to share tenantry, to cash tenantry, and finally for some to farm owner. While in 1900 there were only thirty-nine Japanese farmers in the United States (thirty-seven of whom were operating in California) with an aggregate holding of 4,698 acres, by 1910 there were 1,816 *Issei* farm operators in California alone.[26] In 1904 the Japanese in the State owned 2,442 acres, leased 35,258 acres for cash and 19,572 acres for a share of the crops. By 1909 the corresponding figures had risen to 16,449, 80,232 and 59,001 acres.[27] By 1920 the Japanese had been written off as an appreciable source of farm labor. . . .

For the Japanese farmers the struggle was not only against the elements but also against discrimination. Having inherited the prejudices which the Chinese had earlier aroused, the *Issei* were made the focus of attack from various political and economic groups. Systematic opposition began with the formation in May, 1905, of the Asiatic Exclusion League which had the avowed purpose of halting Japanese immigration and preventing by legislation the sale of land to Japanese aliens.[28] In 1909 no fewer than seventeen different bills relative to the

25. *Ibid.*, pp. 81–84; U. S. Immigration Commission, *Reports*, XXIV, pp. 635–639.
26. United States Census Office, *Twelfth Census of the United States: 1900. Agriculture*, Vol. V (Washington: United States Census Office, 1902), p. xciv; United States Bureau of the Census, *Thirteenth Census of the United States: 1910. Agriculture*, Vol. V (Washington: Government Printing Office, 1913), p. 176; U. S. Immigration Commission, *Reports*, XXIII, p. 79.
27. *Ibid.*
28. *Ibid.*, p. 169. Among organizations which supported the exclusion movement in California were the American Federation of Labor, American Legion, National Grange, and the Native Sons of the Golden West. For views expressed by representatives of the Asiatic Exclusion League on behalf of Japanese exclusion, see United States Congress, Senate, Committee on Immigration, *Japanese Immigration Legislation*. Hearings before the Committee on Immigration, 68th Congress, 1st Session, on S. 2576, March 11, 12, 13, and 15, 1924 (Washington: Government Printing Office, 1924), pp. 3, 21–38, 38–51, 103–143, 146 ff. Fuller maintains that "general anti-Japanese feeling in the rural districts dates from the years subsequent to 1910 and not before as some writers have supposed." Fuller, *op. cit.*, p. 19837.

Japanese were introduced in the California legislature including an alien land bill and a school segregation measure, neither of which passed.[29] In the campaign of 1910 in California, the platforms of the Republican, Democratic, and Socialist parties contained exclusion planks.[30] In 1913 an anti-alien land bill finally became law. It provided in essence that the Japanese might lease agricultural lands for a maximum of three years, that lands already owned or acquired in the future in satisfaction of existing liens, might be retained but could not be bequeathed to heirs under a citizenship disability though proceeds from the sale of the land would be turned over to such heirs.[31] This was a severe blow, but the Japanese circumvented the ownership provisions of the law by purchasing agricultural land in the names of their minor children born in the United States or by paying American citizens to buy land and hold it for them or their children.[32]

During World War I, economic antagonism against the Japanese ceased as industrial expansion stepped up labor demand. With farm laborers and operators alike leaving the rural areas for factory employment, the Japanese were eagerly sought as tenants. Hence well over 70,000 Japanese aliens entered the country between 1913 and 1920, among whom the farmers and farm laborers formed the largest group. This influx was a reflection of the relaxation in the enforcement of the Gentlemen's Agreement.[33] From 1916 through 1918 nearly 10,000 immigrants of these two categories were admitted.[34] . . .

After the first World War, agitation against the Japanese farmers was revived. Agitators found no difficulty in winning adherents for the anti-alien movement among the stream of returning doughboys

29. U. S. Immigration Commission, Reports, XXIII, pp. 171–172.

30. Ibid., p. 173.

31. U. S. Congress, National Defense Migration, pp. 77–78. For the full text of the land law of 1913, see Eliot Grinnell Mears, Resident Orientals on the American Pacific Coast (Chicago: University of Chicago Press, 1928), pp. 473–475.

32. Ibid., p. 253; U. S. Congress, National Defense Migration, p. 78.

33. Specifically the provisions of the governmental agreement stated that Japan of her own accord would refrain from issuing passports to Japanese laborers desiring to enter territories contiguous to continental United States and would recognize the right of the United States to refuse the admission to continental United States of Japanese of the laboring class whose passports did not include continental United States. Albert H. Elliot and Guy C. Calden, The Law Affecting Japanese Residing in the State of California (San Francisco, 1929), p. 68.

34. U. S. Congress, National Defense Migration, pp. 78–79.

and workers released from war industries, many of whom now felt their own economic insecurity in contrast to the established position of the Japanese. The movement was abetted by Japan's aggressions in Siberia, Manchuria, and Korea, and by the awarding of Shantung to Japan in 1919. American nativists made the best of the situation in California at the expense of the Japanese farmers.

The proponents of Japanese exclusion used a plethora of arguments after 1919, among which the economic was not the least of those stressed. The white farmers were told, for example, that the ever-increasing number of Japanese family farms where the father, mother, and children worked in the field would present unfair competition. V. S. McClatchy, a virulent representative of the Japanese Exclusion League of California, filed a skeleton brief with the Secretary of State of the United States in which he said:[35]

The Japanese possess superior advantages in economic competition, partly because of racial characteristics, thrift, industry, low standards of living, willingness to work long hours without expensive pleasures, the women working as men, etc. Combine with these characteristics extraordinary cooperation and solidarity, and the assistance of the Japanese Government, through associations acting for it or in its behalf, and the Japanese, concentrating in communities or industries, are easily able to supplant the whites.

The Japanese were also accused of having "secured the control of one-eighth of all the irrigated lands of California, which are the State's richest," and that they were organizing a market trust.[36]

The champions of the Japanese argued that the Japanese had taken up much of the worst lands in California and made them fertile, thus helping to reduce the cost of food for the city consumers.[37] Evidence

35. V. S. McClatchy, *Japanese Immigration and Colonization*, Skeleton brief with the Secretary of State, 67th Congress, 1st Session, Senate Document No. 55 (Washington: Government Printing Office, 1920), p. 14.

36. *Ibid.*, pp. 14–15. Besides the economic agreements, the exclusionists charged that the Japanese were unassimilable, that they owed primary allegiance to the Japanese emperor, and that the birth rate of the Japanese residents would enable them in time to outnumber the whites.

37. The American Committee of Justice, *Arguments Against the California Alien Land Law* (Oakland, 1920), p. 11. See also U. S. Congress, *National Defense Migration*, p. 84.

indicates that the Japanese did indeed develop undesirable lands. The refractory hog wallow lands in western San Joaquin Valley were actually shunned by the white man, but the Japanese succeeded in conquering them. Subsequently, vineyards and orchards were to cover such lands from Seville to Lemon Cove. It was the Japanese who pioneered the rice industry and produced the first commercial crop of rice on hard pan and goose lands "that were not worth paying taxes on."[38] These are not isolated examples; they were the general condition throughout the State in areas where the Japanese farmed. Through intensive cultivation and the application of scientific techniques, the Japanese had succeeded by 1920 in producing on improved lands crops valued at $67,000,000.[39]

Despite the presentation of evidence favoring the presence of Japanese farmers in California agriculture, the opposition forces persuaded the State legislature in 1920 to pass an amendment to the land law of 1913. The amended law deprived the Japanese of the right to lease agricultural land and to act as guardian for a native-born minor if his estate consisted of property which the Japanese could not hold under law.[40]

Whether as a result of the land law[41] or not, Japanese agricultural development in California was checked during the third decade of the twentieth century. In 1921, for example, the Japanese produced 12.3 percent of the total farm products raised in the State, whereas in 1925 the percentage had dropped to 9.3.[42] A corresponding decrease is to be noted in the census figures enumerating the number of Japanese farms and acreage under cultivation for the years, 1920 and 1930:[43]

38. J. P. Irish, "Orientals in California," *Overland*, Vol. 75, April, 1920, p. 333.
39. The American Committee of Justice, *op. cit.*, p. 10.
40. For a synopsis of the alien land law of 1920 as amended in 1923 and 1927, see Elliot and Calden, *op. cit.*, p. 25 ff.
41. The effectiveness of the alien land laws has been questioned. One source even goes so far as to say that they actually increased Japanese ownership because landowners who might otherwise have rented to Japanese tenants, after 1920 sold outright to their American-born minor children. U. S. Congress, *National Defense Migration*, p. 86.
42. *Ibid.*, p. 87.
43. United States Bureau of the Census, *Sixteenth Census of the United States: 1940. Agriculture*, Vol. 1 (Washington: Government Printing Office, 1942), p. 684.

	1920	1930
Number of Japanese farms	5,152	3,956
Acreage	361,276	191,427

The decline in the number of Japanese engaging in agriculture in the 1920's is said to have been reinforced by the disinclination of the Nisei to remain on the farms,[44] but this was an insignificant factor. After all, the great majority of the Nisei during this decade were not even in their teens and hence would have had little bearing on the decline of Japanese agriculture.[45] The agricultural depression of that decade may have been a weighty factor in forcing some of the Issei to leave farming, but the legal barriers, the land law and the Oriental exclusion act of 1924,[46] did much to discourage the Japanese from entering farming or expanding their operations.

By the eve of the Second World War, however, the number of Japanese farmers in California nearly equaled that of the 1920 figure although the acreage farmed was much lower. Hence in 1940 there were 5,135 farms operated by this race with a total acreage of 220,094.[47] During the previous decade the maturing Nisei had become a factor in agriculture, and their participation in this occupation undoubtedly accounted for the small increase in the number of farmers classified in census figures as "Japanese"; yet, even at this late date the management and operation of Japanese farms were still in the hands of the Issei male.[48]

With respect to land tenure among the Japanese immigrant farmers only a small percentage of them actually owned their farms. In California only twenty-five percent were owners or part owners, less than

---

44. U. S. Congress, National Defense Migration, p. 87.

45. For a table showing the age by sex of the Japanese population in California, see United States Bureau of the Census, Sixteenth Census of the United States: 1940. Population, Characteristics of the Nonwhite Population by Race (Washington: Government Printing Office, 1943), p. 98.

46. For an explanation of the Immigration Law of 1924, see Elliot and Calden, op. cit., p. 13 ff.

47. United States Bureau of the Census, Sixteenth Census of the United States: 1940. Agriculture, Vol. III, General Report (Washington: Government Printing Office, 1943), p. 224.

48. Leonard Bloom and Ruth Riemer, Removal and Return (University of California Publications in Culture and Society, Vol. IV, Berkeley and Los Angeles: University of California Press, 1949), p. 76.

five percent managers, while the majority of them, seventy percent, rented their farms. In Los Angeles County, where almost thirty percent of all Japanese farms were located, approximately ninety percent of the operators were tenants. In contrast, in the counties of Fresno, Merced, Placer, and Sacramento only fifty percent of the Japanese growers were in this category.[49] Apparently there were more tenant farmers in truck and field-crop-producing areas of the State than in those regions where considerable fruit and other perennial crops were cultivated.

Various theses have been presented to account for the low rate of decline of tenancy among the Japanese farm operators. In 1910, eighty-five percent of them were classified as tenants and thirty years later, in 1940, seventy percent of them were still in the same category. True the laborious method by which they worked up the agricultural ladder had not enabled many of them to accumulate the money necessary to purchase and equip a farm. But the reasons are more fundamental. Students of the problem have stated that although doubt was expressed as to the effectiveness of the alien land laws, the forces which effected these measures deterred many eligible Japanese from acquiring tenure status, particularly farm ownership, in regions where local sentiment was not favorable to the Oriental. Because of this uneasiness, say the experts, many may have preferred tenure of land which would enable them to move on short notice, and a type of farming, i.e., truck farming, which required a minimum of capital investment for permanent structures and perennial crops. The restrictive measures, to the extent that they discouraged farm ownership, probably contributed to establishing an unstable tenure pattern among the Issei agriculturalists with associated undesirable features inherent in short-term leasing, insecurity of land occupancy, and high tenant mobility.[50]

The Japanese, whether farm owner or tenant, usually farmed on a small scale. In 1940 their farms averaged a little over forty acres[51]

49. U. S. Congress, National Defense Migration, p. 117.

50. Adon Poli and Warren M. Engstrand, "Japanese Agriculture on the Pacific Coast," Journal of Land and Public Utilities Economics, Vol. XXI (November, 1945), pp. 354–355.

51. U. S. Bureau of the Census, Sixteenth Census of the United States: 1940. Agriculture, Vol. III, General Report, p. 224.

as compared with the national average of two hundred acres.[52] The *Issei* generally preferred to cultivate small acreages intensively, as did their counterparts in Japan, in order to grow crops with high returns per acre. Consequently only a very insignificant number of the race were engaged in livestock farming which requires extensive acreages of forage crops.[53] ...

The noteworthy aspect of pre-World War II Japanese farming was the ability of the farmers of this ethnic group, each growing on a small scale, to compete successfully with large vegetable grower-shippers. The Japanese were not out-competed because they possessed aptitude for the type of agriculture in which most of them were engaged. They possessed special skill in soil preparation, crop and seed selection, planting, cultivation, irrigation, and spraying. They were also able managers. "Japanese capacity for labor in the fields, growing, cultivating, and marketing truck crops is secondary to their managing ability," said one observer who was acquainted with their ways.[54] Another reason for their success in agricultural competition was their willingness to organize cooperative farm organizations.

A cohesive group, the Japanese immigrants very early in their careers as independent farmers cooperated to meet common problems. The early Japanese farm organizations, local in character, aided their members in finding ranches, served to limit the competition for land by fixing a maximum rental that a Japanese should pay, assisted in marketing the crops and obtaining supplies, interested themselves where disputes arose between a landlord and tenant, and disseminated scientific knowledge of agriculture and horticulture through publications of their own. Many of these local associations served as mutual benefit societies as well.[55]

In southern California, Japanese farmers' associations (*nogyo kumiai*) were more extensive in their operations than elsewhere in the State. Such organizations were connected with marketing associations in Los Angeles for channeling crops from farm to market.

52. *Ibid.*, p. 81.
53. Kūchi Kanzaki, *California and the Japanese* (San Francisco, 1921), p. 97.
54. U. S. Congress, *National Defense Migration*, p. 118.
55. U. S. Immigration Commission, *Reports*, XXIII, pp. 85–86; U. S. Immigration Commission, *Reports*, XXIV, pp. 341–343, 396–397.

The two types of associations were also joined in a service federation which for a fee provided its members with daily newspaper and radio broadcasts of produce prices.[56] . . .

In the course of their rise to a distinctive position in California agriculture, the Japanese immigrant farmers were condemned by their critics for various uncommendable practices. In their desire to become independent farmers, it was asserted, the Issei paid comparatively high rent for land which led to an increase in the rental value of land and to a certain extent caused the displacement of farmers of other ethnic groups.[57] Another charge made against the Japanese was that the value of land diminished in areas where they settled which forced the white population to move away. This was undoubtedly true, especially with respect to residential property, but evidence to the contrary is also available. Hence in a certain section of Fresno County a Japanese was the first to settle and begin farming. Within four years two of his countrymen and four white families moved into the area. While the first settler paid thirty-five dollars an acre for the hay land, the later purchasers were compelled to pay sixty dollars for the same type of land.[58]

Early in their careers the Japanese were also criticized for overspecialization and over-production of crops such as berries and asparagus, a consequence of their eagerness to acquire quick profits. The practice is said to have resulted in the lowering of market prices of such crops which forced non-Japanese farmers to withdraw from producing them. But actually the white farmers did not generally grow the type of crops in which the Japanese specialized, and therefore the effect upon the farmer was minimal. Instances, moreover, in which prices were adversely affected because of Japanese competition were comparatively few.[59]

A further practice attributed to the Issei growers was "mining" the soil. The allegation was not entirely without foundation because, as already indicated, the Japanese were predominantly tenants, not owners, a situation which inevitably affected their attitude regarding land improvement. But at the same time it is important to note that

56. Poli and Engstrand, op. cit., p. 358.
57. U. S. Immigration Commission, Reports, XXIV, p. 309.
58. Ibid., p. 643.
59. Ibid., pp. 307–308.

a soil scientist of the United States Department of Agriculture minimized the seriousness of the charge by stating: "I am inclined to believe the thorough and excellent cultivation given land under Japanese farming, which favors aeration and biologic processes promoting soil fertility, may in a large measure offset deterioration through removal of plantfood materials."[60]

Finally, during the early years as farmers the Japanese were taken to task for failing to honor contract agreements.[61] No adequate explanation has been given for this, but the fact that East and West differ in the stress each places upon the inviolability of contract may be a partial reason. No sweeping generalization should be made about the Oriental, however, because the Chinese farmers were not generally accused of breaches of contract.

Various other pertinent data are available which help to form a clearer picture of the Japanese immigrant farmers in California. The standard of living of the average *Issei* farmers prior to 1941 was definitely below that of other ethnic groups engaged in the same occupation.[62] They did not, generally speaking, improve property or build a better class of homes. Most of them were merely rough, unplastered frame structures of three or four rooms.[63] An acute observer has described Japanese farm life in the following words:[64]

In California I met for the first time large groups of Japanese, industrious farmers, fruit growers, and poultry raisers, in the Sacramento and San Joaquin Valleys, from El Centro to Colusa, in and around Los Angeles and Fresno and Sacramento. It was comparatively easy to distinguish between the Japanese ranches and

60. Mears, *op. cit.*, pp. 245–246.

61. U. S. Immigration Commission, *Reports*, XXIII, pp. 87–88.

62. A comparison of the data for the Japanese and Italian truck gardeners around Sacramento prior to 1910 reveals that the Japanese farm homes were generally rated from bad to fair in repair while those of the Italians were rated fair to good. In Los Angeles County the Japanese homes were in fairly good repair. The Scandinavian farmers in Santa Clara County and the Germans in Anaheim had homes kept in good condition. Cf. Tables 119, 209, 255, and 289 in U. S. Immigration Commission, *Reports*, XXIV, pp. 838–840, 864–865, 884–889.

63. *Ibid.*, p. 399.

64. Konrad Bercovici, "The Japanese in the United States," *The Century*, CX (September, 1925), p. 608.

the white man's farm ... Either because of the insecurity with which the Japanese has regarded his holdings in this country, the farm home of a Japanese, even of a wealthy farmer, is far below that of a home of a white man owning a similar piece of ground or of similar wealth.[65] The neatness of the field ... is in direct contrast with the flimsy, improvised condition of the living quarters of the Japanese.

This is a faithful picture of Japanese farm houses in the 1920's and, in general, it had not changed considerably by 1941. The shifting and unsettled nature of the Japanese farmers induced by the land law and the inability of the Issei to become naturalized citizens prevented many from establishing themselves permanently in any community. Under such conditions there was little incentive to build permanent homes. In the settled districts, however, chiefly around Fresno, where there were large Japanese landholdings, the standard of living was surprisingly high.[66] ...

By 1941 the Japanese immigrants in agriculture, the majority of whom had come to America as "birds of passage," intending to make enough money and then to return to Japan, had settled down in various farm communities. They were rearing their native-born children in the American tradition. For most of the Issei there was now no longer any strong desire to leave the country in which they had resided the greater part of their lives. ...

... Very few, however, even among the Japanese themselves, realize the important role the Japanese immigrants collectively played in California agricultural history. Coming in large numbers after the turn of the twentieth century, they filled the farm labor vacuum and thus prevented a ruinous slump in those lines of agriculture for which California is noted, namely, in the growing and harvesting of intensive crops. As independent farm operators, the Japanese with

65. In the 1930's the writer had occasion to visit the home of a Japanese operator of one of the largest growing and shipping concerns in California. The owner of a large packing shed and a grower of crops on thousands of acres of well-tilled land, this operator lived in a humble unpainted frame home surrounded by huge sheds housing hundreds of thousands of dollars worth of trucks, tractors, and other farm equipment. The picture, in view of his wealth, was incongruous to say the least.

66. E. Manchester Boddy, Japanese in America (Los Angeles, 1921), p. 107.

their skill and energy helped to reclaim and improve thousands of acres of worthless lands throughout the State, lands which the white man abhorred, and made them fertile and immensely productive. They pioneered the rice industry and planted the first citrus orchards in the hog wallow lands in the San Joaquin Valley. They played a vital part in establishing the present system of marketing fruits and vegetables, especially in Los Angeles County, and dominated in the field of commercial truck crops. From the perspective of history, it is evident that the contributions of the *Issei* to California's economy far outweigh the evils that have been attributed to their agricultural activities. They were undeniably a significant factor in making California one of the greatest farming states in the Union.

Part VII
Struggle for Status,
1940 to the Present

Struggle for Status, 1940 to the Present

At the mid-point of the twentieth century in the United States, nonwhites grappled with material and psychological obstacles. During the years from 1940 to date some progress seemed evident to casual observers, but particularly in relation to the white population, cold statistics showed improvement to be largely illusory. Spurred on by heightened expectations and growing bitterness and abetted by an awakening white conscience, nonwhites embarked on a sustained drive to upgrade their status and achieve coexistence and equality with the white world.

The effort to improve the lives of nonwhites borrowed heavily from the tactics of earlier militants who had appeared intermittently during the previous two hundred years, only to be ruthlessly put down. The new approach emphasized pride in their color, heritage, and culture. Nonwhites rejected those values of the white culture which seemed inappropriate to their experience. But for many the most important consideration continued to be subsistence; rat-infested housing, inadequate food and clothing, and unemployment persisted as daily problems.

Black Americans led the struggle for status, and many of their tactics were adopted or modified by other nonwhite groups. From A. Philip Randolph's threatened march on Washington in 1941 to the Black Panther party program of 1971, black Americans organized and confronted the white establishment. Their techniques included the legal battles of Roy Wilkins, the political activities of Shirley Chisholm and Julian Bond, the nonviolent demonstrations of Martin Luther King, the religious and nationalistic appeals of Elijah Muhammad and Malcolm X, and the black power program of Stokely Carmichael. Some joined forces with white Americans while others aligned themselves with the Third World; some were violent while others insisted on peaceful protest, but all were determined to create an equitable place for the black man in American society.

Other nonwhites developed similar patterns of resistance. The new American Indian created a "red power" movement which exhibited his disenchantment and militancy; the invasions of Alcatraz Island and the other efforts to reacquire land by force, as well as by legal means, epitomized their strategy. The success of the grape strike at Delano, California, initiated by Filipino farm workers and carried through by Cesar Chavez and his Mexican-American followers, illustrates another kind of resistance through labor union organization and methods. While the family structure and living habits of Orientals who have remained within the culture work toward separation from the currents that often agitate American life, young people such as the Maoist-leaning youth guards and the alienated Wah Ching, the Hong Kong born young men of San Francisco's Chinatown, have asserted a militancy not shared by their parents.

The objectives of minorities were not confined to a demand for parity with the white world; nonwhites also called for self-determination within their communities, and particularly for the control of schools and businesses. The movement for community control ironically was fostered by the isolation of nonwhites in ghettos and more recently by the movement of economically secure whites to the suburbs. The growth of ghettos led to an enlarged nonwhite population in the great central cities of the nation and a concomitant increase in the political influence which nonwhites could assert. Thus by midcentury nonwhite mayors and congressmen were placed in office by city electorates.

The discriminatory policies that herded nonwhites into ghettos opened the way to the development of alternative life styles and promoted the pluralism which Americans have simultaneously prized and attempted to prevent by homogenizing their white population.

The structural assimilation of which Milton M. Gordon (Part I, "Assimilation in America: Theory and Reality") speaks did not apply to nonwhites, and the effect was the promotion of separate cultures that often had only a tangential relationship to that of the majority.

Nonwhite demands for correcting the imbalance between their world and that of the whites created a population that was no longer quiescent. Nonwhites gave voice to their frustrations and unhappiness in a manner that shook the foundations of the nation. For not only did they demand equitable treatment by the economic and political system, but some also confronted the social system and rejected it in favor of a culture that derived from their own experience.

Ronald O. Haak,
"Co-opting the Oppressors:
The Case of the Japanese-Americans"

The attack on Pearl Harbor which brought the United States into
the Second World War had disastrous results for those Japanese-
Americans who lived on the west coast. A wave of fear and hatred
produced hysterical rumors of sabotage and Japanese-American-
aided invasions of the coast. A flagrant violation of human rights
occurred as over 117,000 people, two-thirds of them American
citizens, were moved to ten relocation camps in the interior of the
nation solely because of their race. The Japanese submitted peacefully
and, professing their loyalty, aided in running the camps and
laboring in surrounding areas. Ronald O. Haak, in "Co-opting the
Oppressors: The Case of the Japanese-Americans," argues that the
Japanese drew on their cultural heritage in order to endure the
oppression and emerge from the ordeal.

Co-opting the Oppressors:
The Case of the
Japanese-Americans

Ronald O. Haak

"A Jap's a Jap," stated Brigadier General John L. DeWitt. As commander of the Western Defense Command in 1942, he was testifying before a congressional committee on the vulnerability of the West Coast to invasion from Japan. Indeed, former Supreme Court Chief Justice Earl Warren, then attorney general of California, testified that the American-born Japanese were even more dangerous to the security of the United States than the alien Japanese. There was a pervasive fear that the Japanese-Americans' knowledge of the English language and American customs would make them excellent saboteurs. To Walter Lippmann the very lack of sabotage and espionage on the West Coast was cause for alarm. Innocuous behavior was merely a ploy to disarm American suspicions, he warned. Plans were soon under way for the harsh resettlement of 112,000 persons of Japanese ancestry. In sealed trains they were dispatched to ten relocation camps, where they were allowed to bring only as much baggage as they could carry in their hands.

The authority for this vast roundup of "undesirables" on the charge of potential treason lay in Executive Order 9066, which

Abridged from Ronald O. Haak, "Co-opting the Oppressors: The Case of the Japanese-Americans," *Transaction*, VII (1970), pp. 23–31. Copyright © 1970 by Transaction, Inc., New Brunswick, New Jersey. Permission to reprint.

President Franklin D. Roosevelt signed on 19 February 1942. The order marked off military areas "from which any or all persons [might] be excluded." General DeWitt, who was made responsible for implementing the executive order, had already recommended "evacuation of the Japanese and *other subversive persons* from the Pacific Coast" (my italics) and had specified that "the word 'Japanese' included alien Japanese and American citizens of Japanese ancestry." In later proclamations and directives, General DeWitt referred to the American-born group, euphemistically, as "American-born persons of Japanese lineage" or as "nonalien persons of Japanese ancestry," and in the *Final Report* of the Western Defense Command, "nisei" was defined as "any person of Japanese ancestry not born in Japan," while the meaning of "Japanese ancestry" was clarified to cover "any person who has a Japanese ancestor, regardless of degree."

The stereotyping was racial, rather than political, since none of America's other so-called enemies-in-residence were so categorized. Germans and Italians in the United States faced no such charges and as a group were never subjected to more than a curfew in the very first days of the war. Moreover, the ideology behind the action had a domestic flavor, even a regional one. The Japanese third of Hawaii's population, 3,000 miles closer to the emperor's charisma, were generally allowed to go about their business, as were the Japanese populations in the Middle West and on the East Coast. For 112,000 people on the western seaboard, however, constitutional guarantees were suspended, and the civilian enclave was subjected to treatment usually reserved for prisoners of war.

Despite this alarming start, within little more than a decade the Japanese were welcomed back into the pantheon of good American immigrants. The oppressed minority, against overwhelming odds and with little hope their efforts would do them any good, induced the white majority to erase the stigmata. How did it happen?

Before the war, the Japanese had earned grudging respect. Neatness, diligence, respect for property, low delinquency rates and an aversion to the dole won them favor so long as they were kept out of the larger competition. Their educational record, for example, compared favorably with the white population at large and exceeded that of any identifiable minority. Yet the fact remains that by 1939 in San Francisco and Los Angeles only one in ten nisei (Japanese:

ni = second, sei = generation) employed in trade or nondomestic service was actually working for a "Caucasian" firm. Significantly, their strivings did not seem to require reinforcement from the larger society. In the 1930s, when even members of favored minority groups could find no jobs, the nisei went to school and avidly prepared for that one chance in a thousand. But then came Pearl Harbor and the vicious "preventive detention" of the war years.

Yet it was precisely their wartime record of camp cooperation and combat valor that finally broke down the accusations against Japanese-Americans. Political loyalties were shown not to be fused to ancestry; this was fact. But society, in exonerating this minority, went a step further and attributed the group's performance to Americanization, to the fact that it had assimilated "our" standards and way of life. Moreover, the truth of this explanation seems to have been accepted even by the Japanese-American Citizens League (JACL) which has also consistently stressed the theme of Americanization in its representations to Congress and to the nation at large. In a statement before the West Coast hearings of the House of Representatives in 1954, the JACL stated:

> In spite of threats and intimidation by the disgruntled and disillusioned, as the records show, several thousand Japanese-Americans whose loyalty had been questioned by their own government volunteered to fight, and if necessary to die, for our country. This we submit was a demonstration of *real faith in America and the American way* seldom if ever surpassed (my italics).

Today, the JACL version is probably the standard version of what happened. (Indeed, it may be the only one the majority is willing to accept.)

If, as in the film *Rashomon*, we look at events through the memory filters of the participants, the entire perspective shifts. The California nisei with whom I spoke regard the camp period as attesting to their worth as Japanese. Postwar acceptance by the larger society was tremendously important, but the nisei view it as belated recognition of peculiarly Japanese virtues, virtues that this nation had ignored for 70 years. In short, they attribute their admirable performance to ethnic intensification, not ethnic renunciation.

These findings suggest that when groups are forced into confrontation each takes what it needs from that confrontation and does not perceive it in the same way even when both are moving toward a satisfactory rapprochement. Far from representing this as a lapse in communication, I would generalize that a happy outcome requires each faction to salvage its self-esteem under the common umbrella of mutual misunderstanding.

The Japanese-Americans know they were misjudged from the start. That may be why their recollections are more bemused than indignant. Of Japanese farmers suspected of planting their vegetable rows toward neighboring airfields for the benefit of Japanese bombing runs, they can laugh, "That farmer didn't know anything but his vegetables." Again, Caucasians hidden in bushes reported that farmers stared intently at passing aircraft, coordinating traffic volume, flight schedules and regional air strength. The truth, it turned out, was that the farmer welcomed an excuse to straighten his back and relieve the monotony of his day. There is still much enjoyment over the story of the Japanese hotel proprietor who returned from his roof-top laundry lines with basket and flashlight to find his hotel filled with police searching for "the spy on the roof."

A strong, overbearing, gullible figure is always good fun, and Japanese folk plays (kyogen) dramatize the discomfiture of many. It is embarrassing when a powerful authority brings a cannon to bear upon a flea, while splashing around huge sums of money for guards, camp maintenance, bookkeepers, administrators—not a bit of it necessary. It softens the blow to reflect that the qualities carried here from an old and illustrious civilization should escape the notice of a newcomer like the United States.

But more importantly, Japanese see no point in nursing even grave grievances if there is an appropriate apology. In their view, postwar indemnification, though partial, qualifies as a proper apology and relieves them of all onus. Once again, they see themselves as rewarded not for renunciation of Japanese traits, but for the very tenacity with which they clung to them.

Many first-generation immigrants grew up in the rural Japanese village, with its deeply entrenched tradition of subservience and cooperation. Long before Japan dreamed of modernization, her villages consisted of small, family-centered production units disciplined to the exacting, labor-intensive techniques of wet rice cultivation. Communal performance was severely monitored, and ostracism meant substantial psychological and economic dislocation. When Japan lunged toward modernization, the agrarian sector was chosen to bear the full brunt of initial capitalization. From 1868 until the upturn of Japan's economic growth in 1886, taxes on farm production accounted for 78 percent of the total national revenue. During this period of rather pitiless extraction, class divisions did not appear in the villages, and the farmers did not challenge the directives. They performed according to expectations.

The immigrants, who in America turned to truck farming, flower raising and other related pursuits characteristic of Japanese endeavors on the West Coast, came from a milieu where duty and sacrifice were demanded almost as in war. Rural commitments in Japan were not made provisionally, in the context of interest politics or a battle for subsidies. Rice cultivators have for centuries worked prodigiously for their immediate hierarchical superior. Commentators on Japan often use the term "moral style" to get at just this readiness of the Japanese to invest themselves in an enterprise that brings them no commensurate gain, none even in sight. The rewards are present, of course, in the security and interdependence of the group cocoon, and this is especially pronounced in the rural sector. Urban girls recruited to weave kimonos in Japanese cities prior to World War II kept themselves aloof and moved on to better jobs after their training or contract was over. Rural girls recruited for the same jobs invested themselves lavishly in the small companies, even to bearing the boss's children and bringing them up as little apprentices, with marriage foreclosed from the start. This rural predisposition for self-sacrifice without hope of reward molded the character of the immigrants in this story. It helps explain how they and their children could stick to these priorities of cooperation under the most tremendous provocation, a fidelity the adopted country could account for only by the self-flattering notion of "Americanization."

The camps gave many Caucasians their first contact with Japanese outside the movie houses. A nisei recalled the day the sealed trains delivered their human cargo to an Arizona camp. Nisei girls in crisp, fresh blouses set up registration points, and family representatives queued up to offer data for rosters. The arrival scene slowly acquired some signs of voluntary order and purpose. "Are these the Japanese people?" a government bystander asked in wonder. "Yes," replied the nisei, "that's the way the Japanese are."

The nisei share a common fund of knowledge about the fates and reputations of the ten garrison settlements that stretched from eastern California to Arkansas. The Arizona camp was well known for the prodigious resourcefulness of its people. The internees faced a blazing sun and harsh soil, but gradually they learned that castor beans were viable. Humble as it was, this crop was marketable and brought money into the camp. Cereals were garnered from the nearby Navaho, who startled the Japanese with the specter of minority ruin. The new arrivals quickly came to fear reservation poverty and apathy, particularly among the sansei (san = third, sei = generation) who would be growing up in a potentially demoralizing milieu. This furnished an incentive for the Japanese to do more than merely adjust to their desert exile.

To appreciate the initiative of the Japanese internee, place him in the context of the wardship that was his for the asking. The government assumed the task of providing food and shelter, while conduct of internal camp affairs was in the hands of the Japanese membership. Specialists such as cooks, nurses, doctors and police earned salaries of $12 to $19 a month. There were no additional allowances for clothing replacements and toiletries. Food shipped in was charged against daily allocations of 29¢ to 45¢ per person. The Japanese could have lapsed into sullen and passive dependence, for which the Navaho provided a vivid precedent, but these new arrivals fared better.

Incentives need not be lofty to be effective. The Japanese had no voice in menu composition, and they found the pork hocks, ox hearts and mutton (the most vividly remembered foods) too different from their traditional fare to be palatable. Private purchases of preferred foods from the neighboring countryside outran the capacities of $12 to $19 incomes for specialized workers. The others had even less money, as bank assets had been frozen before the evacuation.

From conferences with nearby Indians, the Japanese learned that where sagebrush grew, vegetables would too. Before their tenure was over, the Japanese were raising all manner of vegetables. Chickens provided plenty of eggs for the whole camp, and even cattle were in evidence. Their initiative produced a bounty that extended beyond the camp. From the year-round growing season of Arizona they were able to ship their surplus to camps in the north.

Timber parties left under escort and returned with harvests that appreciably lowered government coal bills. With 120,000 internees, trimming a dime a day per capita meant $12,000 saved daily from the federal outlay. From nisei recollections, many dimes were pared from maintenance costs by Japanese diligence. As camp food production grew to supplement the official menu, the cooks found themselves able to cut their food purchases. At the end of the first year, a delegation approached their captors and volunteered the money left over from the food budget, all carefully saved and meticulously recorded.

Rumors of the Japanese performance seeped into the Arizona governor's mansion. With the establishment of the camps, the governor had guaranteed to his people that not one Japanese would be allowed to remain in the state when the war was over. The irony of the situation was not lost on the internees who met the governor's reserve, some of them recall, not head-on, but with characteristic finesse. Their response was a gift of three yellow and three white camp-grown chrysanthemums coaxed from the desert soil. The flowers, "big as cantaloupes," waved from two-foot stalks and were replete with rapprochement symbolism. "Did such flowers grow inside *that* camp?" the outsiders asked one another as the present made its way to the statehouse. Soon a local fire department visited the camp for a picnic. The police took the next tour, and finally the governor himself put in an appearance. "They all thought we would be living like Indians, but they found out the Japanese were different," one man remembers. The guests found the sandy glare softened by trees, flowers, a pond, walks and improvised landscaping. (Some internees devoted half their precious hand baggage to prize bulbs, cuttings and the like. Thus, camps favored with better soil sported Chinese elm trees and even manicured lawns.) "How do you keep everything so clean?" the Caucasian visitor of the moment might ask. "Who picks up all the paper?" Shrugging diffidently, the nisei would reply matter-of-factly, "Oh, everyone looks after himself."

By the war's end, the governor was won over. He invited six nisei agriculturalists from the camp to inspect a parcel of property under consideration for his own venture into commercial flower raising. Of the 25 acres, the Japanese judged 15 as promising, and they agreed to develop this acreage as employees of the governor-turned-businessman. Two refrigerated trucks were purchased the first year to convey the flowers to California winter markets. Needless to say, the Japanese are now welcome in Arizona, as they are welcome everywhere.

It would be inaccurate to attribute the Japanese cooperative drive to a spirit of docility. When the government accountant accepted the donation of savings from the food budget, the Japanese did not withdraw, content with a down-scaling of funds for the following year. They requested a hike in the very next allocation for clothes and travel fares so they could "help the war effort" by repairing railroad tracks and harvesting in the fields that had lost workers to the army or higher paying war industries. Although they often met hostility, they traveled throughout the country doing farm work.

Such cooperation has all the earmarks of sheer identification with the American war effort. But within the camps, the elected leadership had their hands full "calming down the people" so as to deal prudently with the Caucasian administrators. Regional and generational fissures, temporarily closed during the stress of evacuation, were reopened inside the camps. Rumors of FBI inquiries and arrests aroused suspicions that there were informers among the internees, and cooperation with the administration was branded as collaboration. Every faction found its convenient scapegoat. Suspected informers were ostracized, threatened or even beaten by their fellow evacuees. Revolt against the administration took the form of major strikes or minor work stoppages during the fall of 1942, and in two projects, Poston and Manzanar, revolt assumed the proportions of riots and was met with force by the administration. . . .

Detention, first considered as a transitory phase in the larger scheme of evacuation and resettlement, bogged down and took on the earmarks of a permanent program. The War Relocation Authority (WRA)—rather more human than the other agencies involved—sought to reinstitute the objectives that its name implied. It sought to extract from the War and Justice Departments the necessary authority to move its people out of the camps. When the War Department decided to reopen the army to loyal Japanese-American volunteers, the WRA saw its chance. It decided to capitalize on the War Department's interest in the male nisei by expanding the loyalty inquiry into a general liberalization of the stalled relocation policy. The War Department was to "process" the male citizen, while the WRA would process the rest of the adults.

For all its good intentions, the questionnaire was clumsily conceived and cast the internees into a state of alarm and consternation. The three points that caused the trouble dealt explicitly with the issue of "loyalty": 1) Are you loyal to the United States, abjuring allegiance to the emperor? 2) Do you hope the United States wins the war? 3) Would you serve in the combat forces of the United States, wherever ordered?

Some nisei found these questions irrelevant to their own feelings of "loyalty" toward the United States, for they perceived them as glossing over legitimate reservations based upon prior violation of their own civil rights. A nisei informant who answered yes in good conscience to questions 1 and 2 could recite in detail his civic reasons for giving a negative answer to the third. Yet this qualified his loyalty. Another nisei recalled that his response to question 2 had been: "There is no winner in a war." Administrator response: "We know that." Nisei rejoinder: "Then why ask me?" This is not as slippery as it may appear, for it is good Buddhist doctrine, but it compromised his status as a loyal citizen in the administration's view. Other nisei were uncertain how they could renounce allegiance to the emperor when they were American citizens and had no contact with Japan. Was this a "Do you still beat your wife?" question?

But the camp debates raged longest about question 1 which, as a condition of loyalty, required alien issei who were barred from American citizenship by statute, to forswear allegiance to the country wherein their citizenship was assigned. If they complied and America lost the war, then what would become of them?

Belatedly, the issei were permitted to affirm that they would "abide by the laws of the United States" and "take no action that would in any way interfere with the war effort of the United States." But their American-born off-spring were required to affirm the original "wife-beating" statement, despite their American citizenship. . . .

As a counterweight to this sketch of uniform Japanese cooperation, I should mention here the militant and outraged Japanese who railed at their imprisonment, refused to take an oath of sympathy toward the United States war effort, beat up the emissaries and the president of the JACL and accused advocates of moderation of being collaborators and informers. They sorted themselves out by their defiant performance on questionnaires and were segregated in a special camp at Tule Lake. It was made possible for these American-born Japanese to renounce their citizenship, and some of them did, though it was later ruled that this renunciation was not binding. A high proportion of these militants were kibei [Japanese born in America but educated in Japan].

Though the West Coast Japanese were thrown back as a group upon their own resources for solidarity and self-worth by harsh outside verdicts, the kibei recoil was compounded by their recent education in Japan. Their memories were fresh and vivid, and their militancy tended to be proportionally stronger. Tanaka, one of my informants, had the added misfortune to be drafted into the army before the war, at a time when he still knew no English. . . .

The vast bulk of the population remained stigmatized throughout the war and were treated "like Japanese." Their forced exile and the cause célèbre of their identity predictably intensified their ethnic consciousness. In conversation today they refer to their wartime capacities and performance as distinctively Japanese solutions to a minority, not a political, problem.

Their solution was an ancestral reflex pattern of self-sacrifice and cooperation with no reward in sight. This was not new. A nisei recalls the exhortations she received from her parents even before the war:

We were abused at school, we were told never to fight back. We were told never to bring disgrace upon our family. Instead, we were told to rise by working hard. We had to do better than Caucasians to earn even equal treatment. We saw our parents had sacrificed everything for us children, and we couldn't disgrace them.

Isn't this a strategy to urge on all minorities striving for a breakthrough? Shouldn't they all follow the Japanese example? Initially, it sounds good, but the more the nisei reveal of themselves, the more they reveal an inheritance that is nontransferable. The diligence, the corporate performance, the respect for authority and parental wishes, shame (more than guilt) as a deterrent to nonsanctioned behavior, the importance of keeping up appearances—all these desirable traits have different roots than their American counterparts, which they outwardly so closely resemble. The Japanese did so well in school, for example, because of their on to their parents, their community and the giri to their name. Already in 1858, Japan's literacy rate of 50 percent outdistanced that of Great Britain, the leading industrial power of that day. In Tokyo (then called Edo), which boasted the world's greatest urban population until London pulled ahead in the early nineteenth century, 85 percent of all children spent at least four years in school despite the low per capita incomes. Throughout Japan, reverence for learning was a national characteristic, and the teacher was held in high esteem. The immigrants brought it with them.

What helped them most in the long run was the way they chose to earn recognition by performance, rather than by claiming it on principle. They steered clear of demands for radical revisions in the national power structure, in the distribution of wealth, in the ethnic composition of political and policy-making bodies. They simply worked and endured until their performance overwhelmed, without contentiousness, society's negative definitions of their worth....

The Japanese cooperated with their captors into submission, but the process was slow. After the close of the war, with the release of the internees and the combat record of the 442nd Regimental Combat Team plainly set forth for all to see, the following discriminatory prohibitions still obtained:

The issei were ineligible for citizenship.

All property was subject to escheat under the alien land laws upon failure to adhere to the legal minutiae of scrupulous reporting procedures. Tenants who improved property after years of hard labor were regularly dispossessed upon the termination of their lease.

There was no equality under law for immigration quotas and procedures.

Intermarriage was prohibited.

Claims for indemnification were unresolved.

General acceptance by their neighbors was still retarded by long-standing majority resentments.

After the close of the war, the Japanese in America chipped in $325,000 to lobby for redress in Congress and were successful on all six points.

Was their wartime performance a calculated strategy? Did the Japanese in America create an impressive record between 1942 and 1945 with explicit intent to silence their critics when the day of adjudication dawned? The clamor over the loyalty questionnaire suggests this was far from the case. Nor is it realistic to expect any minority to trample the response pattern that sustains its identity and self-esteem. The Japanese were faithful to theirs throughout. When the close of the camps was imminent, representatives from each of the garrison settlements convened in Salt Lake City to draw up an agenda for repatriation to the larger society. Caucasians were excluded, but all camp representatives agreed that the last contact with the government should be conciliatory. Demands were minimal. Larger questions of equity under law and economic redress were deferred. From the convention emerged 24 articles providing for such matters as housing and care of the sick and aged. "The government man told us we wouldn't have to sleep under bridges, and he was right." In a California camp of thousands of trailers the Japanese set up their last temporary settlement. The government man arrived weekly with subsidy checks to find many already off securing a beachhead, to speed the day when they could send for their families. The trailers became empty one by one, with the sick and the aged the last to go. Relocated, this time without supervision of forced scheduling, the relief checks were no longer needed. "The Japanese don't like relief," my informant noted. He added, after a pause, "This saves the government money."

How was consistently Japanese behavior reconciled with prevailing American expectations? Not by intent. When projected on the ethnic screen, Japanese values and psychological commitments presented a favorable Rorschach. The majority society read its own priorities into the ethnic tenacity of the Japanese and saw no reason to debate the diverse background and motives that inspired them. Indeed, it is far more flattering to concede that the Japanese had been Americans all along than to entertain the suspicion that ethnicity is admirable in its unredeemed state.

Joan Ablon,
"American Indian Relocation: Problems of Dependency and Management in the City"

Nowhere, perhaps, is the clash of cultures in modern America more apparent than in the case of Indians who have migrated from the reservation to the city. As Joan Ablon emphasizes in "American Indian Relocation," traditional Indian values and reservation life have ill-prepared these newcomers for urban survival. American Indians, schooled in dependency as wards of the government and accustomed to communal life by their heritage, find it difficult to make their way in a complex white urban society which places a heavy value on independence and individualism. While some Indians have managed a successful transition to city life, many others return defeated to their reservations or subsist, unemployed and impoverished, in urban slums. If the movement of Indians to cities is not to constitute simply another disastrous "relocation," much more must be done to make it possible for them to adapt to the demands of urban life while retaining their unique cultural heritage.

American Indian Relocation: Problems of Dependency and Management in the City

Joan Ablon

The diverse population groups that are migrating into metropolitan areas are offering formidable challenges to community agencies who must attempt to understand the particular needs of widely varying groups. More than 60,000 American Indians have immigrated to large urban centers in the last decade to seek stable employment and a new life. American Indians present a peculiar new urban group, a tribal people who have left the primary relationships and cultural world of the folk society to enter a complex industrial order whose basic values violate many of the premises of Indian life. It is the fact of the persistence of tribal and folk values that differentiates the rural, unskilled Indians from other such population groups that are moving into urban centers over the country. This paper will attempt to point up some of the factors involved in the relocation experience, and to analyze typical Indian attitudes of dependency and modes of coping with problems in the new urban milieu.

Most Indian reservations are economically underdeveloped areas. The lack of steady employment opportunities and the prevalence of widespread social and domestic problems have motivated many per-

Abridged from Joan Ablon, "American Indian Relocation: Problems of Dependency and Management in the City," *Phylon*, XXIV (1965), pp. 362–371. Reprinted by permission of the publisher.

sons to relocate to urban areas. For some the venture has proven successful but for many others it has been another contemporary trauma to add to the list of those in Indian history.

Many Indians have moved into urban centers on their own resources and initiative through the years. A great many of these decided to remain in areas where they were stationed or had worked during World War II. However, the greatest impetus for Indian relocation has been recent programs sponsored by the Bureau of Indian Affairs. The Employment Assistance Program (formerly called the Voluntary Relocation Program), which began in 1952, provides financial assistance for the Indian individual or family unit for transportation from the point of origin to ten Field Relocation Offices throughout the country, maintenance and living expenses until the first wages are in hand, and services in the areas of orientation, employment, housing, and general counseling. The Adult Vocational Training Program, a potentially more successful program because it has offered wide educational opportunities for young people, was first broadly implemented in 1957. This program brings Indians between the ages of 18 and 35 to schools across the country where they will receive training in specific marketable skills. The pragmatic sink or swim nature of a move to areas distant from family and community differs qualitatively from all other Bureau programs. The character of the program and its demands requiring certain initiative and independence in thought and action from a people long in wardship status has produced complex and varying responses.[1]

While other rural Americans or even European immigrants who move into urban societies are segments of the broader Western European tradition and share in some part its values and accepted moral system, American Indians, though differing from tribe to tribe in some accepted values and patterns, almost all hold to certain common values which differ from or are completely contrary to those of the dominant white society. Most Indians are not aggressive toward others.

1. This discussion is based primarily on a two-year study (1961 to 1963) of the general adjustment complex and the persistence of Indian values and tradition in the course of the relocation process among government-sponsored and self-relocated Indians in the San Francisco Bay Area. The findings are similar to those of other investigators in other areas. There are, unfortunately, few published works on urban Indians. For more detail on Indians in the San Francisco Bay Area see Joan Ablon, "Relocated American Indians in the San Francisco Bay Area: Social Interaction and Indian Identity," *Human Organization*, Vol. 23, No. 4, Winter 1964.

They do not like to compete. In conflict situations they are more likely to withdraw than to speak out. They would rather share their money and goods than to budget and save. A man's prestige was based traditionally on what he had given away and not on what he had accumulated for himself. The functional realistic time dimension is short and the deferring of educational or economic goals is alien.

Relocatees exhibit a wide variety of tribal backgrounds, educational experiences, and histories of contact with whites. Most have attended all-Indian schools and many have had nominal vocational training in school or in the service, but proportionately few make use of this. Almost half of the relocatees who came in the early years of relocation were veterans, and most have had some form of prototypic work experience in which they were forced to deal with whites. Although the chief reason for relocation is the incentive to find steady employment, this goal is usually compounded by a variety of personal and family problems that the relocatees wish to escape.

Most Indians bring few vocational skills with them, and the unskilled job market is small and uncertain. Lay-offs are common and expected. Many Indians who do remain in the city have treasured the security of jobs in "dirty work" that more educated acculturated persons would not endure. Indeed personal attitudes toward work and a craving for security often appear to be more important in the retention of jobs than previous training or sophistication in the complexities of the job and union markets. Indians tend to live in working-class neighborhoods where a variety of other ethnic and minority groups are also represented. Although dispersed among this general population, they do not often associate with their neighbors and most frequently turn to other Indians, usually tribesmen, for their intimate social relocationships, and to pan-Indian social activities.

Most Indians exhibit temerity and ambivalence in dealing with whites. Often they have experienced great discrimination in the areas peripheral to their reservations and many have been ill-used by whites leasing their lands. Thus in the city they are pleased by the relative freedom from the blatant forms of discrimination they have known. Nonetheless, most Indians never feel relaxed among whites,[2] and true egalitarian relationships with whites occur infrequently. A com-

2. For a penetrating and informal discussion of characteristic personality differences between Indians and whites, see Rosalie Wax and Robert K. Thomas, "American Indians and White People," *Phylon*, XXII 1961, Fourth Quarter, 305–317.

mon type of friendship may be noticed in the form of young Indians being adopted in a dependency relationship by older whites who help them with money, services, and emotional support. This dependency relationship is a distinct carryover from the relations with white federal or local officials that they experienced on the reservation.

Certain gross cultural-tribal common personality characteristics are often readily apparent in the responses of relocatees of the same tribe. Certain of these common tribal characteristics may be highly selective for success or failure in the city. For example, some tribes who have experienced great disorganization and heavy alcoholic problems on their reservations have sent many families on relocation, but these families frequently have grave difficulties in simple survival in the urban situation. Uncontrollable drinking problems which prohibit steady employment and compulsive hospitality and sharing patterns which further complicate an already impoverished condition are common. For instance, most Sioux who have remained and are doing well on relocation have generally been sober and not inclined to follow the hospitality and generosity patterns which their tribe traditionally has emphasized to an extreme. In general it may be said that many Indians tend to exhibit severe ambivalent "marginal man" characteristics which often seem to paralyze action and preclude efficient relations with whites.[3]

There is, however, a wide range of personal characteristics unique to individuals of the same and differing tribes. The importance of the personal psychological characteristics of the individual relocatee cannot be overstated in their influence on the future of the relocation experience, and are so varying that they can rarely be figured in as a generalized "given" when planning for the individual or family unit.

It is indeed difficult to speak in generalities about Indians and the

3. The "marginal man" as an individual caught between the values of two cultural worlds, and often finding himself unable to function acceptably in either, has been treated as a sociological phenomenon by a number of scholars. The original classic article by Robert E. Park, "Human Migration and the Marginal Man," *The American Journal of Sociology*, No. 6, May 1928, 881–893, has been reexamined by others such as Milton Goldberg, "A Qualification of the Marginal Man Theory," *American Sociological Review*, VI, No. 1, February 1941, 52–58; Arnold Green, "A Re-Examination of the Marginal Man Concept," *Social Forces*, XXVI, No. 2, Dec. 1947, 167–171, and Steven Polgar, "Biculturation of Mesquakie Teenage Boys," *American Anthropologist*, LXII, No. 2, April 1960, 217–235.

relocation experience. Each family represents a differing cultural and educational situation, further complicated by the nature and amount of experiences with whites the families have had, and the personal psychological characteristics of the individual relocatees. Often crippling personal problems or drastic homesickness are the factors that finally break the relocation, in spite of a happy employment situation. The treatment by the Bureau and the process of relocation as it occurs is highly significant, as are the simple factors of chance and luck which may determine the pickings of the job market and housing just at that particular time that the relocatee arrives.

Most Indians do not like the city, although they appreciate the many conveniences of urban life. They do not like the crowds, the traffic, the many buildings pushed together, the constant restraints, the bills, the lack of privacy. Yet most enjoy the varied amusements a metropolitan area can offer them, as well as the educational experiences of seeing new things. Indians come to the city seeking work, not to become white men, nor to stop being Indians. Most of them sorely miss their families and reservation life. Their feelings about returning are ambivalent, and negative and positive attitudes occur in their every utterance. If comparable job opportunities at home were available, it is probable that more than 75 percent of the Indians who have relocated would choose to return to their reservations as soon as possible.

The decision of returning to the reservation is a complex blend of objective economic and social factors, and of shifting emotions for most relocatees. In some cases, aside from and secondary to employment opportunities, men think of the much longed-for open spaces, woods, fishing and hunting that they enjoyed at home; women think of the household conveniences of running water, lights and heating, to which they have grown accustomed in the city and which are so painfully important with a large family. They also think of the better educational opportunities available for their children in the city. Many persons argue the pros and cons of easier control and discipline of children in the city as opposed to rural areas. Some fear that their children will become delinquents in the city by being caught up in school, neighborhood, or housing project gangs. Most prefer to raise small children in the country, but say that there the adolescents have more opportunity to run wild and that they will not be able to control their wanderings or drinking. A complicating dimension of both alternatives of reservation and city life is the alcohol problem, which may be more threatening at home where drinking relatives surround one, or more dangerous in the city where anxieties caused by new and alien pressures cause one to wish to lose himself....

The immediate decision to return home may be made in a few minutes or hours, precipitated by illness, death, an overwhelming medical bill, a sudden lay-off, or a traffic offense. It takes only a short time to activate the fever for home in the blood, and one may not stop to think clearly, to remember or care that employment opportunities have not improved, nor have reservation shanties been provided with running water or lights or easy heating. The time for second thoughts will come after the glad return.

The Bureau of Indian Affairs estimates that some 35 percent of those persons who have relocated for employment return to their reservations. Other investigations suggest that although this figure has been accurate for the past several years, in the early years of relocation the return rate was about 75 percent. Some returnees eventually apply for a second or even third relocation, but there is careful screening of these cases, and generally only such objective reasons for return as major illness or death are accepted as a justifiable basis for subsequent sponsorship for a repeat location.

Most Indians still retain vestiges of what may be called a former "primitive world view," which recognized an important and precious relation between man, his fellows, nature and the gods. Man was part of an interdependent harmonious whole.[4] He was a cog in the larger order of his community and nature, and he did not have an individual and independent career. His thoughts were pervaded with mysticism. A person molded in this culture is not equipped to readily adjust to an individualistic, anonymous existence and to the nuclear-family, self-sufficiency pattern of the city-dweller. Members of the middle-class urban society have come to see themselves as objects to be shaped to fit into the requirements of complex modern culture, and to be changed to meet goals which hold promises of rewards. For Indians to become efficient managers of their life situation is a complex process which may never occur. This requires an amount of introspection and

4. For excellent expository discussions of this subject see Robert Redfield, "The Primitive World View," in *The Primitive World and its Transformations*, 1953; and Laura Thompson, "Attitudes and Acculturation," *American Anthropologist*, No. 2, April–June 1943, 200–215.

self-awareness of being a unique and malleable entity that is not common to the Indian personality or view of life. An Indian already *is* so to speak; he *is* a Navajo, a clan member, a son, a father, etc.—all stations existing only in relation to his tribe, his family, or the universe.

The nature of governmental relations with Indian communities has compounded the potential for dependency of the tribal man whose resources with which he could maintain his own way of life were rapidly and forcibly removed. The many reservations over the country differ in the detail of their history of federal administration; however, governmental policies have been generally ill-planned and inconsistent. A pervading paternalistic orientation and preemption of decision-making has characterized government policies toward Indian communities. The continuing effect of these policies has been extreme economic deprivation and psychological crippling to most of the several hundred Indian tribes. Two of the more obvious manifestations of this crippling have been a deeply entrenched dependency, and widespread and chronic drinking.

Life in the city is a difficult and puzzling experience for most relocatees. Reservation life has little prepared them for the credit temptations and varied monetary pitfalls of urban society. On reservations Indians have a wardship status and have become accustomed throughout their lives to depend on governmental doles in the forms of money, commodities, and free medical services. They frequently paid little or no rent. In the city they suddenly encounter seemingly endless bills. . . .

Complexities in almost every aspect of life and various sorts of red tape are part and parcel of the urban existence. City dwellers are used to dealing with and manipulating both the small daily problems of life and also larger long-range issues. Middle-class persons usually put emphasis on practical problem-solving through work, thrift, and legal means. Lower socio-economic groups likewise put importance on manipulating their environment; however, they often choose methods such as conning or stratagems of chance, rather than stable employment or long-term education.[5] Such ingenious forms of "alley smart-

5. For an analytic discussion of lower-class values see Walter B. Miller, "Lower Class Culture as a Generating Milieu of Gang Delinquency," *Journal of Social Issues*, XIV No. 3, 1958, 5–19.

ness" contrast sharply to the traditional more pedestrian planning and action patterns of Indians, who may have great knowledge about hunting, farming and other areas not applicable to city life. Also it may be observed that many ethnic groups develop communities with indigenous leadership with urban know-how, and these persons serve as clearing-houses of information and skills for less sophisticated persons and new arrivals. Indians have not developed such functional urban structures, primarily because of tribal differences in political procedure and values.

The most important characteristics that appear to be common to almost all the Indians who have remained in the city are a conformity to white standards, at least on the economic level, by a striving for employment stability and security, and an ability to manage for themselves and to control their life situation. In less crucial aspects of their lives they have made various kinds of adjustments. Families who have made successful relocations exhibit great differences in home atmosphere, life ways, values, and activities that they consider pleasurable and worthwhile. The differences in these homes are far greater than would be found in white homes of the same economic brackets. . . .

Those Indians who have been able to take active control of their situation in the city have separated their own identity as a separate and inviolable entity that does not substantially change, while on the other hand they have mastered the techniques of handling and manipulating their environments. There is no doubt but that the roads through which the development of this control come about are many. A first step is a self-awareness of Indian identity, and a certain introspection about the implications of this. Some persons were fairly sophisticated in dealing with whites before coming; others learned through harsh experience. Members of most tribes can be counted among the controllers, full and mixed bloods, relatively highly educated and sophisticated persons to those less educated and sophisticated.

Those who consciously and actively have controlled their urban life, even if torn by great desire to return to the reservation, will not generally do so until they believe they will be able to control their reservation situation once there, by having a secure job, ridding themselves of dependent relatives, etc. It is probable that a sizeable number of those who have developed sufficient mastery to give them a realization of choice and the meaning and possibility of alternatives have also made the decision to return home, preferring not by default of inability, failure and subsequent withdrawal, but through conscious choice to return home.

Many Indians have survived in the city for years, but exist essentially in the same manner as their relatives on the reservations rocking from daily problem to problem with little ability to better their situation.What criteria can be set up then to distinguish survival from success? The Bureau of Indian Affairs has had no program to followup relocatees except through chance encounters or by the "grapevine," and has not followed the progress of self-relocatees at all. Therefore, they tend to almost categorically label a unit they hear has remained over a period of years and has not frequently called on them for aid (which is often a hopeless gesture, as the Indians are well aware) as being a successful relocation.

The crucial question that must be faced is how success is to be defined pragmatically as opposed to mere elemental physical survival in the city. I would suggest that the fact of active mastery of one's everyday situation on a daily operational level is the functional definition of success for a family. Are persons who have developed this control the less Indian for it? On the basis of my observations and interviews which almost universally encountered an everpresent psychological and social awareness of Indian identity, I would suggest that these persons are not less Indian, but are Indians of a little different quality—an urban neo-Indian type. This neo-Indian has a more acute awareness of himself, of the general implications of his identity, and how, as an Indian, he must be able to meet the everyday problems of city living with some equanimity and measure of control to shape the mundane features of his new life....

Alphonso Pinkney,
"Black Power"

Beginning with the 1954 Supreme Court decision, Brown v. Board of
Education of Topeka, which declared that segregated schools
were inherently unequal, and the Montgomery bus boycott of 1955
and 1956, blacks with the aid of some whites, embarked on a
new drive to improve their living conditions. However, by the
middle sixties it become apparent to many blacks that the Negro
Revolt, or the Civil Rights Revolution, had not been particularly
successful. Compared to the rest of the population, blacks lost
ground economically; southern whites were especially unwilling to
permit change, and conditions in the North seemed to be
deteriorating. "Black Power" became a popular slogan, emphasizing
black pride, black nationalism, and self-help. The Black Power
movement alienated some white supporters of the Civil Rights
Revolution because its advocates threatened violence as opposed to
the nonviolence of the earlier struggle, attacked racism in the
North as well as the South, and insisted on black direction and
leadership. In the following selection from his book, Black
Americans, Alphonso Pinkney defines Black Power and explains
its rapid acceptance in the black community.

Black Power

Alphonso Pinkney

For all practical purposes the civil rights movement ended in 1965. The following year civil rights organizations appeared to be searching for some cause around which to rally as a means of continuing their protest activities. Although implementation was lagging, they had won important victories: the Civil Rights Act of 1964, the Voting Rights Act of 1965, and, perhaps most important of all, the recognition by Americans that the low status of black people posed a serious social problem in a world where oppressed people were fighting for freedom and self-determination. The question "Where do we go from here?" was being asked by the leaders of the major civil rights organizations. In June 1966 James Meredith was shot as he started his freedom march through Mississippi. Immediately thereafter the leaders of several civil rights organizations gathered in Memphis, Tennessee, and made plans to turn the aborted march into a major civil rights campaign. During this march Stokely Carmichael, the chairman of SNCC, introduced a new and controversial slogan into the nomenclature of the movement to achieve greater civil rights for Negroes. The concept of Black Power was first used in this context when the marchers reached Greenwood, Mississippi.[1] Field workers from SNCC had worked in this community, and, at a mass rally, when Carmichael proclaimed, "What we need is black power," he was cheered by the crowd of poor Mississippians.

The introduction of the concept of Black Power was debated by the leaders of CORE, SCLC, and SNCC. Martin Luther King and his associates from SCLC disapproved of its use, but the leaders of CORE and SNCC supported its use. A compromise was reached—that the concept was not to be used as the official slogan of the march—but it gained worldwide usage and generated a heated debate among the major black organizations.

Somehow the combination of the words "black" and "power" seemed to offend and frighten white Americans, especially some "liberal" white persons who had contributed time and money to the civil rights movement. To them the concept implied black supremacy (or reverse racism) and black violence. Consequently they resigned from membership and withheld financial support from the more militant organizations. Similarly the more moderate civil rights organizations, such as the NAACP and the National Urban League, expressed their disapproval of Black Power. The organizations which had led the civil rights movement and which had cooperated in the major campaigns and demonstrations in the South were divided along ideological lines.

Those leaders advocating Black Power have attempted to define the concept, but such attempts have usually been lost in the growing debate in the mass media of communications. To Stokely Carmichael of SNCC the concept speaks to the needs of black people at the present time. It is a call to black Americans to liberate themselves from oppression by assuming control over their lives economically, politically, and socially. He has said:

Black Power means black people coming together to form a political force and either electing representatives or forcing their representatives to speak to their needs. It's an economic and phys- ical bloc that can exercise its strength in the black community instead of letting the job go to the Democratic or Republican parties or a white-controlled black man set up as a puppet to

1. Martin Luther King, Jr., *Where Do We Go From Here?* (New York: Harper & Row, 1967), pp. 23–32.

represent black people. We pick the brother and make sure he fulfills our needs. Black Power doesn't mean antiwhite, violence, separatism, or any other racist things the press says it means. It's saying, "Look, buddy, we're not laying a vote on you unless you lay so many schools, hospitals, playgrounds, and jobs on us."[2]

Later he and Charles Hamilton elaborate on the concept of Black Power:

It is a call for black people in this country to unite, to recognize their heritage, to build a sense of community. It is a call for black people to begin to define their own goals, to lead their own organizations, and to support those organizations. It is a call to reject the racist institutions and values of this society.

The concept of Black Power rests on a fundamental premise: *Before a group can enter the open society, it must first close ranks.* By this we mean that group solidarity is necessary before a group can operate effectively from a bargaining position of strength in a pluralistic society.[3]

Floyd McKissick of CORE sees the following as elements of Black Power: increased political and economic power for Negroes, improved self-image, the development of young, militant black leadership, the development of black consumer power, and strong resistance to police brutality in black communities.[4]

Although Martin Luther King, Jr., opposed the use of the concept of Black Power for a variety of reasons, he acknowledged that it had what he called a "positive meaning."[5] He saw it as a "cry of disappointment" and of despair with the present state of black-white relations. He also interpreted it as "... a call to black people to amass the political and economic strength to achieve their legitimate

2. From "Stokely Carmichael: Young Man Behind an Angry Message," by Gordon Parks, *Life Magazine*, May 19, 1967; copyright © 1967 Time Inc., p. 82.
3. Stokely Carmichael and Charles V. Hamilton, *Black Power: The Politics of Liberation in America* (New York: Random House, Inc., copyright 1967), p. 44. Reprinted with permission.
4. See Fred C. Shapiro, "The Successor to Floyd McKissick May Not Be So Reasonable," *The New York Times Magazine*, October 1, 1967, p. 102.
5. King, *Where Do We Go From Here?*, pp. 32–44.

goals." Finally, he saw Black Power as "a psychological call to manhood." Despite its many positive features, King felt that the concept had too many negative values for it to serve as the basic strategy with which to meet the problems faced by black people at the present time.[6] He believed that it embodied a philosophy of hopelessness about achieving basic changes in the structure of American society. In addition, as an integrationist, King saw the Black Power movement as one based on separation of the races in the United States. He rejected the notion that any group within the larger society could achieve equality through separation. Finally, as a foremost exponent of nonviolence, he felt that the concept was often a call for retaliatory violence, which, he maintained, could only serve to impede progress in race relations.

The more moderate leaders of civil rights organizations have opposed the concept of Black Power from its inception. The leaders of the NAACP and the Urban League joined five other prominent black spokesmen and responded to the militant organizations by placing an advertisement entitled "Crisis and Commitment" in numerous newspapers.[7] In response to the advocates of Black Power they enumerated what they considered to be the "principles upon which the civil rights movement rests." They included four points: (1) a commitment to the principle of racial justice through the democratic process, (2) the repudiation of violence, (3) a commitment to the principle of integration, and (4) a commitment to the principle that the task of bringing about integration is the common responsibility of all Americans, both black and white.

One of the leading critics of Black Power rejects the concept in favor of coalition politics. Bayard Rustin feels that the concept is harmful to the movement for greater civil rights for America's Negroes because "It diverts the movement from a meaningful debate over strategy and tactics, it isolates the Negro community, and it encourages the growth of anti-Negro forces." As an alternative to Black Power, Rustin advocates a "liberal-labor-civil rights coalition which would work to make the Democratic Party truly responsive to the aspirations of the poor, and which would develop support for programs (specifically those outlined in A. Philip Randolph's $100 bil-

6. *Ibid.*, pp. 44–63.
7. *The New York Times*, October 14, 1966, p. 35.

lion Freedom Budget) aimed at the reconstruction of American society in the interests of greater social justice."[8]

Supporters of Black Power reject the notion of forming coalitions with predominantly white liberal, labor, and religious organizations. They insist that those who advocate such coalitions proceed on the basis of three fallacious assumptions: (1) that at the present time the interests of black Americans are identical with the interests of these groups, (2) that a viable coalition can be established between groups with power and powerless Negroes, and (3) that it is possible to sustain political coalitions on a "moral, friendly, sentimental basis; by appeals to conscience."[9]

The debate over Black Power continues. The more militant organizations, CORE and SNCC, are its chief proponents; the more moderate organizations, the NAACP and the Urban League, are strongly opposed; and SCLC takes a middle position. In keeping with their position that Black Power means black consciousness and solidarity, the militant organizations have urged their white supporters to form parallel organizations and to work with the white community to rid it of the racism which is endemic to American life. A coalition between black and white Americans at the present time is seen as unworkable. The major impediment to equality for black people is seen as the resistance of the white community. Consequently, CORE and SNCC have urged their white supporters to work within their own communities.

Less than one year after the concept was first introduced, it had gained widespread prominence. In July 1967 the first National Conference on Black Power was held in Newark, New Jersey. This conference was attended by more than 1,000 black delegates from 42 cities in 36 states. They represented a broad cross section of black leaders, ranging from the militant black nationalists to employees of government agencies. One of the most significant aspects of the conference was its bringing together for the first time a wide assembly of black people who met in workshop sessions to define the concept of Black Power and who agreed to implement its components. When the conference ended, a series of resolutions had been passed, in-

8. Bayard Rustin, " 'Black Power' and Coalition Politics," *Commentary*, Vol. 42 (September 1966), pp. 35–40.
9. Carmichael and Hamilton, *op. cit.*, Chap. 3.

cluding the following: (1) the establishment of black financial institutions such as credit unions and nonprofit cooperatives, (2) the establishment of black universities, (3) selective purchasing and boycotting of white merchants in black communities, (4) the demand for a guaranteed annual income for all people, (5) a boycott by black athletes of international Olympic competition and professional boxing, in response to the stripping of the world heavyweight boxing title from Muhammad Ali, (6) boycotts of Negro churches which are not committed to the "black revolution," (7) boycotts of Negro publications accepting advertisements for hair straighteners and bleaching creams.

Meanwhile, Black Power gained wider acceptance among more radical white Americans. In November 1966 students at Oberlin College, in Oberlin, Ohio, held an intercollegiate conference entitled Black Power in the Urban Ghetto, in an effort to "eliminate the emotionalism which clouds the debate on Black Power and to try to point out the basic issues involved." At its annual meeting in August 1967 the National Student Association, the largest organization of college students in the United States, resolved to support the implementation of the concept of Black Power "through any means necessary." In September the delegates attending the National Conference for New Politics in Chicago voted by a margin of more than two to one to support all resolutions of the Newark Black Power Conference and to support "black control of the political, economic, and social institutions in black communities."

Current interest in the concept of Black Power is perhaps too recent in its origin to gain wide acceptance on its relevance to the problems faced by Negroes. It has emotional implications which white Americans fear, but, stripped of its emotional connotations, it appears to mean the amassing by black people of the economic, political, and social power necessary to deal effectively with the problems they face as a powerless people relegated to a life of poverty in an affluent society. Furthermore, it is a call to black people to reject the social values (especially racism) which are responsible for their low status in the United States and to replace them with an ideology which embraces dignity and pride in blackness. Black solidarity is seen as a precondition to the achievement of these ends. Integration, it is felt, is much more likely to be achieved from a position of strength than from one of weakness.

The concept of ethnic power is not alien to American society. Historically, many ethnic groups have managed to improve their status through the process of organizing themselves into power blocs. Indeed, historically, ethnic solidarity has been a fundamental aspect of American minority relations. One writer has defended Black Power as follows:

> .... to the extent that "Black Power" expresses a determination to build a Negro community which would be something more than euphemisms for the ghetto, it is a valid and necessary cry; to the extent that it expresses a despair of the one-by-one absorption of "deserving" Negroes into the general society and puts its faith instead in collective action aimed at dealing with collective fate, it is an intelligent response to the reality of American life.[10]

He sees the attempts to establish group loyalty among Negroes, which is a fundamental aspect of Black Power, as an essential means of dealing with a basically hostile society. Although other minority groups have effectively organized themselves along religious and ethnic lines into political and economic power blocs as a means of improving their status, once this goal has been achieved, they effectively combine forces and join what Negroes call the white power structure, which serves to perpetuate the low status of Negroes. They may be of Irish, Italian, Jewish, or Polish extraction, but in encounters with Negroes, racial homogeneity serves to solidify them. In short, black subordination was achieved and has been maintained by the unabashed use of "white power."

Another writer, who sees Black Power as "the acquisition of power by Negroes for their own use, both offensively and defensively," defends the concept, especially its emphasis on black nationalism and black consciousness, as follows:

> It *is* important to establish a positive black identity in a great many sectors of the black communities, both North and South, rural and urban, lower and middle class. Indeed, it is both im-

---

10. "In Defense of 'Black Power'," by David Danzig, *Commentary*, Vol. 42 (September 1966), p. 46. Reprinted from *Commentary*, by permission; copyright © 1966, by the American Jewish Committee.

portant and legitimate to teach black people (or any other ethnic minority) about their history, placing special emphasis upon the positive contributions of other black people. This black consciousness has the potential to create unity and solidarity among black people and to give them hope and self-confidence.[11]

She reports that Black Power has achieved success among Mississippi Negroes because attempts at racial integration in that state have failed.

The use of black political power to achieve Negro rights is not new. In 1941 black leaders effectively forced the President to issue an executive order banning discrimination in employment in industry doing business with the federal government. Such organizations as the Negro American Labor Council of the American Federation of Labor–Congress of Industrial Organizations and the all-Negro organization within the New York City Police Department exist to protect the interests of their members. The idea underlying the concept of Black Power, then, is not a new one. It has, however, gained new strength within the last two years. In 1967 a nationwide organization of elected Negro public officials was formed to develop methods of utilizing their combined power to improve the status of black citizens. A nationwide group of Negro ministers met in November 1967 in an effort to make Black Power a force in American Protestant church policies. They are organizing to serve as a pressure group within the National Council of Churches in an effort to increase the number of Negroes in policy-making positions and to "bring the resources of white churches into urban ghettos in such a way as to enhance Negro leadership."[12]

The civil rights movement was basically reformist, aimed at changing some aspects of the structure of American society insofar as black people were denied some of the rights guaranteed citizens in the Constitution. It was directed toward establishing the principle of legal equality as public policy and toward the responsibility of the federal government in protecting the constitutional rights of citizens. To a degree these goals have been achieved, or, at least, they have

11. Joyce Ladner, "What 'Black Power' Means to Negroes in Mississippi," *Transaction*, Vol. 5 (November 1967), p. 14. Reprinted by permission of the publisher.

12. *The New York Times*, November 2, 1967, p. 52, col. 2.

been accepted as a matter of principle. The Black Power movement, on the other hand, goes beyond social reform. If the demands for political, economic, and social control by black people over the institutions which are responsible to them, along with the other changes necessary for the "liberation" of American Negroes, are achieved, American society will have undergone revolutionary changes. The civil rights movement did not address itself to the complex, deeply rooted problems facing black people in the slums of the United States. The Black Power movement does. In this sense, the Black Power movement might be said to be the logical extension of the civil rights movement. Where the civil rights movement ended, the Black Power movement begins, and it might be said that the death of the civil rights movement gave birth to the black liberation movement. . . .

Joseph L. Love,
"La Raza: Mexican-Americans in Rebellion"

During the 1960s Mexican-Americans displayed a new determination
to acquire legal and civil rights, land, protection of agricultural
workers, and a voice in community and educational activities. Their
increased aggressiveness and sense of unity created a heightened
awareness in the nation of their organizations and leaders. Perhaps
the best known movement was that led by Cesar Chavez and
the National Farm Workers Association, whose successful strike and
boycott of the grape growers in Delano, California, demonstrated
the benefits of organization. Other new and dynamic alliances
included the Political Association of Spanish-Speaking Organizations
(PASO) and the Mexican-American Political Association (MAPA).
In "La Raza: Mexican-Americans in Rebellion," Joseph L. Love
examines the attempts of one of the new militant organizations
to secure land grant rights to millions of acres in New Mexico.

La Raza:
Mexican-Americans in Rebellion

Joseph L. Love

In early June, 1967 a group of Spanish-speaking Americans who call themselves the *Alianza Federal de Mercedes* (Federal Alliance of Land Grants) and claim that they are the legal and rightful owners of millions of acres of land in Central and Northern New Mexico, revolted against the governments of the United States of America, the State of New Mexico, and Rio Arriba (Up River) County, formally proclaiming the Republic of Rio Chama in that area.

On June 5 an armed band of forty or more *Aliancistas* attacked the Tierra Amarilla courthouse, released 11 of their members being held prisoner, and wounded a deputy sheriff and the jailer. They held the sheriff down on the floor with a rifle butt on his neck, searched for the District Attorney (who wasn't there) and for an hour and a half controlled the village (population 500). They took several hostages (later released when the getaway car stuck in the mud).

Despite some of the melodramatic and occasionally comic opera aspects of the affair, both the members of the *Alianza* and the local and state authorities take it very seriously. This is not the first time the Aliancistas have violated federal and state law, attempting to ap-

Abridged from Joseph L. Love, "La Raza: Mexican-Americans in Rebellion," *Transaction*, VI (1969), pp. 35–41. Copyright © 1969 by Transaction, Inc., New Brunswick, New Jersey.

propriate government property (in October, 1966, for instance, their militants tried to take over Kit Carson National Forest, and to expel the rangers found there as trespassers); nor is it the only time their activities have resulted in violence. In this case the state government reacted frantically, sending in armored tanks, 300 National Guardsmen and 200 state police. They rounded up dozens of Spanish-speaking persons, including many women and children, and held them in a detention camp, surrounded with guns and soldiers, for 48 hours. The raiders got away, but in several days all of them—including their fiery leader, former Pentecostal preacher Reies López Tijerina—were captured.

It has become common to associate these actions of the Alianza with other riots or revolts by poor, dark-skinned and disaffected Americans—with Watts, Newark and Detroit. Tijerina himself helps reinforce this impression by occasionally meeting with, and using the rhetoric of, some leaders of the black urban revolt. The fact is, however, that the Alianza movement is really a unique example in the United States of a "primitive revolt" as defined by Eric Hobsbawm, a kind almost always associated with developing nations, rather than advanced industrialized countries—and which includes such diverse phenomena as peasant anarchism, banditry, and millenarianism (the belief that divine justice and retribution is on the side of the rebels and that the millenium is at hand). The attack on the courthouse, in fact, had more in common with the millenarian Sioux Ghost Dance cult of 1889–91 than with Watts.

As the Aliancistas see it, they are not violating any legitimate law. The territory around Rio Arriba belongs to them. They demand the return of lands—primarily common lands—taken from *Hispano* communities, most of which were founded in the Spanish colonial era. Their authority is the famous *Recopilación de leyes de los Reinos de Indias* (*Compilation of Laws of the Kingdoms of the Indies,* generally shortened to *The Laws of the Indies*) by which the Crown of Castile governed its New World possessions. They claim that according to these laws common lands were inalienable—could not be taken away. Since most of such lands were in existence when the Treaty of Guadalupe Hidalgo was signed in 1848—and since in that treaty the United States government pledged itself to respect property rights established under Mexican rule—the Alianza insists that those land grants remain valid. The members speak primarily of common lands, rather than individual heirs, and define the towns in question as "closed corporations, with membership restricted to the descendants and heirs of the founding fathers and mothers"—that is, themselves.

The Alianza's interpretations of law and history are, of course, selective, and tend to ignore inconvenient facts and other interpretations. It claims that *The Laws of the Indies* were not abrogated when "Mexico invaded and occupied New Mexico," nor when the United States did the same in 1846. The Aliancistas are the early settlers, the legitimate heirs.

The Alianza and its actions cannot really be understood without knowledge of its background and its leader. First, the people from whom it draws its members and its strength—the Mexican-American minority in the U.S.—and specifically New Mexico; second, the rapid economic changes throughout the area since World War II that have so greatly affected their lives; and last but surely not least the dynamism, determination and charisma of Reies Tijerina, without whom the movement would probably never have arisen.

In the 1960 census Mexican-Americans, though they make up only 2.3 percent of the population of the United States, constituted 12 percent of the population of Texas, New Mexico, Arizona, Colorado and California—almost three and a half million persons.

Generally they are a submerged minority that have only lately begun to articulate their demands. They formed "Viva Kennedy" committees in 1960; since then three Mexican-American Congressmen have gone to the House, and New Mexico's Joseph Montoya sits in the Senate. The end of the *bracero* program in 1964 opened the way to a successful unionization drive among agricultural workers; and the celebrated "Huelga" strike in Delano, California in 1965 was a symptom of and stimulus to the new awakening. The federal and state poverty programs, and the example of the Negro revolt, have also undoubtedly had their effects.

New Mexico is a distinctive area of Latin culture. It was the last state in the Southwest to be overwhelmed by Anglo-American civilization, and is the only one with two official languages. The Mexican-American population has been traditionally located along the Rio Grande and its tributaries, and extends into southern Colorado.

Until recent years, the Mexican-Americans of New Mexico have been isolated from other members of *la raza* (the Mexican-American "race"). Texas and California have more than 80 percent of the

Mexican-American population of the Southwest, yet most of these crossed over from Mexico after 1900, or descended from persons who did. But, the New Mexican *Hispanos* (the local name) have resided there for many generations, and some strains go back to the seventeenth century (Santa Fe was founded in 1609). Moreover, large numbers of English-speaking Americans only began to compete seriously for rural property in the 1880's, and appropriation continued into the 1920's.

In the 1960 census New Mexico had a higher percentage of "native born of native parents" than any other Southwestern state (87.4 percent). The mobility of Hispano males between 1955 and 1960 (defined in terms of changing residence) was lower in New Mexico than elsewhere. In 1960 New Mexico had the highest percentage of rural non-farm inhabitants with Spanish surnames.

In absolute numbers New Mexico's Anglo population was for many years roughly in balance with the Hispano. It is now surging ahead as a result of the economic boom which began with the atomic testing program of World War II. In no other Southwestern state was the disparity between the growth of Anglo and Latin populations greater from 1950 to 1960 than in New Mexico, where the former increased by 59.1 percent and the latter by a mere 8.1 percent. Yet in spite of this, New Mexico in 1960 still had a greater proportion of Mexican-Americans than any other state: about two-sevenths of its inhabitants had Spanish surnames, compared to one-seventh of Texans, and one-eleventh of Californians.

The job situation for the Hispanos of New Mexico has also worsened more rapidly than in other states. In 1950 male Mexican-Americans had a greater percentage of jobless in California, Colorado, and Arizona than in New Mexico; but ten years later the Hispanos of New Mexico had the dubious distinction of leading the list.

As some observers have noted, in certain ways New Mexico resembles Quebec: Both are centers of Latin culture founded in the seventeenth century, and both are subject to an increasing degree of Anglo domination. And like the Quebeckers, the New Mexicans have their fringe-group separatists—the *Alianza Federal de Mercedes*.

The Alianza was born in 1963, partly to combat the alienation and isolation of the Hispanos, but specifically to reclaim lands taken from the Spanish-speaking population since 1848. In colonial New Mexico (1598–1821), Spanish officials made land grants of indeterminate size to both individuals and to communities as commons, and the latter were respected through the era of Mexican rule (1821–1848). When Anglo-Americans began to enter New Mexico in significant numbers in the 1880's, they found it possible to wrest lands from the native inhabitants through the legal and financial devices of land taxes, mortgages, and litigation over disputed titles. By 1930, through legal and extralegal means, the Anglos had taken over most of the farming and ranching land in the state, and the state and federal governments appropriated much of the common lands that had previously belonged to the incorporated towns and villages. The Spanish-speaking population ultimately lost 1.7 million acres of community lands and two million acres in private holdings. The Hispanos sporadically reacted to this process by forming secret societies and vigilante groups; but at most this constituted harassment rather than effective resistance.

The Alianza now demands the return of these lands.

Yet in all probability, the Alianza would not exist but for the efforts of a single man, a leader who devotes his life to his cause, and inspires his followers to do likewise. Reies López Tijerina is a man of rare charisma who is most in his element when haranguing a large crowd. Of average height, he seems to have great physical strength as he grasps a microphone with one sinewy arm and gesticulates artfully and furiously with the other. He sometimes shouts violently as he asks rhetorical questions of his audience in Spanish—the language he uses by preference—and gets "Sí!" and "No!" bellowed back in appropriate cadences. The author witnessed a Tijerina performance last fall on the steps of the state capitol in Austin, Texas, where the Alianza leader told a group of Mexican-American Labor Day marchers he supported their demand for a state minimum wage of $1.25 an hour, but did so "with shame." Why should Mexican-Americans in Texas ask so little of the Anglos, whose government had repeatedly broken the Treaty of Guadalupe Hidalgo?

Reies Tijerina uses a demagogic style before a crowd, but he holds the tenets of his faith with unshakable conviction: "It's something in me that must come out," Tijerina proclaims. His followers regard him with awe. He is "Caudillo" (leader) of the Alianza, but disclaims any desire to be dictator. He points out that a Supreme Council has ultimate control—though he, clearly, makes the decisions. It seems obvious that no one could step into his shoes, nor has anyone been groomed to do so. In any event Tijerina has no doubt that his followers require strong and able leadership. He justifies this by arguing that the Hispanos are a "young" race. They were "born," he explains, by virtue of a royal decree in 1514 allowing Spaniards to marry Indians; the term "Hispano" or "Spanish American" therefore can generally be equated with "mestizo." This young race is still learning, painfully, how to defend itself and requires strong direction. It is not an ancient and clever people like the Jews, he says.

Recognizing the diverse historical experiences of Texas, New Mexico, and California, the Caudillo realizes that his constituency for the foreseeable future will be limited to New Mexico. He does believe, however, that the land grants to Mexican-Americans in California can still be identified and claimed like those of New Mexico.

It is no coincidence that Tijerina's style and language recall Pentecostal protestantism. He has been a minister in the Assembly of God, and was an itinerant revival preacher for many years to Mexican-Americans throughout the Southwest.

But, unlike the vast majority of his followers, he was not born in New Mexico but in Texas ("A prophet is not without honor save in his own country"). One of seven children of a migrant farm family, once so desperate that they were reduced to eating field rats, he picked crops and preached in Illinois and Michigan as well as in Texas and Arizona. He did not settle in New Mexico until 1960; and, with his five brothers, formed the Alianza three years later.

The quasi-religious fervor of Tijerina has strongly shaped the aspirations and style of the Alianza. However, there is greater emphasis on Old Testament justice than New Testament love. *Justicia* is a word frequently on the Caudillo's lips.

The Alianza now claims to have 30,000 dues-paying members paying at least $2.00 per month. A scholar guesses that 10,000 may be closer to the true figure. It seems clear that Tijerina's computation includes sympathizers or at least persons who have only occasionally contributed funds.

As with some sectors of the American Negro movement, the Alianza's programs began with an emphasis on litigation; and when that failed, frustration and a disposition toward violence emerged.

In April 1966 the "President and Founder" of the Alianza journeyed to Spain in order to gather materials on the registration of

New Mexican land grants in the colonial era; from such documents he hoped to generate a strong legal case to present in federal courts.

In July Tijerina presented a petition to the Governor of New Mexico, Jack Campbell, and stated, "We do not demand anything. We just want a full investigation of the issue." Yet Governor Campbell would do little more than receive Tijerina and hear him out.

In January 1967, the Caudillo, one of his brothers, and a self-styled legal expert in the Alianza named Gerry Noll made a trip to Washington, D.C., where they "limited" their claims to 500,000 acres in the Kit Carson National Forest and to an area around the city of Albuquerque. He only obtained a brief hearing with a State Department attorney and a sympathetic interview with New Mexico's Senator Montoya.

In 1966 the Alianza had already begun to give up hope of legal redress. The Supreme Council of the Alianza "passed a resolution of non-confidence in the Courts of the State of New Mexico and of the United States of America" because of "corruption" and "low standards of knowledge of law."

On October 22, 1966 the Aliancistas proclaimed the existence of the Republic of San Joaquín del Río de Chama (in Rio Arriba County) with Tijerina as "city attorney" (procurador) of the community; they simultaneously attempted to take over Kit Carson Forest, which covers most of the county. They arrested U.S. Forest Rangers for trespassing, decided to print hunting and fishing licenses, and commandeered government vehicles. The rebels were quickly dispersed by local authorities, and Tijerina and four lieutenants were charged on counts of assault, converting government property to private use, and conspiracy.

Demonstrations and protest meetings continued. On January 15, 1967 the Alianza declared it would seek redress in the United Nations if the U.S. Congress failed to act. On April 17 several hundred Aliancistas paraded before the State House in Santa Fe, and Reies Tijerina, out on bond, delivered an ominous message: "We will ... issue to the public and the federal government and the world the last human legal notice exposing the truth. ... The government is being warned and advised if anybody is found trespassing on these land grants they will be arrested and punished. ..."

At the beginning of June the District Attorney of Santa Fe, Alfonso Sánchez, expressed concern about the "communist philosophy" of the Alianza and alleged that Aliancistas were amassing "machine guns, M-1 rifles, and 15,000 rounds" of ammunition. Eleven members of the Alianza were promptly arrested and jailed in Tierra Amarilla, an Alianza stronghold and the seat of Rio Arriba County.

The reaction was swift and violent: On June 5, as noted, the Aliancistas launched their revolt and attacked the Tierra Amarilla courthouse. This time, when caught, the Caudillo and his principal aides were charged with kidnapping, three counts of conspiracy to commit murder, and bombing a public building (the courthouse). Despite the gravity of the charges, Tijerina and some of his men were released on bond after six weeks in prison. The failure of the attack by no means dampened the spirits of the Aliancistas.

In the months following, Tijerina traveled throughout the Southwest to gain backing. He found it, both in radical organizations of Mexican-Americans and Negroes, and in some Mexican-American associations with more traditional reformist leadership.

On October 15, Tijerina was in Los Angeles, linking his cause to the peace movement at an anti-war rally. Labeling the United States' involvement in Vietnam "the most criminal in the history of mankind," he contacted radical Negro and Mexican-American groups in the Los Angeles area. One week later, at a convention of the Alianza de Mercedes on October 21, Tijerina announced that a "Treaty of Peace, Harmony, and Mutual Assistance" had been contracted between his organization and SNCC, CORE, and the Black Panthers. The Caudillo also obtained statements of support from the Crusade for Justice, a Mexican-American organization of slumdwellers in Denver, and from MAPA, an important Mexican-American political action group in California.

While gathering support from non-Anglo groups outside New Mexico in the here and now, Tijerina and his deputies have not discouraged the movement's latent tendencies toward millenarianism[1] and belief in special divine favor back home on the Upper Rio Grande. During the raid at Tierra Amarilla, several Aliancistas witnessed the appearance of a double rainbow, a sure sign of God's grace. According to others, the Caudillo is the prophet of Montezuma who

---

1. Nancie Gonzalez was the first to note millenarian tendencies in the Alianza.

will miraculously return in the imminent future to punish the Anglos for their appropriation of Hispano lands.

Another legend has it that a leader will come "from the east" and expel the foreigners who took the Mexican-Americans' lands. (Tijerina fits, since Texas is east of New Mexico.)

In the "*Corrido de Rio Arriba*," which appeared shortly after the June raid, the balladeer told his audience that when bullets started flying "*Las mujeres y los niños/iban corriendo y llorando,*

Y en este instanite pensamos/Que el mundo se iba acabando.*"

("Women and children/Ran about in tears

And at that moment we thought/The world was coming to an end.")

Although the "free city-states" which Tijerina hopes to erect are of this world, they clearly represent a sort of secular paradise, a recaptured golden age, somewhat along the lines prescribed in *The Laws of the Indies*. The inhabitants will be able to do any work they please, explains the Caudillo; but most will be herdsmen using the common lands (*ejidos*) of the pueblos. Tijerina himself will simply become City Attorney of the Republic of Chama.

If "la raza" is specially favored and will come into its millenium, why is it suffering so now? This is explained as the result of a "fall from grace" which occurred after the Anglo-American invasion of New Mexico in 1846 and the collusion of certain Hispanos with the alien conquerors. An allegorical mural at Alianza headquarters tells the story: A sacred temple in the center of the mural represents paradise entwined by a serpent, which also clutches three figures symbolizing the oppressed races—the Negro, the Indian, and the Hispano. The snake personifies the "Santa Fe Ring"—the Anglo and upper-class Hispano politicians who appropriated the poor Hispanos' lands in the 1880's and later. Figures on the right side, representing the People, begin to emerge from the Darkness and a reptile-devouring secretary bird, personifying Justice, arrives to attack the snake. At the top of the canvas is a rainbow (a symbol of God's blessing) and the phrase "Justicia." Just below this emblem is the City of Justice, which will once more be reconstituted on earth.

Yet there is a sinister element in the apocalypse which must precede the millenium: Anglos must be driven out. And Hispanos will be judged by whether they aided, stood aside from, or hindered the cause. Those who hindered will be treated harshly....

Helen Wheeler,
"The Puerto Rican Population of New York, New York"

Puerto Ricans have been citizens of the United States since 1917, but denial of statehood limits the influence of their island in national politics as well as its share of national revenues. Poor employment opportunities in their homeland led many Puerto Ricans to migrate to New York City where they numbered about one million by 1970. Cultural and racial barriers impeded employment and acceptance of Puerto Ricans and forced them to occupy the lower rungs of the economic ladder. In Puerto Rico color does not constitute an important social or economic disadvantage, so that prejudice toward darker-skinned islanders on the mainland was an unexpected and perplexing experience for them. Although Helen Wheeler wrote "The Puerto Rican Population of New York, New York" twenty years ago, her observations on the difficulties encountered by the migrants on the mainland are unfortunately descriptive of the situation today.

The Puerto Rican Population of New York, New York

Helen Wheeler

The people who migrate to this country from the Spanish-speaking countries of this hemisphere are frequently grouped together in one category. This is unfortunate, because it hinders an understanding of their motives for coming and their reasons for staying or leaving. Those who migrate from the most economically "underdeveloped" republics do so, obviously, for the purpose of seeking better living standards, and these come in considerable numbers. On the other hand, there probably are not many more Argentinians, Uruguayans, Colombians, and Chileans here than there are Americans in those countries. Their reasons for being here are the same as those of the Americans for being there, namely, study, business, or simply travel.

Although there are no immigration quotas for Latin Americans, as there are for Europeans, American visas are hard to get. A very limited number of persons from each country get a "permanent" visa, and the length of other visas varies according to the purpose of the visit. Therefore, the number of Latin Americans who have arrived in this country during the past ten years, intending to live here permanently, is relatively small. The exception to this is the Puerto Ricans, who,

Abridged from Helen Wheeler, "The Puerto Rican Population of New York, New York," *Sociology and Social Research*, XXXV (1950), pp. 123–127. Reprinted by permission of the publisher.

being American citizens, are free to come and go. They play, therefore, an interesting part in Spanish-American immigration into the city of New York, since they represent the impact of two cultures and its transfer to a great metropolis.

Puerto Rico is more closely associated with United States ways than any other Latin-American country, and the Puerto Ricans are the largest Spanish-speaking group in the city of New York.

Ceded to the United States as a result of the Spanish-American War in 1898, her people were made United States citizens by the Jones Act in 1917. Since that time, Puerto Rico has become the object of interest to many sociologists and historians who see in the island the actual taking place of the impact of two cultures, the tropical and the temperate, and of two races, the Latin and the Saxon. This conflict, together with extreme economic depression in Puerto Rico, has precipitated one of the greatest migrations in New York City's history.

Puerto Rico, with a population of about two million inhabitants, ranks among the most densely populated regions of the world; it is the third most densely populated agricultural spot on the earth, with six hundred people per square mile. More than two thirds of the inhabitants reside in the rural zones, and the population in general depends almost completely on agricultural activities. Seventy-six percent of the population is composed of "whites," and the remaining 24 percent, principally, of Negroes and mulattoes.

On passing into the hands of the United States, a marked increase in the island's population was produced, due in part to the high natality rate, but due principally to the lowering of the mortality rate. The high percentage of unemployed is due to three important factors: the density of population, the scarcity of raw materials, and the almost complete absence of large industrial enterprise. In September 1942 about 37 percent of the active population was jobless.

The workers' movement has not had a great development in Puerto Rico because of the great number of laborers and the relatively poor standard of living of the population. Even during the prosperous years between 1920 and 1927, the number of employable persons always far exceeded the number of vacant jobs. Moreover, the farmers and planters, flattered by the high prices, sold their lands and transferred to the towns.

At the beginning of the [thirties] the island found itself in the midst of the greatest economic crisis in its history, so that the Puerto Ricans by 1931 composed the entire Spanish-speaking group in the city of New York. In August 1933 the Puerto Rico Emergency Relief Administration was established, and dedicated itself to the economic reconstruction of the island; in 1935 this agency was replaced by the Federal Relief Administration. By 1939 this Office had effected a reduction in the number of unemployed, but in that year Congress failed to extend new allocations for it.

The Bureau of Applied Social Research of Columbia University believes that there are about 160,000 Puerto Ricans in New York City at the present time [1950] and that the average age is twenty-four. The main reason these migrants give for coming to New York is their search for economic betterment. In more recent years the Puerto Ricans have come in search of *better* jobs, rather than *just* employment.

Other reasons for migrating refer to their desire to join their families, to attend schools, and to utilize hospitals and other facilities which the city offers. Puerto Rican migration to New York is an example of movement of a people who hope to better their condition. The Puerto Ricans find themselves landless, unemployed, herded into towns, and they look to the United States and New York as means of escape from these economic conditions.

The Puerto Ricans come to New York because of better steamship facilities and rates between Puerto Rico and New York as compared with the Gulf ports. They come to New York to earn the comparatively high money-wages that used to go to the European immigrant groups which are now restricted. The fact that this migration results from population pressure is the greatest difference from the reason for the migration of other Latin-American countries represented in New York. They also come in large numbers by plane.

In addition to the great difference in wages and opportunity which draws the Puerto Rican to this country, he is attracted by the higher standard of living he observes in American movies. Unfortunately, many distorted ideas are also given by these same pictures. Relatives and friends already living in the United States have a strong influence. They draw him here, whether or not they have prospered, for he may simply come to join them, and then too a little appears as a lot. It is customary for Puerto Ricans to share whatever they have with relatives. Ease of movement here is the fifth main motive for the Puerto Rican's migration to New York.

Most of those in the labor force arrive in New York without prior arrangements for a job. Contrary to the recent speculation that Puerto Rican migrants have been brought here by labor contractors, most of them arrive with only great hopes; they do increase their earning power, however, immediately. The migrants consistently earn more money on their first job in New York than they had earned in Puerto Rico.

The New York State Employment Service places Puerto Ricans in industrial and domestic positions. Most of the males find work as assemblers of various products; heavy laborers in the sugar factories; pressers and floor boys in the garment industries; dishwashers, bus boys, pantrymen, and countermen in the hotels; laundry workers, porters, elevator operators and janitors in building maintenance; and many, in shipbuilding, as cleaning, scaling, and painting workers. The International Ladies' Garment Workers Union reports a membership of over five thousand Puerto Rican women workers. In the garment industries they find employment as hand sewers, floor girls, cleaners, and beginning sewing machine operators; in hospitals, as ward aides; in addition, they do piecework at home assembling jewelry and toys, making artificial flowers, and doing hand embroidery and sewing on blouses, underwear, and lampshades.

Most of the Puerto Ricans agree that their greatest handicap in gaining employment is their lack of knowledge of the English language. Other barriers are lack of vocational training, New York City licenses, tools, and local references. Unfamiliarity with New York's streets and with transportation facilities limits the employment of many to the immediate neighborhood in which they live; but, in general, they are quick to become familiar with the city's transportation, hospital, clinic, public welfare, and entertainment facilities. The Puerto Rican encounters a color line which does not exist in Puerto Rico. He is also at a disadvantage because he is not organized with his fellow Puerto Ricans here, and he is subject to sickness, particularly parasitical diseases and tuberculosis. The professional class and business and trades people are practically nonexistent. Almost all fall into the unskilled labor class, depending upon the weekly wage.

The Puerto Ricans in New York are distributed widely throughout the three boroughs of Manhattan, the Bronx, and Brooklyn, with per-haps half of the total population being concentrated in East Harlem and the South Bronx. It is in these neighborhoods, particularly in East Harlem, that the conditions exist which give rise to the articles and photographs which have appeared in the newspapers and maga-zines. These conditions are part of the whole problem of slum dwell-ings—a problem of the city as a whole, and not confined to Puerto Ricans. The general characteristic of their housing is that it is bad, but not worse than the way most of them lived in Puerto Rico, or, if in some cases it is, the Puerto Rican feels compensated if he is able to find the position and opportunity he expected. Many do, and a surprisingly small number return to Puerto Rico permanently.

Free to come and go as a United States citizen, the depressed Puerto Rican sees this great city in motion pictures and thinks it is not difficult to make good money here. Moreover, conditions in Puerto Rico at the present time are such that practically any living conditions and rate of pay would be better than those to which he is accustomed. One reads and hears accounts of the unhealthful crowded tenements in the Puerto Rican sections of Harlem, and it is difficult to realize that many of the occupants still consider themselves better off than they were in Puerto Rico. True, most of these people miss home—they long for the tropical climate and scenery, for their fami-lies and friends, and, above all, for the slower, more easygoing life—but they do not miss the old standard of living....

John H. Burma,
*"The Background of the Current Situation
of Filipino-Americans"*

The United States' acquisition of the Philippine Islands after
the Spanish-American War paved the way for a new immigration.
Although the movement was minimal at first, by 1930, there
were about thirty thousand and by 1970, seventy thousand Filipinos
living in California where they have concentrated. Employment
opportunities were limited; even today over 50 percent of the men
are either farm laborers or service workers. Writing in 1951, John H.
Burma described "The Background of the Current Situation of
Filipino-Americans," explaining the historical development of
the difficulties of adjustment faced by these immigrants to the
United States. According to Burma, the Filipinos of 1950 considered
themselves white, but the majority society generally viewed them
as nonwhite. On the other hand, today's younger Filipino-Americans
often identify with the Third World, rather than with whites.

The Background of the Current Situation of Filipino-Americans

John H. Burma

The last Asiatic group to migrate in any number to the United States was the Filipino. Prior to 1920 there were not over 5,000 Filipinos in the United States at any one time, although during the previous decade they had begun to immigrate into Hawaii as contract laborers in the sugar and pineapple industries. After 1920 their movement from Hawaii to the mainland increased and was augmented by a stream of direct emigration from the Philippines. During the 1920's well over 50,000 Filipinos came to the mainland from both sources.[1] Possibly one-fourth of this number came via Hawaii. This was a two-way stream, however, the number leaving the United States in any given year being from one-half to one-sixth as great as the number entering. No restrictions were placed on such immigration and emigration as the Filipinos were nationals of the United States (until 1935) and so not subject to any quota restrictions.

The result of this relatively short-time migratory movement was that by 1930 there were some 45,200 Filipinos on the mainland of the

Abridged from John H. Burma, "The Background of the Current Situation of Filipino-Americans," Social Forces, XXX (1951), pp. 42–48. Reprinted by permission of the publisher. Some footnotes have been renumbered.

1. See Louis Black, Facts About Filipino Immigration into California, California State Department of Industrial Relations, Special Bulletin No. 3, 1930.

United States. This immigration was quite effectively cut off by the exigencies of an immigrant making a living during the depression. Then, when the Philippines were promised their independence in 1935, a formal quota of fifty was set up. This quota was in effect until 1945. At this time the Philippines received their complete independence and were given an immigration quota of one hundred, commensurate with the number of Filipinos then in the United States. Because of the practical and then official limiting of immigration, the number of Filipinos in this country has slightly decreased, so that it is expected that the 1950 census will report 40,000 or less.

The majority of Filipino-Americans are under 55 years of age. Most of them came as young men in their early twenties or later teens, unaccompanied by wives or families.[2] This meant a very disproportionate sex ratio, which in 1930 was 143 to 1. By 1940, because older men had returned to the islands and younger families were having children, this disproportion was down to about 7 to 1 for the group as a whole. For 19 years and under, the sex ratio was about even, but for 20 years of age and up, the sex ratio was approximately 20 to 1.[3] A marriageable Filipina hence is a rare sight.

Most Filipinos did not intend to stay permanently in the United States; they came in order to secure savings large enough to set themselves up in business at home, to get an American education, or just out of a spirit of adventure. More often than not their plans to return have never materialized. Many have never accumulated the desired "nest egg," others have failed to achieve the education they sought; they are failures in their own eyes, and their pride will not permit them to return home until that failure has become success. Because they have intended to return home, most Filipinos have sought acculturation but not assimilation.

The Filipino-Americans landed on the West Coast, and nearly all of them have remained there. Outside this area, only New York City has any appreciable number of Filipinos; Seattle, Portland, and San Francisco have sizeable Filipino-American colonies. Stockton, California, with some 4,000 fairly permanent residents and a "floating"

2. Cf. Grayson Kirk, "Filipinos," *Annals of the American Academy of Political and Social Science*, 223 (Sept. 1942), pp. 45–48.

3. Sixteenth Census of the United States, 1940—*Population: Characteristics of the Non-white Population by Race* (Washington: Government Printing Office [1942]), Table 3, p. 7.

population of about twice as many more, is considered the center of Filipino-American concentration, with its "Little Manila" probably the most highly developed Filipino ethnic area in America. Vying with it is Los Angeles, with 3,000 to 4,000 permanent residents, and a "floating" population of about double that number. Prior to the 1930's, in Los Angeles, they nearly all lived on the outskirts of "Little Tokyo," but during the depression there began a movement away from the First Street area over toward Figuroa and Temple Streets. Japanese relocation accelerated this movement, which is now virtually complete.[4] . . .

On the West Coast the chief occupational opportunity open to the new Filipino immigrant was some form of agricultural labor, and from the beginning to the present, casual, migratory, agricultural labor has been the occupation at which the largest number of Filipino-Americans have been able to find employment. Young, male, and single, they migrate easily, working as a racial group, usually under some variety of the *padrone* system. They are likely to travel in groups of five to fifteen, in battered cars or trucks, and have been found chiefly on the larger ranches. Although widely used in agricultural labor, no special area or crop is actually dependent on Filipino labor, nor are the *Pinoy*[5] dependent on any one crop. . . .

To find a Filipino-American employed in industry has been rare. In Alaska they have worked in rather large numbers in the fish canneries, and occasionally elsewhere in vegetable canning. They have been employed in the Merchant Marine in considerable numbers, and even before World War II some four or five thousand were in the United States Navy, mostly as mess attendants. During the winter months, and sometimes throughout the year, they work in West Coast cities as cooks, dishwashers, bellboys, elevator boys, house boys, or gardeners. Some are engaged in service occupations to their fellows, in barber shops, pool halls, hotels, cafes, taxi service, and the like. During the war many secured employment in shipyards, airplane factories and other war-stimulated industries. A surprising number were hired by movie studios as extras. This, plus the number in the army meant that the war period was the best period economically which the Fili-

4. R. T. Feria, "War and the Status of Filipino Immigrants," *Sociology and Social Research*, 31 (Sept. 1946), pp. 48–53.
5. Their own name for themselves.

pinos have experienced since the beginning of their migration to the United States.[6] Unfortunately most so employed were "marginal workers," and were among the first to lose their jobs after the war stimulation ceased.

All those except the disillusioned and disheartened look forward to moving out of the migratory labor, domestic service, etc., to better jobs, but discriminatory hiring plus their own lack of qualification make this a rather unlikely step for most of them. In short, the Filipino-American has filled, in his own way, a function in the economic life of the Pacific Coast similar to that which different waves of migration always have filled on the Atlantic Coast.[7] . . .

The living conditions of most Filipino-Americans have been far from satisfactory. They usually do not form permanent ethnic settlements, but live in the cities during the winter and work on farms in the summer. In the city, in order to save money, several will live in one room, usually in an old house which makes no pretext of being anything except a place to sleep. In the rural area they move about week after week, always living in "temporary" housing—poor houses, made-over barns, barracks, or just sheds. Typical furniture includes only cots, a table, and a few chairs. Sanitary facilities may be at an amazing minimum. Hence, winter or summer, urban or rural, the Filipino-American is a slum dweller, with all the problems that such residence entails. . . .

As a group, the Filipinos have been subject to a full quota of social problems. The great preponderance of young males, absence of older persons, extensive lack of family life, and living conditions in labor camps promote not only restlessness and migratoriness but also instability of personality and abnormal social life. . . .

Most states where Filipinos live have passed laws prohibiting the marriage of "Caucasians" and "Mongolians,"[8] and the court arguments have been over whether the Filipino, who is predominantly Malay, is therefore also a "Mongolian." In California where most Filipinos have lived, such marriage was first considered legal, then

6. Feria, *op. cit.*

7. Bruno Lasker, *Filipino Immigration* (Chicago: University of Chicago Press, 1931), p. 65.

8. Cf. N. Foster, "The Legal Status of the Filipino Intermarriages in California," *Sociology and Social Research* (May–June, 1933), pp. 441–54. Also, I. B. Buaken, "You Can't Marry a Filipino," *Commonweal*, 41 (March 16, 1945), pp. 534–37.

illegal, with the county clerk of each county serving as judge of race,[9] and then in 1948 California's anti-miscegenation law was declared unconstitutional. That no more Filipina intermarriages have occurred is no doubt chiefly due to the desire of most Filipinos to return home and marry Filipinas, plus the fact that discrimination and social distance prevent intimate friendships which might lead to marriage, and often prevent the acceptance of the husband. Rural intermarriage seems to work somewhat better than urban, probably because there is somewhat less public opposition and discrimination and because the rural environment seems more conducive to stable marriage than the disorganized area of city slums. In either case discrimination, language handicaps, and wide cultural differences are potentially disorganizing factors.[10] . . .

The fact that Filipinos are dark-skinned foreigners (plus living on the West Coast) is sufficient to expose them to discrimination.[11] Such discrimination has followed the usual pattern of social rejection, attitudes of superiority, difficulty in securing housing, difficulty in securing jobs above the labor category, refusal of service in cafes, segregation in movie balconies, being "frozen out" of local or campus social activities, and objections to Filipino-white dating. To these are added the individual slights and injustices which unpremeditatedly occur when one group feels itself superior to another. There are, of course, wide differences in treatment from region to region, from town to town, and from individual to individual. When the Filipinos are few in number they are usually thought of as Latin Americans, because of their color and the fact that they speak Spanish. If few in number and inconspicuous they usually suffer no discrimination. When they arrive suddenly and in large numbers, unfavorable reports are circulated and believed, and discrimination results.[12]

The crux of the most active and bitter discrimination and dislike seems to be the Filipino's refusal to accept his "place" as an inferior.

9. Cf. Emory S. Bogardus, "What Race are Filipinos?" *Sociology and Social Research* (Jan.–Feb. 1932), pp. 274–79.

10. Denicio T. Catapusan, "Filipino Intermarriage Problems in the United States," *Sociology and Social Research* (Jan. 1938), pp. 265–72.

11. Cf. Emory S. Bogardus, "American Attitudes toward Filipinos," *Sociology and Social Research*, 14 (May–June 1930), pp. 469–79.

12. Cf. M. Buaken, "Where is the Heart of America?" *New Republic*, 103 (Sept. 23, 1940), p. 410.

He typically considers himself white, with all the perquisites thereto appertaining in our culture. He has been taught in the Islands that all men are created equal, and his pride and sensitivity will not permit him to passively assume the role of an inferior as did the Chinese coolie a generation or two before him. Most "incidents" seem to stem from the Filipino's conviction that he is as good as any one else, and his consequent behavior.[13] Between 1928 and 1930 there were about a dozen disturbances of significance in Washington and California. Most of these disturbances occurred in small towns and villages and included beatings, dynamitings and near-riots. Although the pattern differed slightly from one to another, the underlying causes were either economic or social. Economically, the Filipinos were often opposed by local labor units or unions on the grounds of lowering wages, and occasionally opposed by employers for striking at a critical time in order to get better wages. Socially, the most prominent difficulty was the attentions paid by Filipinos to white girls, attentions which usually were of alarm to the white men rather than to the white women. In general the vocal objections raised were the same as those voiced against Orientals: they cause low wages by having a low standard of living, they could not become citizens,[14] they could not be assimilated, and contact with them would endanger our racial purity. It is unfortunate that the Filipinos were and are concentrated in an area especially sensitive to the "Oriental Menace," particularly since this concentration prevents the rest of the nation from knowing the facts in the situation.

One result of the above conditions and accusations was the early demand for the exclusion and deportation of Filipinos. In 1924 Congress declared that they were not aliens, but being neither Caucasian nor Negro they were ineligible to citizenship. Hence they possessed the hybrid status of nationals or wards. As nationals, however, their forced deportation was likely to be illegal, and their exclusion was also of doubtful legality. Of those who sought Filipino exclusion and deportation, labor unions and California "Native" organizations were the most prominent. Deportation and exclusion were opposed by

13. Cf. Donald E. Anthony, "Filipino Labor in Central California," *Sociology and Social Research*, 16 (Nov.-Dec. 1931), p. 156.

14. This was true at the time, but Filipinos now may become citizens just as can other immigrants.

those employing Filipino laborers and by the Filipinos themselves. A third suggestion, that Filipino immigration be limited to students and to "better class" Filipinos was supported by intellectual and semi-intellectual groups and hence received less Congressional consideration than either of the other two. The solution came in 1935 with a federal act providing for voluntary repatriation at government expense of any Filipino who would return home.[15] No more than one in forty took advantage of this opportunity, partly from the injury it would do their pride, and partly because such repatriation prohibited their ever returning to the United States. In the same year the granting of partial independence to the Philippines, with the promise of full independence in 1945, helped quiet Filipino complaints and removed their hybrid political position.[16]

The Filipino always doubted whether he would spend the rest of his life in America, yet he did not know when he could return home, for he had to have either money or an education before he could return without disgrace. Then World War II in most instances made him make up his mind to return soon or to stay permanently here; either decision decreased significantly the instability, indecision, and partial goallessness which had been seriously disorganizing factors.[17] . . .

15. Cf. Emory S. Bogardus, "Filipino Repatriation," Sociology and Social Research (Sept.–Oct. 1936), pp. 67–71. Also, "Lovers Departure; Subsidized Exodus," Time, 27 (April 13, 1936), p. 17; Carey McWilliams, "Exit the Filipino," Nation, 141 (Sept. 4, 1935), p. 265.
16. They are now "Aliens eligible to citizenship."
17. Feria, op. cit., p. 52.

Selected Bibliography

A. General Works

Allport, Gordon W. *The Nature of Prejudice.* New York: Anchor, 1954.

Bennett, Lerone. *Before the Mayflower.* New York: Penguin, 1962.

Burma, John H., ed. *Mexican-Americans in the United States.* Cambridge, Mass.: Schenkman, 1970.

Farb, Peter. *Man's Rise to Civilization, As Shown by the Indians of North America From the Primeval Times to the Coming of the Industrial State.* New York: Avon, 1968.

Franklin, John Hope. *From Slavery to Freedom.* New York: Vintage, 1967.

Glazer, Nathan and Daniel Patrick Moynihan. *Beyond the Melting Pot: The Negroes, Puerto Ricans, Jews, Italians, and Irish of New York City.* Cambridge: M.I.T. Press, 1963.

Gordon, Milton M. *Assimilation in American Life.* New York: Oxford University Press, 1964.

Gossett, Thomas F. *Race: The History of an Idea in America.* New York: Schocken, 1963.

Grebler, Leo, Joan W. Moore, and Ralph C. Guzman. *The Mexican-American People: The Nation's Second Largest Minority.* New York: Free Press, 1970.

Hagan, William T. *American Indians.* Chicago: University of Chicago Press, 1961.

Handlin, Oscar. *Race and Nationality in American Life.* New York: Anchor, 1957.

Kitano, Harry H. *The Japanese-Americans: The Evolution of a Subculture.* New York: Prentice-Hall, 1969.

Kovel, Joel. *White Racism: A Psychohistory.* New York: Vintage, 1970.

Lee, Rose Hum. *The Chinese in the United States of America.* Hong Kong: Hong Kong University Press, 1960.

McWilliams, Carey. *North From Mexico: The Spanish-Speaking People of the United States.* Westport, Conn.: Greenwood, 1948.

Meier, August and Elliott M. Rudwick. *From Plantation to Ghetto*. New York: Hill and Wang, 1966.

Myers, Gustavus. *History of Bigotry in the United States*. New York: Capricorn, 1943.

Nash, Gary B. and Richard Weiss, eds. *The Great Fear: Race in the Mind of America*. New York: Holt, 1970.

Schwartz, Barry M. and Robert Disch. *White Racism: Its History, Pathology, and Practice*. New York: Dell, 1970.

Spicer, Edward H. *A Short History of the Indians of the United States*. New York: Anvil, 1969.

B. The Seventeenth and Eighteenth Centuries

Blacks

Greene, Lorenzo. *The Negro in Colonial New England*. New York: Atheneum, 1942.

Jordan, Winthrop. *White Over Black: American Attitudes Toward the Negro, 1550–1812*. New York: Penguin, 1968.

Klingberg, Frank. *An Appraisal of the Negro in Colonial South Carolina*. Toronto: Associated Publishers, 1941.

Mannix, Daniel, and Malcolm Cowley. *Black Cargoes: A History of the Atlantic Slave Trade*. New York: Viking, 1962.

Mellon, Matthew T. *Early American Views on Negro Slavery*. New York: Mentor, 1934, 1969.

Quarles, Benjamin. *The Negro in the American Revolution*. Chapel Hill: University of North Carolina Press, 1961.

Robinson, Donald. *Slavery in the Structure of American Politics, 1765–1820*. New York: Harcourt, 1971.

Tate, Thad W. *The Negro in Eighteenth-Century Williamsburg*. Charlottesville: University of Virginia Press, 1966.

Zilversmit, Arthur. *The First Emancipation: The Abolition of Slavery in the North*. Chicago: University of Chicago Press, 1967.

Indians

Lauber, Almon W. *Indian Slavery in Colonial Times Within the Present Limits of the United States*. New York: Columbia University Press, 1913.

Leach, Douglas E. *Flintlock and Tomahawk: New England in King Philip's War*. New York: Norton, 1958.

Milling, Chapman J. *Red Carolinians*. Chapel Hill: University of North Carolina Press, 1940.

Trelease, Allen W. *Indian Affairs in Colonial New York: Seventeenth Century*. Ithaca, N. Y.: Cornell University Press, 1960.

Vaughan, Alden T. *The New England Frontier: Puritans and Indians, 1620–1675.* Boston: Little, Brown, 1965.

Wallace, Anthony F. C. *King of the Delawares: Teedyuscung.* Philadelphia: University of Pennsylvania Press, 1949.

C. The Nineteenth Century

Blacks

Aptheker, Herbert. *American Negro Slave Revolts.* New York: International Publishers, 1943.

Carroll, Joseph C. *Slave Insurrections in the United States.* Westport, Conn.: Negro Universities Press, 1938.

DuBois, W. E. B. *Black Reconstruction in America.* Cleveland: Meridian, 1935.

Elkins, Stanley. *Slavery: A Problem in American Institutional and Intellectual Life.* Chicago: University of Chicago Press, 1959.

Genovese, Eugene. *The Political Economy of Slavery.* New York: Vintage, 1961.

Litwack, Leon F. *North of Slavery: The Negro in the Free States, 1790–1860.* Chicago: University of Chicago Press, 1961.

Logan, Rayford W. *The Betrayal of the Negro: From Rutherford B. Hayes to Woodrow Wilson.* New York: Collier, 1965.

McPherson, James. *The Negro's Civil War.* New York: Vintage, 1965.

Meier, August. *Negro Thought in America, 1880–1915.* Ann Arbor: University of Michigan Press, 1963.

Quarles, Benjamin. *Black Abolitionists.* New York: Oxford University Press, 1969.

Stampp, Kenneth. *The Peculiar Institution.* New York: Vintage, 1956.

Starobin, Robert S. *Industrial Slavery in the Old South.* New York: Oxford University Press, 1970.

Wade, Richard. *Slavery in the Cities.* New York: Oxford University Press, 1964.

Wood, Forrest G. *Black Scare: The Racist Response to Emancipation and Reconstruction.* Berkeley: University of California Press, 1968.

Woodward, C. Vann. *The Strange Career of Jim Crow.* New York: Oxford University Press, 1955.

Indians

Abel, Annie. *The Slaveholding Indians,* 3 vols. Glendale, Calif.: Arthur H. Clark, 1915–1925.

Andrist, Ralph K. *The Long Death: The Last Days of the Plains Indians.* New York: Collier, 1964.

Brown, Dee. *Bury My Heart at Wounded Knee.* New York: Holt, 1970.

DeRosier, Arthur Jr. *The Removal of the Choctaw Indians.* Knoxville: University of Tennessee Press, 1970.

Downes, Randolph C. *Council Fires On the Upper Ohio.* Pittsburgh: University of Pittsburgh Press, 1940.

Ewers, John C. *The Blackfeet: Raiders on the Northwestern Plains.* Norman: University of Oklahoma Press, 1958.

Foreman, Grant. *Indian Removal: The Emigration of the Five Civilized Tribes of Indians.* Norman: University of Oklahoma Press, 1953.

Fritz, Henry E. *The Movement for Indian Assimilation, 1860–1890.* Philadelphia: University of Pennsylvania Press, 1963.

Hagan, William T. *The Sac and Fox Indians.* Norman: University of Oklahoma Press, 1958.

Horsman, Reginald. *Expansion and American Indian Policy, 1783–1812.* East Lansing: Michigan State University Press, 1967.

Priest, Loring B. *Uncle Sam's Stepchildren: The Reformation of United States Indian Policy, 1865–1887.* New Brunswick: Rutgers University Press, 1942.

Prucha, Francis P. *American Indian Policy in the Formative Years, 1790–1834.* Lincoln: University of Nebraska Press, 1962.

Tucker, Glenn. *Tecumseh.* Indianapolis: Bobbs-Merrill, 1956.

Wallace, Ernest and E. Adamson Hoebel. *The Comanches: Lords of the South Plains.* Norman: University of Oklahoma Press, 1953.

Mexican-Americans

Burns, Walter Noble. *The Robin Hood of El Dorado: The Saga of Joaquin Murietta.* New York: Coward-McCann, 1932.

Greenwood, Robert. *The California Outlaw: Tiburcio Vasquez.* Georgetown, Calif.: Talisman Press, 1960.

Pitt, Leonard. *The Decline of the Californios: A Social History of the Spanish-Speaking Californians, 1846–1890.* Berkeley: University of California Press, 1966.

Chinese-Americans

Barth, Gunther. *Bitter Strength: A History of the Chinese in the United States, 1850–1870.* Cambridge: Harvard University Press, 1964.

Chiu, Ping. *Chinese Labor in California, 1850–1880.* Madison: Historical Society of Wisconsin, 1963.

Coolidge, Mary. *Chinese Immigration.* New York: Henry Holt, 1909.

Miller, Stuart C. *The Unwelcome Immigrant: The American Image of the Chinese, 1785–1882.* Berkeley: University of California Press, 1969.

Sandmeyer, Elmer C. *The Anti-Chinese Movement in California.* Urbana: University of Illinois Press, 1939.

D. The Twentieth Century

Blacks

Cleaver, Eldridge. *Soul On Ice.* New York: McGraw-Hill, 1968.

Cronon, E. David. *Black Moses: The Story of Marcus Garvey.* Madison: University of Wisconsin Press, 1955.

Jackson, Kenneth T. *The Ku Klux Klan in the City, 1915–1930.* New York: Oxford University Press, 1967.

Kellogg, Charles F. *NAACP: A History of the National Association for the Advancement of Colored People,* vol. 1. Baltimore: Johns Hopkins Press, 1967.

Lester, Julius. *Look Out Whitey: Black Power's Gon' Get Your Mama.* New York: Grove, 1968.

Lomax, Louis. *The Negro Revolt.* New York: Signet, 1962.

Malcolm X. *Autobiography of Malcolm X.* New York: Grove, 1964.

Osofsky, Gilbert. *Harlem: The Making of a Ghetto, 1890–1920.* New York: Torchbook, 1966.

Spear, Allan. *Black Chicago: The Making of a Negro Ghetto, 1890–1920.* Chicago: University of Chicago Press, 1967.

White, Walter. *Rope and Faggot: A Biography of Judge Lynch.* New York: Arno, 1928.

Indians

Deloria, Vine, Jr. *Custer Died for Your Sins: An Indian Manifesto.* New York: Macmillan, 1969.

Embry, Carlos B. *America's Concentration Camps.* New York: David McKay, 1956.

Kahn, Edgar, ed. *Our Brother's Keeper: The Indian in White America.* Cleveland: World Publishing, 1969.

Levine, Stuart and Nancy O. Lurie, eds. *The American Indian Today.* Deland, Fla.: Everett-Edwards, 1968.

Steiner, Stan. *The New Indians.* New York: Dell, 1968.

Mexican-Americans

Dunne, John Gregory. *Delano: The Story of the California Grape Strike.* New York: Farrar, Straus, 1967.

Heller, Celia S. *Mexican-American Youth: Forgotten Youth At the Crossroads.* New York: Random, 1966.

Kibbe, Pauline R. *Latin Americans in Texas.* Albuquerque: University of New Mexico Press, 1946.

Matthiesen, Peter. *Sal Si Puedes: Cesar Chavez and the New American Revolution.* New York: Random, 1969.

Nabokov, Peter. *Tijerina and the Courthouse Raid.* Albuquerque: University of New Mexico Press, 1969.

Peattie, Lisa Redfield. *The View From the Barrio.* Ann Arbor: University of Michigan Press, 1968.

Tuck, Ruth D. *Not With the Fist: Mexican-Americans in a Southwest City.* New York: Harcourt, 1946.

Japanese-Americans

Daniels, Roger. *The Politics of Prejudice: The Anti-Japanese Movement in California and the Struggle for Japanese Exclusion.* New York: Atheneum, 1962.

Grodzins, Morton. *Americans Betrayed: Politics and the Japanese Evacuation.* Chicago: University of Chicago Press, 1949.

Hosokawa, Bill. *Nisei: The Quiet Americans.* New York: Morrow, 1969.

Rademaker, John. *These Are Americans: The Japanese-Americans in Hawaii in World War II.* Palo Alto, Calif.: Pacific Books, 1951.

Puerto Ricans

Chenault, Lawrence R. *The Puerto Rican Migrant in New York City.* New York: Russell and Russell, 1938.

Lewis, Oscar. *La Vida: A Puerto Rican Family in the Culture of Poverty—San Juan and New York.* New York: Random, 1966.

Senior, Clarence. *The Puerto Ricans: Strangers—Then Neighbors.* Chicago: Quadrangle, 1961.

Sexton, Patricia Cayo. *Spanish Harlem.* New York: Harper and Row, 1965.

Wakefield, Dan. *Island in the City.* New York: Corinth Books, 1959.

Filipinos

Bulosan, Carlos. *America is in the Heart.* New York: Harcourt, 1946.

Lasker, Bruno. *Filipino Immigration to Continental United States and to Hawaii.* Chicago: University of Chicago Press, 1931.

Index

Index

Index

Ladner, Joyce, 352 n.
Lamar, John, 148
Land rights, government's policy 1783, 97
Larpenteur, Charles, 140
Lasker, Bruno, 374 n.
Latin Americans, immigration quotas and visas, 365
Laws of the Indies. See Compilation of Laws of the Kingdoms of the Indies
League of Nations, 272, 279
Lee, Arthur, 99 n.
Lee, Richard Henry, 83 n., 86 n., 90 n., 92 n.
Leonis, Miguel, 223
Leslie, Sam, 93 n.
Lewis, Lloyd, 167
Lewis, M. G., 153, 156
Liberty, 81
Limón, José, 293
Lincoln, Abraham, 212
Linton, Ralph, 30 n.
Lippmann, Walter, 322
Little Turkey, 63
Little Turtle, 110
Locklear, William R., 236–251
"Lodging House Law of 1876," 246
London, Jack, 190
Lopez, Henry, 293
"Lord Dunmore's Ethiopian Regiment," 90
  See also John Murray
Los Angeles
  Chinatown in, 240
  Chinese population, 239
  decline in Spanish-speaking, 233
  1871 massacre of Chinese, 241–242, 249
  influence of Californios, 222, 225, 230
  See also Anti-Chinese movement in Los Angeles
Los Angeles Woolen Mills, 247
"Lost Cause," 220
Louisiana, restricting Negroes, 211, 212
Louisiana Purchase, 109
Love, Joseph L., 354–363
Lowrie, Samuel Harman, 163, 164
Ludlam, Richard, 69
Ludlow, Thomas, 54
Lugo, Antonio Maria, 224

Lurie, Nancy Oestreich, 27–44
Lyell, Sir Charles, 148, 158 n.
Lyttelton, William, 69

McCarran-Walter Act of 1952, 10
McClatchy, V. S., 307
McDonnell, W. L., 136 n.
McDowell, W. L., 63 n., 65 n., 67 n.
Machumps, 40
McIlwaine, H. R., 51 n., 58 n., 88 n.
McKelvey, Blake, 223 n.
McKissick, Floyd, 347
McLaughlin, James, 200, 201
McWilliams, Carey, 161–172, 377 n.
Malcolm X, 319
Malingering of slaves, 154
Manahoac, 38, 40
Mangum, Charles S., 215 n.
Maoist-leaning youth guards, 319
Marcus Garvey's Back-to-Africa movement, 254
Margold, Nathan R., 259 n.
Maroons, 68, 69
Martin, Paul, 32 n.
Matoki society, 143
Mattaponi, 38
May, Ernest, 228 n.
Meade, George C., 167
Meade, Richard Kidder, 90 n.
Medina, Harold, 293
Melting pot, 5, 6, 10–12
Meredith, James, 345
Meriam, Lewis, 259 n., 264, 266 n.
Meriam Report, 264 n., 266
Meriwether, Robert L., 64 n.
Merritt, Joe, 120, 128, 265
Mexican-American Political Association (MAPA), 354, 362
Mexican-Americans, v
  attitude toward, 162
  civil rights of, around 1848, 130
  following Civil War, 188, 190
  1960 census, 357, 358
  present number, 161
  pre-World War II, 286–296
  process to despised minority, 286–287
  and prosperity, 285
  seeking land grant rights, 355–363
Mexican-American War, 161–163, 166–169
"Mexicanized gringos," 231

Index

PRINTED IN U.S.A.